THE NATIONAL SOCIALIST LEADERSHIP AND TOTAL WAR 1941-5

THE NATIONAL SOCIALIST LEADERSHIP AND TOTAL WAR 1941-5

Eleanor Hancock

Lecturer in History
Monash University, Australia

St. Martin's Press
New York

First published in the United States of America 1991

Printed in the United States of America

ISBN 0-312-07202-3

Library of Congress Cataloging-in-Publication Data
Hancock, Eleanor.
The National Socialist leadership and total war, 1941-5 / Eleanor
Hancock.
    p. cm.
Includes bibliographical references and index.
ISBN 0-312-07202-3
1. World War, 1939-1945—Germany. 2. Political leadership—
Germany—History—20th century. 3. National socialism. I. Title.
D757.H297 1992
940.53'43—dc20

91-31201
CIP

For my husband,
Ted Wilson

CONTENTS

PREFACE

This study expands on my doctoral thesis, 'Mobilizing for Total War: The National Socialist Leadership and Social and Labour Prerequisites for Intensifying the German War Effort, 1941-1945,' submitted to the Australian National University in 1988. It is largely based on research completed before 1988 but takes in some later research and significant publications after that date. My doctoral supervisor, Dr Bruce Kent, History Department, the Faculties, Australian National University, and my adviser, Professor Peter Dennis, History Department, University College, University of New South Wales, provided assistance, criticism and advice during the writing of the thesis. I would particularly like to thank Professor Dennis for his help as my thesis adviser. My examiners, Professor Klaus Hildebrand, Friedrich-Wilhelmsuniversität, Bonn, Dr R. J. Overy, King's College, London, and Dr Geoffrey Jukes, Australian National University, Canberra, offered helpful advice and criticisms. The preparation of the manuscript has been made easier by thoughtful and perceptive comments and suggestions from Professor Gunther Rothenberg of Purdue University, Indiana, Professor Ferenc Feher of the New School of Social Research, New York, and Dr Robin Prior, History Department, University College, University of New South Wales. I wish to thank my departmental head at the University College, Professor Alan Gilbert, for his personal encouragement and for creating an intellectual atmosphere which facilitated my research. I am also grateful to my departmental head, Professor Merle Ricklefs at Monash University, for supporting my research.

Papers based on my research were presented in 1985 to seminars in the History Departments of the University College, University of New South Wales, and the Australian National University, to the 1986 meeting of the Australian Association of European Historians and in seminars and conferences in 1988 and 1989 at Monash University. For helpful suggestions and detailed comments on later versions of the thesis, I would like to thank Professor Reinhard Meyers, Westfälische Wilhelms-Universität, Münster, and Dr Robin Prior, History Department, University College, University of New South Wales. The late Dr Martin Broszat, Director of the Institut für Zeitgeschichte, Dr Elke Fröhlich of the Institut für Zeitgeschichte, Professor Peter Hüttenberger, Düsseldorf University, Professor Alan Milward, European University of Florence and Mr David Adams, Political Science Department, Australian National University, provided helpful advice and guidance at an early stage of my research. Useful written advice was also received from Professor Gustav Schmidt and Dr Hans Mommsen, Ruhr University Bochum, and Dr Carole Adams, University of Sydney. For stimulating and helpful comments and suggestions, I wish to thank my former colleagues, Professor Alan Gilbert, Professor John McCarthy, Dr Roger Thompson and Dr Jeff Grey, and my colleagues, Dr Marian Aveling, Dr David Cuthbert and Dr Elizabeth Boross. My friend, Philippa Horner, and my mother, Eva Hancock, both helped by generously providing me with accommodation in Canberra in 1987 and 1988. Financial support from the Dean's Fund of the University College, the Dean's Fund of Monash University and an Australian Research Council Grant permitted three research trips to Germany in 1985, 1986 and 1989. The Library of the University College, University of New South Wales, also funded my research.

At the Bundesarchiv I would like to thank Dr Real and Dr Werner for their assistance. The staff of the Bundesarchiv reading room, particularly Mr Scharmann, Mr Schneider and Mr Rösser, and the staff of the Bundesarchiv Militärarchiv, in particular Mrs Müller, were always helpful.

I am deeply grateful to my husband, Ted Wilson, for his love, support and encouragement during the writing of this study.

Eleanor Hancock

ACKNOWLEDGEMENTS

The author and publishers gratefully acknowledge permission to reproduce tables from Willi A. Boelcke, *Die deutsche Wirtschaft 1930-1945: Interna des Reichswirtschaftsministeriums* (Droste Verlag GmbH, Dusseldorf, 1983); Ulrich Herbert, *Fremdarbeiter: Politik und Praxis der "Ausländer-Einsatzes" in der Kriegswirtschaft im Spannungsfeld von Politik, Ideologie und Propaganda 1939-1945* (Verlag H.W. Dietz Nachf., Bonn, 1985, 1986); Raul Hilberg, *The Destruction of the European Jews*, revised and definitive edition (Holmes & Meier Publishers, Inc., New York, 1985); Paul Kennedy, *The Rise and Fall of the Great Powers: Economic Change and Military Conflict from 1500 to 2000* (Random House Inc., New York, 1987 and HarperCollins Publishers Limited, London, 1987); R.J. Overy, *Goering the 'Iron Man'* (Routledge and Kegan Paul, London, 1984); Dieter Rebentisch, *Führerstaat und Verwaltung im Zweiten Weltkrieg: Verfassungsentwicklung und Verwaltungspolitik 1939-1945* (Franz Steiner Verlag Wiesbaden GmbH, Stuttgart, 1989); and Rolf Wagenfuehr, *Die deutsche Industrie im Kriege 1939-1945*, second edition (Duncker & Humblot GmbH, Berlin, 1963). The author and publishers gratefully acknowledge permission to reproduce lists of leaders from Dietrich Orlow, *The History of the Nazi Party, 1933-1945* (University of Pittsburgh Press, Pittsburgh, 1973); and Gerald Reitlinger, *The Final Solution*, second edition (Vallentine Mitchell & Co. Ltd., London, 1971).

ABBREVIATIONS, GERMAN AND SPECIALISED TERMS

Allgemeines Heeresamt—general army office.

Arbeitseinsatz—mobilisation of labour.

av.—arbeitsverwendungsfähig—fit for work, capable of work in staffs, offices and units and garrison battalions.

av. H.—arbeitsverwendungsfähig Heimat—fit for work, capable of work in staffs, offices and units and garrison battalions on the home front.

AWA—Allgemeines Wehrmachtsamt—general armed forces office.

AZS—Aktion Auskämmung des zivilen Sektors zugunsten der Rüstungsindustrie—programme combing out the civilian sector of the economy to transfer staff and production to armaments.

BA—Bundesarchiv—German Federal Archives, Koblenz.

BA MA—Bundesarchiv Militärarchiv—German Federal Military Archives, Freiburg.

BDM—Bund deutscher Mädel—League of German Girls; National Socialist youth organisation for all girls between 14 and 18.

Bereitstellungsschein—certificate showing availability for call-up.

Bildungsoffizier—instruction officer.

Chef. H.L.—Chef Heeresleitung—head of the army leadership.

Chef. H. Rüst u. BdE—Chef Heeresrüstung und Befehlshaber des Ersatzheeres—head of army armaments and commander of the Replacement Army.

class—term used for call-up group where the year denotes the year of birth, for example, 'class of 1901' is men born in 1901.

DAF—Deutsche Arbeitsfront—German Labour Front.

Dolchstoss—so-called 'stab in the back' of the German army by the German revolution of 1918.

Dreier Ausschuss—Committee of Three.

Einsatzgruppen der Sicherheitspolizei und des SD—literally, action groups of the security police and the SD; mobile SD and security police units used for special operations.

Ersatzheer—Replacement Army.

Frauenschaft—Women's League of the NSDAP.

Führerhauptquartier—main Führer headquarters.

Führerinformation—literally Führer information; submission.

Gau—region, the main territorial division of the NSDAP.

Gaubeauftragten—Gau deputies.

Gauleiter—Nazi Party functionary responsible for administration in a province or federal state.

GBA—Generalbevollmächtigter für den Arbeitseinsatz—General plenipotentiary for employment.

GBK or GBTK—Generalbevollmächtigter für den Totalen Kriegseinsatz or *Generalbevollmächtigter für den Totalen Krieg*—General plenipotentiary for the total war effort; shortened to general plenipotentiary for total war.

GBV—Generalbevollmächtigter für die Reichsverwaltung—General plenipotentiary for Reich administration, Interior Minister.

GenGouv—Generalgouvernement—General Government, administration of unannexed sections of central occupied Poland.

Gestapo—Geheime Staatspolizei—Secret State Police.

gv.H.—garnisonsverwendungsfähig Heimat—capable of serving in a garrison on the home front.

Gliederungen—Formations or divisions; the collective name for paramilitary groups and other sections, including the Hitler Youth.

Handwerk—trade, handicrafts, artisans.

Hauptamt—Main Office.

HWaA—Heereswaffenamt—army weapons office.

Heimarbeit—outwork.

Hoheitsträger—'bearer of sovereignty'; title given to territorial chiefs in the Nazi Party's political organisation.

HSSPF—Höhere SS- und Polizeiführer—Higher SS and Police Leaders.

IfZ—Institut für Zeitgeschichte, Munich.

Jägerstab—fighter staff.

Kampfzeit—literally period of struggle, period before the NSDAP came to power.

KDF—Kraft durch Freude—Strength through Joy, a DAF programme for worker recreation.

Kreisleiter—district Nazi Party leader.

Kristallnacht—night of broken glass, government sponsored anti-Semitic pogrom in November 1938.

kv.—kriegsverwendungsfähig—fit for active service.

LK-Mitteilungen—Luftkrieg-Mitteilungen—air war bulletins.

Luftkriegsschädenausschuss—air war damage committee.

Luftschutzpolizei—air defence police.

Machtergreifung—NSDAP seizure of power in 1933.

Meldepflicht—compulsory registration for labour duty.

Ministerratsverordnung—ministerial council decree.

NSDAP—Nationalsozialistische Deutsche Arbeiterpartei—National Socialist (Nazi) German Workers' Party.

NSFO—Nationalsozialistischer Führungsoffizier—National Socialist leadership officer in the armed forces.

NS-Führungsstab—National Socialist leadership staff.

NSKK—Nationalsozialistisches Kraftfahrer-Korps—National Socialist Automobile Corps.

NS-Reichskriegerbund—National Socialist war veterans' league.

NSV—Nationalsozialistische Volkswohlfahrt—National Socialist welfare organisation.

Oberster Gerichtsherr—supreme justice authority.

OKH—Oberkommando des Heeres—Supreme Command of the Army.

OKL—Oberkommando der Luftwaffe—Supreme Command of the Air Force.

OKM—Oberkommando der Marine—Supreme Command of the Navy.

OKW—Oberkommando der Wehrmacht—Supreme Command of the armed forces.

ORBs—Oberste Reichsbehörden—Supreme Reich authorities.

Ostministerium, or RMO—Reichsministerium für die besetzten Ostgebiete—Reich ministry for the occupied Eastern territories.

OT—Organisation Todt—building organisation involving state building administration and private firms.

Panzerfaust—anti-tank weapon.

Persönlicher Stab Reichsführer SS—Personal Staff of the Reichsführer of the SS.

Planungsamt—planning office.

PO—Politische Organisation—political organisation; cadre for mobilizing NSDAP political activists.

RAD—Reichsarbeitsdienst—Reich Labour Service.

Reichmesseamt—Reich trade fair office.

Reichsbevollmächtigter für den totalen Kriegseinsatz or *Reichsbevollmächtigter für den totalen Krieg*—Reich plenipotentiary for the total war effort, shortened to Reich plenipotentiary for total war.

Reichskulturkammer—Reich Chamber of Culture.

Reichspostdirektionen—Reich post management offices.

Reichspropagandaring—Reich circle for propaganda; organisation co-ordinating propaganda of the Party branches and affiliated organisations.

Reichswirtschaftsverordnung—war economy decree.

RFSS—Reichsführer-SS—Reich leader of the SS.

RK—Reichskommissar—Reich commissioner; title of a Nazi chief of civilian administration in the occupied areas of Europe.

RKFDV—Reichskommissar für die Festigung Deutschen Volkstums—Reich Commissioner for the Strengthening of Germandom.

RKO—Reichskommissariat Ostland—Reich commissariat Eastland, the territorial administrative area for the Baltic countries.

RKU—Reichskommissariat Ukraine—Reich commissariat Ukraine.

RM—Reichsmark—German unit of currency.

RPÄ—Reichspropagandaämter—Reich propaganda offices.

RPL—Reichspropagandaleitung—propaganda leadership; NSDAP propaganda office.

Rüstungsrat—Armaments Council.

SA—Sturmabteilungen—Storm troops.

S-Betriebe—Sperr-Betriebe—blocked firms, in the occupied territories whose employees were protected from transport to Germany

Scheinarbeit—illusory employment, nominal employment designed to prevent the employee from being called on for actual labour.

Schlüsselkräfte—key workers, protected from call up because of their importance to the war effort.

Schnellplan—accelerated armaments plan.

Schwerpunkt—literally focal point; programme concentrating on armaments priorities.

SD—Sicherheitsdienst—Security Service (SS secret intelligence unit).

SE—Sondererziehung—special call-up programme (known as SE 1, SE 2, etc.).

SS—Schutzstaffel—Guard squadrons.

SS-Führungshauptamt—SS Leadership Main Office.

SS-Helferinnen—female assistants to the SS.

uk—unabkömmlich—indispensable workers.

Umschulung—retraining of unskilled workers for skilled or semi-skilled work.

USSBS—United States Strategic Bombing Survey.

Verordnungsblätter—literally decree paper; official gazette.

Versorgung—supply, care.

Volksgemeinschaft—national community.

völkisch—national, racial, of the folk.

Volksgrenadier—literally people's infantry or people's grenadier; name given to new divisions founded in 1944, more like a militia than ordinary army divisions.

Volkssturm—'People's Storm'; militia organisation.

VWHA—*Verwaltungs- und Wirtschafts-Hauptamt*—Main Office for Administration and the Economy of the SS.

WaA—*Waffenamt*—Weapons Office.

Wehrersatzamt—armed forces' replacement office.

Wehrersatzdienststellen—armed forces' recruiting offices.

Wehrersatzplan—armed forces' replacement plan.

Wehrgeistige Führung—military ideological leadership.

Wehrhilfsdienst—armed forces' auxiliary service.

Wehrkreis—defence district.

Wehrmachthelferinnenkorps—female auxiliary armed services corps.

Wehrmachtssanitätswesens—armed forces' medical service.

Wehrpflichtigen—those liable for military service.

Wehrwirtschaft—defence economy.

WFSt.—*Wehrmachtsführungsstab*—armed forces' leadership staff.

WiRüAmt—*Wehrwirtschafts- und Rüstungsamt*—war economy and armaments office.

WVHA—*Wirtschafts- und Verwaltungs-Hauptamt*—Main Office for Economy and Administration in the SS (reorganisation of VWHA).

Zentrale Planung—central planning; committtee set up to allocate resources to industry.

LIST OF LESS WELL-KNOWN LEADERS*

Amann, Max—Head of NSDAP publishing house, 1933-45.

Backe, Herbert—State Secretary in the Reich Ministry of Agriculture, 1933-42; acting Minister of Agriculture, 1942-5.

Berger, Gottlob—Head of the SS main administrative office, 1938-45; Himmler's personal liaison officer with the Ostministerium.

Brandt, Rudolf—Himmler's personal adjutant; second in command of the Reichsführer-SS Persönlicher Stab.

Bürckel, Josef—Gauleiter of the Palatinate, 1933-44; Reich commissioner in Lorraine, 1940-4.

Daluege, Kurt—Head of the Ordnungspolizei (state police), 1936-45.

Darré, R. Walther—Reich Minister of Agriculture, 1933-42.

Dietrich, Otto—Reich Press Chief, 1933-45.

Eichmann, Adolf—Head of the Jewish section of the Gestapo, 1940-5.

Florian, Karl—Gauleiter of Düsseldorf, 1933-45.

Frank, Hans—Governor-General in Poland, 1939-45.

Frick, Wilhelm—Interior Minister, 1933-43.

Friedrichs, Helmuth—Head of the Party division of the Party Chancellery, 1934-45.

Funk, Walther—Reich Minister of Economics, 1938-45.

Ganzenmüller, Theodor—State Secretary in the Transport Ministry.

Guderian, Heinz—Commander in Chief of the Second Panzer Army, 1941-2; Inspector-General of armoured troops, 1943; Chief of the Army General Staff, 1944-5.

Hanke, Karl—State Secretary in the Propaganda Ministry, 1933-40; Gauleiter of Lower Silesia, 1941-5.

Henlein, Konrad—Gauleiter of the Sudetenland, 1938-45.

Heydrich, Reinhard—Head of the SD, 1933-42; Reich Protector in Bohemia and Moravia, 1941-2.

*Reprinted from "Checklist of Less Familiar Nazi Leaders", from The History of the Nazi Party, *1933-1945*, by Dietrich Orlow, by the permission of the University of Pittsburgh Press. ©1973 by the University of Pittsburgh Press.

Hildebrandt, Friedrich—Gauleiter of Mecklenburg, 1933-45.

Hildebrandt, Richard—Head of the SS Race and Settlement Office.

Hoffmann, Albert—Deputy Gauleiter of Upper Silesia, 1941-3; Gauleiter of Westphalia-South, 1943-5.

Holz, Karl—Acting Gauleiter of Franconia, 1940-5.

Ifland, Otto—Party Chancellery official since 1938; Party Chancellery representative on von Unruh commission, 1943.

Jüttner, Hans—Head of the leadership office of the SS.

Kaltenbrunner, Ernst—Head of the Security Police and SD, 1942-5.

Kaufmann, Karl—Gauleiter of Hamburg, 1933-45.

Klopfer, Gerhard—Head of the state division of the Party Chancellery, 1938-45.

Koch, Erich—Gauleiter of East Prussia, 1933-45; Reich commissioner in the Ukraine, 1941-5.

Krüger, Friedrich W.—Head of the SS in occupied Poland, 1941-3.

Meyer, Alfred—Gauleiter of Westphalia North, 1933-45; State Secretary in the Ostministerium, 1941-5.

Milch, Erhard—Luftwaffe Field-Marshal and Chief of Staff of the Luftwaffe.

Model, Walter—Tank commander; commander of Army Group North, 1944; commander of Army Group Centre, 1944; Supreme Commander in the West, 1944-5.

Mutschmann, Martin—Gauleiter of Saxony, 1933-45.

Ohlendorf, Otto—Head of SD Amt Inland; head of Einsatzgruppe D.

Pohl, Oswald—Reich treasurer of the SS, 1936-45; head, SS economic administration office, 1942-5.

Prützmann, Hans—HSSPF to Southern Army Group, Kiev, 1941-3; head of the Werewolf organization, 1945.

Rafelsberger, Walter—Gau economic adviser, Vienna, 1940-5.

Sauckel, Fritz—Gauleiter of Thuringia, 1933-45; Reich plenipotentiary for labour, 1942-5.

Simon, Gustav—Gauleiter of Koblenz-Trier, 1933-45; chief of civil administration in Luxemburg, 1940-5.

Stuckart, Franz—State Secretary in the Interior Ministry.

Tiessler, Walter—Party Chancellery liaison officer to the Propaganda Ministry, 1940-3; director of the Reich Circle for National Socialist Propaganda and Popular Enlightenment.

Wagner, Robert—Gauleiter of Baden, 1933-45; Reich commissioner in Alsace, 1940-5.

Wahl, Karl—Gauleiter of Swabia, 1933-45.

Walkenhorst, Heinrich—Head of the Party Chancellery personnel office, 1942-5.

Wegener, Paul—Gauleiter of Weser-Ems, 1942-5.

Weiszäcker, Ernst von—State Secretary in Foreign Ministry to 1943; Ambassador to the Vatican, 1943-5.

Zander, Wilhelm—Head of the Party Chancellery section on mobilisation, 1937-45.

Zeitzler, Kurt—Chief of the Army General Staff, 1942-4.

Introduction

'The German example should have provided an adequate lesson of the results of initiating war measures too late,' Germany's Propaganda Minister Joseph Goebbels wrote in 1945.[1] As the National Socialist government faced defeat, both Goebbels and Armaments Minister Albert Speer claimed the leadership had not done enough to mobilise German society for the war effort. Where suitable measures were adopted, they came too late. They suggested that these failings arose from Hitler's leadership style, the opposition of other key leaders and the regime's administrative structure. Since 1941 both men had advocated policies to which they gave the overall description of 'total war,' designed initially to ensure German victory and later to avert defeat. Their criticisms were based on an alternative model of total war, sometimes explicit and sometimes implicit.

Many historians have echoed Goebbels' and Speer's criticisms of the regime's commitment to total war and have argued that the regime only reluctantly adopted a policy of total mobilisation of Germany's resources for war at the end of 1941. Studies of total war in Nazi Germany have so far concentrated on armaments production; the use of propaganda to mobilise public support for the war has also been studied. The role of specific ministries and organisations, in particular the Armaments Ministry, the Economics Ministry, the economics and armaments office of the supreme command of the armed forces (OKW), and the railways have been examined in several recent books.[2]

Drawing on archival sources, this work examines the commitment of the German leadership to total war, which may be defined as the complete orientation of society in its political, economic and social life to the pursuit of the war effort.[3] It does so by analysing the policies designed to achieve total war and the strategies for their acceptance pursued from 1941 to 1945 by four powerful National Socialist leaders—Martin Bormann, Secretary to the Führer and head of the Nazi Party Chancellery, Heinrich Himmler, the Reichsführer-SS, Joseph Goebbels, Propaganda Minister, and Albert Speer, Armaments Minister.

Age 41 in 1941, Martin Bormann became head of the Party Chancellery, when Hitler's deputy in the Nazi Party, Rudolf Hess, flew to Britain in May of that year. Bormann had risen through the Nazi Party administration in the 1930s, displacing Hess and strengthening his position by his constant presence at Hitler's side. During the war, as Hitler became increasingly preoccupied with military matters, he was content to let Bormann handle many other issues, seeing him as a reliable servant of his will. Bormann gave every sign of being Hitler's fervent admirer. In 1943 Bormann was appointed Secretary to the Führer, a position of co-ordination between the ministerial level and Hitler's personal staff. The sources of his power were the trust Hitler placed in him, his access to Hitler and his ability to impede the access of others to Hitler. He could influence Hitler's decisions by the manner in which he raised issues. Bormann preferred to work behind the scenes, leaving centre stage to others, and as a result his views have to be inferred at times. His relative obscurity meant that his power was not always recognised at the time. Contemporaries and historians as a result have differed in their interpretations of his influence, specifically whether he controlled Hitler or was Hitler's tool. Hitler's secretary, Christa Schroeder, and the head of the Reich Chancellery, Hans Lammers, both judged Bormann to be a faithful executor of Hitler's wishes; Speer claimed that in the 1930s Goebbels and Bormann always sought to radicalise Hitler ideologically, while in wartime Bormann was slavishly dependent on expressions of Hitler's views.[4]

Joseph Goebbels, age 44 in 1941, had been Minister for Popular Enlightenment and Propaganda since March 1933, Gauleiter of Berlin since 1927 and Reichspropagandaleiter of the Nazi Party since 1929. As Propaganda Minister he saw his ultimate task as winning the entire population over to the side of the regime. He was able, hardworking and capable of dispassionate analysis of problems. With the exception of his organisation of the anti-Semitic pogrom, the *Kristallnacht*, Goebbels had not played a prominent role in policymaking outside his area of control in the 1930s. His main responsibility in wartime was the organisation of enthusiasm for the war and the maintenance of morale. The regime's increased need for propaganda strengthened his position. In 1941 Goebbels was emerging from a period of disgrace after Hitler ordered him to end his affair with the actress Lida Baarova in 1938. According to Hitler's press chief, Otto Dietrich, this was the only time Hitler's friendship with Goebbels was strained.[5] Like Bormann, Goebbels and his wife, Magda, were members of Hitler's private circle. Goebbels combined his formal and informal access to Hitler with a strong personal commitment to Hitler.

Dietrich described Goebbels and Himmler as two men of whose loyalty Hitler felt absolutely certain. Age 41 in 1941, Heinrich Himmler had led the *Schutzstaffel* (SS) since 1929. The SS had begun as a Nazi Party bodyguard for Hitler but developed into a powerful political police force. Himmler held the positions of *Reichsführer-SS* (RFSS) and Chief of the German Police in the Ministry of the Interior. He was responsible for the Reich's internal security, including the secret police, *Geheime Staatspolizei* (Gestapo), and security service, *Sicherheitsdienst* (SD), and also controlled the country's network of concentration camps. Himmler's power was strengthened during the war by the wartime growth of the *Waffen-SS*, the SS armed forces, and by expanding SS economic interests. Himmler's position was strengthened by his partnership with his most able subordinate, Reinhard Heydrich, head of the SD. Contemporaries and historians disagree whether Himmler saw himself as implementing Hitler's ideas or developed policies independently. He certainly developed a far more comprehensive and coherent world view derived from national socialism than either Goebbels or Speer.[6] Unlike Bormann, Goebbels and Speer, Himmler was not a member of Hitler's private circle.

Albert Speer had been a member of Hitler's private circle since 1933. Age 36 in 1941, he was Hitler's architect. His political responsibilities had increased in the 1930s; by 1937 he was made Inspector General of Building for the Capital of the Reich, entrusted with preparing a complete urban renewal plan for Berlin. In 1939 Speer had made his construction staff available for war purposes and as a result assumed responsibility for erecting buildings for the armed forces, repairing bomb damage, building air raid shelters and later repairing rail connections in the USSR. In this capacity, Speer was responsible to Fritz Todt, Reich Minister of Armaments and Munitions since March 1940. Speer was close to Hitler and had shown the ability to prosper in the National Socialist in-fighting. A close associate, Luftwaffe Field Marshal Erhard Milch, described Speer as 'highly intelligent, artistic in temperament, and ambitious to the point of power-hunger; . . . Always unpredictable. . . . Personally courageous.'[7] Historians have tended to accept Speer at his own valuation as either an apolitical artist linked to Hitler by their common architectural interests or an apolitical technocrat.

This study sets out how and why the leaders' views changed and competed, comparing their proposals to Hitler's views and to the measures which Hitler approved. In studying these leaders' views, the work seeks to answer the following questions. What were the proposals of the four leaders? What concepts of total war were they based on? How did the leaders seek to have their ideas implemented? If they failed, why was this so? Were Goebbels and Speer correct in perceiving a lack of commitment to total war on the part of the leadership and a delay in adopting total war policies?

The book concentrates on the period from winter 1941 to the end of the war in 1945; this period witnessed the deterioration of Germany's military position and the National Socialist political system coming under increased stress; it was a time in which resources were becoming scarcer and competition for them accordingly fiercer, and in which options were steadily decreasing.

The four leaders whose views and policies are examined were all important and powerful members of the regime, and their powers and responsibilities increased in the period under study. All four men had direct access to Hitler, enjoyed his confidence and gained powers directly relevant to any pursuit of total war in the period: Bormann was the leading member of the Dreier Ausschuss, a committee set up in 1943 to implement total war measures; Speer became the minister in charge of armaments production; Himmler was leader of the regime's police and secret police, and as such led an organisation with its own economic enterprises and captive labour force; Goebbels controlled the regime's mobilisation of enthusiasm for the war effort and was appointed plenipotentiary for total war in 1944. While there has been considerable study of the organisation of the German economy and the armaments industry during the war, particularly based on the files of the Armaments Ministry and Speer's recollections, there has not been an examination of the policies, concepts, competition and cooperation of these four men. Individual aspects of Goebbels' campaign for total war have been studied, by Herbst and Longerich in particular;[8] this is the first study which sets his ideas in a broader comparative perspective by also studying Bormann and Himmler's views. The views of other leaders and officials will be included where relevant.

For Goebbels, proposals for total war were part of a more wide-ranging policy aimed at avoiding defeat and seeking a political solution to the war. Accordingly, proposals for a compromise peace, debates on the treatment of people in the occupied territories and the extermination of the Jews will all be considered where they are relevant either to this wider policy or the debate on total war. The study is not a specific reexamination of the details of German economic mobilisation for war, wartime armaments production or labour policy, all of which have been examined by other historians, but it will use the results of these studies to set out relevant details of German policy and how they affected the leaders' changing conceptions of total war. Combining these details with an examination of the leaders' concepts and policies, it gives a new view of the mobilisation of the German economy and society for the war effort.

It also contributes to current historical debate on the nature of the National Socialist political system and sources of authority within it. There are two main interpretations of the National Socialist political system. The 'monocratic' or 'intentionalist' interpretation argues that Hitler's intentions and power were of central importance to the development of policy. Policies were adopted because Hitler ordered them or agreed to them. In the final analysis, this was a system based on the personal authority of one man. Conflict and confusion arose at lower levels of the political system, because Hitler chose to 'divide and rule' in order to maintain his authority.[9]

The second interpretation—the 'polycratic' or 'functionalist' interpretation—suggests that Hitler's personal role was not as crucial. It argues that the role of the Führer achieved functional importance as a unifying factor only because of the lack of agreement on ideology. Historians supporting this interpretation contend that various organisations, notably the SS and the Nazi Party (*Nationalsozialistische Deutsche Arbeiterpartei*, NSDAP), developed an independent power base. Hitler's power, and competition among leaders and organisations, was not the result of deliberate policy but arose from political and institutional divisions. The competition hampered co-ordination, and increased the radicalisation of policy and the emphasis on the negative elements of the regime's ideology. Historians of both interpretations agree that Hitler allowed large accretions of power to men he trusted; but they disagree about the autonomous power of these empires. They also agree that at the level below Hitler, the regime was marked by an institutional Darwinism; they disagree as to its causes. Lack of evidence on many central aspects of Hitler's rule, due to his unsystematic style of working and reliance on verbal decisions, suggests that there can be no final resolution of these differing interpretations.[10]

Like some other recent studies, this work derives a model for understanding Hitler's power, and the style of leadership and political system which developed, from Weber's 'ideal type' of charismatic authority. Hitler's authority derived from his charisma, which made his followers willing to subject themselves unconditionally to his leadership. Hitler's hostility to routine, his delegation of powers for special tasks, the need to prove loyalty to the leader, the unchecked struggle for power waged by the organisations of subordinate leaders and the difficulties of co-ordination among the rival organisations and leaders were all consequences of Hitler's charismatic authority. Hitler could delegate authority to his followers. 'Territorial limits, the personal charisma of the follower, and the ability to secure the confidence and favour of the leader alone determine how much power he [the follower] can wield.'[11] Hitler's practice of delegating aspects of his authority temporarily to trusted followers meant that 'institutional dynamics in the NSDAP [were] little more than the personal relationships and clashes of individual party leaders.'[12] These practices did not diminish Hitler's ultimate authority.

An interpretation of Hitler's authority as charismatic allows a synthesis of the two differing interpretations. The gap between the 'monocratic' and 'polycratic' interpretations has become exaggerated. The Third Reich was both monolithic and pluralistic, and the functioning of its leadership should be seen as a combination of both. Polycratic competition reigned among the competing secondary leaders at the same time as they acknowledged and were bound by Hitler's authority where and when he exercised it. Secondary leaders tried to, and did, influence Hitler's decisions, but they were willing to submit themselves unconditionally to his leadership. Hitler could be influenced from case to case but he could not be directed for long, and his reactions could not be predicted. It was in the nature of Hitler's rule that his decisions were not final: this prevented his authority from becoming in-stitutionalised. A recognition of Hitler's ultimate authority need not exclude the possibility that his individual orders could be 'interpreted' in a way which suited the secondary leader.[13]

Charismatic authority is inherently unstable, because it is dependent upon the person of the charismatic leader. It is eventually transformed into traditional or bureaucratic authority. Additional elements of instability arose from the particular circumstances of National Socialist rule. The dictatorship had not existed long enough to overcome many traditional structures and values. Hitler's institutionalised irrational charisma was superimposed on the pre-existing, rational bureaucratic system. Hitler stood at the apex of various power systems. Combining the offices of President and Chancellor, he stood at the head of the political and administrative system; he was also commander in chief of the armed forces; he led the Nazi Party as its Führer. The administrative system of the Weimar Republic and its ministries contin-ued formally, but was paralleled by the creation of new authorities and the assumption of powers by various National Socialist organisations and office holders. A tension existed between the bureaucracy, which gained greater power with the end of parliamentary scrutiny of its activities, and the Party leadership who saw themselves as revolutionaries. While National Socialist rule had some centralising tendencies, regionalism was strengthened by the power of the Gauleiters, regional NSDAP leaders with the right of immediate access to Hitler. Gauleiters were directly responsible to Hitler and were capable of originating policies, and ignoring or transforming central directives.[14]

Historians who see the National Socialist regime as polycratic tend to see Hitler's charismatic authority as incapable of being combined with a rational and stable government. 'Even in the final war years . . . the Hitler regime was certainly capable of generating astonishing energy, but it had long been incapable of the rational exercise of power.'[15] Such interpretations may overestimate the rationality of the more conventional parliamentary and bureaucratic system and underestimate the extent to which inter-organisational conflict is normally present in such a system. As Murray has pointed out, historians have tended to see the existence of competing authorities exclusively as a weakness rather than as a possible sign of flexibility in a dictatorship. The organisational conflict of National Socialism served as, and was used by Hitler as, a substitute for the checks and balances of a parliamentary system. It could pit organisations and leaders against each other in a quest for optimum performance. Mierzejewski's comment on the National Socialist economic system can also be applied to its political system: its 'informality, "planlessness", and lack of centralised control and systematic growth at once limited its overall potential and conferred upon it considerable flexibility.'[16]

Despite the rivalries encouraged by the system, National Socialists shared 'institutional solidarity . . . shared assumptions and beliefs, commonly accepted norms, and . . . unquestioned general values'[17] which allowed them to work together for common goals. One such shared assumption is of crucial importance to understanding their approach to total war. In *Der Totale Krieg und die Ordnung der Wirtschaft*, Ludolf Herbst has demonstrated that in National Socialist Germany 'total war' as a concept implied more than economic rationality in the orientation of national life to wage a modern war. For National Socialism, 'total war' was an ideological as well as economic and military concept. Historians usually emphasise its economic aspects. The fundamental economic tasks of a government in wartime have been defined as 'to absorb into productive industry all employable resources of brain and muscle, material and plant' and 'to switch over to immediate war purposes as large a proportion of these resources as could be spared from

peacetime activities.'[18] Since the middle of the nineteenth century, organisation of industrial capacity has become increasingly important for the conduct
of total war. The organisation of a modern industrial economy for a long war
is constrained by certain factors. All resources cannot be diverted to armaments production: a balance has to be struck between the resources necessary
for maintaining the efficiency of the armed forces and those needed for the
efficiency of the civilian population. Morale and effectiveness require the
standard of living to be kept at a certain level. Some consumer goods still
need to be produced, and some 'inessential' goods and entertainments are
necessary to maintain productivity.

As a concept, total war also implies total destruction of the enemy and
the 'organisation of enthusiasm' for the war effort.[19] The demands of these
varying components may compete and contradict one another: for example,
resources needed for propaganda may have to be diverted from armaments
production or vice versa. Since the wars of the French Revolution, the idea
of 'the nation in arms,' a revolutionary or popular war supported by the
efforts of the entire nation, has been part of the concept of total war. The
levée en masse of the French Republic in 1793, a universal call-up in a state
of national emergency, involved the use of ideology, political indoctrination
of officers and men, and propaganda in a new kind of warfare.

For National Socialist leaders, as will be seen in later chapters, effective
and efficient pursuit of the war relied not only on the organisation of
economic production but also on the adoption of political policies, based on
ideological analyses, which would allow the nation to pursue the war without
treason or dissent. As Herbst has shown, Hitler saw total war as a realisation
of German ideology. The resources allocated to anti-Semitic policies, propaganda and maintaining public morale, and ideological education were part
of the 'German doctrine of total war.' Not all these policies would be
considered part of total war if a more narrow, economically rational, model
is used, but they are rational for this model. In understanding the leadership's
approach to total war, 'the total claim of the ideology . . . must be taken into
account just as much as the striving to achieve more efficient forms of
armaments production.'[20] The tension between these two goals was part of
making the war more total.

The origins of this model in Germany's World War I experiences are
discussed in Chapter 1, which also summarises the course of German
preparation for war and notes the differing interpretations of German preparedness for war. Chapter 2 deals with the German attack on the Soviet
Union and its consequences which for the first time raised calls from the
leadership for a more 'total' war effort. Chapters 3 and 4 analyse the response

to Stalingrad—Chapter 3 concentrates on the setting up of the Dreier Ausschuss and Chapter 4 on Goebbels' attempts to change policy on total war. Chapter 5 looks at the response to Italy's leaving the war, and further moves in 1943 to introduce total war on the home front. Chapters 6 and 7 examine renewed attempts to have total war measures adopted in 1944. Chapter 8 covers the results of Goebbels' appointment as *Reichsbevollmächtigter für den totalen Krieg*. Chapter 9 looks at the last attempts to pursue such policies in 1945.

1

'Redressing the Sins of the Generation of 1918': Total War and the Path to World War

The National Socialist movement itself, and its concepts of organising for war, arose from the German experience of World War I. The National Socialist analysis of Germany's organisation for war from 1914 to 1918 and of the reasons for Germany's defeat strongly influenced its leaders' planning for and organisation of the home front in World War II. During the Czech crisis in September 1938, Goebbels commented after a speech by Hitler, 'One thing is sure: 1918 will never be repeated!'[1] Later, during the war, Goebbels suggested that the population was redressing 'the sins of the generation of 1918.'[2]

World War I had marked a further stage in the development of total war. The involvement of entire populations meant that the war had to be fought for aims beyond maintaining the balance of power, and this made the scope and length of the war greater by reducing the possibility of compromise. Popular involvement led to the use of propaganda to motivate the home front, to influence neutral states and to undermine enemy morale. World War I saw extensive mobilisation of economic and social resources for war production and the widespread employment of the civilian population of both sexes in war production. Civilians on the home front were also the objects of air attack. This war created an economic and social model of total war. Conduct of the war required large-scale government intervention in the economy, increased taxation and borrowing and the diversion of resources and labour from other purposes for war production. It removed the former limits on the industrialisation of war.³

In Germany from 1914 to 1918 the organisation of the home front for war was beset by difficulties, largely caused by weaknesses of the Imperial political and social system and an unbalanced emphasis by Germany's wartime leaders on armaments production at the expense of other aspects of economic life. The armed forces, led by Hindenburg and Ludendorff, placed demands on the economy which aimed at a total orientation of effort and resources solely for direct war purposes, but which were divorced from economic reality. Resources were squeezed from the home front to supply the soldiers. Military dominance in decision making and the class and political divisions of the Imperial regime led to attempts to 'command' labour, while profiteering by industrialists went uncontrolled due to lack of regulation. As a result, political and social tensions grew. Disorganisation, particularly of the transport and distribution networks, problems in German agriculture and the enemy blockade of Germany meant hunger and starvation by 1917. Food shortages, popular desire for peace and political reform led to strikes in 1917 and 1918, and mutinies in 1918.⁴

German right wing and conservative opinion blamed this unrest and the subsequent revolution of 1918—the so-called 'stab in the back' (*Dolchstoss*)—for the country's defeat. The model of waging a future war which they derived from this experience has been described by Herbst as the 'German variation of the doctrine of total war' or 'the *völkisch* doctrine of total war.'⁵ In this doctrine Ludendorff, other former military leaders and theorists combined the social and political requirements of modern warfare and policies designed to prevent a collapse of the home front as in 1918. The doctrine was particularly influenced by the belief that the German home front had not proved as reliable as those of Britain and France. Propaganda and ideological mobilisation of the people would, accordingly, given high priority in future wars. In the 1930s Ludendorff, Carl Schmitt and Ernst Jünger publicised the concept of 'total war.' Ludendorff called for a total orientation of the state for waging war before and during wartime. He wanted politics subordinated to the war effort and envisaged Germany in the next war as a country under an emergency dictatorship, economically oriented for security from blockade and socially organised by means of general labour service. Ludendorff concluded that creating national unity by excluding Jews would ensure the loyalty of the home front.

Publicly, the National Socialist leaders blamed Germany's defeat on the collapse of the home front. In *Mein Kampf*, Hitler argued that Germany's

collapse was caused by Marxist agitation, specifically organised and fo-
mented by Jews, who had exploited internal divisions. 'The ultimate and
most decisive [reason for Germany's defeat] remains the failure to recognise
the racial problem and especially the Jewish menace,' he claimed.[6]

As early as 1922, Hitler saw a need for a deep process of regeneration
and political education in Germany to overcome Marxism, create national
unity and prepare the people for war. Propaganda and ideological education
of the armed forces were to play an important role in this process. The
National Socialist and armed forces leadership believed that Imperial Germany had been completely outmanoeuvred by British propaganda, which
had contributed to the collapse of the home front. Better propaganda in 1918
would have been able to prevent defeat, according to Goebbels. As a result
of the importance the regime placed on propaganda, its direction remained
in Party hands with Goebbels as Propaganda Minister and Otto Dietrich as
Reich Press Chief. Attempts by the armed forces in the 1930s to seek control
of the overall direction of propaganda in wartime were unsuccessful.[7]

With the 1918 mutinies as a warning, high priority was also given to
ideological education of the armed forces. Such education had been pion-
eered by Ludendorff in 1917-18 in an attempt to strengthen morale. Ideological education remained the responsibility of the armed forces. But the Party
claimed, and the military conceded, a role in providing the ideological
justification for combat. Soldiers could not be apolitical. Hitler ruled out the
option of a party army or militia in 1934, when he moved against its main
proponent, *Sturmabteilungen* (SA) leader Ernst Röhm. The notion of a
militia or people's army, and of political commissars, was not entertained in
the 1930s.[8]

If Germany's collapse in 1918 was publicly blamed on the revolution, the
policies National Socialist leaders pursued after 1933 suggest that they were
privately aware that the failings of the Imperial leadership contributed to
defeat. Efforts to create a feeling of social solidarity and overcome class
barriers in a national community (*Volksgemeinschaft*) were an attempt to
overcome the failings of Wilhelminian Germany. In contrast to the social
conflict and division of the Second Reich, Hitler emphasised the need to
ensure that the working class was fully part of the nation. The National
Socialist government's emphasis on crushing the left-wing parties after
1933, and on overcoming unemployment, aimed at ensuring this.[9]

Government concern to ensure adequate food supplies during World War
II derived from its awareness of the political consequences of hunger in
World War I. In World War I popular morale had been dependent on the
food situation. The National Socialist government's political and social

strategy was to provide a minimum standard of living for all Germans in wartime. To do so it was prepared to sacrifice the lives of people in the occupied countries. It monitored popular reaction to cuts in rationing. The government was justified in its emphasis on the food supply. The German public judged the war's progress by the adequacy of the food supply.[10]

The National Socialist leaders were aware of the Imperial Government's failings on the home front. Their concepts of total war contained an implicit recognition of these failings but concentrated on the political rather than the economic or strategic problems. Hitler indicated in *Mein Kampf* that Germany's enemies had been numerically and technically superior from the onset. This was not a significant concern since a state was built by heroic virtues and a spirit of sacrifice, not the 'egoism of shopkeepers.'[11] A German victory should have been possible in 1917 after the collapse of Russia, he believed.

The lack of a successful model from World War I for the economic and social organisation of war may have made organising the home front in World War II more difficult, just as the British Government was helped by the existence of a successful model. The stresses placed on the German working class gained attention at the expense of other problems, such as the profiteering and waste resulting from allowing industries to organise their own production. Little attention was given to the wider use of women in military capacities in Great Britain.

Tim Mason has argued that the National Socialist leadership's ability to organise the home front in World War II was hampered by the spectre of the revolution of 1918. Hitler did not dare to ask the population to make sacrifices. Speer recalled that Hitler was particularly concerned to avoid any repetition of 1918, but there are few specific cases, aside from pay policy at the outset of the war, where Mason can show this to have affected wartime policymaking. It has been suggested that the employment of women was one such case.[12]

The experience of 1918 is crucial to understanding the emphasis placed on some policies during wartime. But the regime's policies were specifically designed to allow it to wage war without a repetition of 1918. The resources diverted into anti-Semitic policies, propaganda, political education of the troops and the population were a contribution to 'the völkisch model of total war.' The regime's policies, including the adoption of the Final Solution, reduced the leadership's concern at such a repetition.

The suffering of Germans as a result of the British naval blockade, the eventual failure of economic production and the World War I defeat also heightened awareness of Germany's economic vulnerability. The Treaty of

Versailles severely restricted the size of the German armed forces and weakened Germany's economic position by the loss of Alsace-Lorraine and Upper Silesia. The only raw material the country possessed in any amount was coal; Germany did not contain the other raw materials needed for a wartime economy. 'Because of its importance to every phase of economic life . . . the coal industry was the decisive factor shaping Germany's economy.'[13] This led to dependence by industry on this source of energy, and the location of industry around it. The main source of coal and centre of manufacturing was the Ruhr; the secondary area was Upper Silesia. Both areas were on Germany's borders, on the west and east respectively. A long war could not be conducted without the Ruhr. As a protective measure in 1934 the *Heereswaffenamt* (Army Weapons Office) recommended the general evacuation to inner Germany of all armaments industries lying on the borders, creating new armaments centres about Berlin and in the area Magdeburg-Merseburg-Bitterfeld, Hanover and on the lower Elbe. Little progress appears to have been made on this; and it would have required a large-scale reorganisation of the German economy to succeed in any way.

In the inter-war period the German military developed the concept of a defence-based economy, a *Wehrwirtschaft*, which would devote all economic resources for a future war. In *Wehrwissenschaft* the geo-politician Ewald Banse drew the conclusion from World War I that a state waging war had either to possess all raw materials necessary for economic production, or ally itself to a state which had them. In a modern war a state could not hold out economically without allying itself to one of the three giant economic empires of Great Britain, United States or the Soviet Union. Hitler was aware of these difficulties and concluded from Germany's economic weakness that the country needed to secure its economic position by expanding to control the resources of the European continent. The conquest of living space (*Lebensraum*) in the East would overcome these problems and weaknesses.[14]

• • •

The Treaty of Versailles had restricted German forces to seven divisions and 100,000 men. Accordingly, rearmament began from a low base. From 1933 to 1936 it was designed to overcome the treaty restrictions and accompanied by economic policies designed to create employment and overcome the effects of the depression. The pace of rearmament was stepped up in 1936. The August 1936 armaments programme aimed for operational readiness of the field army by 1 October 1939. This programme aimed for a peacetime army of 830 000 men and a field strength of 102 divisional units with 32 infantry divisions, 3 armoured divisions and 4 motorised infantry divisions.[15]

The adoption of the Four Year Plan in 1936 and the appointment of Göring as Commissioner for the plan marked a decisive move by Hitler towards accelerating the process of rearmament. In 1936 Göring had been commissioned to review and improve Germany's situation regarding raw materials and foreign exchange. The Four Year Plan provided for exploitation of all raw materials available in the Reich and the expanded production of synthetic materials without regard to cost; it aimed at achieving a high level of self-sufficiency in four years. In appointing Göring, Hitler instructed him that the German army had to be operational within four years and the German economy prepared for war. Göring specifically stated that the Four Year Plan had to prepare the German economy for total war. Costly long-term processes were used to develop artificial raw materials such as Buna, a rubber substitute, and artificial substitutes for petrol. Increases in the production of all raw materials followed. In 1938, recognising that all goals of the Four Year Plan would not be fulfilled, the regime opted for an accelerated plan (*Schnellplan*), which increased resources to key industries including munitions.[16]

Göring's appointment marked the beginning of the process by which control of the armaments economy passed from the armed forces to the state. Three organisations shaped the scope of rearmament in this period. The first was the military. Expansion of the armed forces and the ordering of their equipment was neither systematic nor co-ordinated. Hitler's directions simply consisted of orders to produce more and went beyond the capacity of the economy. Each service drew up its own programme of expansion based on its immediate needs and competed for limited resources. The scale of the plans was limited only by the raw materials shortages. Attempts by officers in the armed forces supreme command (the *Oberkommando der Wehrmacht*, or OKW) to co-ordinate planning foundered partly on the ability of the head of the Luftwaffe, Hermann Göring, to go directly to Hitler. The OKW possessed a war economics and armaments office, the *Wehrwirtschafts- und Rüstungsamt*, led by General Georg Thomas. It employed armaments officers (*Rüstungsoffiziere*) and defence economy officers (*Wehrwirtschaftsoffiziere*) in each of Germany's military districts to allocate contracts and raw materials check that armaments firms received the necessary labour and materials and report on armaments production. But Thomas was marginalised because of his strong opposition to Hitler's policy of rapid rearmament. Thomas has been seen as an advocate of rearmament in depth, based on a thorough build-up of the armaments economy, rather than rearmament in width, based on a relatively high level of ready armaments. In practice there appears to have been little difference between the policies Thomas favoured in 1939 and those Hitler adopted.[17]

The second organisation with responsibilities relating to rearmament was the Reich Economics Ministry (*Reichwirtschaftsministerium*). The Economics Minister held the position of plenipotentiary for the economy, *Generalbevollmächtigter für die Wirtschaft*, under the Reich Defence Law of 1938, and was responsible for securing the economic preconditions for armaments. The ministry set up a series of organisations to control the economy, which involved industry representatives in economic chambers and groups. Its political position, however, was weak. Its new minister, Walter Funk, appointed in 1937, did not have a high political profile and was content to play a subservient role to Göring and the Four Year Plan.[18]

The Office of the Four Year Plan under Göring was the third organisation shaping rearmament policy and directing the economy in the 1930s. Göring set up a large economic apparatus to control the allocation of resources to industry and to provide the general planning framework for investment, but it did not become an effective steering organisation. Overy suggests that Göring was hampered in exercising these powers by the lack of a central administration and a national network to ensure policies were implemented locally.[19]

In 1938, 52 per cent of government spending and almost 17 per cent of gross national product were devoted to armaments. The government's emphasis on preparation for war led to falls in consumption and shortages. Consumption as a share of national income declined from 71 per cent in 1928 to 59 per cent in 1938. Investment in consumer industries in 1939 was less than in 1928. German consumption patterns and living standards were low in the 1930s compared with the United States or Britain.[20]

Serious problems were created by the rapid expansion of German armaments. Despite the attempts to stockpile raw materials and to create substitute materials, shortages continued and were intensified by the armed forces' demands for raw materials. On 1 January 1937 rationing of non-ferrous metals was introduced. The takeover of Austria and Czechoslovakia provided some resources and armaments. But by 1939 only 80 per cent of minimum food supplies were assured. Germany still imported 70 per cent of its iron ore, 80 per cent of its copper, 65 per cent of its petroleum and rubber. Rearmament was constrained by foreign exchange shortages which hindered Germany's ability to buy raw materials overseas to produce more. Attempts

to promote exports failed because of the priority given to fulfilling armaments orders.[21]

By autumn 1939 Germany mobilised an army of 2.7 million men in 103
units. An aircraft industry, which had only employed 3000 people in 1933,
had expanded to produce an air force of over 4000 front-line aircraft with
302 operational squadrons. The navy concentrated almost completely on the
construction of a battleship fleet, with no carriers and only 26 oceangoing
submarines. In January 1939 Hitler had approved the so-called Z plan which
gave priority to building a large fleet of ten battleships, three battle cruisers
and three heavy cruisers. Continued large-scale military production was
planned, and German mobilisation plans all aimed for a long war and a total
orientation of the economy to war.[22]

As a result of these difficulties, German forces were not as well prepared
for war in 1939 as was assumed at the time. Munitions stocks were low;
Germany had fewer tanks than Britain and France combined; by the beginning of the war German and British aircraft production rates were running
at the same monthly level. Only 13 per cent of the army was motorised and
less than 6 per cent armoured, partly due to fuel and steel shortages. Many
of the economic and administrative preparations for the reorganisation of the
economy were incomplete.[23]

Historians differ in their interpretations of the extent and purpose of the
National Socialist organisation for war from 1933 to 1941. Initially, drawing
on the findings of the United States Strategic Bombing Survey, historians
argued that Hitler tried to wage a kind of war, the *Blitzkrieg*, which did not
require total organisation of the economy for war purposes. In *Germany's
Economic Preparations for War*, Burton Klein suggests that Germany could
have used a much larger share of national product in 1938 for war purposes
by cutting back further on civilian production. Klein argues that the rise of
production and consumption of consumer goods above 1928-9 levels by the
late 1930s indicated that the level of civilian production was high. The
German economy produced 'more butter and less guns.'[24] The government
avoided a greater economic effort because of its fear of deficits and a
disinclination to ask for civilian sacrifices.

In *The German Economy at War*, Alan Milward argues that Germany was
geared to 'armament in width,' not 'armament in depth': 'armament in width'
is a relatively high level of ready armaments, while 'armament in depth' is
the investment and redevelopment necessary to produce the level of armaments for a war against larger mass-producing powers. Milward develops
the concept of a 'Blitzkrieg economy,' derived from the tactical definition
of lightning war as 'a quick knockout blow against the enemy's forces from

a position of strength.'[25] Milward saw the German economy in the Blitzkrieg period (September 1939 to December 1941) as marked by a fairly steady overall armaments production, switched from one type of production to the other as the need arose, while the total output of consumer goods did not fall. '"Guns and butter" was Hitler's aim.'[26] Carroll too argues that the German government only switched to a more comprehensive war economy reluctantly in winter 1941-2.

This interpretation still finds much support among historians. Herbst has extended it to suggest that the government wanted to abolish the distinction between a peace and war economy, by replacing them with an intermediate state of a defence economy (*Wehrwirtschaft*), an economy always partly mobilised. He agrees that the transition to a full war economy was delayed because of the Party's fear of the effect of such measures on popular morale.[27] This view is supported by Tim Mason in *Arbeiterklasse und Volksgemeinschaft*. War—by capturing other sources of raw materials—was the only way out to avoid workers' hostility to the regime. Mason argues, controversially, that the economic overheating caused by rearmament forced the regime to seek war in 1939. Most historians argue that Mason has over-estimated the extent of working-class hostility to the regime and the extent of the economic over-heating of 1938-9. Mason's argument is followed and extended by Stephen Salter, who suggests that the unpopularity of the war and working-class resistance forced the regime to maintain consumer production at a higher level than was needed.[28]

Mason's account, however, contains evidence which supports a different interpretation. He states that arguments that Hitler's strategy did not require the highest possible concentration on armaments cannot be sustained. Hitler wanted Germany to make the greatest possible efforts to strengthen its military potential by 1942. Despite claims that consumer production was high, Mason points out living standards were already being sacrificed before the war. Food consumption by working-class families fell from 1927 to 1937. Consumption of eggs, milk and butter was lower in 1938 than in 1930. The anecdotal evidence of contemporary observers also testifies to a decline in living standards before the war.[29]

More recently the 'Blitzkrieg economy' interpretation has been challenged by R. J. Overy, beginning with his seminal article 'Hitler's War and the German Economy.' Other historians, such as Mierzejewski, Boelcke and Müller, have also followed Overy's 'total war' interpretation. Overy proposes an alternative model of the German economy as consciously, even if inefficiently, mobilised from the outset for total war. He points to Hitler's long-term plans for a major war with the great powers by the mid-1940s.

Because, contrary to Hitler's expectations, wider conflict began in 1939, the regime's plans for rearmament in depth were not complete. According to Overy, the conversion of the economy began in 1939 with sharp and sustained increases in military spending and cutbacks in consumer goods production. By 1941 per-capita civilian consumption had fallen by 22 per cent from its already low 1938 level.[30]

Overy suggests that Göring and the regime sought to mobilise all necessary resources, using material captured from occupied territories. He concedes that bureaucratic competition, and the lack of any system of central control, hampered the war economy. Organising for war was also hampered by the reluctance of many industrialists to co-operate and by Hitler's lack of understanding of the way an economy worked. Overy's work suggests that historians may have been misled into assuming a lack of commitment to total war by the regime's administrative inefficiency, its need to build up a military infrastructure before expanding armaments production beyond a certain point and by high German standards of armaments production. Overy has since suggested that women were employed to a far greater extent than previously assumed.[31] (This question will be examined further in later chapters.)

The historians who favour the 'Blitzkrieg economy' interpretation see political constraints as forcing the government into a certain kind of rearmament. Murray suggests that economic constraints meant that Germany could rearm only in the way it did and that the German armaments effort was at a far higher level than those of Britain and France. But the prewar German economy was limited by its dependence on imports and the inability of German industry to boost foreign exchange earnings significantly. Even if the regime had been willing to cut back more on food imports or consumer industries, the lack of skilled labour and raw materials would have meant that armaments production could not expand further. Germany could not have rearmed in depth because it did not possess the raw materials, industrial base or financial resources to do so. 'The only possible course, taken by Hitler, was to build German forces up as rapidly as possible and then, with that short-term military advantage, conquer the raw material and financial base for a long war.'[32] Murray's account therefore explains the perception of an apparent 'Blitzkrieg' economic strategy, a concept he criticises. National Socialist rearmament was incomplete not because Hitler wanted it incomplete, but because it could not become complete until it had access to the wider European economy. Germany was able to expand production in the period 1942 to 1944 because it controlled the resources of almost the entire continent. For example, in 1941 close to 40 per cent of Germany's steel production took place outside the 1938 borders of the Reich.

• • •

Although the German government had established extensive plans for economic mobilisation in the event of war, these were not fully implemented because of the restricted and swift Polish campaign and the fact that a major war came earlier than planned. Hitler believed that Britain and France would not seriously pursue war in 1939.[33]

When war began, Göring was in charge of armaments production and economic organisation. In addition to being Commissioner for the Four Year Plan, he held the position of Chairman of the Ministerial Council for Reich Defence and could issue decrees with statutory effect. This body soon lapsed. Hans Kehrl, then a senior official of the Economics Ministry, wrote that Göring had been given all the powers of deputy Chancellor but that he did not use them methodically. Instead he was distracted by his duties as commander of the Luftwaffe.[34]

Difficulties soon arose in the coordinating measures taken by the 16 Reich defence commissioners, chosen from among the regional Nazi Party leaders, the Gauleiters. To overcome some of the difficulties of co-ordination, Göring made Fritz Todt Inspector-General for Special Tasks in the Four Year Plan on 23 February 1940. Todt, a convinced National Socialist, had made his name by building Germany's super highways, the *Autobahns,* and headed the Organisation Todt, which carried out building. As Inspector-General, Todt was to investigate the success or failure of measures taken by the Reich authorities for the war effort. He subsequently set up 'combing out' commissions which inspected firms' use of labour. Some 84,000 workers were freed by July 1940 while 137,000 workers were freed in the consumer goods industry. On 17 March 1940 Todt was appointed to the newly created position of Minister for Armaments and Munitions to supervise munitions production. Here he introduced the beginnings of the system of industrial self-responsibility, giving industrialists an official role in distributing munitions contracts. Todt's policy of seeking to harness industry's profit motive to ensure greater armaments production broke with the tendency of the military, including Thomas, to try to 'command' the economy.[35]

The regime was waging war under certain constraints. The leadership itself had been divided about the decision to attack Poland in 1939; Goebbels and Göring opposed war, while Speer and Bormann supported it. Goebbels had warned openly about the danger of war at the time of the Nazi-Soviet pact, and urged that Germany adopt peaceful policies.[36]

The war was not popular with the German people. Contemporary reports clearly indicate the population entered the war in a mood of 'reluctant loyalty.'[37] Public attitudes were strongly influenced by memories of the privations of World War I. As a result, fluctuations in food supply had a considerable effect on morale. Problems emerged as early as winter 1939-40 due to shortages of food and coal. Morale stabilised with the military successes of 1940, reaching its high point after the German victory over France in 1940, but the popular mood remained fragile and easily shaken.

The organisation of the home front from 1939 to 1941 faced other constraints. Planning continued to be hampered by Hitler's shifting armaments priorities. In 1940 Hitler stressed to Thomas' staff the need for great flexibility in the control of the economy and the impossibility of setting down long-term production programmes. He wanted to be able to shift production according to his military priorities. In addition, Hitler had unrealistic expectations of the economy. While he spoke of a long war he continued his building projects.[38]

Nonetheless, restriction of the economy began with the start of the war. On 4 September 1939 a war economy decree (*Reichswirtschaftsverordnung*) was promulgated, which included pay and price freezes, tax increases and stopping of overtime payments. In practice this meant drastic pay cuts. A strong working-class reaction against these measures led to the Party and small businesses putting pressure on ministers to back down on these policies. By November 1939 most of these policies, particularly the bans on overtime, had been quietly abandoned. The higher tax rates remained. Historians disagree about the reasons for the working-class resistance, whether it was a symptom of a general working-class opposition to the regime and the war or whether the workers were willing to bear the burdens imposed by the decree and only became restive when the end of the Polish campaign, and the apparent need for the measures, passed.[39]

Food and clothing rationing was introduced in 1939. Businesses involved in non-essential activities were cut back or closed, although historians disagree about the extent of these moves. Herbst claims that in the first two months of the war 100,000 small artisan and craft businesses (*Handwerk*) had been closed down, and their employees reduced by almost one million; while Boelcke suggests that only 100,000 workers were freed. The regime sought to achieve industry restructuring by closures rather than by open bans, which were opposed by the Gauleiters and the civil service. Further indirect controls were used to restrict consumer production. In December 1940, for example, raw materials were withheld from producers of small consumer goods. A scarcity of consumer goods was reportedly depressing morale in 1941.[40]

The German leadership faced demographic problems which worsened the existing labour shortage. Low birth rates in World War I meant that the size of the main military classes was smaller than usual. Germany went into the war with full employment because of the rearmament programme of the late 1930s. Unlike in Britain, the German labour offices had no slack to take up but had to find extra workers from those with no previous interest in paid employment. In addition, the German armed forces called up a higher proportion of men in the main age groups for military service than did any other combatant. Foreign workers were already being used to fill vacancies. In the late 1930s the government and industry encouraged programmes of retraining (*Umschulung*), training unskilled workers to do skilled and semi-skilled work. The effectiveness of these policies in the war is hard to trace and needs further investigation.[41]

Although National Socialist ideology emphasised women's natural place in the domestic sphere, the number of women in employment remained high by international standards. At least 44 per cent of women were employed in 1933 and at least 46 per cent in 1939. Koonz's figures suggest 49.2 per cent of adult women were in employment in 1939. Women predominated in agriculture and as assistants in family businesses. In contrast, at the beginning of the 1930s in the United States 17.7 per cent of women were employed; in the United Kingdom the figure was 26.9 per cent and in France, 37.1 per cent. The differences in rates arose partly because of differences in statistical measurement. German statistics of employment included women assisting in family businesses, even if unpaid. These categories were not always included in other countries.[42]

Once war broke out, women proved to be reluctant to seek employment for a number of reasons. Women's work in industry tended to be unskilled and boring, thus reducing their interest in remaining in the workforce. The government's pro-natalist policies of the 1930s had also resulted in a slight increase in the birth rate, thereby reducing the number of women likely to make themselves available for employment. Full employment meant that most women who wanted paid employment had already found it. Fear of coming into the labour registration system and then being unable to leave or change jobs was a disincentive for those still outside paid employment.[43]

Generous levels of government financial support for the families of soldiers also discouraged women from seeking employment. In World War I German financial support for soldiers' families had been extremely low.

The new rate set in 1938 was generous, designed to prevent a repetition of problems in World War I, and Labour Ministry warnings that it would discourage female employment were ignored. The one group excepted were farmers' wives, who could receive the allowance only if they could show that farm income had decreased since the husband left. At least 300,000 women were estimated to have left the work force permanently as a result. Later efforts to encourage and threaten these women to return were unsuccessful. Efforts were made to get the women who left the work force since the war to return, by threatening a substantial reduction of their family support, but this only resulted in the return to work of 14,000 women. In 1940 Göring rejected a draft decree obliging women to report for employment. The proposal would cause too much public unrest, he believed. Labour requirements could be met by employing prisoners of war. A comprehensive Party publicity drive to encourage women to volunteer for work, using the slogan 'German women help victory' ('*Deutsche Frauen helfen siegen*'), failed in 1941.[44]

Social attitudes to women's roles restricted their wider employment. Many women preferred to accept reductions in their family support than work; men were often the strongest opponents of the employment of their wives. Industry did not appear to take up Thomas' suggestion in 1940 that they encourage female employment by adapting the work environment to their needs. While women were included in the Umschulung programmes, there was no particular awareness on the part of either government or industry for the need for specific policies to ensure women were trained. Armed forces' investigations suggested that firms tended not to make full use of training for women, only training them to a semi-skilled level. The regime did, however, use compulsion for some women. Labour service was introduced in 1938 for unmarried women between 17 and 25. In 1941 the period involved was lengthened and the numbers involved increased.[45]

The regime turned to the employment of foreign workers and prisoners of war. The number of foreign workers employed increased to 1.5 million by the end of April 1941. The labour shortage led to 300,000 men being temporarily released from the armed forces. Civilian conscription had been used for both men and women before the war, and was used in 1939 and 1940. The poor productivity of these workers, particularly if they were forcibly transferred from their home areas, led to the winding down of this programme after January 1940.[46]

The two interpretations of the German economy at war differ most markedly in their analysis of the German war economy of 1939 to 1941, a period which requires still further investigation, as most studies do not examine it closely. Overy has suggested various problems which arose in the period 1939 to 1941 without discussing them in detail. Müller's new study, 'Die Mobilisierung der deutschen Wirtschaft für Hitlers Kriegsführung,' in *Das Deutsche Reich und der Zweite Weltkrieg*, provides the most thorough and persuasive interpretation so far presented. Müller categorises the German economy in this period as a 'transitional economy' (*Übergangswirtschaft*).[47] Although the regime and the leadership from Hitler down went into the war intending to wage a total war, there were considerable problems in achieving this from 1939 to 1941. First, Hitler decided to implement the war economy step by step in 1939, and this allowed opposition to these policies greater scope. Secondly, rivalry between civilian leaders and organisations and the military hampered German armaments production. The military fought to retain their primacy, even though it became increasingly clear that Hitler favoured control of the economy by civilian businessmen. Thirdly, the quick German victory over France and widespread popular expectations of peace created difficulties for the regime in 1940, even though Hitler continued to plan for a long total war. The problems of German production were not due to a strategic or economic concept of the Blitzkrieg economy, but due to 'weakness of the leadership, bureaucratism and an inefficient decisionmaking structure.'[48]

Problems of sources and reliability of statistics may prevent a definite answer to the debate about the extent of German war production in 1939-41.[49] The evidence put forward by Overy, Murray and Müller suggests that, if the German economy was not effectively mobilised before 1942, this was not necessarily due to a lack of will on the part of the leadership.

The lack of unified central control of the economy seems to have influenced Klein, for example, into believing that priority was not given to the armaments industry. Carroll has pointed out that civilian consumption was the same proportion of gross national product (GNP) in 1940 as in 1937. She looks at the volume of production rather than its allocation. Nevertheless, while the absolute amount of consumer production was not reduced, it was reduced by one third per head of the civilian population. A large percentage of those consumer goods still produced was used by the armed forces. The fact that consumer spending in the 1930s was allowed to rise back to its 1928 levels led some historians to believe that the economy was geared only to Blitzkrieg and that the regime was not planning long campaigns. Historians' judgements may also have been influenced by the absence of a drastic alteration of the economy on the outbreak of war, in contrast to Britain. Herbst's concept of a Wehrwirtschaft can be drawn on to explain this absence. Such a sharp shift of course was necessary in an economy largely oriented to civilian production in 1939, such as the United Kingdom; in an economy already considerably oriented to armaments production, a more steady increase of war production was possible.[50] The idea that National Socialism was unable to command sufficient popular support to mobilise effectively may also exercise a disproportionate appeal to historians.

By July 1941, 68 per cent of the industrial work force were engaged on direct military orders, a proportion higher than in the United Kingdom. The growth of war production was blocked by a lack of raw materials, equipment and skilled labour, which could be made up only partly by exploitation of the occupied territories. In 1941 the German economy could be described as 'overtaxed.'[51]

Notwithstanding the problems of the German economy in 1941, the German Government had access to the resources of the greater part of Europe, with only Great Britain still unconquered. Despite increasing British organisation of its economy for a long war, the threat from Britain could be contained. The German-Soviet pact had overcome many raw materials problems. The regime had begun to exploit the resources of the conquered territories and to incorporate their economies into the German war effort. The conquered territories, France in particular, represented a great addition to Germany's productive capacity. This exploitation was initially inefficient, and Germany did not begin to benefit economically from its victories until 1942-3. Germany could also draw on the economies of the neutral countries, particularly Spain, Sweden, and Turkey. Germany lacked the resources for a war of the scope it had embarked on. The period from 1940 to 1941 was not long enough to incorporate European production into the German war effort. There was always a tension between the need for foreign labour in Germany and the desire to make the optimum use of the economies of the occupied territories.[52] Military success made Hitler less rather than more likely to listen to the cautions of his advisers when planning for the attack on the Soviet Union began.

2

'Dangerous Illusions'? 1941-2

In 1941 Hitler's strategic and political decisions—to invade the Soviet Union and declare war on the United States—altered the nature of the war. These decisions strengthened the ideological component in the war and the regime's pursuit of total war, particularly with the beginning of the extermination of the Jews. They also reduced Germany's chances of victory. As the war in the East continued, the German government was faced with a military and economic crisis, which led to policy changes.

On 22 June 1941, in 'Operation Barbarossa', Germany invaded the USSR, attacking with three separate forces, aiming at Leningrad, Moscow and the Ukraine. Initially, as German propaganda emphasised, German forces achieved spectacular victories in the air and on the ground. Soviet forces, however, continued to resist and to produce reinforcements. They were given time to regroup when, after four weeks, the German advance was halted while the German leadership debated their future course of action.[1]

The German leadership believed the campaign would not last long. In *Mein Kampf* Hitler argued that Russia was ripe for collapse because it was ruled by Jews. Hitler told von Rundstedt, 'You have only to kick in the door and the whole rotten structure will come crashing down.'[2] Himmler too claimed the USSR was not a military threat. Its army was badly equipped and trained, and its officer corps were not as competent as German non-commissioned officers. The leaders' assessment that the Soviet army was incapable of prolonged resistance was influenced by ideological interpretation of the Soviet system, including Hitler's use of race to judge military strength.

Most leaders were unaware of the economic and military significance of the decision to attack the Soviet Union. Estimates of the 1930s suggest that the regime lacked information about the USSR's resources and power. A 1939 paper noted the recent creation of armaments firms on the Volga and in the Urals, but concluded that the armaments industry centred on Moscow and Leningrad. More cautious intelligence assessments were ignored.[3]

It could be argued that Germany lost the war against Russia from the start, because Soviet productive and military capacity was greater. The possibility existed, however, that the capture of Moscow or Leningrad might induce the collapse of the Soviet political system. Lack of clear military objectives hindered the campaign in late 1941. Disputes between Hitler and the High Command, particularly over the priority of capturing Moscow, ensured that the chances of such a capture had faded by November 1941. The same month Hitler told Goebbels that developments in the East could be viewed positively. The enemy had lost its great armaments centres. But the situation on the Eastern front was less favourable than Hitler's confident assertion suggested. German offensives floundered, and Soviet forces retook Rostov on the Don on 29 November 1941; the first Soviet counter-offensive followed in December 1941. At Hitler's order, German forces held fast during the severe Russian winter. Hitler may have recognised that his strategy had failed, but he did not alter it. By the end of December Hitler had made himself Supreme Commander of the Army in place of General Brauchitsch.[4]

At the same time as German forces encountered difficulties in the East, Hitler declared war on the United States. Historians disagree about the reasons for this decision. Some argue the decision reflected over-confidence, or an unrealistic assessment of US military and economic potential. It seems that Hitler was conscious of US power and believed by early 1941 that war between the United States and Germany was only a matter of time. The United States was already involved in an undeclared war with German submarines in the Atlantic. Hitler's declaration of war aimed to avert immediate United States involvement in the war in Europe by ensuring it was preoccupied with the Pacific war and to split US forces to prevent a quick victory over Japan.[5]

The Nazi leadership underestimated American political and economic potential and therefore generally did not recognise the significance of declaring war. Goebbels' only concern was the psychological effect of the news on the German people. Göring was largely responsible for Hitler's inaccurate picture of enemy economic capacity. Those who tried to present a more accurate view of US production were disbelieved. In early 1942, Göring and Hitler still rejected SD reports of American economic capacity as 'nonsense.'[6]

War against the Soviet Union marked a significant escalation of the ideological element in the war and was accompanied by a qualitative change in the conduct of the war. Expansion to the East, extermination of Bolshevism and the destruction of Jewry became linked in the war against the Soviet Union. From the beginning the campaign was cast as an ideological war and a war of annihilation. This radicalisation began with the Commissar Order that Red Army, and some civilian, commissars were to be shot on the spot, and led to the deaths of Soviet POWs by starvation, disease and shooting in 1941-2. Some 3.3 million Soviet POWs died out of a total of 5.5 million.[7]

The ideological aims of the campaign and expectations of a quick victory meant no political appeals were directed to the Soviet people. In 1941 there were no attempts to gain the support of the population in the occupied territories, even though a skilful attempt to win them over might have yielded substantial results.[8]

Ideological radicalisation was expressed above all in the extermination of Soviet Jews and the extension of this policy to the Jews of conquered Europe. The 'Final Solution' was well underway by winter 1941. That year approximately 1.1 million Jews were killed, mainly in mass shootings carried out by the *Einsatzgruppen*, mobile SD and security police units. Adoption of genocide was a sign of commitment to an ideologically based concept of total war. Genocide could not be economically rational: it diverted valuable materials and equipment and destroyed a large potential labour force. Such considerations were irrelevant to a leadership that believed that these potential workers would inevitably work for the Reich's destruction. Accordingly, Jewish workers in General Government armaments firms were deported, despite the armed forces' objections. 'Economic interests should fundamentally be left out of consideration with the settlement of the [Jewish] problem.'[9]

As Germany's strategic position weakened, the regime stepped up its campaign against what the leadership perceived as its deadliest enemy. It 'rationalised and industrialised mass annihilation.'[10] The war against the Jews was a 'total' war. From a National Socialist viewpoint, resources allocated to the pursuit of the 'Final Solution' strengthened the war effort and reduced the chances of internal revolt. In May 1942 Goebbels pointed out to Hitler how much more favourable the German internal position was than in 1917. Hitler replied that the German workers did not think of stabbing him in the back. 'The Germans only participate in subversive movements if the Jews seduce them.'[11]

If the campaign against the USSR in 1941 was accompanied by an irrevocable commitment to the ideological model of total war, it also brought the first questioning of the conduct of the war and the first doubts of victory. Goebbels was one of the first political leaders to express caution about the Russian front. Initially he was confident, believing that Soviet industrial capacity had either been captured or was within German grasp. He did not, however, share the belief common in Hitler's headquarters that the campaign would be finished in November, and he was angered by Dietrich's announcement in October 1941, at Hitler's instigation, that the war in the East had been won. He called this 'the greatest psychological mistake of the war.'[12] It would make the continuation of the war hard to explain to the people. To prepare the population for an extended campaign, in August 1941 Goebbels proposed a public collection of winter clothing for the troops. General Jodl rejected this, explaining that by winter German troops would be safely quartered in Moscow and Leningrad. Consequently Goebbels had to introduce the winter clothing appeal in late December 1941, when it served to alarm, rather than reassure, the population.

Goebbels correctly believed Germany had misjudged Soviet military potential. He considered that the Soviet Government's control of its population meant they had considerable reserves to mobilise. Despite lack of access to exact information, Goebbels recognised the growing difficulties in the conduct of the war. The origins of his greater realism are unclear. His assessment of the Soviet regime may have been influenced by his sympathy with the USSR in the 1920s; he may have wanted to avoid exaggerated optimism from diminishing the credibility of his propaganda. Goebbels saw his task as preparing the people for another winter of war. He did so partly by introducing more caution and realism into reporting of the campaign in the East.[13]

Goebbels was also quickly persuaded of the need to alter the political policies followed in the East. As early as September 1941, he considered this 'the main problem' of the Russian campaign—a positive policy towards the Russian people was needed.[14] At the urging of experts on the Soviet Union, Goebbels prepared a memorandum to Hitler on the issue. Its fate is not known. He unsuccessfully raised the matter of the overall treatment of the Soviet peoples, and the treatment of Soviet prisoners of war, with Hitler in November 1941. Hitler responded that prisoners of war received better treatment in Germany than they had in the USSR and that overall treatment of the Soviet peoples was the responsibility of Alfred Rosenberg, minister for the occupied Eastern territories. Goebbels attempted to use his subordinates to counter these policies but was hindered in these efforts by his poor relations with Rosenberg.

By the end of 1941, at least one leader had begun to advocate a compromise peace. Armaments Minister Todt began the Eastern campaign with the same optimistic assumptions as other leaders. Yet, after visiting the front in November 1941, he judged that the Germans were neither physically nor psychologically tough enough to withstand the rigours of the campaign. Todt was impressed by Soviet military ability and concluded that American productive capacity was so great that Germany could not win the war. 'The decisive fact for him [Todt] was that Germany had to adapt itself to a *long* war and that with this the prospect of ending the war favourably dwindled from month to month.'[15]

Todt arranged for the industrialist Walter Rohland to brief Hitler on American armaments production. Todt told Hitler that the war was already lost militarily and in production: he had to seek a political end to the war. Hitler's reply suggested that he was prepared to consider peace only with the West. He answered that he had tried to make peace earlier, but had exhausted all political possibilities. Todt made further efforts to convince Hitler to take these steps in January and February 1942. Todt died in an aircraft accident after his last visit to Hitler's headquarters in February 1942. To Rohland, this 'eliminated from the government the only man at that time, who had a complete overview of the situation because of his connections with other countries and his clear judgement.'[16]

Todt's proposals involved 'a fundamental re-ordering of German strategy'.[17] He advocated peace, not intensification of the war effort; he recognised that this latter course was futile. Hitler does not appear to have discussed Todt's ideas with other leaders or have taken any further action on the proposals. There are various possible explanations for Hitler's inaction: Todt may not have persuaded him of the seriousness of the situation; Hitler may not have believed there was any solution to Germany's strategic problems; or he may have hoped renewed military success would solve these problems. In December 1941 Hitler had reportedly rejected a peace offer from Stalin, because he was convinced of ultimate victory.

Todt had shown that he did not believe the war could be won, even if armaments production increased. Hitler refused to alter his overall strategy for the war but was willing to alter other policies to increase armaments production. Throughout 1941 Hitler had continued to switch priorities in armaments production. For example, belief in a quick victory over Russia led him in July to expand air and sea armaments to prepare for possible war with the United States. The armaments economy remained hampered by the lack of a clear overview of German economic potential. Todt's powers continued to expand: he was made Inspector-General for Water and Power on 29 July 1941. On 11 September Hitler ordered a transfer of the power to inspect and reduce armaments claims to Todt and Keitel. The co-operation Hitler expected did not materialise: disputes between Todt and the armed forces, and within the armed forces over priorities for production, continued. Müller argues that this hastened the collapse of the power of the military and their command economy.[18]

By the end of 1941 there was growing awareness in the leadership not only of military difficulties on the Eastern front but also of a crisis in armaments production. Hitler rejected attempts by Ley and Goebbels to gain influence in armaments production and pursue more anti-capitalist policies. He preferred to rely on industrialists rather than on military or Party direction of the economy. At the end of 1941 Todt persuaded Hitler to extend the system of industrial self-responsibility from munitions to all war equipment. A series of committees, staffed mainly by factory managers, was created, responsible for allocating munitions orders and developing weapons. Other changes were also made in the armaments economy. Todt introduced a price-fixing system for war contracts by December 1941; the previous system, where industrialists received a percentage of their costs as profits, had been no incentive to cut costs. On 4 February Todt announced the appointment of Zangen, head of the Reich Industry Group, to rationalise the civilian economy further. In his final talks with Hitler on 7 February 1942, Todt probably discussed reorganisation of the war economy.[19]

Historians' judgements of Todt's achievements differ. Milward sees him as an important figure who established the structures Speer was later to use so successfully. Mierzejewski is more critical. Todt's role in the economy was 'creditable' but 'utterly inadequate'; he should have introduced more far-reaching reforms.[20] Müller's more extensive study favours Milward's assessment. Todt spent some 18 to 24 months in disputes with the military. The armed forces had been able to prevent the rise of a civilian armaments minister for 18 months. Todt took the opportunity of the winter 1941 crisis and Hitler's growing distrust of the military as a result of his disputes with them over the battle of Moscow to convince Hitler of the need for fundamental changes.

Hitler granted Albert Speer, Todt's successor as Minister for Armaments, the wide-ranging powers he had already decided to give Todt. Speer later claimed that his appointment was surprising, since he had no professional experience for the position. But he had already been involved in organising work in the construction industry for Todt. Speer was nominally responsible to Göring in the Four Year Plan in his capacity as *Generalbevollmächtigter für Rüstungsaufgaben*. On taking office Speer had to establish his authority against attempts by Göring, Funk and *Deutsche Arbeitsfront (DAF)* leader Robert Ley to gain power at his expense. These efforts soon collapsed because of Hitler's clear support for Speer, prompted by his personal friendship with Speer and by his recognition that clear authority was needed for armaments production. In a clash between Speer and Rosenberg over control of the economy in the occupied East, Hitler not only decided in Speer's favour but also declared that he would sign anything which came from Speer. 'For a considerable time I found myself moving in a kind of vacuum that offered no resistance whatsoever,' Speer later observed.[21]

Hitler advised Speer to use industry as much as possible in his work. Although Speer had not originated the system of industrial self-responsibility, he continued and extended it. He argued that bureaucracy killed improvisation. He created new co-ordinating organisations such as the *Zentrale Planung* (Central Planning) committee, staffed by himself, Milch and Koerner. Zentrale Planung allocated resources to industries and thereby partly overcame the lack of a central office for the German war economy. Speer extended his ministry's power. Most notably, the Wehrmacht's War Economy and Armaments Branch (Wehrwirtschafts- und Rüstungsamt, or WiRüAmt) and its armaments inspectors were subordinated to Speer on 7 May 1942. Thomas supported the amalgamation but was soon frozen out by Speer.[22]

By the end of 1941 the two main non-military priorities of the regime were to increase armaments production and to replace manpower losses. As a result of fighting in winter 1941-42, German losses from June 1941 to March 1942 were 295,000 killed or missing, and 823,000 wounded. On 25 January 1942 Hitler ordered the administration to make all available workers free for the armed forces and armaments and to end planning for peacetime tasks. Administrative simplifications resulted, but the number of staff saved thereby are not listed.[23]

Some leaders had already been reducing or reallocating their staff on their own initiative. These efforts give some indication of their commitment to total war. In January 1942 Goebbels began his own programme to reduce staff and substitute female for male workers in the Propaganda Ministry. Women were employed as drivers and messengers, and for routine administration. Goebbels had already released 650, or 36 per cent, of his ministry's 1770 employees to the armed forces and armaments by the end of 1941. By March 1942, 59 per cent of the remaining 1400 staff were women. In reporting these measures to Hitler, Goebbels did not explicitly suggest other departments adopt similar policies. He did point out that while the Propaganda Ministry now had a ratio of 32 per cent men to 68 per cent women, the Armaments Ministry employed 35 per cent women to 65 per cent men. The Propaganda Ministry adopted other measures of simplification, but Hitler overruled Goebbels' plan to reduce the positions of indispensable (*unabkommlich* or *uk*) workers in the arts, stating that cultural life was necessary to maintain morale on the home front and prevent pessimism.[24]

During the winter of 1941-42 Goebbels originated a wider plan to mobilise labour, the exact details of which have not survived. He planned to concentrate all industrial capacity on armaments; Göring apparently persuaded Hitler it was unnecessary. Goebbels' diaries suggest he intended as well to recruit one million additional workers voluntarily. Hitler told him he preferred to use Soviet prisoners of war rather than German workers. On 31 October 1941 Hitler had ordered the use of Soviet prisoners of war to solve German labour problems. The initial victories in the USSR opened up the prospect of unrestricted labour resources and led to judgements based on an illusion of plenty, as in Hitler's response to Goebbels' plan. These potential resources were prodigiously wasted through the ill treatment, starvation and shooting of the majority of Soviet POWs. Himmler later commented that it was 'regrettable' that in 1941 the Germans had not valued their Soviet prisoners of war as they did in 1943.[25]

• • •

Germany's leaders had reason to regain confidence by mid-1942. The failure of Soviet offensives in the Crimea in April and May appeared to improve Germany's position. In May Hitler again told Goebbels he viewed the military situation positively. The Soviet internal situation was precarious and Stalin had exhausted his armaments potential. German forces continued to advance in the southern USSR and North Africa, taking Sebastopol on 1 July and Tobruk on 21 June. Hitler told Halder on 10 July 1942, that 'the Russian is finished.'[26] The German Sixth Army aimed for the Caucasus and for Stalingrad. The first serious attempt to storm Stalingrad began on 16 August, and the Germans came close to controlling the southern half of the city. Early Japanese military successes had reduced disquiet about the strength of Germany's opponents. By November 1942 Goebbels had abandoned earlier hopes of British disintegration. He commented that the Germans often indulged in such 'vain' hopes because of their experience in 1918, where they foundered 'because of our ideologists and because of our own lack of political education.'[27] As late as December 1942 Goebbels still believed US armaments production claims were exaggerated. Those who knew of the United States' superiority in raw materials and volume of production were comforted by the superior quality of German armaments.

Yet public morale remained vulnerable, and war weariness grew. By summer 1942 the food supply and quality of goods available was worsening. During 1942 Hitler adopted measures to strengthen control of the home front. He received full powers from the Reichstag on 26 April 1942 as supreme justice authority (*Oberster Gerichtsherr*), which allowed him to overrule decisions of judges and legal authorities. The administration of justice became more ideological and stricter, particularly after Otto Thierack became Justice Minister on 20 August 1942.[28]

The ideological nature of the war continued to intensify. By 1942 Goebbels linked the struggle against Jews with decisiveness and thoroughness in the war effort. In May 1942 he gained Hitler's permission to evacuate Jews from Berlin. Hitler gave Speer the task of replacing Jews employed in the German armaments industry by foreign workers as far as possible. Goebbels commented that 40,000 Jews at liberty with nothing to lose were a security threat.[29]

The SS's tasks of extermination of the Jews and repression, and Himmler's views as expressed in his speeches, indicate that Himmler was more deeply committed to the ideological concept of the war. Like Hitler, he saw total war as the realisation of German ideology. For Himmler the war was an ideological war, a war to the death between the Germans and subhuman Slavs governed by Jewish Bolshevism. Accordingly, though he did not say so explicitly, the implementation of the Final Solution would be consistent with his commitment to total war. An estimated 2.7 million Jews were exterminated in 1942.[30]

In that year there was a growing willingness among members of the leadership to pursue a compromise peace. Himmler had not shared Goebbels' and Todt's concern about military developments in the East in 1941. He considered the war with Russia 'the most necessary war' which prevented a Soviet attack on Germany.[31] He still claimed to be certain of victory in the East in 1942, although he warned that it would not be easy. Stalin used the most modern weapons and had no regard for human life. He still considered that subordinates like Schellenberg overestimated Russian strength.

Walter Schellenberg, the head of the SD's foreign section, learnt in March 1942 of Japanese attempts to arrange a compromise peace between the USSR and Germany. Judging that Himmler was too much under Hitler's influence to act independently, Schellenberg had the SD leader, Reinhard Heydrich, raise the matter with Hitler, unsuccessfully. Further Japanese efforts were rejected in April and June 1942. It is possible that, confident of victory, at this time Hitler also neglected to take up a Soviet compromise peace offer.[32]

By summer 1942 Schellenberg concluded Germany could no longer win the war. He planned to open negotiations with both the western allies and the Soviet Union and play one side off against the other. When he approached Himmler, Himmler admitted that he was worried about Germany's prospects once US armaments production took off, and they discussed possible peace terms. Schellenberg suggested a return to the status quo of 1 September 1939, allowing Germany to pursue its goals peacefully. Himmler agreed to Schellenberg's plan. He believed that nothing could be achieved while Ribbentrop was still Foreign Minister, and wanted the scheme kept from Bormann, whom he believed made Hitler more uncompromising. Schellenberg claimed contact was made with the British, but the scheme foundered on Himmler's nervousness. Himmler decided he had to inform Ribbentrop and Hitler, who stopped Schellenberg from pursuing the contacts. Hitler rejected proposals for a compromise peace by the Japanese in June and October, from the Italian leadership in November and December and from General Fritz Fromm, the head of army armaments and commander of the Ersatzheer, at the end of 1942. Hitler turned down Rommel's plan to reduce German military commitments by withdrawing from North Africa.[33]

Goebbels too was willing to contemplate a compromise peace by July 1942, telling Propaganda Ministry officials that the opening of a second front would not serve German interests. 'Germany by no means intends to continue fighting Stalin under all circumstances; should Stalin . . . be prepared one day to come to an arrangement which would offer us a strategically good frontier and security against Russian rearmament, then such a possibility will certainly not be rejected out of hand on the German side.'[34] It is not known whether Goebbels discussed these ideas with Hitler. Whether he did or not, the preference for peace with Stalin rather than the West was Goebbels' and not Hitler's.

These abortive peace negotiations suggest that unease about Germany's prospects in the war was spreading among the leadership, and this lack of confidence developed quickly. Moves for a compromise peace could serve either as an alternative to total war or as part of a strategy of total war. Todt's moves were an alternative to total war, since he had decided that this would not bring victory. For Goebbels total war was designed to make Germany a more threatening opponent and thereby make a compromise peace more attractive to the enemy.

While overall strategy was under question, both armaments production and labour supply continued to be crucially important to Germany's war effort. Armaments production increased by 55 per cent between February and July 1942, probably as a result of Todt's reforms; production rose again after October. Speer reallocated resources to armaments production and introduced a series of production efficiencies.[35]

In a speech to Gauleiters on 24 February 1942, Speer urged them to end any planning for peace and told them not to be influenced by what they saw as the exceptional circumstances of their region (*Gau*). It was not the Party's task to determine and organise the remaining industrial economy; this was the task of armaments. The Party's task was to increase the German worker's productivity. The Party's influence on war production was extended in 1942, when all Gauleiters were made defence commissioners and the boundaries of other organisations were revised to correspond with the Gaus.[36]

Labour shortages expanded the SS's role in economic production. Himmler could promise a large labour force even though the actual work force he commanded has been estimated to have been no more than 500,000 at any one time. Himmler proposed in July 1942 that a factory should be built in Buchenwald to produce 55,000 carbines; the Neuengamme camp would make the .08 pistol; and an SS company would be established to produce communications equipment in women's concentration camps. On 15 September 1942 Speer agreed to set up 300 more barracks at Auschwitz and to use concentration camp inmates for large armaments production; in exchange the SS abandoned their principle that all such production should be within the camps. Instead, the staff of factories outside would be replaced by the SS's prisoners. Fifty thousand Jews would be employed. The SS offered Speer other production as well. These plans were opposed by representatives of the army and industry, who saw the SS as competitors. Later in September Speer, Saur and Sauckel persuaded Hitler to put an end to the plan. Hitler agreed, because he felt Sauckel had solved the question of labour supply. Himmler retained some production for armaments but not to the extent he and Pohl had planned.[37]

Although Speer viewed the SS's economic production as a considerable obstacle to rational planning of production and resented the empire building it involved, Himmler saw SS economic production as part of his contribution to total war. 'Every internee had to be employed in the armament industry to the extreme limit of his forces. The Reichsführer constantly and on every occasion kept this goal before our eyes,' testified the commandant of Auschwitz, Rudolf Hoess.[38] Himmler combined his support for total war with his ideological priorities. Despite his desire for increased production,

Himmler tried unsuccessfully to remove ethnic Germans from civilian and military tasks for political activities, even though they were needed as interpreters in the armed forces.

Germany continued to need to replace losses on the Eastern front. By 21 June 1942 these losses amounted to 271,612 dead and 65,730 missing; and 851,053 wounded by 10 May 1942. A wide range of measures was adopted. Hitler made two appointments intended to ensure the labour supply. On 19 March 1942 Fritz Sauckel, Gauleiter of Thuringia, was appointed general plenipotentiary for labour with extraordinary powers (*General-bevollmächtigter für den Arbeitseinsatz* or *GBA*). Speer had convinced Hitler that such a position was needed, since Gauleiters had been unwilling to transfer workers to other Gaus for armaments purposes. As a political problem, this could not be solved by the Labour Ministry's bureaucrats. Speer proposed his friend Karl Hanke, Gauleiter of Lower Silesia, for the position, and claimed Hitler agreed. Bormann intervened, persuading Hitler that an experienced Gauleiter, who would have the necessary authority to get agreement, should be appointed. In his first few months as plenipotentiary, Sauckel effectively identified and mobilised labour reserves; Bormann's support helped him overcome Gauleiters' resistance. Sauckel appointed the Gauleiters as his special plenipotentiaries for manpower in the Gaus in April 1942. He launched a programme to recruit foreign workers to Germany, both voluntarily and by force. By 31 December 1942 Sauckel claimed to have brought 1,480,000 workers into the Reich and to have employed 1,725,000 prisoners of war. In addition, 2.7 million German workers were transferred to the armaments economy in 1942. His figures were possibly exaggerated, but nonetheless represent a considerable advance.[39]

Hitler, secondly, appointed General Walter von Unruh as 'special commissioner for the supervision of a purposeful war effort' on 26 April 1942.[40] Von Unruh was to examine the armed forces' use of staff behind the lines and in the occupied territories. A commission, which included an SS officer, With, and Party Chancellery representatives (Ifland and Hoffmann), was set up to assist von Unruh in this task. The von Unruh commission inspected organisations in occupied territories in the East from May to July 1942. Von Unruh's own reports do not set out the overall numbers saved or provide an overview of his methods for simplifying administration. They indicate he freed staff, made simplifications and suggested administrative and organisational improvements. The commission uncovered waste of raw materials and corruption, and discovered many staff surpluses and inefficiencies caused by overlapping organisational responsibilities. German firms were found to have moved their younger men into positions in the General Government to avoid call-up. The commission gave no exemptions from call-up to workers born in 1914 and later. It reduced staff in some of the Reichskommissariats, the major territorial divisions of the German civilian administration in the occupied USSR (Reichskommissariats Ukraine and Shitomir), by one third and reduced the civilian staff of the Kiev Generalkommissariat, the intermediate level of administration, by between 1200 to 1500 people. As well, an estimated 3000 men were freed from the civilian sector in the General Government for the Wehrmacht or armaments. The numbers freed were not great in comparison to German losses, but the findings indicate that there was excess capacity in the administration. Bormann was advised that more positions could be cut. Hoffmann warned that there was a danger that offices might fill up again with workers when the commission's work ended. A limit on staff would need to be set from the top.

Von Unruh's commission was extended to inspecting the use of staff inside Germany, because of his success in the occupied territories. Bormann advised Party leaders that von Unruh enjoyed Hitler's 'particular trust.'[41] Between November 1942 and April 1943 the commission examined each level of administration inside Germany; in co-ordination with Speer it also inspected the use of labour in the economy. Unfortunately the results of the commission's examinations, and the numbers it removed, do not appear to have survived. Extant files contain only lists of employees, provided for its deliberations, classified by skill and fitness grading for various departments. National Socialist leaders were divided in their opinion of the commission's work. While Hitler had confidence in von Unruh, Bormann, Speer and Goebbels all criticised von Unruh's effectiveness. The Reich Chancellery was also sceptical about von Unruh's capacities and the possibilities of freeing staff. One official described the numbers saved as 'not overwhelming.'[42] Only Post Minister Ohnesorge was willing to give up large numbers of staff, while von Unruh met quiet resistance from other ministries. Yet a neutral observer, the Swedish journalist Arvid Fredborg, considered the commission effective and ruthless. 'He spared nobody. Both State authorities and the Party organisations had to give up their people. . . . He also succeeded in sending complete garrisons to the front, replacing them by old . . . reservists. Women were taking the men's jobs in great numbers in barracks and police offices.'[43] Officially, it was claimed von Unruh freed 2.5 million men, but Fredborg assessed between 1 and 1.5 million men were freed. By 1943 some organisations were relying on men called back from retirement.

Hitler also decreed on 29 July 1942 that girls employed by the Labour Service would be transferred to the Wehrmacht and administration for a further six months war service; and the OKW announced in late 1942 that all wounded soldiers capable of military service were to take the places of men fit for active service in the Replacement Army (*Ersatzheer*). In December Keitel ordered that soldiers who were not able-bodied or who were World War I veterans should replace younger fit soldiers in reserved positions.[44]

The one million foreign workers who came to Germany between May and October 1942 did not satisfy the economy's need for labour. More use had to be made of prisoners of war and concentration camp inmates. The issue of women's employment was raised frequently. Goebbels had favoured increased employment of women at the beginning of 1941, and he and Ley had unsuccessfully urged the compulsory registration of women for employment in September 1941. Hitler declined, saying he would consider it if America entered the war. In March 1942 Goebbels' staff investigated the issue of greater women's employment. They did not envisage use of compulsion, but hoped that moral pressure to work would be sufficient. They anticipated public hostility to such a policy. The policy would be most successful if the women were initially employed in administrative jobs, and if the OKW cooperated in a propaganda campaign to persuade men at the front that such an innovation was necessary. Goebbels' staff also prepared a propaganda campaign to encourage women to take over their husbands' businesses.[45]

In April 1942 Himmler issued a general order that the wives and female relatives of SS men should volunteer to work with the *Frauenschaft*, the women's league of the National Socialist Party. He did not accept the draft prepared by Gottlob Berger, leader of the SS main office (*SS-Hauptamt*), which placed the measure in the context of total war and would have 'required' all SS men to ensure female family members reported to Frauenschaft offices. Himmler's order omitted all mention of total war and wider questions of women's employment; it merely 'asked' the female relatives to report to the Frauenschaft.[46]

In a meeting with Berger about the draft decree, Frauenschaft leaders raised wider issues which Himmler did not comment on. They claimed the reluctance of privileged women to work diminished their credibility with working women and reported that Hitler and Göring had overruled Sauckel's plans to introduce a requirement for women to work. (Hitler's views probably influenced Göring's opposition, since in the 1930s Göring had favoured the use of female labour in wartime.) In a speech in November 1942 Sauckel stated he had planned, on taking up his position, to increase female employment, but had changed his mind after discussions with Hitler and Göring. They persuaded him it was necessary to restrict women's employment 'for biological reasons,' to increase the birth rate.[47] Unfortunately, he continued, it was not possible to correct the resulting injustice to women in paid employment. Hitler ordered 400,000 to 500,000 Ukrainian women to be recruited as domestic servants; but ultimately only some 100,000 Ukrainians were employed in this capacity.

The clear indications from Sauckel and the Frauenschaft that Hitler opposed moves for greater female employment deterred further moves to introduce compulsion. Employment of women nonetheless increased, including in the SS. The leadership was divided between those who supported an ideologically based model of women as childbearers and those who favoured a greater use of women in paid employment, in a model based on economic efficiency. This very division may have caused Hitler's reluctance to decide on this issue.[48] A combination of other factors probably influenced his attitude in 1942: his conservative view of women's role, his desire to free women for reproduction, continued confidence in German military success, his fear of a repetition of the unrest of 1918 and a desire not to alarm the regime's middle- and lower middle-class supporters. Conquests in the East seemed to offer access to an almost unlimited supply of labour, which may also have influenced Hitler. Some leaders were not as persuaded by these considerations, or, like Goebbels, were willing to set them aside for wartime expediency. Göring, Ley, Goebbels, Sauckel and Berger had all tried in turn to increase the employment of women, seemingly unconcerned at the prospects of another 1918-style revolution. Indeed, Goebbels believed that his propaganda would have averted such an uprising.

Many leaders appeared to have been content to leave responsibility for saving staff with von Unruh's commission; others adopted their own initiatives. In winter 1941-42 Himmler attempted to ease labour shortages by expanding use of the concentration camps as an SS-owned source of compulsory labour. He wanted to use the SS to develop new weapons. Himmler was also willing to cut his staff to support the war effort. By June 1942 he placed a high priority on freeing more men for the front, and called on senior SS officers to reduce continuously the numbers of men in their offices and headquarters. Eventually perhaps only the wounded would be employed at headquarters. Himmler was not prepared to tell Hitler that more troops could not be provided. 'We can never use the word impossible.'[49]

Himmler claimed to favour administrative simplification and took steps to decentralise and streamline various SS administrative procedures and reduce bureaucratic infighting. His overall approach to solving domestic political and administrative problems was punitive. Germany suffered from the jurisdictional disputes of its ministries and offices; he called on his commanders to send the 'useless bed bugs' who made a living from these disputes to the Eastern front.[50] Those who over-indulged in alcohol were to be strictly punished; while those who made gains while the soldiers bled were to be eradicated.

Himmler thus favoured administrative simplification and the creation of a 'lean' behind-the-lines organisation. He did not oppose the wider employment of women. His actions at this time, and those of Bormann, show no wider or more coherently expressed concept of total war. Bormann spent this period after May 1941 consolidating his power as chief of the Party Chancellery. He made some staff cuts and simplified administrative procedures. At the beginning of 1942 he advised the Party that military requirements made it impossible to ease the ban on creating uk positions. The Party would have to give up more men and restrict its uk positions as much as possible. The number of uk Party leaders was reduced from 20,319 to 15,458 in the first ten months of 1942. By the end of 1942 the Party employed some 85,327 full-time functionaries: more than one sixth were uk but of military age. At the same time the Party laid claim to greater responsibilities. Hoffmann's reports recommended expanded Party activities in the East together with restraint for other organisations.[51] Bormann consolidated his position in 1942, as Hitler increasingly concentrated on military policy.

Even though Goebbels viewed military developments at Stalingrad optimistically in October 1942, he continued to reduce the Propaganda Ministry. He commissioned one of his officials, Ministerialdirigent Haegert, to comb through its staff and those of related organisations. Haegert proposed to end 81 uk positions in the Ministry, free 100 of 550 uk positions in publishing and close nine organisations. Goebbels agreed to close these offices and a radio station (*Reichssender Köln*) and to reduce staff in the Reich trade fair office (*Reichsmesseamt*), freeing 218 workers and saving 3,028,000 Reichsmarks. By the end of the year, 2598 uk positions had been removed from the Ministry by this voluntary process. On 1 June 1942 the Ministry and its related offices employed 19,033 people, 17,683 on 1 October 1942 and 16,435 on 1 January 1943.[52] Goebbels always tried to keep his ministry relatively small, but these reductions were a particular sign of the importance he attached to total war. The effect of air raids on civilian morale could easily have justified expansion of the Propaganda Ministry because of the importance of mobilisation of enthusiasm in total war.

Some of the distinctive elements of Goebbels' approach to the issue of total war were beginning to emerge by 1942. He appears to have proposed simplification of economic life in 1939 and stressed the need for a positive war aim, the creation of a large continental European living space. He believed the population's loyalty could be relied on and that they could be urged to greater efforts if this was accompanied by a reduction in privileges. It was psychologically important, he believed, for each citizen to feel he or she was contributing to the war effort. He regarded developments like the black market as the inevitable consequences of a long war, rather than as harbingers of another 1918. Goebbels was using the Party crises of 1930 and 1932 as models of the situation the regime faced and admiring the more radical Soviet war effort. He planned to make closer contact with the Gauleiters by December 1942. Although Goebbels was later to claim he had begun to urge more vigorous policies at this time, there is little extant evidence of the measures he proposed. In winter 1941 he apparently approached Hitler to argue for more radical action but met with little response. Goebbels and Ley both wanted greater involvement of the Party and the DAF in armaments, and closed regulation of industry. In March 1942 Goebbels claimed Hitler agreed with his proposals that the war should be conducted in a more radical manner but he noted opposition from the bureaucracy.[53]

Intensified bombing of Germany in 1942 meant air defence became an additional priority for the regime. Even Himmler abandoned his usual avoidance of areas outside his jurisdiction to suggest improved air protection and to create three SS building brigades for repairs and clearance after air attacks. Bombing absorbed resources which might otherwise have been spent on war production. A certain level of consumer production was needed to replace household goods lost in bombing and to meet the increased demand of foreign workers. The leadership could not guarantee sufficient production to issue a ration card for household goods: Goebbels pointed out to Kehrl that the regime could not meet all the requirements of the existing clothing card, let alone honour a new card. The two agreed instead on increased control over, and allocation of, such goods to bombed districts. Bombing intensified shortages of goods: in December 1942 shortages of clothing and shoes worsened; by January 1943 metal household articles were rationed. Bombing not only weakened the effectiveness of propaganda but also worsened morale. The German civilian population tended to over-estimate the effectiveness of Allied bombing. Various steps were taken to improve morale, including a decree from Hitler asking the leadership to ensure that it observed all wartime restrictions.[54]

Goebbels proposed that the Propaganda Ministry create an air defence section to prepare broad guidelines for, and co-ordinate, repair measures. Helmut Friedrichs, the head of the Party Chancellery's political department, opposed this because it would tie down more staff and further complicate responsibilities. Such measures could be carried out by the Gauleiters. Despite this opposition, Goebbels gained responsibility for introducing immediate measures in all bombed areas where the Gau's own resources were insufficient. By January 1943 he had set up the *Luftkriegsschädenausschuss*, an inter-departmental bomb damage committee, to 'centralise, coordinate and above all to activate civil measures of the Reich'[55] against bombing. Goebbels' persistence on this issue brought him success; he was the only member of the leadership willing to take on so potentially difficult a task.

• • •

The invasion of the Soviet Union and the German declaration of war on the United States intensified the ideological component of the war. Hitler's decisions removed Germany's chances of victory unless it could split the enemy coalition, force the political collapse of the Soviet Union or establish overwhelming technological superiority. The economically rational model of total war became crucial as a means of buying time for the regime to pursue these options. It could not, however, lead to victory on its own.

What is interesting is that members of the leadership realised this so quickly. This may have been because they were less committed to the war's goals than Hitler, or because they had not been as involved in the decision to go to war and they could therefore judge the situation more rationally. Two among the regime's most influential and able leaders, Fritz Todt and Reinhard Heydrich, died in 1942. They had been the first leaders to advise Hitler to seek a compromise peace, indicating that they believed more effective use of German resources for the war effort would not give Germany victory. Their task was difficult because they were attempting to change the basis of the war to one for limited goals.

The years 1941-2 were a time of lost opportunities to seek a compromise peace. Hitler's responses to the efforts of Todt, Heydrich, Himmler and others indicated that he was not willing to consider a compromise peace, even though there was a growing belief in the leadership that it was necessary. The irony was that while the war could not be won militarily, Soviet peace feelers suggest Germany still had the cards to seek a political settlement. There was still territory to be traded, and the United States had not yet begun land operations against Germany.

Those leaders who wanted German policy to change did not seek support among their peers. Rather they tried to convince Hitler: he alone had the authority to pursue a compromise peace. Particularly after the beginning of the Russian campaign, Hitler's preoccupation with military campaigns meant that those leaders who were based at his headquarters in East Prussia and Winniza (as Bormann was), who had their headquarters near his (Himmler, Keitel)[56] or had frequent business at his headquarters (Lammers, Speer, Todt) had more chance to influence him. Goebbels, the most firmly based in Berlin of all these leaders, had less frequent access to Hitler.

These leaders were all civilians. If they experienced disquiet about the conduct of the war, they were in a difficult position to challenge the professional expertise of the armed forces. For example, Goebbels' later attempts to warn Hitler about the failings of the German air force were dismissed. He was told that he was a pessimist and an ignorant civilian who did not comprehend military questions.[57] Above all it was psychologically and politically difficult to question Hitler. These men had reached their positions as the loyal followers of a charismatic leader: Germany's series of victories to the end of 1941 increased their reliance on Hitler's judgement and encouraged a tendency to think of the winter crisis as a temporary setback. Accordingly they concentrated on their own spheres of influence.

Of these leaders, only Goebbels showed great concern at Germany's military position, but he had not yet articulated any analysis of the overall situation. His initial interest appears to have arisen from his general approach to problems. 'The watchword must be: keep one's nerve and a cool head. And prepare everything down to the last detail.'[58] He and Himmler undertook simplifications in their own spheres of authority. Himmler stated his commitment to total war and sought to have his subordinates act on it, but did not try to extend these policies beyond his own area of responsibility. Their efforts to simplify were also affected by a psychological factor. At the beginning of such a process, many cuts would appear too drastic or impossible; even minor simplifications and closures would appear considerable initially. Only later, once these changes had been absorbed, would greater cuts become possible.

Bormann and Speer initially paid less attention to wider issues of total war. Bormann's response probably reflected the more optimistic atmosphere at Hitler's headquarters, while, by concentrating on his new tasks, Speer could hope to influence Germany's chances of victory directly. His position in itself was a contribution to total war. The different reactions of Todt and Heydrich may stem from their ability to gain the information to make a wider judgement, especially of enemy capacity.

Looking back on this period in 1943, Goebbels claimed that 'total war leadership should already have been introduced one and a half years ago.

But then we had unfortunately not drawn the necessary hard consequences from the terrible winter crisis, and when the sunshine woke again the ghosts of dangerous illusions woke again and gave themselves hopes which unfortunately could not be fulfilled.'[59] This judgement may have been excessive. This was a period of missed opportunities for pursuing a compromise peace and in labour policy. The relative abundance of a captive labour force in the Soviet Union created an illusion of plenty and encouraged wasteful use of this labour. It encouraged Hitler to delay introducing compulsory registration for work for women.

Yet in this period a wide range of measures was introduced to intensify organisation for war on the home front, and leaders could readily assume Hitler would support such moves. Hitler responded to the resulting military crisis of 1941-2 by appointing von Unruh to remove waste and find manpower for the armed forces; by appointing Sauckel to obtain more labour for armaments and economic production; by ordering government and Party to simplify further their staffing and administration; and by agreeing to give Todt, then Speer, additional control over the economy. Hitler's appointment of Speer as Armaments Minister, the clear support he gave him in the position and his close interest in the details of armaments production, suggest he was committed to total war. He was willing to adopt measures to reorganise the home front. But the second winter of the Russian campaign shook confidence in Hitler's leadership and his commitment to total war.

3

The Dreier Ausschuss and the Response to Stalingrad

At the beginning of 1943, the worsening military position on the Eastern front and the end of the battle for Stalingrad prompted Hitler to take further decisions designed to mobilise the home front for the war effort. A committee of three, composed of Bormann, Keitel and Lammers, was set up to implement these measures. The measures taken were wide ranging but took time to take effect. Hitler's initiatives met an initially enthusiastic response, but before long pressure developed, particularly from Goebbels, to do more.

The German Sixth Army of some 250,000 men had been surrounded at Stalingrad since 23 November 1942. The Luftwaffe's attempts to supply the army by air, and attempts to relieve it in November and December 1942 led by von Manstein failed. Speer suggested Hitler still hoped Stalingrad could be held or relieved. Outside Hitler's headquarters and the armed forces, the true seriousness of the situation was not quickly grasped. Goebbels' diaries for December 1942 do not exhibit undue concern. The leaders' reactions suggest that difficulties were initially seen as temporary. Hitler ordered the army to hold Stalingrad at all costs, but the area in German hands was steadily reduced until the final surrender of German forces on 2 February. Some 100,000 German troops passed into captivity. Soviet forces then tried unsuccessfully to bottle up German troops in the Caucasus.[1]

After the defeat at Stalingrad the National Socialist leadership paid greater attention to total war. Why did Stalingrad have so great an effect on these leaders? It could be argued that the turning point for the German armies on the Eastern front came earlier, in winter 1941. However, Stalingrad was militarily and psychologically important. It was strategically important because Hitler made it so. It became a clash of wills between him and Stalin, a 'Verdun on the Volga.' Stalingrad signalled that, despite the renewed victories of summer 1942, winter 1941 had been the harbinger of things to come. The growing material as well as numerical strength of the Soviet armies was demonstrated. The battle marked the first surrender of an entire German army to the enemy in the war. The Germans lost some 209,000 men from November 1942 to February 1943.[2]

Psychologically, it demonstrated to the Germans and their enemies that the Germans could be beaten. Stalingrad removed illusions about German arms. Early propaganda on the fight for Stalingrad had been optimistic, and the German public was not advised about the course of the battle in December 1942. By mid-January 1943 Hitler approved Goebbels' proposed propaganda treatment of Stalingrad, which emphasised the troops' sacrifices. For three days German radio suspended normal programmes and observed a period of mourning. The defeat was a tremendous shock to German public morale. Propaganda now emphasised waging war totally for final victory, a true people's war borne by the entire nation.

Other decisions had meant some leaders were ill-informed. Early in 1943 Hitler decided that ministers should no longer be briefed about the military situation. He may have feared a weakening of his position had such briefings continued: after Stalingrad Hitler became reluctant to meet with Party leaders, meeting the Reichs- and Gauleiters only three times in 1943. Goebbels disapproved of Hitler's decision: ignorance led to many leaders not drawing the correct conclusions about the policies to be adopted.[3] Goebbels' position as Propaganda Minister meant that he was exempted from the decision and continued to receive such information, which helped him to see events in their context. The publicity given to the sacrifice of the German army in Stalingrad meant that even the most ill-informed leaders realised that the nation's situation had worsened and some action had to be taken.

Attempts continued to change the regime's policy towards the occupied areas of the Soviet Union. Schellenberg unsuccessfully tried to persuade Himmler to adopt different measures in the East. In early 1943 he prepared a report, which found no support from Himmler, advocating the abolition of the Reich commissioners (*Reichskommissars* or *RKs*) and Einsatzgruppen, creation of autonomous states and the overhaul of the economic administration.[4]

Goebbels too favoured more constructive policies in the East and was dismayed by the leadership's lack of flexibility concerning political questions in the East. He compared this unfavourably with Nazi tactics before their seizure of power. In his 'first clear-cut "pro-Easterner" statement,'[5] Goebbels issued a proclamation as Reich propaganda leader (*Reichspropagandaleiter*) stating that National Socialist propaganda had to convey to those under Bolshevik control that German victory was in their interests. Leaders should avoid inept and inappropriate references to the inferior racial status of the Eastern peoples or plans to convert their countries into German colonies. In agreement with Bormann, he requested strictest observance of these guidelines. Himmler did no more than pay lip service to this proclamation. He told SS offices he considered it 'very important'[6]—all SS offices had to obey it to help win the war—but a month later he opposed Propaganda Ministry attempts to stop the distribution of a SS pamphlet depicting the Russians as subhuman.

Goebbels saw great propaganda opportunities in General Vlasov, the captured Soviet general who was seeking to set up a Russian 'liberation movement' on the German side. But he was aware of Hitler's lack of interest in such moves. In March Himmler noted that Wehrmacht propaganda for Vlasov's Russian committee was against Hitler's wishes. Vlasov's advice on policy towards the Soviet Union was ignored. Goebbels was aware that Hitler's strong stand against a political declaration on the Eastern question made it impossible for him to raise the issue again quickly. Goebbels' pressure for this declaration may even have led Hitler in March 1943 to decide against the Propaganda Ministry and in favour of Rosenberg's Reich ministry for the occupied Eastern territories (*Ostministerium*) in their disputes over responsibility for propaganda in the East.[7]

Stalingrad also prompted further efforts to persuade Hitler to conclude a compromise peace. He rejected a further attempt by the Japanese to mediate with the Russians and forbade Ribbentrop to speak of negotiations. The announcement by US President Roosevelt at Casablanca on 24 January that the Allies would insist on the 'unconditional surrender' of Germany further discouraged advocates of a separate peace.[8]

Soviet success at Stalingrad appeared to prompt doubts whether the German regime's approach to waging the war was sufficiently radical. From Hitler down the army's lack of ideological commitment was criticised. Political indoctrination was seen as one of the keys of Soviet military success, and the belief that similar education would improve German military effectiveness grew. Waffen-SS ideological education had been stepped up in May 1942. By February 1943 Berger advised Himmler that the Soviet army reserved eight hours a week for political indoctrination, even in the front lines. This was the reason for the Soviet soldier's 'incredible will to resist.'[9] Himmler agreed to Berger's proposal that the Waffen SS introduce more extensive ideological education, issuing a decree to this effect on 24 February.

From Hitler down the regime gave a higher priority to total war on the home front in January 1943, even before the end of the battle for Stalingrad. Even Göring, who played a less active role in formulating policy and was discredited by the Luftwaffe's failure to supply Stalingrad, expressed concern about the levels of German employment of women in comparison to Britain and the United States and about US armaments potential. Gauleiters, and other state and Party leaders, responded. They proposed that rival organisations be closed or have their functions reduced. For example, Ley proposed the closure of the greater part of German cultural societies and the merging of their functions into the DAF. Such proposals not only served the goals of total war but also could be used to further the power of one leader at the expense of another.[10]

Goebbels had sent Hitler a memorandum proposing total war measures in December 1942, and he discussed policies to encourage the war effort on the home front with Bormann that month. While details of these proposals have not yet come to light, they were probably similar to the suggestions he passed to Lammers on 2 January 1943. These proposals were intended to increase labour supply and reduce the civilian sector of the economy by introducing labour service for women, completely suspending production of luxury and a large proportion of consumer goods, closing department stores, redirecting at least 60 to 70 per cent of Germany's transport personnel to war purposes and completely transferring industries from civilian consumption to war production. Rebentisch describes these proposed measures as composed with an eye to their propaganda effect and not politically practical: 'Goebbels did not possess a practical concept for an efficient use of all economic forces.'[11] His proposals, aside from the introduction of women's labour service, were extreme, as were some of Speer's later proposals. Both men had an over-simplified concept of total war which was too prone to judge resources devoted to items other than weapons and feeding the population as non-essential.

Action followed quickly. A meeting of ministers on 8 January discussed the need for more workers in the armaments industry; among the suggestions were employing more women and calling up all able-bodied men to the army. Workers in department stores and shops should be transferred to the armaments sector. Sauckel was the only dissenter. He claimed that it was not necessary to employ more women, either because he believed that he could continue to meet labour requirements from the occupied territories or because he was mirroring Hitler's views.[12]

On 13 January Hitler signed a decree ordering the total mobilisation of the home front for the war effort and setting up a three-man committee (the *Dreier Ausschuss*) of Bormann, Keitel and Lammers to implement the measures. The decree's first priority was to provide more manpower for the forces and armaments production. It did so by three means—compulsory registration for employment, further simplification of the administration and the closure of inessential businesses. For the first time all men aged between 16 and 65 and all women aged between 17 and 50 had to report for employment. The upper age limit for women was later lowered to 45. The only exceptions granted were for men and women working in agriculture or the civil service, women with one child below school age or two children below 14. Members of religious orders and the clergy were exempted from the scope of the decree, presumably for political reasons. Keitel for the armed forces and the heads of all Supreme Reich authorities (*Oberste Reichsbehörden*—ORBs) had to inspect uk positions and abolish those not necessary to the war economy or the production of essential goods. The staff freed were to be transferred to armaments and the forces. Secondly, all inessential work in the administration was to stop: Hitler reiterated his 25 January 1942 order that planning for peacetime tasks should cease. Thirdly, the Reich Economics Minister, in agreement with Sauckel, and working through the Reich defence commissioners, was to close firms and businesses which did not serve the war economy or secure essential needs. The Ausschuss was to supervise the implementation of these measures and to investigate whether further measures were needed. They were to maintain close contact with Goebbels in view of his important, but unspecified, tasks in connection with the decree. In Bormann's view the purpose of the decree was to reorient the economy to supply the necessary replacements to the armaments industry and the armed forces, by freeing those already at work through simplifying their tasks and employing those not previously employed. The creation of the Ausschuss would not affect von Unruh's investigation, which the Party was to support 'most energetically.'[13] In practice the work of the Ausschuss mainly fell to Lammers and the Reich Chancellery.

The Ausschuss drew on preliminary work by the Reich Chancellery staff which proposed an end to the duplication of work by various Party organisations and the state, concentration of work in fewer agencies, possible elimination of some middle and lower layers of administration and decentralisation and abolition of appeal rights. A subsequent submission suggested closing the Prussian Finance Ministry, removing responsibilities from the Ostministerium, which had already been reduced from 1312 employees to 812 by von Unruh, and transferring support of army dependents from the military to the Labour Ministry. The last measure would replace 4000 military officials with an estimated 1700 to 1800 civilian officials.[14]

A meeting, attended by Keitel, Frick, von Unruh, Bormann, and others, was held on 4 February to implement the 13 January decree. The weakest ministries and those with the least popular constituencies were the first to lose staff. The meeting unanimously agreed to recommend the dissolution of the Prussian Finance Ministry to Hitler. Judging a dissolution of the Church Ministry to be politically impossible, it agreed that von Unruh should reduce its personnel as much as possible. The Ostministerium's role should be restricted to overall leadership of German policy in the East. Keitel agreed to begin the handover of responsibility for armed forces' dependents to the Labour Ministry, and Bormann agreed to institute further reductions in the personnel and responsibilities of the Party Chancellery.[15]

By 23 February 1943 the following measures were underway. A decree had been sent to the Supreme Reich authorities amplifying Hitler's decree of 13 January; Sauckel had issued a decree governing labour registration; and the Ausschuss had issued an order making workers available for war work. In the occupied territories, measures similar to those planned for the Reich were to be introduced: inessential shops, such as jewellers and stamp dealers, were to be closed; tobacco, textiles and household goods stores were to be restricted; nightclubs, bars, luxury hotels and unimportant handicrafts firms were to be closed. Various pay and taxation measures had been simplified; the Justice Ministry had dissolved 150 local courts and the Post Ministry 12 regional offices (*Reichspostdirektionen*). The number of staff freed was not stated. Various ministries reported the savings they had made; their reports suggest that the administrative sector had given up almost all possible staff. The most notable savings were achieved by the Post Ministry, which offered to give up 25,000 staff from the classes of 1901 and younger. The measures adopted were a mixture of the practical, mainly measures to make staff available, and the symbolic, such as restricting decorations to those relevant to the war effort and the honour cross of the German mother.[16]

Although Hitler's decree coincided with at least some of Goebbels' proposals, Goebbels was soon worried by insufficient progress. In his opinion, this was virtually inevitable, the result of appointing a committee rather than one man to oversee the changes. He was concerned that 'forces are at work already in order to spare, on the one hand, the party, on the other the administration and to act on the principle of "skin washing but not wetting".'[17] He derived some comfort from a discussion with Bormann about the functions of the Dreier Ausschuss on 18 January. He concluded that his work on total war had defined that of the Ausschuss more precisely and would have considerable influence. There was no danger that he could be outmanoeuvred.

Shortly after this meeting, Goebbels spent a day at Hitler's headquarters, where he suggested a programme of total war measures to Hitler. This involved labour duty for women, disbanding all organisations and concerns not important to the war effort and the complete focussing of civilian life on the war's requirements. Hitler and Goebbels agreed that shops, department stores and luxury restaurants would be compelled to shut, and the age limit for female labour service was set at 45. Hitler promised that no obstacles would be put in Goebbels' path where total war was concerned; he would not listen to any complaints but refer them all to Goebbels. In turn Goebbels promised these measures would provide some 1.5 to 2 million soldiers available. He claimed that Hitler not only agreed to all his proposals but also was more radical on many points. Goebbels' record of the meeting does not indicate how this programme differed significantly from that of the Ausschuss.[18]

Goebbels' initial criticisms of the Ausschuss came four days after Hitler's decree, before it had really had time to start its activities. His criticisms stemmed from a number of motives; the main reason was that he was not made a member of the committee. He was disappointed at Hitler's seemingly inexplicable decision not to make him a member of the Ausschuss. As late as 5 January 1943 he had clearly expected to be a member of the committee. His criticisms may also have been due to his assessment of the individuals on the committee. He described Lammers as a wet blanket. His sense of urgency about the measures he thought necessary was genuine: every day lost was a loss for them all. He continually compared the inadequacy of German measures with the Soviet example.[19]

Historians have disagreed about Goebbels' role in originating the concept and policies of the Ausschuss. Many historians have given Goebbels considerable credit for the overall concepts, but more recently Rebentisch has strongly argued that this credit is misplaced. He claims that Hitler, not Goebbels, was the originating force. As he had widened Todt's powers under the impetus of the military crisis of winter 1941, so too, on 25 December 1942, under the influence of the siege of Stalingrad, Hitler ordered more radical measures to use all possible resources for armaments. On 27 December Bormann travelled to Berlin to advise Lammers and Goebbels of Hitler's wishes; Goebbels developed his proposals as a result.[20] Rebentisch's evidence that the impulse came from Hitler reinforces Overy's overall interpretation that the National Socialist system was committed to total war. Rebentisch is, however, too hasty in dismissing Goebbels' influence, in keeping with his generally negative judgements of the Propaganda Minister's policies. Goebbels had been urging more radical policies on Hitler earlier in 1942 with little success; he had already demonstrated that his commitment to total war.

Hitler partly explained Goebbels' omission from the Ausschuss to him when Goebbels visited his headquarters in late January. He claimed that he did not want Goebbels to join the Dreier Ausschuss himself, so as not to be burdened by the administrative work involved; but he wanted Goebbels to attend all meetings of the Ausschuss, be present at any reports to him and play the role of a galvanising motor on the issue. No submission was to go to Hitler which had not received Goebbels' approval: this way he would know that the submission was radical enough. After his meeting with Hitler Goebbels referred to the Ausschuss as the *Vierer Ausschuss* (Committee of Four) in his diary, reflecting his view that he was a de facto member. He saw his task as intensifying and radicalising measures, using Naumann, the head of his ministerial office, to prepare the ground.[21]

There is no direct evidence of Hitler's actual reasons for not making Goebbels a member of the Ausschuss. The reason Hitler gave Goebbels—the burden of excessive administration—is unlikely to have been genuine, since the members of the Ausschuss themselves would have had greater administrative burdens than Goebbels. Hitler may still not have been persuaded of the need for the drastic policies which Goebbels envisaged, or may have wanted them interpreted differently. He may have believed that the Ausschuss itself was better suited to implementing the measures needed. Hitler may have seen Goebbels as primarily a propagandist and not an administrator and believed that the three Committee members were better equipped to carry out the measures. The honorary position was probably designed to placate Goebbels. Goebbels was to claim in 1944 that Lammers and Bormann had outmanoeuvred him. They had led him to believe he would be on the Ausschuss, while Bormann told Hitler that Goebbels was content with the role of herald of total war and would leave the implementation to specialists. In this context, it is significant that all Ausschuss members were based at Hitler's headquarters, so he could, if need be, closely supervise their activities. Bormann, and possibly Hitler himself, may have been nervous of concentrating power in Goebbels' hands. Goebbels' own activities could have given rise to these suspicions. He saw his task as relieving Hitler of the cares of internal politics. Berger, Chief of Staff of the SS-Hauptamt, had already interpreted Goebbels' proposals as an unsuccessful attempt to be made Führer of the Home Front.[22]

Goebbels' early readiness to criticise the Ausschuss, and his personal motives for doing so, raises the question of how justified or realistic his criticisms were. By February there seemed to be some justification for his complaints about the Ausschuss. Its bureaucratic structure seemed to slow decision making. The records of its meetings suggest its members tended to respond to reports of abuses by denials of responsibility rather than by investigating the reports, or by concentrating on small-scale issues rather than large-scale decisions. The committee structure itself may also have reduced the leaders' sense of personal responsibility for measures taken. On the other hand, Goebbels failed to allow time for the measures to take effect before he criticised them. His disappointment may have been a result of exaggerated expectations of the results.

Evidence of reluctance to act can be seen from Goebbels' claim that when he put his views to other leading men, they agreed with him, but passive resistance began as soon as two or three of them met together. This explained to him why most heads of organisations would not get things done; they declared themselves unable to overcome the difficulties. Even his own State Secretary, Gutterer, had not adjusted to the new course and was creating difficulties for Goebbels' plan to send uk film and theatre artists to entertain the troops.[23] Goebbels may have been able to persuade leaders by argument in private conversation, but when they left his presence inertia, further reflection or self-interest, particularly the need to protect their own administrative fiefdoms, prompted resistance. His proposals met opposition because their successful implementation would require National Socialist leaders to reduce the size of their organisations and the range of their powers. In a system marked by intense competition for power, this would be seem a loss of influence.

Publicising labour duty for women encountered some difficulties. Goebbels proposed to issue an explanatory circular. He believed that the regime would be able to persuade all except the habitually lazy. The draft prepared by Tiessler, the leader of the Reich circle for propaganda (*Reichspropagandaring*), called for the home front to take its fair share of burdens and drew attention to the willing service of working women, who were calling for total mobilisation. The Party was aware of the difficulties for women who had not worked before, but these sacrifices were small compared to those of the front, and those already made by working women. 'Common work is . . . the requirement of the hour.'[24] The Party Chancellery altered the text to omit the pointed references to working women's complaints about unequal treatment. As part of his efforts to encourage women's work, Goebbels had his officials participate in plans to employ 40,000 of the women called up in day care centres for the children of those called up.

Goebbels hoped to be able to publicise the employment of the wives of prominent Party members. He believed that burdens had to be seen to be borne equally to maintain morale. An emphasis on public equality did not of course prevent private privilege. His attitude carried over into his private behaviour. While his household had a large staff and he decorated his homes lavishly, his wife, Magda, ran the household on official rations for the first six months of the war and continued to entertain on rations. Goebbels cut back on his staff in 1943. For a time after Stalingrad, Magda Goebbels worked at a Telefunken factory, but she abandoned the work when no other leaders' wives followed her example. Later she did some outwork for industry.[25]

Goebbels expected that women's registration for work would allow at least two regiments to go to the front, but on 27 January he learnt that Lammers had persuaded Hitler to change the provisions of women's registration. Hitler agreed with Lammers that women with one child under six or two children under 14 were to be exempted, even if they had adequate domestic service, Goebbels observed. Goebbels described Lammers as 'a complete canker' because he saw the issue of women's employment from a comfortable middle-class perspective.[26] (Speer described Lammers as 'a government official without initiative or imagination'.)[27] Hitler later rejected attempts by Sauckel and Goebbels to have the exemptions interpreted more strictly, but he did agree that Sauckel could remove superfluous domestic staff from households. The policy led to popular discontent, as Goebbels anticipated.

Goebbels saw these concessions as a sign of weakness, but they were considerably less generous than the British guidelines of spring 1942. These guidelines exempted a woman from paid employment if she lived in her own house and looked after at least one other person. Women with children still living at home did not have to take paid employment.[28]

Goebbels blamed Lammers for Hitler changing his mind on women's labour duty; Lammers' own account suggests that the initiative for these changes came from Hitler. The secondary leaders had been divided on the question of guidelines for women's work: Goebbels and Sauckel wanted them stricter, excluding only pregnant women and women with three children under 14, while Frick and Lammers wanted a more lenient policy. But it was Hitler who decided to set the age limits for registration at 17 and not

16, and at 45. Goebbels had earlier claimed that he had the support of the armed forces and the Party for total war, and the elite of the state had to be forced, if necessary, to adopt the correct policy. His explanation of the change of policy suggests he saw it as originating in the social and political conservatism of the bureaucracy.[29] Explaining Hitler's change of mind in this way did not threaten Goebbels' belief in National Socialism's revolutionary potential.

By 1943 there are indications of Goebbels' differences with Hitler in his diaries, and even more in his discussions with other leaders. Goebbels did not canvass the reasons why Hitler changed his mind and changed measures he had agreed to. Did Goebbels misinterpret or exaggerate Hitler's support for his ideas? Hitler's motives are unclear. Did Goebbels misinterpret the reasons behind some of these changes? Soon after relaxing the regulations on women's employment, Hitler called on the Gauleiters, at Goebbels' and Speer's suggestion, to remember the *Kampfzeit*, the period of struggle before the National Socialists came to power, and proceed with similar measures for total war. He criticised the continued existence of luxury restaurants, such as Horchers, and stated that women's and sporting magazines needed to be dissolved. He called on the Gauleiters to mobilise all national strength for the war effort.[30]

Goebbels interpreted the policy changes as watering down, due to conservatism or ignorance of the true situation. He now viewed the Gauleiters as insufficiently aware of the gravity of the situation and still living as if Germany were at peace. (Hitler's restrictions on the dissemination of information about the course of war may of course have contributed to this.) The Gauleiters were crucial for the implementation of centrally decreed measures at the regional level;[31] it was a matter of concern if they assessed the situation so differently from the senior levels of the leadership.

But differences of opinion could arise from different views of total war. At a meeting of the Ausschuss, on Hitler's instructions, Bormann opposed measures to close down inessential business activities, unless their staff were needed immediately. Goebbels considered this view incorrect: he had claimed at an earlier meeting that closures could free 20,000 men from hotels and inns and 40,000 from restaurants. The question at issue was whether shops should be closed only where there was a possibility of their employees being used elsewhere, the view supported by Bormann and Hitler; or whether it was better, for partly symbolic reasons, to proceed with closures at all costs, the view Speer and Goebbels supported. Bormann's opposition clearly reflected Hitler's view that action should be taken only when it would be of direct help to the war effort. This view did not necessarily imply lack of commitment to total war. Speer's and Goebbels' view prevailed for a time and resulted in some cases of loss of employment for workers too old, unfit or immobile to be redeployed.[32]

Hitler agreed to other measures to provide the army with new manpower. Industry had to free 50,000 men born between 1908 to 1922, with the fitness grading *kv* (*kriegsverwendungsfähig* or fit for active service), for call-up within two months, while Sauckel would both provide 50,000 specialists for industry and provide a further 30,000 workers available to the army. In addition industry had to supply the army with 150,000 kv men born between 1908 and 1922 in the exchange action '*Rü. 43 Tausch*' (Armaments Exchange '43) to conclude by 31 March 1943. The army would make available as replacements for at least a year soldiers less suitable for active service, classed as *av* (*arbeitsverwendungsfähig* or capable of work), and *gv.H.* (*garnisonsverwendungsfähig Heimat* or capable of serving in a garrison on the home front). A further 100,000 men were to be called up from mid-January to bridge the gaps which the exchange would create for the army. These measures would involve a further 180,000 men being withdrawn from the economy. This call-up of armaments workers was the first special call-up, *Sondererziehung* or *SE*. No organisation was exempt; the Party too would have to lose some personnel. Bormann explained that the Gau and Kreis offices would be exempted from releasing workers, since their remaining uk positions were so few that they could not sustain losing them. Accordingly the Party's central offices would have to lose more staff.[33]

Hitler extended the von Unruh commission's responsibilities to cover the entire German civilian administration. Von Unruh based his work on two principles: no male born in 1901 or later should be employed on the home front unless he was classified gv.H. or less; and women workers were to be used to the greatest extent possible. His investigations covered all areas of administration and resulted in simplifications and reallocation of staff. In areas which were politically vulnerable or less able to justify their continuing functions during the war, he was able to achieve greater savings, such as his reduction of the Ostministerium staff by 500. It is not clear how many workers the von Unruh commission freed. Some examples survive: he made ten female workers of the Presidential Chancellery available to the Labour Office and freed some 45 employees after inspecting 18 educational offices. The absence of detailed records for the commission's work does not allow an overall assessment of the numbers freed for war work. Those savings contained in the commission's files seem tiny when set against the loss of 200,000 men at Stalingrad and are low in comparison to the numbers the commission had removed in the East. They suggest that the administration had already given up most suitable staff.[34]

Speer, Goebbels and Bormann criticised von Unruh's effectiveness. Speer's office diary, the Speer Chronik, described the results of von Unruh's 'combing out' of civilian offices as 'somewhat inferior' to his results with the military offices.[35] Goebbels believed that as a general, von Unruh was not capable of inspecting the armed forces rigorously enough. He soon clashed with the commission over his failure to provide his quota of 3400 men to the army, despite his professed desire to save manpower. He told von Unruh that he was meant to sweep out the Wehrmacht with an iron broom and lead fat, well-fed majors to useful occupations. The Propaganda Ministry subsequently pointed out to the general army office, *Allgemeines Heeresamt*, of the OKW that it was not able to make 3400 men available but could free 309 kv men from the age groups 1901 and younger. Probably as a result of this disagreement, Hitler issued an order on 10 February that the performing arts were to be exempted from the combing out of uk positions, and Goebbels received the necessary powers to ensure this. Hitler prohibited the closure of theatres and orchestras. There were 7145 men liable to military duty, rated kv and born in 1901 and later, in the three protected sections (radio, film, theatre and orchestra). Goebbels' success in persuading Hitler of his case was helped by the importance Hitler attached to the arts and to propaganda in wartime, an importance which had led Hitler to dissuade Goebbels from cutting uk positions in the arts before.

Goebbels' protection of his staff against von Unruh reduced the number of workers he had to give up, ensured part of his area of responsibility was protected from further 'combing-out' actions and re-emphasised his power in the cultural sphere. His main motive was probably a desire to protect his jurisdiction, since the Propaganda Ministry continued its own measures to cut staff. Non-artistic personnel were to be made available to the Wehrmacht.[36] As the Propaganda Ministry pointed out to the Allgemeines Heeresamt, the ministry had already combed out its offices considerably, giving up over 2000 people in 1942. It had also increased the percentage of female staff compared to other ministries. Nonetheless, Goebbels sought, and obtained, a privilege which, if extended to other ministers, would have made a mockery of cutting staff on the home front. He would also have been among the first to criticise other ministers if they had sought the same exemptions.

By implication, Bormann also criticised von Unruh's effectiveness. In a circular to the Gauleiters he pointed out that repeated reports indicated the Wehrmacht did not apply the same staffing restrictions in its own offices which civilian organisations did. Such reports were denied by the OKW. Von Unruh claimed to follow similar principles in inspecting OKW offices as inspecting civilian offices. Bormann asked the Gauleiters to report any such overstaffing of military offices discreetly.[37] Surviving Party Chancellery records do not indicate the results of this call.

Both Bormann and Goebbels assumed that there was still considerable overstaffing in the armed forces, behind the lines. Von Unruh was criticised by officials of the Reich Chancellery and others, even though more disinterested observers saw him as very effective. These judgements were based on impressions and rumours rather than facts. Another example of a judgement based on personal impression is Goebbels' comment that he was not persuaded by Sauckel's argument that there were not many men listed as uk; the number of healthy young men who could be seen in the cities proved this wrong.[38]

Stalingrad gave an added impetus to simplifying the administration. In his own ministry, Goebbels continued to implement a variety of measures restricting administrative tasks and use of material. He discussed closing all gourmet restaurants, bars and night spots, and restriction of the restaurant trade in general with Esser, state secretary for tourism in the Propaganda Ministry. In addition he proposed to use the head of publishing, Max Amann, to intervene on the total war issue not only because of his ruthlessness but also because of his thorough reorganisation of the printing industry.[39]

Bormann also increased measures inside the Party to rationalise administration. He suspended the operations of six subsidiary organisations for the duration of the war and subsequently dissolved a further organisation, the NS-Reichskriegerbund, the National Socialist war veterans' league, freeing some 270 staff. Bormann successfully used these simplifications to centralise authority in the Party Chancellery.[40]

Bormann called for Party leaders to use the Party's telegram network rather than hold unnecessary meetings. By Hitler's 'strict order' meetings should only be held if matters could not be settled in writing and should not go for more than two days.[41] Leave for male staff in the Party was restricted. This policy was introduced, despite Bormann's opposition, as the result of pressure from Goebbels and Tiessler. Gauleiters were also urged to support Speer in his task of increasing tank production immediately. Hitler ordered that the Party appeal to workers' consciences and sense of responsibility: Gauleiters were to read Hitler's call to the work force at a tank factory during working hours.

Following Stalingrad, Himmler continued to favour reductions in staffing and abandoning matters inessential to the war effort. He exempted policies serving ideological goals from this latter category. Himmler decreed in January 1943 that all Waffen-SS officers aged 40 and below had to be released for active service. The resulting inconvenience had to be endured or mitigated by lengthening working hours or merging offices. 'All forces must be given up to the front and all comfort must take a back seat to this duty.'[42] To win additional labour he ordered the responsible SS and Police Leaders of Ukraine and Russia-Centre to take the entire working population and all men of military age with them when evacuating districts. In no cases were men whom the enemy could use to fall into their hands. Despite these orders, 30,000 potential workers in the area of the Army Group Don on the lower Volga were left behind. Various decisions Himmler made on minor issues also signified a desire to focus on essentials. Yet he persisted in his attempts to have ethnic Germans made available for settlement in the East, although they were needed in armaments factories to interpret for Eastern workers.

Himmler's main tasks continued to be the extermination of the Jews, the maintenance of the regime's security and the use of concentration camps for forced labour. In 1943 an estimated 500,000 Jews, mostly from Western Europe, were exterminated. He planned to expand SS armaments factories in the General Government. He ordered the Higher SS and Police Leaders (*Höhere SS- und Polizeiführer, HSSPF*) to refrain from setting up their own local concentration camps, since the prisoners' labour power must be used systematically and centrally to fulfil the SS's armaments tasks. Despite the increased need for labour, large transports of Jews from Berlin, including Jews employed in armaments factories, began. In January 1943 Hitler and Goebbels had again agreed that the Jewish question in Berlin had to be solved as quickly as possible. As long as there were still Jews in Berlin, Germany did not have internal security.[43]

Speer also supported measures to simplify the administration. He simplified licensing for building from five processes to one and sought the Interior Ministry's approval of lengthened working hours for all officials. 'Next to armaments issues, the Minister occupied himself with measures for the reduction of procedures unimportant for the war and for greater labour entry into armaments concerns,' the Speer Chronik noted.[44]

Goebbels' criticisms of the various measures give some indication of his attitude to total war. He wanted to use improvisation to overcome the difficulties in calling up large numbers. He believed an atmosphere of crisis was needed to make the measures work; relying on orderly development would be ineffective.[45]

Goebbels praised Speer's achievements in raising armaments production. He believed that Speer was obtaining everything possible from the armaments industry and that he had Speer's full support in radicalising the conduct of the war. Goebbels and Speer formed an alliance in which each man could use the other's skills and demands to secure his goals. Goebbels could use Speer's demands for more workers to support his calls for the restriction of inessential economic production. Speer could support Goebbels' demands to restrict the economy as a means of gaining more staff for armaments. Goebbels' own concept of total war extended beyond armaments production to labour policy, administrative simplifications and introducing a 'spirit of total war' among the regime and the population. For the purposes of his propaganda and to ensure that he could help muster public opinion behind the increased effort, Goebbels wanted measures in keeping with the 'optics' of total war, which would create the impression that burdens were being shared equally. Stalingrad increased the urgency and importance with which Goebbels viewed the question of total war. He considered that news of the battle provided the right psychological moment among the population for more drastic measures. He planned to use public opinion as an ally should he run up against greater difficulties in the Ausschuss.[46]

Stalingrad prompted a swift reaction from the leadership, including the introduction of some measures which Goebbels had urged for some time. With the creation of the Ausschuss, Hitler had publicly placed his authority behind additional mobilisation of the home front. The leadership had agreed to the principle of women's labour service and had set up additional mechanisms to pursue measures of simplification and rationalisation. The policies were wide ranging but their chances of success were difficult to judge in early 1943. While Goebbels was perhaps too quick to judge that the Ausschuss had not been effective, its slow progress did justify his criticisms to some extent. The tendency to soften the measures adopted also aroused the suspicions of Speer and Goebbels. The creation of the Dreier Ausschuss did not gain Goebbels the powers he believed necessary or result in the radical measures he advocated being adopted. Goebbels did not intend to accept this: he considered the situation too urgent and began to plan alternative strategies. He was seeking allies in the leadership and among the population to help him counter this situation.

4

Overcoming the Führer Crisis?

From February to June 1943 the policies of Hitler's 13 January decree were implemented. Goebbels tried to give total war policies additional momentum and moved unsuccessfully to have Hitler take a more active role in domestic politics. He sought to do so by four means—securing allies, proposing a change of Foreign Minister, seeking Hitler's intervention on the home front and seeking to revitalise Göring.

On the Eastern front, the March 1943 thaw allowed the Germans to recapture Kharkov and retain most of the Donets basin. The Soviet victory at Stalingrad had not yet proved decisive. The German position, however, began to deteriorate on other fronts. Anglo-American forces had landed in Morocco and Algeria on 8 November 1942. After initial German success at the Kasserine Pass, Field-Marshal Rommel was defeated at the battle of Medenine in Tunisia on 6 March. Hitler refused Rommel's proposal to evacuate the Tunisian bridgehead, and the last remnant of German and Italian forces surrendered with some 150,000 men going into captivity. During early 1943 the British bombing campaign against the Ruhr was stepped up and extended to Hamburg and Berlin. From March to June 1943 British bombers concentrated on the Ruhr, destroying two of three dams there in May.[1]

As the military situation worsened and rations were cut, popular morale continued to decline. There was growing criticism of the leadership and the Nazi Party, even of Hitler. The increase in air attacks unsettled the population and made them more fearful. German propaganda increasingly had to find

ways of making a deteriorating situation palatable, and as a result it lost more
and more credibility with the German public.[2]

By mid-January 1943, despite the creation of the Dreier Ausschuss,
Goebbels continued to be concerned with the regime's position and with
insufficient movement on the issue of total war. He tried four methods of
overcoming this—securing allies, suggesting that Hitler replace Ribbentrop
as Foreign Minister, seeking Hitler's intervention on the home front and
trying to revitalise Göring. In order to overcome what he saw as Hitler's
inertia and the Ausschuss's unsatisfactory approach, Goebbels sought allies
within the National Socialist leadership. From December 1942 he had met
Ley, Funk and Speer regularly; in 1943 he widened this group to include
Milch, Sauckel and Backe in a Wednesday night salon. With the exception
of Speer, these men were of the second level of the leadership. They agreed
with Goebbels that Germany's conduct of the war needed to change.[3]

Goebbels concluded that Hitler's isolation from domestic policymaking
allowed Bormann too much power and that Bormann opposed total war. On
27 February he told a group of leaders that domestic politics were controlled
by Bormann, who allowed Hitler to feel he was still in charge. Bormann was
guided by ambition, and his doctrinaire approach meant that he represented
a danger to any policy change. (Himmler had reached a similar conclusion
in 1942.) Bormann's influence had to be reduced and Hitler persuaded to
come to Berlin more often and take charge of policies. Goebbels hoped they
could then influence Hitler more. Goebbels concluded: 'We are not having
a "leadership crisis," but strictly speaking a "Leader crisis"!'[4] Speer believed
that Goebbels' moves demonstrated his lack of faith in victory. His criticisms
suggest that Hitler's charismatic authority was being weakened by German
military and diplomatic failures.

Goebbels criticised Bormann for reinforcing Hitler's doctrinaire approach and preventing the development of more 'realistic' policies. Goebbels
here admitted that whatever he could temporarily persuade Hitler to do on
total war, his arguments had no lasting effect. His criticisms of Bormann may
have been a means of avoiding criticism of Hitler and the realisation that
Hitler's views of total war and his were not the same. By criticising Bormann,
Goebbels did not have to recognise that total war policies had not had the
effects he hoped for and believed necessary.

The plans of Goebbels' group included replacement of Ribbentrop as
Foreign Minister. Goebbels hoped to split Germany's enemies by highlight-
ing the threat Bolshevism posed to Europe and by signalling, in adopting
total war, that Germany was willing to make any sacrifice to win. He tried
to appeal to the Western powers by raising the spectre of a Bolshevik victory

in his 18 February 1943 speech on 'total war.' Afterwards he sought to turn Hitler against Ribbentrop. In response Hitler described Ribbentrop as 'greater than Bismarck' and forbade Goebbels extending any more such feelers.[5] From this time on, Hitler showed no interest in plans to exploit differences among the enemy, commenting that Germany had burnt its bridges.

Hitler continued to reject attempts to follow more politically flexible policies in the East. In a discussion on 8 June, he indicated that, like Bormann, he favoured hard-line policies, such as those of Erich Koch, Commissioner for the Ukraine. He ruled out a political end to the war in the East and warned against the false hope that nationalist movements fighting on the German side would win the war. As in World War I, they would simply pursue their own national interests. The Russians would be better used as workers to free Germans for military service. Here Hitler rejected a short-term advantage for Germany because of the likely later political consequences. Herbst has argued that this was a general problem for the regime during the war: policies adopted to assist the war effort appeared to set the agenda for post-war policies and were therefore not acceptable either to the regime or its middle-class supporters.[6] Goebbels did not consider this an obstacle. His approach possibly reflected his activities as a propagandist—promise whatever was necessary for victory, but do not draw any conclusions from this about long-term policies. He did not share Hitler's apparent desire for consistency.

Goebbels believed that a strong authority was needed to give direction to domestic policy. He planned to counter Bormann's and Lammers' influence by persuading Göring to use his powers as 'Chairman of the Council of Ministers for Defence of the Reich.' In this position Göring could issue decrees independently of Hitler. Goebbels was seeking to overcome any lack of co-ordination of measures on the home front by using Göring's powers as de facto deputy Chancellor. Previously Göring had had considerable influence over Hitler. He had been, and possibly still was, the most popular National Socialist after Hitler; he had a prestige and popularity with the public and in the Party which Goebbels or Speer lacked. In Goebbels' opinion, Göring's authority was essential for any future reorganisation of the Reich's leadership. Although Göring's nominal powers and responsibilities were still great, since 1941 his position diminished. His power had dissipated, weakened by his failure in the Four Year Plan to create an effective administrative alternative to the military/economic apparatus, by the defeats of the Luftwaffe and his retreat into self-indulgent hedonism. Yet to

Goebbels Göring may have seemed reliable because he was a long-standing member of the leadership group, a known quantity compared to Bormann.[7]

Goebbels wanted to form a more radical group. He believed that in any union of a more and a less radical group or policy, the more radical one would always win the upper hand.[8] He may have thought that if a more radical group could guide Göring in the increased assertion of his powers, it would soon dominate him.

Göring's view of the situation in 1943 was somewhat similar to Goebbels' and Speer's view. Göring considered that the German position was retrievable, provided the population recognised how serious it was. His suggested solution was 'economise on soldiers, women as replacements everywhere it is possible.'[9] But relations between Goebbels and Göring were strained: as part of his post-Stalingrad measures in the Berlin Gau, Goebbels shut down Horchers, the Berlin luxury restaurant patronised by Göring. Therefore, Speer, who claimed that he and Milch originated this means of countering Bormann, made the first approach. He met Göring at the Obersalzberg on 28 February. Göring responded positively and criticised Bormann's influence on Hitler. Progress was smooth and a 'fundamental political' meeting of Speer, Goebbels and Göring took place on 1 March.[10] During this meeting they discussed the need to replace Ribbentrop with someone who could persuade Hitler to adopt a rational foreign policy. Victory had to be pursued politically as well as militarily. When Goebbels next met Hitler, however, recent heavy enemy air raids led Hitler to criticise Göring strongly. Goebbels and Speer therefore judged it politic not to raise these proposals for the time being. Two further meetings with Göring were held during March.

The group of allies, headed by Goebbels and Speer, planned to use Göring to call Sauckel to account for allegedly using false figures about the work force he supplied for industry. They believed that Sauckel created false hopes in Hitler and the Party by exaggerated claims of the labour force he could provide. At a meeting on 12 April, Göring supported Sauckel and attacked Milch, so that no light was thrown on the question of Sauckel's figures. Various reasons have been put forward for Göring's changed position. Speer suggested Bormann used bribery and evidence of Göring's drug addiction to blackmail Göring into changing sides. Göring's biographer Overy attributes Göring's stand to distrust of the group seeking to revitalise him and a hesitation to attack Sauckel because he had SS support. Göring's fear of Hitler may also have played a part.[11]

While Goebbels still wanted to revive Göring's authority in April, his efforts to do so had clearly failed. Göring's own lethargy had contributed to the failure. He recognised the need for altered policies but was no longer willing to take a stand. In addition he was increasingly discredited by Germany's deteriorating position in the air war in 1943 and the failure of the Luftwaffe. These developments progressively weakened his standing in Hitler's eyes. By August 1943 Goebbels considered that 'politically Göring might as well be dead.'[12] Other factors also contributed to the failure. Speer and Reimann have suggested that Lammers and Bormann were wary of Goebbels because they knew that, if given new powers, he would use them, thus upsetting the established balance of power. The leaders Goebbels was planning to counter, particularly Bormann, were probably more powerful than he realised. Therefore his move came too late.

Thus Goebbels' wider political strategy had failed. He had been able to create a bloc of members of the secondary level of the leadership who agreed with his plans to intensify the mobilisation of the home front. However he was unable to persuade Göring to take a stand against Bormann; nor was he able to set aside Bormann's influence and persuade Hitler to conduct the home front in the manner he considered necessary. Goebbels could not understand why there was not enough power in an authoritarian state to achieve what he believed was necessary. He blamed Hitler's advisers for his failure to convince Hitler. Perceptions of a Führer crisis arose when Hitler was undecided on an issue or when observers saw they had no influence over Hitler.[13]

Goebbels may also have failed because he misjudged Hitler's own views. Alterations Bormann and Hitler made to a speech Goebbels delivered on 5 June 1943 made his references to the preceding crises, the possibilities of surrender or defeat, and the existence of weapons of retaliation less specific. Goebbels' claim that the number of workers available to the English and Americans 'scarcely' compared to those available to the Germans was altered to 'could not' compare.[14] An entire section dealing with the 'setback' in North Africa was removed, including Goebbels' justification that this bought time for Europe to consolidate its defences. These alterations indicate differences of emphasis on how far the public should be kept informed; they may also demonstrate differing assessments of the seriousness of Germany's position. Differences of opinion on policy matters between Hitler and Goebbels existed, for example, on the question of housing. Goebbels favoured compulsory seizure of unoccupied homes to solve housing problems in bombed areas. In the same month, April 1943, Bormann advised that Hitler had rejected the introduction of compulsion for the moment and had opted for an appeal for second homes and houses not being fully used. Here Hitler and Bormann may have been influenced by earlier SD reports that public opinion opposed compulsion.

Goebbels' failure raises the further possibility that he did not understand Hitler's position. He saw Hitler's opposition to the measures and/or tempo he advocated as evidence of lack of understanding of or support for total war, when it may have reflected a different understanding or definition of total war. In April, for example, Speer reported that, under the influence of Austrian Gauleiters Eigruber and Uiberreither, Hitler supported total war.[15] Hitler and Bormann increased their instructions to the Party on total war, for example. At the beginning of March Bormann advised Party leaders of Hitler's direction that total war measures could be implemented only with the full support of the National Socialist movement. 'The personal example' of each leading Party member was of decisive importance.[16] Hitler called for Party members to practise as well as preach the virtues of the Kampfzeit. There was, for example, no justification for teas or receptions unless they were needed for foreign policy purposes. Individual National Socialists had to become 'the motor' for the changes on the home front. A later decree advised that members whose comments betrayed doubt or defeatism were to be expelled from the Party.

Hitler repeated similar orders in May and June 1943, prompted by a loss of heart among Party members. He further expected that the wives and children of leaders who reported for work should not be given lighter or fake work (Scheinarbeit). Those who did not have to report to work because of their age or the size of their family should undertake voluntary work. The instructions reflect a fear of the effects on public morale on any evasion of total war policies by Party members and a concern for morale within the Party itself. The Party in Bavaria was discredited because the population believed the leadership led a life largely untouched by the war.[17]

Bormann conveyed Hitler's desire that the use of adjutants by leading state and Party officials be considerably reduced, and where possible able-bodied men be replaced as adjutants by war wounded. In March Bormann advised that Hitler wanted the National Socialist Motorist Corps (Nationalsozialistisches Kraftfahrerkorps or NSKK) to train women as quickly as possible to replace men as civilian motor vehicle drivers. Bormann advised that Hitler himself had decided that all newspapers and magazines serving political, intellectual and material war leadership would continue to be produced. In other areas only one specialist magazine would appear. This was a wartime solution; a general end to competition was not envisaged. The publication of 53 papers was discontinued, and the number of specialist magazines reduced from 125 to 40. Bormann asked that Party leaders intervene only in particularly important cases, noting that the changes would save lead and free workers.[18]

Goebbels' policies and their failure raise a number of interesting considerations about his proposals and the National Socialist system. Historians have differed in their judgements of Goebbels' proposals. Ulrich Herbert considered that Goebbels was 'the only one within the National Socialist leadership who linked a clear view of Germany's actual military and economic situation at the turn of the year 1942-3 with a total concept of domestic and foreign policy.'[19] Some of Goebbels' biographers agree that he genuinely sought to mobilise economic effort for the war. Carroll, Herbst and Janssen are more critical of Goebbels' sincerity, but none of them have subjected his proposals to close scrutiny. Carroll claims his design for total war 'was simply a prolonged, shrieking demand for "sacrifices" on the part of the German public.'[20] Indeed she suggests he was involved in the Ausschuss's sabotage of total war measures. Herbst sees Goebbels' moves to adopt total war in 1943 as a response to a crisis of confidence in the regime's propaganda; he does not study it in a wider context. Janssen suggests Goebbels' views were less soundly economically based than Speer's.

In his speeches in early 1943 Goebbels spoke of total war as involving the complete preparedness of the population to concentrate all its energies on the fight for victory. Germany needed to give up all comfortable middle-class customs; a significant degree of voluntary sacrifice of living standards was necessary. He stressed his belief that the public would be prepared to bear burdens if they were treated equally. The specific measures which Goebbels stated were necessary were similar to those imposed by the Ausschuss: women were to replace men wherever possible; businesses not needed for the conduct of the war were to be shut temporarily; the population should work a 14- to 16-hour week if necessary; offices were to stay open until their tasks were finished, however long it took.[21]

Goebbels also signalled that some measures would be taken which were not directly linked to victory but were needed to maintain morale, to secure the 'optics of war.' He foreshadowed the shutting of bars, nightclubs, luxury restaurants and shops, while retaining some means of relaxation (theatres, cinema, sport). Goebbels' concept of the optics of war reflects his background as a propagandist and seems designed to overcome public suspicion that burdens were being borne unevenly. Development of a public image of austerity would also overcome problems of inequality, problems which damaged public morale in World War I and which did affect morale in 1943. As Gauleiter Goebbels banned horse racing and betting in Berlin. Bormann and Lammers submitted the matter to Hitler, who decided that horse racing and sporting competitions should not be stopped since they were one of the few remaining popular entertainments and absorbed excess purchasing power. Goebbels approached Hitler again and succeeded in having the decision on racing left to individual Reich defence commissioners.[22]

In Goebbels' concept of total war, there were definite elements of radicalism for its own sake, of wartime socialism and levelling, even if only rhetorical. He believed that a more egalitarian approach to total war policies was psychologically correct and would result in the population being more willing to make the sacrifices needed. This view was probably drawn from the SD reports on morale and is reinforced by SD leader Kaltenbrunner's comment to Himmler that most German workers met the requirements of total war more willingly than 'a great part' of well-to-do German circles.[23] Additionally Kaltenbrunner suggested that the leadership had to subordinate itself still more to the requirements of total war.

As it referred to social and economic organisation, Goebbels' concept of total war was one of the rationalisation of manpower and resources so that the greatest possible number of staff could be employed in armaments and the greatest possible number of soldiers freed for the front. For Goebbels the economic model of total war involved simplifications to free workers and soldiers and the dismantling of structural obstacles to production. He specifically spoke of the Germans needing to counter the ruthless Soviet methods of mobilising the population with equally valid measures, which were not Bolshevik in spirit.[24] He apparently saw no need to alter the provision or allocation of raw materials, or the organisation of the economic infrastructure as a precondition for increased production. Nor was he openly advocating a different military strategy. His attempts to lead Hitler to a compromise peace, however, indicated his private judgement about the course of the war: Germany needed to find a way to end it quickly.

Goebbels tended to see his disagreements with other leaders about total war as evidence of their lack of commitment to the concept. Yet often these disputes were on questions of implementation. He appeared only to trust action actively pursued and closely supervised from the top; this was in keeping with his own style of administration in the Propaganda Ministry. He saw disagreement as opposition, sabotage or conservatism, rather than recognising it as a different approach to the same goal. For example, he criticised the extraordinarily lax approach of Sauckel and his officials, which he claimed restricted women's employment in Berlin. Out of 150,000 women liable for service in Berlin, only 78,000 were classified as employable. He feared the bad effect such half-measures would have on women already employed. Goebbels judged this result so low that he explained it by deficiencies of the officials involved. His disappointment at this result, which classed 52 per cent of those reporting as employable, suggests he may have had unrealistic expectations of the results of such registration. In 1943, when the British extended registration of women for work to the 45- to 50-year age group, a total of 1,737,000 women were included but the net increase in those employed was only 10,000, or some 0.5 per cent of the total.[25]

Despite Goebbels' suspicions, Bormann, for example, was committed to the policy of total war. Indeed Bormann claimed to his wife that he was responsible for the total war decrees of January 1943. 'I started the whole thing, I set it in motion, and now I have to see to it that . . . the necessary results are achieved.'[26] He may have been exaggerating his role, but his comments and actions, such as his views on the closure of businesses, suggest that he did see himself as introducing total war measures and indeed as leading the entire process. Differences arose between Bormann, on the one hand, and Speer and Goebbels on the other, for two reasons. Bormann certainly, and Hitler probably, was opposed to the creation of a central authority outside Hitler's headquarters. In addition, Bormann possessed different priorities about the measures to be taken.

Bormann's influence was seen in the Ausschuss's consideration of the proposed dissolution of the Prussian Finance Ministry, which would have freed some 232 men. Hitler opposed the dissolution but left it to Lammers to discuss the matter with Göring. In the June meeting Lammers reported on his conversation with Göring. Bormann considered a dissolution of the ministry to be psychologically correct, and the remaining members of the meeting agreed.[27] Bormann probably believed that he could change Hitler's mind. The continued existence of the ministry in June 1944 indicates that he was no more successful than Lammers. This example shows that at least some of the restrictions on closures came from Hitler himself. In this case all members of the Ausschuss agreed, but Hitler's opposition prevented action being taken.

The manner in which Goebbels set about having his ideas accepted demonstrated his understanding of the sources of power and decision making in the regime. He was aware of Hitler's importance as a source of authority. Like Todt, he began by seeking to persuade Hitler in private conversation. Goebbels described the method which had to be used to persuade Hitler. According to Goebbels, hardly anyone in the armed forces could handle Hitler correctly because they believed that when they brought a matter before him once, it was settled. This was not so. A matter had to be brought to Hitler's attention repeatedly and not abandoned at the first refusal. Hitler insisted on his own point of view; to convince him otherwise required tenacity and a strong belief in one's own point of view.[28] Goebbels continued his efforts to persuade Hitler of his preferred solutions; his efforts to win support from secondary leaders would ensure that Hitler received similar advice on important issues from other leaders. When Goebbels found that others interceded with Hitler to have his preferred policy options changed, he identified the problem as being with Hitler's advisers and sought to circumvent them. He was not prepared to counter Hitler openly. In choosing Speer as his main ally in the leadership and in seeking to reactivate Göring, Goebbels demonstrated either an intuitive or a conscious gravitation to the men to whom Hitler had already delegated the most authority on the home front.

Goebbels was advocating some alterations to the National Socialist political system—the introduction of greater co-ordination and supervision. He wanted a National Socialist senate to criticise incorrect decisions and to supervise the Gauleiters. He also wanted to use Göring's powers to establish a stronger central authority on the home front. These proposals suggest that in theory he was willing to concede some authority to others if the required policies were implemented. Just as from 1920 to 1923 Hitler may have seen himself as the 'drummer' of a nationalist revival rather than its leader, so too Goebbels now may have seen himself as the 'drummer' of total war. Suspicion that he sought a greater position for himself existed, typified in Berger's comment that Goebbels wanted to be the Führer of the home front.[29] He may have concealed from himself the extent to which he meant his own policies by total war. He suspected the success and rigour of measures he was not involved with and suspected the radicalism and commitment of others on the issue, with the notable exception of Speer.

This period saw Bormann's position strengthen rather than diminish, as Goebbels intended. On 12 April 1943 Hitler named Bormann Secretary to the Führer, giving him the right to transmit Hitler's orders to ministers and thereby giving him much of the power Lammers had previously enjoyed. Bormann explained to Himmler that this appointment would not create a new office. For years he had been given tasks outside the Party Chancellery's area of responsibility. Bormann was aware that Goebbels was not pleased with this announcement. Bormann could now intervene in any field he wished, and Goebbels believed that Bormann would not allow the adoption of less doctrinaire policies.[30]

In his memoirs Speer stated that, when their plans had failed, Goebbels resigned himself to the extent of Bormann's influence and made an informal alliance with him. Speer claimed to have declined similar overtures from Bormann. Contrary to this assertion, Goebbels did not resign himself to Bormann's influence but continued to be concerned about total war. The reopening of three casinos in April indicated to him that spring was bringing the resurgence of dangerous 'illusions.'[31] He continued to express anxiety about attempts to weaken total war. The same month he observed that unnamed people at Hitler's residence on the Obersalzberg, possibly either Bormann or Lammers, were attempting to undermine press restrictions. He believed that he would be able to persuade Hitler that it was an inappropriate time to start a film magazine.

Goebbels' attempts to publicise the employment of Party leaders' wives met with continued resistance and appear never to have been successful. On 17 March the Party Chancellery objected to the proposal because it would highlight that these women had not worked before. Tiessler responded that Goebbels was unlikely to accept this argument. The population was aware that on the whole the leaders' wives had not previously been employed in factories. The announcement would pacify those who suspected total war was not genuine. At the same time as his office resisted this publicity, Bormann criticised press publicity of visits to the wounded by the wives of prominent citizens as 'aping the customs of an epoch of society made outmoded by National Socialism.'[32] They should do such duties with less publicity.

• • •

As attempts to supersede the Ausschuss by a more radical group had failed, its work continued. Eleven formal meetings were held between January and August 1943. A meeting on 16 March discussed various proposals aimed at cutting down staff, such as reducing the staff of the environmental planning office from 56 to 12 and restricting the range of activities carried out on the home front, including restricting horse racing and a proposed tax on theatre and cinema tickets. The Chronik commented that Speer barely participated in the discussion since 'hardly any useful help for armaments could be expected from the proposals advanced.'[33] Speer refrained from pointing this out at the meeting and did not advance other proposals which he considered more useful.

A 24 June meeting of the Ausschuss, attended by Goebbels, Frick and Seldte, again dealt with a mixture of important and trivial issues. The most important decision was that business closures would be extended from the original end date of 15 May to 30 September 1943. Probably to counter the public unrest which had developed as a result of these measures, an announcement would indicate that such closures took place solely because of total war: recognising the importance of maintaining a healthy middle class, the government would encourage these firms to reopen as soon as possible after the war. The Reich Chancellery record of discussion does not bear out Carroll's claim that this marked a retreat by Goebbels from the realistic introduction of total war. Goebbels had earlier agreed with Speer that it was more important to close down affected businesses completely, but by April he had come to believe, perhaps in response to the public unrest, that such measures had to be taken with an eye to their overall aim—freeing staff.[34]

Businesses had been divided into four categories: first, food stores and other businesses which were exempted from the order; secondly, various household goods producers which were allowed to retain enough capacity to allow for repairs; thirdly, other businesses were either closed or, fourthly, a restricted number allowed to remain open. The extent of business closures seems to have varied from region to region, according to local enforcement of the guidelines. They appear, for example, to have been strictly enforced in Nuremberg and Wurttemberg. Some businesses that continued to pursue peacetime production were closed. It has been suggested that closures acquired a momentum of their own beyond any employment gains and served to rationalise various areas of business. Shutdowns freed materials and power as well as labour but did lead to unemployment, particularly in regions without an armaments industry or among people ill-suited to other work. The policy caused considerable unrest among middle-class business owners, tradesmen and the middle class in general. Many suspected that it was the forerunner of post-war plans designed to eliminate private enterprise permanently. Ill feeling was created as well by actual, and perceived, inequities in the application of the policy across Gaus. The change in policy in June—to close only those businesses whose staff could be redeployed—caused resentment among workers whose businesses were closed under the earlier stricter guidelines, particularly those who could not find any new employment. The public response led Tiessler to suggest Goebbels implement a propaganda campaign to demonstrate that national socialism supported the middle class; this would counter any confusion of wartime measures with long-term policy. The state secretary of the Interior Ministry, Stuckart, claimed that the political porcelain being broken was irreplaceable. Civil servants such as Lammers and Stuckart seem to have been more fearful of the political consequences of this policy and that on women's employment, and more conservative in their attitudes than Party leaders. While some Gauleiters combatted closures, most seem to have used the policy to launch a strong new combing out of firms. The Gauleiter of Mark Brandenburg, Emil Stürtz, told Lammers he had received a flood of complaints from businesspeople about the closures, but he wanted all authorities to stand firm. Bormann claimed the process had been 'without friction and successful' but complained about 'misplaced leniency' in some areas.[35] The Party had to guarantee that Hitler's order was carried out quickly and without compromise.

The Ausschuss was most active from January to June 1943. Its measures resulted in an estimated 2 million more men being called into the armed forces and some 2.5 million workers entering the workforce or being freed from less essential activities. In 1944 Lammers claimed that the Ausschuss had freed 2,506,000 workers from the following programmes:

Compulsory reporting	1,126,000
Inspection of uk positions	830,000
Business closures	150,000
Combing out	400,000

These figures may be exaggerated or inflated; but even so, they represent a considerable achievement. Lammers could not provide an overall figure of all savings made by individual organisations, because he had no record of them. Post-war comments from Reich Chancellery officials suggested that it was not possible to overcome the strong resistance of some offices without Hitler's intervention. Even if some organisations were not very conscientious or could justify most of their activities as relevant to the war effort, the figures recorded suggest that further considerable savings were made by individual organisations. Rebentisch has estimated that some 560,000 staff were given up by all levels of the administration. Some ministries shed large numbers of staff and instituted substantial simplifications. The Reich Labour Service (*Reichsarbeitsdienst* or *RAD*) gave up 54.6 per cent of its leaders to military service, despite its role in training the classes of 1925 and others due to be called up. By the end of February 1943 the Post Ministry, which gave considerable priority to total war, freed 121,000 employees.[36] Where records permit, further studies of each ministry are needed to gain greater knowledge of the results; a complete overview may not be possible.

Hitler had not agreed to some of the Ausschuss's proposals; others had foundered on the resistance of the ministries. In some cases, however, where it has been claimed that Hitler weakened the measures, he merely altered the means of implementing them to avoid strong public reaction. He wanted production restricted without disturbing the population unnecessarily by open bans. For example, instead of maintaining the open ban on hair permanents, he aimed to achieve the same effect by stopping the repair of the relevant machines. These difficulties lead Rebentisch to see the Aus-schuss as a failure. He considers it an attempt to set up a rational form of co-ordinated government in the National Socialist political system, a rather surprising judgement since he also believes it was originated by Hitler. Because it did not achieve its aim, he judges it a failure, even though he considers it was reasonably successful in freeing staff.[37]

Some of the gains from the Ausschuss's measures were only fleeting. Many of those freed by the closure of businesses were old; only one third proved re-employable, mostly outside armaments. Of the 1.6 million women who were brought into the work force, some 500,000 had left again by the end of 1943. A further 0.7 million could be employed only part time. (Similar problems arose in Britain.) Some organisations showed imagination in encouraging women's employment. The railways decided to use the wives of their workers for all railway work, because they would already have a considerable knowledge of the work required. The two largest public service employers, the railways and the post office, seemed strongly committed to expanding women's work.[38]

Others, however, were less enthusiastic. Industry was often reluctant to employ or train women. Sauckel ordered Labour Ministry officials to inspect carefully women's objections to being called up. In some cases Labour Ministry officials were reluctant to enforce rigorously the decree on women's labour duty; public opinion certainly believed this was the case. Enforcement of the policy depended on the Labour Ministry officials and on the varying attitude of individual Gauleiters. Gauleiter Bürckel of Westmark took a strong line and ordered Party leaders to report any women still avoiding work to the labour offices. There do appear to have been problems with lax enforcement or uneven interpretation of the guidelines and lack of a mech-anism to ensure that women did not slip out of the system again. Several studies have shown that many women tried to evade industrial work by organising light work or sham work (Scheinarbeit) and by faking illness.[39]

But supporters of greater employment of women such as Speer and Goebbels also had unrealistic expectations of the numbers who would become available. They were therefore prone to suspect sabotage when these expectations were not fulfilled. Often women who had not participated in paid employment before, or who had spent a long time away from it, were physically and/or psychologically unsuitable for long-term employment. Many women eligible to work did not live in the areas where labour was most needed. A comparison with the British experience suggests that large numbers of women would not become available by registration. In August 1941, 1.5 million women in Britain registered for employment, but only

61,400, 4.09 per cent, were actually employed as a result.[40] The German figures suggest that they were employing a considerably greater proportion of the women registered.

Despite Goebbels' hope that compulsory reporting for labour would overcome public perceptions of unequal treatment, these perceptions were, if anything, strengthened by the Ausschuss' activities. The registration of women for work had not stilled working-class resentment of perceived upper- and middle-class evasion of labour duty; the closure of businesses and compulsory reporting for women, on the other hand, caused middle-class unrest. Goebbels failed in the attempt to use class animus to introduce stricter policies, as he seems to have intended, because the measures did not appear radical enough. Herbst has argued that the regime was forced to introduce total war measures as a result of the incongruence between its propaganda and reality. He concluded that the halfheartedness of the measures meant that the support of neither group was secured and that the measures in fact weakened public support for the regime.[41] Reports and studies of public morale suggest that this was indeed the case. Increased British and American air attacks were directly attributed to the proclamation of total war by some of the German public.

The belief that only upper- and middle-class women evaded employment was probably false. The majority of women not in paid employment (58 per cent in 1939) had working class husbands.[42] Yet the misconception persisted, and may have reflected both working-class suspicions of the regime and a more general lack of social solidarity. Not only hostility to the regime but also World War I memories appear to have contributed to a fragility in German morale, which manifested itself most markedly after the defeat at Stalingrad. This brittleness of public opinion vindicated Goebbels' unsuccessful efforts to publicise leaders' wives working.

Aside from the Ausschuss' policies, other policies were also followed to win additional labour. In 1943 Sauckel's recruitment of foreign labour met increasing difficulties, and greater use made of force. By June Sauckel could report to Hitler that he had recruited 846,511 workers from January to May 1943. After suspending its activities for a few weeks in March 1943 to allow the Ausschuss' measures to take effect, the von Unruh commission continued its work. It continued to encounter difficulties when it proposed to abolish duplicated work. For example, General Fromm opposed proposals that Speer take over the raw materials offices of the Head of Army Armaments and that of the Army Weapons Office (Heereswaffenamt or HWA). His staff suggested changes to save some 150 out of the 480 men in the HWA. Von Unruh authorised the call-up of as many men as possible from the General Government. SS officials subsequently complained that many of the positions he had abolished had been re-created by the civilian administration and suggested that therefore von Unruh's reduction of staff in the General Government had not been great. The administration argued that younger men were needed in the positions because of the security situation in the General Government.[43] This did not necessarily represent failure on the commission's part; Hoffmann's earlier reports indicated that continual vigilance at the top was needed to prevent the return of excess staff. On the other hand, the refilling of positions might also have been evidence that von Unruh cut too harshly and that some of the positions abolished were necessary and had to be replaced.

Hitler continued to have faith in von Unruh. He authorised von Unruh to unify the building organisations of each section of the armed forces in January 1943. A proposal to merge them with the state building organisation, the Organisation Todt or OT, for the duration of the war was developed and forwarded to Speer and Keitel by May. Göring had already ordered that the air force's building section should go to the OT.[44]

Organisations encountered difficulties in meeting the quotas Hitler ordered, as seen in the example of the Post Ministry. Even though only 16,000 men were required, Post Minister Ohnesorge had impulsively volunteered 25,000 men to von Unruh. In Berger's opinion Ohnesorge would do anything in his power to win the war. When Ohnesorge had second thoughts and wanted 4000 men waived from the quota, Keitel told him he could not do so and would not count men already made available to the army as part of the quota. Ohnesorge appealed to Himmler for help, pointing out that his increased quota would mean giving up men from the telecommunications service. The OKW's reinforcements section refused to include the men he made available to the Waffen-SS as part of the quota. Himmler's staff supported Ohnesorge. Berger commented that it would be understandable if Ohnesorge never volunteered help again. Himmler asked Berger to instruct the SS officer on the von Unruh commission, With, about the case.[45] This case illustrates some of the pitfalls for organisations and leaders who were willing to make substantial sacrifices of personnel for the war effort: their commitment was vulnerable to exploitation.

On 28 April von Unruh had discussions with Speer, Sauckel and Rail Minister Dorpmüller to review gaps which had arisen in the fulfilment of a programme to deliver 800,000 men to the armed forces, the so-called 800,000 man programme. Bormann commented that unfortunately von Unruh had 'very weak powers of command, weakest in the armed forces.'[46] Here, as Goebbels had earlier, Bormann voiced the suspicion that as a senior officer von Unruh was incapable of taking a firm enough stand on possible cases of overstaffing in military offices. It is not clear whether these suspicions were justified, or whether they were merely symptoms of internal rivalries and suspicions, engendered by the competition for power and resources.

Hitler did not appear to share, or be influenced by, this suspicion. On 10 May he decreed that von Unruh should examine whether all Germans in the occupied territories in the north and west and in Italy were engaged in tasks necessary for the war effort. This new investigation was designed to prevent German staff from being moved into the occupied territories to avoid military service. After his first inspection in France, von Unruh reported to Bormann that the administration was quite economically staffed, but that duplication existed between various offices and the military commander's office. These inspections, it has been claimed, were insufficiently rigorous.[47]

Surveying five months of the von Unruh commission's activities, Ifland suggested to Bormann that the methods of finding men for the armed forces needed to be changed. The different approaches of individual Gauleiters led to varying results. Gauleiters Wegener and Kauffmann had done nothing; a lot had been done in North Westphalia and nothing in South Westphalia. Ifland criticised the Wehrmacht's disorganisation and reluctance to surrender soldiers, even if they could be better used outside the armed forces. He proposed that the Gauleiters, as Reich defence commissioners, have the right to inspect staffing levels in all areas, including the armaments sector and the armed forces. He was suspicious of both sectors' use of staff and claimed that 600,000 men had slipped between the cracks because of Wehrmacht disorganisation. The 800,000 man programme would not be filled as a result of the armaments sector not delivering its quota. Since Speer's sector was the one remaining source of labour, future programmes were less likely to be successful.[48]

Bormann's reply foreshadowed pressure on Speer's area of authority. The armaments industry had been treated 'extremely considerately' and was the only sector which had so far not met its responsibilities.[49] The Party had exceeded its quota by 150 per cent and could not give up any more staff; other organisations were in a similar position. Bormann believed that the remaining uk positions were so few that they were of little consequence; any further drafts had to come from the armaments sector. (Bormann possibly believed that von Unruh had effectively scrutinised uk positions.) In view of Speer's ban on any intervention in armaments, 'coming demands must be raised from the outset not with Pg. Speer, rather with the Führer, so that the Führer takes the decision. As was seen with the progress of the 800,000 man programme to 15 May, no office achieves a result without this Führer decision.'[50] Bormann considered that only Hitler's personal intervention could overrule Speer, an indication of the strength of Speer's position.

The strength of Bormann's own position can be seen in April 1943 when the OKW agreed that all uk positions for male Party employees would be agreed in the future '*without exception.*'[51] Responsibility for the number and length of uk positions lay with the Party, while Bormann's approval was needed for uk positions of men born 1910 and after. Bormann advised senior Party officials that it was their duty to see that no one stayed in a reserved position any longer than necessary. Continuous inspections would free men for the front in exchange for older men, the wounded or other soldiers.

Increasing armaments production continued to be of high priority to the regime. In 1943 Hitler and Speer placed their reliance on the concept of 'qualitative superiority' over the armaments of the Allies, producing technically superior individual weapons. While production continued to rise, bottlenecks in the steel and components industries and in the supply of skilled labour caused problems. German industry worked mainly on a single-shift basis, due to shortages of skilled workmen and foremen. This single shift often lasted at least 60 hours a week, with workers in some firms having a 72-hour week. In June 1943 Speer appointed labour mobilisation engineers to firms with more than 300 employees to maintain their productive capacity.[52]

Speer's responsibilities and power continued to expand: this is an example of Hitler's support for him and for increasing production. Speer won control of foreign exchange questions in the armaments industry from the WiRüAmt, control of price inspections and control of all financial requirements for armaments from the OKW. He opposed the evacuation of armaments firms from Essen, which he insisted had to remain the German armaments centre.[53] This decision was later of great significance to Germany's capacity to continue resistance.

Speer began to express concern at the effects of call-ups of workers on production. He told Hitler and Keitel that proposals to call up 200,000 specialists would prevent continued increases in production. While programmes of training were established in industry to train unskilled workers, these tended to concentrate on bringing them to a semi-skilled level, and German firms proved reluctant to train German women. It was difficult for the central organisations themselves to get an idea of the extent of the training programmes. On 16 February Speer and Sauckel issued a common decree ordering the transfer of technical workers in construction offices and firms to a programme concentrating on armaments priority areas, the *Schwerpunkt* programme. In a later decree they asked the leaders of armaments factories to ensure that new workers were used as quickly and effectively as possible. Speer proposed to Hitler that workers being called up be placed in units which would see action only in large operations. With this and the help of longer working holidays, Speer could use the workers in quiet times for armaments production. He also submitted a proposal to Hitler for more purposeful employment of specialist workers in the army.[54]

The regime had responded to the Stalingrad crisis with a flurry of decisions, aimed at getting more labour for the armaments factories, simplifying the home front and making more men available to the front. The measures adopted suggest commitment to some concept of total war from Hitler down and were accompanied by a propaganda campaign emphasising that the government was serious about total war.

The debates about the measures reveal various models and concepts of total war. They suggest that Goebbels and Speer were motivated in part by radicalism for its own sake. There appears to have been little reason to close down some businesses if their employees could not be re-employed, for example, unless they used large amounts of scarce materials. In his concern for popular morale Bormann represented the own sectional interests of the Party; Speer reflected the sectional interests of the armaments economy in seeking to drive all production into his own power base, armaments. Himmler was not involved in such debates. Instead in this period he pursued both regime's ideological policies, particularly the Final Solution, and the expansion of SS armaments production, both contributions to a National Socialist model of total war.

At a time when more labour was being sought urgently, it is important to note that none of these leaders advocated a greater use of Jewish labour in the economy, except for their use as SS prisoners. Speer tried to restrict the SS's use of building materials, but the overall allocation of resources for the SS's purposes, which included the concentration camp system and the extermination of the Jews, was not questioned.[55]

At least two leaders, Goebbels and Speer, considered that the Ausschuss' response had not been radical enough. The Ausschuss' results suggest that their criticisms were not always well judged. Their criticisms were of two kinds: firstly, that not enough was being done, and secondly, that the measures were being sabotaged at the top. Two points arise in regard to the first criticism. Goebbels and Speer had little reliable information about whether enough was being done or not, whether the measures were effective or not. They did not possess much of an independent system of verification and tended to rely on their perceptions and impressions. What evidence there is suggests that quite a lot had been done, as in the case of the von Unruh commission. Goebbels' and Speer's disappointment with what had been achieved suggests that their expectations were unrealistic. They tended to attribute the shortfalls to sabotage and foot dragging rather than admit that their expectations were exaggerated. A comparison to the British policies reinforces this point.

In response to their second suspicion, the evidence suggests that if there was any weakening of measures, this was being done either right at the top by Hitler or by local officials rather than by other leaders at their level. A number of factors contributed to Goebbels and Speer developing these impressions. The lack of a system of verification and their distrust of the reports of other leaders were weaknesses of the National Socialist system. Their judgements were also affected by their lack of realism in their conceptions of total war and their tendency to overlook considerations of internal politics. Germany's increasing military problems made them want to achieve more than was possible. The regime's options were declining and total war was the last hope.

Goebbels and Speer aimed to supplement total war by creating a more flexible foreign policy, but Hitler was not interested. They also tried to overcome Bormann's influence. Instead the creation of the office of Secretary to the Führer had strengthened Bormann's position. For the remainder of 1943, the regime's attention domestically was focussed on avoiding a collapse of the home front. Despite the beginning of some doubts about the ideological model of total war, application of this model was intensified in late 1943.

5

'Ideological Renovation' (July-December 1943)

In the second half of 1943 the German leadership was not confronted with a military crisis as dramatic as Stalingrad, but encountered more rapid deterioration of Germany's position on the Eastern front and the opening of a new front in Italy. The regime faced a political crisis when Italy left the war, and this led to a heightened emphasis on ideological mobilisation of the population and on the ideological model of total war in general.

The Allies followed their successful campaign in North Africa with the invasion of Sicily on 10 July 1943. In little over a month, they had captured Sicily. Following a vote of no confidence by the Fascist Grand Council, Mussolini was dismissed by the Italian king on 25 July and succeeded by Marshal Badoglio. On 8 September it was revealed that Italy had surrendered, and German forces immediately occupied Italy. The German leadership was surprised by the news of the dismissal of Mussolini and found it difficult to know how to present the news to its people. German propaganda, Baird considers, was at its most equivocal in dealing with the Italian crisis.[1]

Italy's withdrawal from the war was a symbolic blow equivalent to Stalingrad. The fall of Mussolini concerned the National Socialist leadership for a number of reasons. It led not only to the opening of a new front, but also to a further crisis of German morale and loss of support for the government. The level of discontent was such that Steinert suggests that many sections of the population half-expected a coup against Hitler in July

1943. 'Conditions for a revolutionary attempt had probably never been better.'[2] The population now largely saw the war as lost. Himmler subsequently admitted that the fall of Italy, supplemented by the efforts of enemy radio broadcasts, had resulted in a wave of defeatism in Germany.

Discontented elements in Germany might be encouraged by fascism's easy overthrow. Italy's withdrawal from the war as a result of internal political changes had uncomfortable parallels with Germany in 1917-18 for National Socialism, a parallel explicitly drawn by General Alfred Jodl, head of the armed forces' leadership staff, the *Wehrmachtführungsstab*, in a speech to Reichs- and Gauleiters in November 1943. The sudden fall of fascism prompted concern at the regime's effectiveness in re-educating the German people. The leadership agreed that the working class remained loyal, unlike in 1918, and was unlikely to be swayed by the Italian example. But the frequency with which the German workers' loyalty was stressed, especially to Party audiences, suggests the Party needed reassurance on this point. The leaders believed that the middle and upper classes and the intellectuals were less reliable than the working class. Speer praised the exemplary attitude of the German worker as responsible for the favourable armaments situation while describing critics as 'middle class.'[3] Himmler claimed defeatism was more prevalent among the upper classes and intellectuals than the middle or working classes. During their speeches of this period, leaders frequently compared the situation in 1943 favourably to that of 1914-18. On a number of occasions Himmler attributed the difference to the removal of the Jews, who in his opinion had acted as saboteurs and agitators in 1916-17, and to the absence of Communist cells.

A variety of policies was adopted to control the domestic repercussions of the Italian crisis. While Hitler responded more calmly than his entourage, he ordered Himmler to take severe police measures to prevent anything similar happening in Germany. As a further precaution, men married to women from enemy countries, or linked to former ruling houses or to international economic circles were to be removed from positions of influence. Hitler also tried to avert public discontent by reducing leadership privileges. Party leaders who owned more than one house, apart from at their place of work, were ordered to make these extra homes available to evacuees. This order seemingly had little effect, since it had to be repeated in November.[4]

The final measure taken to ensure internal order, recognised as such by the population, was the appointment of Himmler as Interior Minister on 20 August 1943. This symbolised the seriousness with which Hitler viewed the possible domestic effects of the Italian crisis. Himmler saw his tasks as

Interior Minister as restoring the Reich's authority, eradicating corruption and misconduct and decentralising less important tasks. In addition he had to secure the mood and attitude of the home front.[5] The slightest sign of trouble from foreigners in Germany would need to be firmly punished, Himmler told SS leaders.

Himmler moved quickly to check defeatism. He chose not to punish every defeatist but rather to make examples of a few, by carrying out some 150 death sentences. Reporting to Gauleiters in October 1943, Himmler assured them that no uprising or difficulties would occur. They did not need to set up individual troop units to protect themselves against a revolt or paratrooper attack. This would only lead to organisational confusion. In July he and Bormann had agreed that such units could be set up only by Hitler's explicit decree. They showed their commitment to this view by stopping Swabian Gauleiter Karl Wahl's defence forces. Himmler described Wahl's plan as 'well meant but destroying all existing organisation.'[6]

Himmler criticised excessive over-centralisation on small issues but stressed that there had to be clear Reich authority to handle the issues of the war effort. He believed that he had strengthened the state's authority by adopting administrative simplifications in the Interior Ministry (removing two sections and one state secretary), introducing clear responsibility among officials and removing undesirable personnel policies such as nepotism. (In practice, Himmler's orders against nepotism had to be ignored because of the labour shortage.) He told the Gauleiters on 6 October that the views of central authority on the economy and armaments had to be decisive. These comments led Speer to hope that Himmler would provide strong central leadership and overcome the Gauleiters' resistance to his proposals. Speer's hopes were in vain. Himmler continued his policy of not seeking to cut across other responsibilities. He referred Speer's disputes with the Gauleiters about continued production of inessential items to the Party Chancellery rather than having the Interior Ministry investigate them. Similarly he refused to intervene over proposals to simplify German propaganda in France, saying he knew too little about the issue.[7]

Himmler also considered it important to stamp out corruption and alcoholism for the sake of public morale. Since he believed bans or restrictions which could not be enforced were damaging, he must have believed these abuses could be controlled. Nonetheless he told Kehrl that he did not have the power to change the inappropriate behaviour of some Party leaders. There were, however, limits to his concern for morale. Popular opposition in the Niederlausitz district did not stop him displacing farmers to set up a military training area there.[8]

The Italian collapse meant that the leadership placed particular emphasis on reactivating the Party and increasing ideological indoctrination of the armed forces. Energy and fanaticism were seen as secret weapons to combat the enemy. Goebbels appeared to be worried about the possible alienation of the populace from the leadership. Perhaps sensing this, the Party aimed to keep closer contact with the people. Bormann suggested Gauleiters take the Party's experiences in the Kampfzeit as their model. In September Party members were called on to set a good example by showing willing involvement in the war effort and implementing all measures needed for armaments and agriculture. They were warned that Party members not up to these tests were to be expelled. These exhortations reflected Party failings. Party members were becoming reluctant to identify themselves, partly because of the public reception they sometimes met. Goebbels was now critical of Hitler's loyalty to Party members who were not up to the job.[9] The Party's weaknesses may have influenced some of Bormann's attitudes. His reluctance to adopt some total war measures may have been stemmed from an awareness that the Party could not be relied upon to carry them out effectively. The organisation at his disposal was not as reliable or efficient as those at the disposal of other leaders.

In August Bormann agreed to a proposal that the Party hold general parades to provide propaganda orientation for its members and to reactivate the members as soon as possible. The submission noted the trough in public mood and criticised Goebbels' propaganda for the Party. In order to influence public opinion and strengthen the popular will to resist, Bormann ordered the Gauleiters to address general membership parades to be held within four weeks from 15 October 1943. Participation in the meetings was compulsory. Speakers at the meetings emphasised the need for Party members to influence public opinion by word of mouth. Quarterly propaganda marches were made by the Party from October on, partly to increase members' feelings of power and purpose. By the end of the year the Gaus were predictably reporting that the meetings and marches had been well attended by Party members and had had a good effect on public opinion. Bormann claimed in December that these measures had led to a successful Party war effort and that they should be continued without new orders being needed. The effect of these measures is difficult to assess. They did not have any sustained effect on popular morale or on the continuing critical public attitude to the Party.[10] The propaganda campaign may have served as a substitute for more rigorous measures at home. Yet it was probably also necessary to 'mobilise' the Party politically and the people psychologically.

During this period other measures of ideological mobilisation were adopted in the armed forces. The Soviet use of captured German officers for propaganda and appeals to German forces, the National Committee for a Free Germany and the League of German Officers under General Seydlitz may have prompted counter measures. Berger assured army Colonel Hübner that Himmler would support his proposals for three- to four-week ideological training courses for officers. Berger advised Himmler that he supported Hübner because of the army's 'particular ideological plight.'[11] He attributed this plight to the officer corps not being oriented to the ideas of their supreme commander. Hitler himself agreed and undertook to write an introduction to Hübner's paper which was to be distributed among the officer corps.

In November Hitler decided that officers for military ideological leadership (*Wehrgeistige Führung*) were to be renamed officers for National Socialist leadership (*Nationalsozialistischer Führungsoffizier*, or NSFOs). The change of name indicated that they not only had the task of ideological education but were also responsible for explanation and guidance on topical issues. Hitler ordered further strengthening of ideological leadership and troop education in the armed forces on 22 December. In co-ordination with the Party Chancellery, the OKW was to create an office to lead this, the *NS-Führungsstab*. General Reinecke, head of the Allgemeine Wehrmachtsamt, led the office. In calling for all sections of the Wehrmacht to appoint NSFOs, Keitel described this as being of 'decisive significance to the war.'[12] But Reinecke told Bormann that the NSFOs soon ran into difficulties; Keitel's real attitude could be seen from the fact that, with 5000 men in the OKW, he had no NSFO in order to save manpower. These measures gave the Party increased control over the armed forces. Party Chancellery officials believed that the Party had to participate in all aspects of setting up the NS-Führungsstab and in choosing officers to staff it.

These policies were evidence of the strengthening of the ideological model of total war. The increased emphasis on ideological training as a means of securing victory marks the persistent strength among the leadership of the 'German model of total war,' and the continued comparison of conditions and problems to those of 1917-18. The setting up of the NSFOs as well as the appointment of Himmler as Interior Minister are further evidence that Hitler was prepared to make the war more total. These policies reflect Hitler's emphasis on the importance of the will to resist in military engagements and the hope that fanaticism and political reliability would make up for material deficiencies. They reflected a growing radicalisation of policy and opened the way for the 'partification' of the army,[13] greater Party ascendancy over the army.

Bormann's prominence in these campaigns to reactivate the Party and to ensure the political reliability of the armed forces suggests that his concept of total war was primarily an ideological one. The emphasis of these and other measures he initiated was on maintaining the stability of the home front and relying on ideological reliability and commitment as a means of securing victory.

The policy of intensifying ideological education in the armed forces highlights two other influences on the German doctrine of total war as implemented by the National Socialist leadership—the influence of Soviet conduct of the war against Germany and the influence of the experiences of the Kampfzeit. During World War II Soviet society was comprehensively mobilised for war by a leadership whose dictatorship was longer entrenched and who possessed greater control over the economy and population than its National Socialist counterpart. Men aged 16 to 55 and women aged 16 to 45 were mobilised to work for the war effort. Women had been 38 per cent of the civilian labour force in 1940 and were 53 per cent in 1942. Women served extensively in the armed forces, in many instances in combat units. Extreme sacrifices of already low living standards were made by the Soviet population. The regime was able to switch its industrial production almost entirely to military purposes, aided by economic assistance from its Western allies and by successful large-scale evacuation of industry out of German range in 1941-2.[14]

As early as March 1942 Goebbels had written of Hitler's admiration of the more radical Soviet war effort. Goebbels himself continually compared the inadequacy of the Ausschuss' measures to those of the Russians. In early 1943 he had criticised the army's lack of revolutionary spirit. Many Germans claimed that Russian military successes were due to their use of political commissars. Himmler himself attributed some of the Russian successes in winter 1941 to the commissar system. Blaming the armed forces' failure on lack of revolutionary National Socialist spirit was, of course, politically and psychologically easier than facing the fact that Hitler's decisions were responsible for Germany's military problems. Continuing references to the Soviet model and the willingness to contemplate a system similar to the commissars, however, suggests some loss of ideological self-confidence, evidence of a belief that the enemy handled some issues better.[15]

If the Soviet Union's conduct of the war provided an alternative ideological model of how to wage total war, the leadership drew as well on its own experience of the struggle for power before 1933. A fanatical belief in National Socialist ideology came to be relied on as German military strength shrank. Jacobsen suggests perceptively that this marked an attempt by Hitler to transpose the tactics of the Kampfzeit—propaganda, indoctrination, ad hoc weapons—to military conditions. By late 1942 Goebbels used the Party crises of 1930 and 1932 as a model for the situation the regime faced; in October 1943 Bormann referred Gauleiter Wahl to the Kampfzeit as a model. Speer later considered this experience as crucial to explain the Party leadership's continued blind faith that Hitler would lead them to victory. Before their rise to power the National Socialist Party had made electoral gains by a combination of tactics including an extremely skilled use of propaganda and pageantry, street fighting and agitation, and appeals aimed at a wide range of German opinion. Hitler gained power when members of Germany's political elite approached him to form a coalition government; he had held out for this and refused to accept lesser terms, even when the Party's electoral success appeared to be failing. The NSDAP had not come to power with the experience of a long period of underground activity or consolidated its power in a civil war, as the Bolsheviks had. It had come to power in a sense by bluffing Germany's conservative politicians around President Hindenburg into appointing Hitler as Chancellor. The influence of the Kampfzeit may have been misleading for total war. It may have prompted an excessive reliance on rhetorical, propagandistic gestures rather than sober organisation. It may also account for the hopes Goebbels placed on a compromise peace by splitting Germany's enemies, a procedure which bore some similarities to the Party's tactics in 1932-3. Indeed in seeking to persuade Hitler to conclude a compromise peace in September 1943, Goebbels explicitly argued, 'I pointed out to the Führer that in 1933, too, we did not attain power by making absolute demands . . . . Very soon thereafter, however, we forced all our demands through. Most likely similar circumstances prevail today.'[16]

If developments in Italy caused and accentuated emphasis on the ideological model of the war, developments on the Eastern front also presented the regime with problems. Despite careful preparation and initial success, a large-scale summer offensive on 5 July, intended to remove the Soviet salient at Kursk, had failed by 12 July. The Russians took Orel and Kharkov in their counter-attack. The Germans lost half a million men in these battles and almost a million men overall in the fighting to October 1943. The losses of the German army at Stalingrad could not be replaced, and the Eastern front had to give up units for Italy and other areas. Hitler refused to sanction any withdrawals and continued to display confidence in victory. Soviet forces continued to advance and had taken Kiev by November.[17]

Moves were made to pursue more positive policies in the East and to make the regime's military task easier by a compromise peace with either the

Western Allies or the Soviet Union. Himmler's influence over Eastern policy grew, when he allowed Berger's appointment as head of a new operational staff in charge of political issues in the Ostministerium. Reflecting this increased influence, renewed attempts were made to win Himmler over to different policies in the East. Colonel Martin, the OKW's liaison officer with Goebbels, passed on reports criticising current policies to Himmler via Berger; Stuckart, State Secretary in the Interior Ministry, wanted Himmler to help fight corruption among German officials in the Ukraine; and Hildebrandt, head of the SS Race and Settlement Main Office, forwarded to Himmler reports from German officers stationed in the East advocating different agricultural and political policies. Himmler responded that such officers should concentrate on their duties at the front and leave politics to others; he would not be drawn into expressing an opinion on the wider issues raised. He saw dangers in the 'Declaration on the Introduction of Peasant Landed Property' which Rosenberg issued in May 1943, a declaration which recognised peasant landholdings in Soviet communes as private property. But he did not oppose the decree, as Ukrainian Reichskommissar Koch had wanted. He contented himself with objecting to the failure to consult the SS in drawing up the decree.[18]

Himmler continued to lack interest in exploiting Vlasov's movement. He warned SS officers that it would be dangerous if Germans came to believe that only Russian soldiers could defeat the Soviet Union, but he had nothing against use of the Vlasov movement for propaganda purposes only. He was more concerned with ensuring that the retreating Germans took all able-bodied Soviet workers back with them. Himmler's opinion echoed Hitler's comments in a speech to army commanders on 1 July 1943. Hitler told them he could not promise an independent Ukraine, even hypocritically, because of the psychological effect of such a promise. For Germany to say that it would give up the territory it had conquered in the East would be tantamount to saying Germany had no war aims. Such a statement would demoralise the soldier at the front, as similar statements had done in World War I. Bormann too supported hard-line policies in the East. Dallin has suggested that Bormann supported Koch's hard measures and presented issues in such a way that Hitler continued to support Koch.[19] Bormann's attitude to Eastern policy seems to vindicate Himmler's and Goebbels' assessment that he was too doctrinaire.

Goebbels continued to be concerned by the 'extremely critical' situation on the Eastern front.[20] The Germans were experiencing a period where strategy, in Schlieffen's words, was a system of substitutions. While Goebbels had shown considerable interest earlier in 1943 in the need to adopt more flexible policies in the East, he did not appear to have developed his proposals further. He may have realised that Hitler was not interested in such considerations, or he may have believed that it was too late for such measures to have an effect. He certainly judged that his increased powers over propaganda in the East came 'very late, almost too late.'[21]

German propaganda in this period played on the fear of Bolshevism. Goebbels hoped that emphasis on the dangers of Bolshevism would help split the enemy coalition and bring a compromise peace closer. The Japanese made further efforts to mediate between the Germans and the USSR in July 1943. When Japanese Ambassador Oshima raised the matter with Hitler, Hitler claimed that the USSR could still be beaten. Oshima gained the impression that Hitler had no intention of concluding a compromise peace. Hitler also reportedly rejected Göring's suggestions that the Eastern front be completely shut down. Ribbentrop nonetheless continued soundings of the Soviets in the latter part of 1943. The Soviet Union apparently demanded a return to the 1941 borders, but the mood in Hitler's headquarters was still too optimistic to agree to this. German peace feelers with East and West continued unsuccessfully in September and October.[22]

The need for a negotiated peace runs like a thread through Goebbels' diary entries for the second half of 1943 and was an implicit criticism of Hitler's conduct of the war. By 1943 Himmler and Goebbels agreed with General Heinz Guderian, the general inspector of armoured forces, that Hitler should no longer be in direct command of the army on the Eastern front, but neither man was willing to take the matter up with Hitler. After Stalingrad, Hitler had turned on those who came to him advocating peace; now he was willing to discuss the prospects for it with Goebbels at length. But the prospects of a compromise peace satisfactory to the regime were deteriorating as Germany's military position worsened. Hitler still preferred to deal with the Western Allies; Goebbels began by considering that Stalin would be more realistic and approachable, but then came to be persuaded by Hitler that Germany would get a better and longer-lasting peace with Britain. Hitler's views on a compromise peace seemed to fluctuate, since a few days later he was more willing to negotiate with Stalin than with Churchill. He may have been humouring or placating Goebbels in discussing peace prospects, since he took no serious steps to implement these ideas and since he did not believe Stalin could cede what he would demand, the Ukraine. (It was this demand by Hitler which Fleischhauer claims prevented a compromise peace earlier in 1943.) Bormann's views reflected Hitler's change of heart. He was reportedly worried about the course of German foreign policy and the war in general. Only the most senior leaders could discuss or consider such proposals without being accused of defeatism.[23]

Hitler and Goebbels discussed the likelihood of growing British and American war-weariness; Goebbels hoped that the strains in the enemy coalition were increasing. Himmler too awaited a breakup of the enemy coalition. He drew attention to Allied disagreements over the Balkans and commented that these disputes would bear fruit for the Germans. The coalition would break up one day and no longer threaten Germany. Himmler believed that the Germans had to pursue political as well as military means of ending the war, but he did not seem take any initiative on the issue. He did, however, make contact with the opposition to Hitler. Other members of the leadership were aware of his contacts, but historians have suggested that he played a double game, that he toyed with the possibility of turning against Hitler. Himmler as well as Goebbels was doubting Hitler's star, and he was seeking 'insurance' for the future. His position was ambiguous. Some in the SS leadership wanted Himmler to play a greater role. Berger, the head of the SS Main Office, told him that Göring, Goebbels and Ley lacked credibility with the population. The time was not yet ripe, Berger continued, to give Himmler prominence, implying that he saw such a time approaching.[24]

Germany's continuing losses in the East and the opening of the Italian front meant the Germans had to increase their available manpower urgently. By the end of 1943, 30 divisions, 15 per cent of those on the Eastern front, were disbanded for lack of replacements.[25]

Further attempts were made to reduce the numbers of civil servants and the numbers behind the lines in the armed forces. In his capacity as plenipotentiary for the Reich administration (*Generalbevollmächtigter für die Reichsverwaltung*), Himmler ordered a reduction in the numbers of uk positions in the civil service. Each Berlin-based organisation had to give up about 50 per cent of its uk positions by 10 September 1943. At this time, the ministries with the largest number of men aged 46 and younger (the class of 1897 and younger) still in uk positions were the Foreign Ministry with 362, the Justice Ministry with 279, the Ostministerium with 361 and the Armaments Ministry with 241. The lowest numbers were held by the Propaganda Ministry with 131 and the Interior Ministry with 83. These figures suggest that the ministries did not contain large numbers of men who should have been serving at the front, and that such measures would not win substantial additional forces. On Goebbels' behalf, the Propaganda Ministry advised that it could not agree to give up 50 per cent of its uk positions and offered to give up 27 men instead. The Propaganda Ministry's 'repeated *voluntary* combing out actions' in 1942 had already freed all workers possible.[26] A direct approach to General Olbricht at the OKW prevented the call-up of the Propaganda Ministry workers; Goebbels also successfully thwarted attempts by von Ribbentrop and von Unruh to exclude the Propaganda Ministry from responsibility for propaganda in France and thereby save 150 positions. The aftermath of the Italian collapse may have led Goebbels to believe that propaganda's role in maintaining morale was becoming more crucial. These moves may demonstrate a lessening of Goebbels' own efforts to shed staff and his desire to maintain his power base.

The Party too was called on to give up more men in uk positions, of the classes 1897 to 1922, from its central offices. On 1 June 1943 the Party Chancellery still employed 14,677 uk Party leaders. Bormann ordered that no more men could be given up by the Gau and Kreis offices because they had such low numbers in uk positions. Even though the Party's main office had reportedly already given up more than half its personnel to the front, Hitler asked it to give up more personnel in December. Specifically men aged 37 and younger (the class of 1906 and younger) who had not yet served or who had only served for six months were to be made available to the armed forces. Reichs-, Gauleiters and organisational leaders were to be exempted. Hitler had to approve other exemptions. In exchange the Wehrmacht would free some men of lesser fitness to return to the Party. Bormann freed between 1000 and 2000 lower-rank leaders.[27]

In a further effort to find more men for the front, Hitler called for fewer troops to be kept behind the lines. The imbalance between fighting troops and the large numbers of soldiers behind the front threatened to be 'not only a purely military, but also a psychological danger.'[28] Hitler specifically referred to the World War I criticisms of the étappe—the area behind the lines which gained a bad reputation for corruption, overstaffing and malingering. He demonstrated that he shared the belief of Himmler, Goebbels and Bormann that the armed forces were overstaffed behind the lines. These perceptions were reinforced by a study prepared for Himmler by the SS Inspector for Statistics, Dr Korherr, on the use of staff by the armed forces in World War I. The report noted an increasing bureaucratisation, with 3 million men in uk positions, 2.7 million men on the home front and some half a million men in the étappe. In Korherr's opinion this decisively weakened the front in 1918. Professional military officials as a group suffered low losses in World War I and would therefore need particular scrutiny in this war.

The belief that there was overstaffing behind the lines was a common misconception among civilian leaders on both sides during the war and demonstrated ignorance of the need for a large technical and support system behind the lines in modern warfare. Ironically historians have seen the Wehrmacht as comparatively lean and efficiently organised considering its limited resources. Van Creveld judges it to have allocated comparatively few resources to logistics, administration and management.[29]

Since Hitler believed all possibilities of gaining more men from the civilian sector were exhausted, he ordered all sections of the armed forces and the Waffen-SS to find one million men from their organisations at home. At least 25 per cent of their men on the home front either had to fight or free other soldiers capable of fighting. To enable this the 'unwieldy' administrative apparatus of the armed forces was to be simplified.[30] Army group commanders had to set up control commissions which were to abolish any manifestations of the étappe and to scrutinise the number of offices and units in towns. Keitel's supplementary orders indicated that armed forces personnel were to be listed as uk only with the commanding general's authorisation; these listings were to be checked by von Unruh. Soldiers who would not regain their fitness for six months were to be exchanged for fully fit men holding uk positions in armaments. Simplifications of armed forces' pay, health care and uniforms were also undertaken.

The leadership's misguided belief that the Wehrmacht was overstaffed and inefficient led them to believe that more soldiers could be found there than was the case. Hitler's comment in his order that there was no possibility of increasing the numbers from the civilian sector suggests he believed that von Unruh and the Ausschuss had made all possible staff cuts and simplifications. His lack of response, when Speer and Goebbels urged stricter measures to free labour, may have arisen from his belief that reserves on the home front were exhausted.

The employment of women in this period widened, but underlying attitudes to it continued to be ambivalent. To save more staff, Hitler decreed that male and female members of the RAD were to be used for anti-aircraft, the men in RAD anti-aircraft units, the women in communications. A further 5000 women were sought for anti-aircraft units through the Reichsfrauenführung. Subsequent unrest at this move prompted Bormann to issue advice to Gauleiters that there was no intention of sending women to the front or their using weapons. Rumours that the Germans planned to create women's battalions similar to those in the Soviet army were to be strongly countered by Party members. Yet on 21 November 1943 Hitler rejected Sauckel's attempt to have the age limit for women to report for work raised. There are no clear indications of Hitler's reasons; perhaps he did not consider women older than 45 capable of effective labour. Both Bormann and Lammers wanted the age level raised but considered, for unspecified reasons, possibly due to Hitler's known views, that at the moment this was completely inopportune. Bormann and the Gauleiters believed that such a measure would gain only an additional 140,000 to 160,000 women and would adversely affect the work of their husbands.[31]

Additional labour was needed for armaments production. The deteriorating military position reduced the number of foreign workers available for recruitment and reduced the willingness of others to work for a losing power. The amount of foreign labour recruited by Sauckel decreased in the second half of 1943; he met his later 1943 quotas through the internment of large sections of the Italian army. Homze estimated that by November 1943 Sauckel had recruited 1,427,680 workers. Speer and Sauckel disagreed about the preferred method of employing more foreign labour. Sauckel wanted to continue to transport foreign workers to Germany, while Speer wanted to keep them in the occupied territories working for German armaments. On 5 October Speer signed a decree establishing 'blocked firms' (*Sperrbetriebe* or *S-Betriebe*) in the occupied territories. Employees of these firms working on German commissions were protected from transportation. In France alone over 14,000 firms were made S-Betriebe. As the Chronik noted, this broke with the policy previously followed by Sauckel. By the end of the year, Speer had won this dispute with Hitler's support.[32] The policy brought the advantage of temporary rises in production at the expense of later problems. It made Speer more vulnerable to the loss of workers from the opening of a second front or other further losses of territory. Speer may have assumed that German armaments production could continue only while the resources of the occupied territories were available.

Additional labour was gained from the employment of the captured and interned Italian prisoners of war and concentration camp prisoners. Speer approached Himmler to use prisoners from Auschwitz and asked Keitel to help counter the decreasing productivity of POWs. Strict discipline was needed: loafing POWs and their guards should be punished. Speer advised Keitel that assaults on German employees should earn the death penalty. He also commended a suggestion to Keitel as relevant—that escaping foreign workers should become POWs when they were recaptured.[33]

The armaments industry had to rely more than before on German labour as it became more difficult to obtain foreign labour, according to Sauckel. Restrictions on the optical industry and the production of electricity meters had already freed some 9000 workers. Sauckel and Speer set quotas for the delivery of staff for a number of industries—textiles, paper and printing, clothing, construction material, glass, ceramics, leather, wood production—in July. On 2 August Bormann asked the Gauleiters to accelerate filling the quotas because of the increased requirements of the armaments industry. Consumer production was to be taken over by firms in the occupied territories or by use of workers unsuited to armaments employment due to restricted mobility and other reasons.[34]

After the significant increases in armaments production from 1942 to mid-1943, production remained fairly constant from May to December 1943. German production policies aimed to overcome enemy quantitative superiority by producing qualitatively superior armaments. In August Speer planned to shut down less important production, transfer the firms concerned to arms production and allow their previous tasks to be taken over by foreign or by small firms in a combing-out programme (*Aktion Auskämmung des zivilen Sektors zugunsten der Rüstungsindustrie*, or *AZS*). Hitler agreed to Speer's proposals. Speer devoted considerable time to this plan in September, holding discussions with the army's procurement officials about shutdowns in the sector providing army equipment. He offered the civilian production to French firms during a visit by the French Production Minister, Bichelonne. He believed that the industries themselves could not be expected to achieve these reductions so he planned to implement them by using men from those areas of the armaments industry which needed staff. By October Speer claimed to have freed 40,000 workers by this means. Here again, in transferring production to the occupied territories, Speer opted for an immediate solution without too much dislocation, at the expense of future problems. In August 1944 Bormann was to claim that events had proved Sauckel right and had shown how wrong Speer's agreement with Bichelonne had been. It would have been better to move the workers to the Reich than to move the machines to France and lose both workers and machines. As Ley commented, Speer's plan was 'more elegant' but Sauckel was more 'farsighted.'[35]

Speer told the Gauleiters in October that their requests for exemptions from shut-downs showed a lack of understanding of the current situation. If a Gau did not comply with his orders within 14 days, he would announce the closures himself. Himmler would deal appropriately with Gaus which did not carry through his measures. (This was Speer's unsuccessful attempt to mobilise Himmler against the Gauleiters' obstruction.) He also used SD reports to select firms for possible closure and to combat cases of corruption in firms.[36]

Speer gained additional powers to pursue his goals. By September he had gained control over electricity production and sole power to use Italian armaments capacity. On 2 September he was given control over all production decisions, while Funk, the Economics Minister, remained responsible for the supply of consumer goods, for foreign trade questions and finance. Funk became a member of Central Planning. The decree was accompanied by a change of title for Speer to Reich Minister for Armaments and War Production. It allowed Speer to set up a planning office (*Planungsamt*) headed by Hans Kehrl which could plan measures for Central Planning and supervise their implementation. These changes marked the high point of Speer's accumulation of power. Bormann explained to the Gauleiters that the general war situation made these powers necessary. He assured them that Speer would order all workers to leave a firm only if there was a guarantee of employment by an armaments firm. Such changes would occur only with artisan and craft (*Handwerk*) firms of more than 50 employees and industrial firms with more than 100 employees. Speer planned to close firms in armaments centres where staff could be quickly redeployed and delegate their tasks to firms in smaller towns.[37]

Speer made three speeches in September and October 1943, explaining and justifying his policy of shut-downs by pointing to the excessive production of inessential goods for the Wehrmacht and for civilian consumption in general. He made much of the production of typewriters, cameras and boots for the Wehrmacht. Where he conceded that such goods were necessary, his proposed solution was that they should be confiscated from people or firms who had them. Any further production for civilian use would have to be the simplest styles possible. Sauckel was later to describe these plans as 'crazy.'[38] Speer may have assumed too readily that production, which was not under his direct control, was inessential and excessive.

The spartan and restrictive conditions of the German home front indicate Speer's claims about the extent of consumer production were exaggerated. Clothing, shoes, paper and soap were all almost unattainable. Shoes were now made of straw and wood. No Party leader below the rank of Kreisleiter could obtain a new uniform. In addition, 'the fall of 1943 marked the beginning of really serious cuts in rations.'[39] Production of consumer goods of elastic demand was no more than one third of the pre-war level or less, even though the German population was greater. Supplying the needs of over 12 million bombing victims was becoming more and more difficult. As a result, much of the resistance from Bormann and the Gauleiters against further closures in the consumer goods industry was rational. They were aware that loss of the little production remaining would make it even more difficult to counter the effects of bombing.

Speer's proposals for confiscation contained a number of flaws. Once again this was a short-term solution, not a long-term solution for a war which could be expected to last for several more years. Politically it was a high-risk strategy, as the hostile public reaction to rumours that excessive clothing would be confiscated demonstrated. It was not likely to gain support of any of the agencies whose help would be needed for it to succeed, particularly the Party, and it would unnecessarily attract opposition from the public. It was not possible to keep the Germans at such a primitive level and expect rising productivity: it might reduce the standard of living below the level needed for morale and efficiency. The results of bombing in particular made some continued civilian production unavoidable. There was a danger that this would repeat the mistakes in treatment of the home front made by Germany's leaders in World War I. Speer's own focus on armaments production may have been serving to narrow his view. Boelcke concludes with some justice that Speer did not recognise the fundamental point that in a long war a well-functioning civilian economy was needed as a basis for the military sector. Goebbels' position was more ambivalent. He criticised inessential production, but at the same time was aware of the need to maintain some production for reasons of morale.[40]

In his speeches Speer sometimes seems to have exaggerated the extent of non-essential production and its dangers for a rational war effort. This was partly a result of the nature of the National Socialist political system. It was not easy for members of the leadership to gain information or an overview of other areas in the state. Speer in addition seems to have had a narrow concept of total war—he did not appear to take much account of other non-economic considerations. At times issues of total war appear to have been a question of control for him. If production was not under his control, he tended to assume it was inessential or wasteful. Goebbels seemed to follow and accept Speer's views on these issues.

In his Posen speech in October Speer asked the Gauleiters to recognise that only the most decisive measures would allow them to master the situation: if the Germans wanted to win the war, then they would also have to make the sacrifices. It was necessary that Germany now pursue total war in the area of production, he argued, implying that the nation did not yet do so. He added, 'I understand by total war (1) adjustment of the home front to the living standard of the front, if this results in an advantage for the front, (2) the highest productivity of all workers, and (3) the utmost economy with the resources available to the nation.'[41] According to the Chronik, in this speech Speer intended to remove any claims by the political leadership that they were unaware of conditions. The speech angered the Gauleiters, but Hitler did not appear concerned about their reaction.

Speer's model of total war was one of efficiency, economic rationality and austerity. His comments in his September and October speeches raise the question whether his concept of total war, and that of Goebbels, included a delight in sacrifice for its own sake, a kind of 'puritanism of total war.' Not only did he show signs of this kind of puritanism, but he also continued to show a tendency to favour short-term gains of increased production at the expense of sustaining this production. But this emphasis was not necessarily shared by all other members of the leadership, and it may have contributed to some of their differences of opinion.

Speer's model of total war additionally involved a tendency to favour measures which brought immediate short-term advantages of increased production over long-term measures. Mierzejewski's research suggests that this is analogous to Speer's overall method of organising the German economy. He did not undertake any major restructuring but instead introduced efficiencies to create savings and increase production. He appeared to seek solutions to his immediate problems with little thought of the long-term consequences. His differences of opinion with Sauckel over the use of foreign labour is one such example. Another is his decision earlier in 1943 not to evacuate armaments firms from Essen. In doing so he averted any immediate disruption of production but increased the effects of bombing and had left the plants vulnerable should a second front open. Because of German industry's dependence on coal from the Ruhr and Upper Silesia, Germany would probably not have been capable of mounting an evacuation similar to that of the Soviet Union in 1941-2 and could not have continued armaments production indefinitely without either of these two areas. Evacuation of factories would have meant a possible loss of several months' production during the relocation. It would also have been difficult to move plants to an area without an existing infrastructure. But a combination of evacuation and plans for stockpiling raw materials might have offered Germany greater opportunities to fight on in an effort to recapture one of these areas.[42]

Speer's short-term emphasis, a policy of 'living for the present,'[43] may itself account for some of his success in raising German production, but this preference for immediate measures may have built a kind of fragility into the system. The various measures which raised production immediately might leave only a slim margin for further changes, might not prove sustainable in different circumstances and may not have been judged best to sustain it in the long term. The fact that other members of the leadership did not necessarily share this emphasis contributed to some of their disagreements.

Labour shortages, restrictions on production, coping with bombing and increased pressure on the civil service all put considerable strain on the regime's remaining resources and led to intensified disputes among organisations. Because of his role in allocating resources, Speer was a particular focus for such conflicts. His role created resentment by those who were disappointed. Opposition to Speer's policies existed but some of it was still latent. It would be incorrect to see all the Gauleiters as opposing Speer. In October the Speer Chronik noted that the Gauleiters could be divided into two groups—those who always made difficulties if firms were shut down in their Gaus and those who never did.[44]

Speer believed that Bormann was undermining his position with Hitler. He considered one example of this to be Bormann drawing to Hitler's attention Speer's decision to close the State Porcelain Factory at Nymphenburg. Speer pointed out to Bormann that he had already approved continued production and asked him not to bother Hitler with such small matters in future. This was another example of Hitler's protection of the arts from the strictures of total war. Similarly Hitler decided not to ban the production of landscape postcards and not to call up staff employed on his building projects. These decisions were in keeping with his refusal in 1942 to agree to Goebbels' plans to give up uk positions in the performing arts. They did not lead to as great a waste of resources as might be expected. Although formal permission was given to the continuation of Hitler's building projects, rivalry between Speer and Hitler's other architects ensured that building in Linz did not get under way. The number of staff protected by these decisions was probably not significant, but they show a continued lack of realism on Hitler's part, a desire to have his cake and eat it too.[45]

Bormann rebuked Speer for by-passing accepted administrative channels. He had submitted the draft decree on the concentration of the war economy to Hitler before getting the agreement of all interested organisations.[46] Speer's tendency to ignore normal bureaucratic procedure and exploit his access to Hitler worsened relations between the two men.

Speer's restrictions on the activities of the Gauleiters encroached on Bormann's power base. Gauleiters were building fortifications in the west and east of Germany when labour shortages meant there were not the weapons to occupy them. Speer emphasised to Bormann that Hitler had to decide which was more important—securing the borders or equipping the troops.[47] Another factor contributing to the clashes between Speer and Bormann was Speer's growing power. Speer's accumulation of offices, justified by the needs of the war, was one of the greatest in the Third Reich. In late 1943 he tended to speak of himself as Hitler's successor.[48] These developments perhaps influenced Bormann's attitude to him.

The two men also differed in their judgement of the measures required by total war. Bormann believed that only measures really needed for the war should be adopted. Hitler, he noted, had repeatedly emphasised the view (shared by Himmler) that the effect of bans had to be considered. It was 'foolish' to impose a ban whose compliance could not be controlled or whose violation could be anticipated. 'More adroit, non-punitive action' should be employed where possible in such cases. 'Precisely to further the course of the war, only such measures as are really necessary for the war should be ordered, not measures which have practically no effect on the outcome of the war.'[49]

Other leaders continued to implement their own policies for total war. Despite Speer's opposition, the SS armaments concerns continued to expand. However irritating this intervention was and however much Speer believed that it frustrated a well-run armaments economy, Himmler clearly saw these measures as contributing to the war effort. He saw the purpose of SS concerns as overcoming difficulties or rescuing firms in a sorry state. Every SS officer had to be educated to intervene where necessary. Despite his reluctance to intervene in Speer's disputes with the Gauleiters, Himmler maintained, 'we want to help irrespective of conflicting responsibilities, for we want to win the war.'[50] To free more men for the front, he had established a school for female assistants to the SS (*SS-Helferinnen*). Himmler continued to advise senior SS officers that he wanted a system of clear authority without disputes over responsibilities.

In November 1943 Otto Ohlendorf of the SD became the head of a sub-division (Ministerialdirektor) and acting State Secretary in the Economics Ministry, increasing Himmler's influence over economic policy. Ohlendorf was a strong defender of the middle class and a critic of the self-responsibility of industry. He was to claim at Nuremberg that the policy allowed individual entrepreneurs to have state authority over their competitors. While Herbst suggests that this gave Himmler power over economic policy, he does not show Himmler influencing economic production. Himmler ignored Berger's suggestion that Ohlendorf be relieved of his position in the SD lest Himmler be held responsible for everything which happened in the Economics Ministry.[51]

Himmler expanded the use of the SS's captive labour force for the war effort. Hitler ordered a greater use of SS prisoners to build the A-4 rocket (subsequently to become the V-2) in August. Himmler advised Speer that he would take over responsibility for the A-4 rocket programme. He gave the task to Pohl and set SS-Brigadeführer Kammler under him as the responsible officer. At Hitler's request Himmler also pursued a programme of building underground factories, after private industry and Speer refused to cooperate.[52]

Himmler responded indirectly to charges that Jewish labour was needed for armaments production in a speech to the Gauleiters at Posen. The Jewish firms in the Warsaw Ghetto were described as armaments firms but, he claimed, they really made fur coats and clothing. He and Speer would clean out the remaining firms. Himmler's defence here is interesting. It suggests by implication that there was more pressure to use Jewish labour in an economically rational manner and that he was feeling this pressure. He now saw it as 'regrettable' that in 1941 the Germans had not valued the Russian prisoners of war as labour and had consequently allowed so many to starve to death.[53] Nonetheless, he still refused to make 30,000 ethnic Germans available to the armaments industry despite a promise to this effect from the liaison office for ethnic Germans, the *Volksdeutsche Mittelstelle*. As in his response to the lobbying for changes in policies to the East and for greater ideological training, Himmler countered criticism of the ideological basis of the war and defended the SS against charges of following economically irrational policies. His speeches and actions show that he was trying to simplify and help the war effort, but, like Hitler, he was not prepared to adopt measures which seemed to him to counter the ideological purposes of the war.

In late 1943 Goebbels appears to have been less active on the wider questions of total war. He was involved in the Party propaganda campaigns to boost morale. He issued 'Thirty articles of war for the German people,' a pamphlet which aimed at maintaining a positive popular attitude to the war and set up an office called 'total war' (*'Totaler Krieg'*) to which members of the public could send suggestions and complaints. Goebbels believed that National Socialism had to undergo a renovation and link itself with the people in a more socialist way than before. The people were the 'very kernel' of the war effort.[54] Goebbels was now critical of the alleged watering-down of the total war measures of early 1943. It was easier for him to criticise the implementation of the measures as diluted than to concede that the measures he had proposed were either inadequate or could not achieve what he hoped for. He could be observed distancing himself from Hitler, an indirect admission that he no longer thought Hitler capable of mastering the situation.

Goebbels was increasingly occupied countering the effects of the Allied bombing campaign, which required more and more resources and attention. During this period bombing was stepped up. The 'firebomb' raids on Hamburg took place in July and August, with over 40,000 deaths. These raids were the most destructive so far, and Speer predicted that six more such attacks would stop German armaments production. Heavy bombing of German cities and the Ruhr disrupted production and civilian life and continued to depress morale. Goebbels assumed more responsibility for mitigating the physical effects of bombing as well as countering its psychological effects by propaganda. He gained popularity because he was the only major German leader to visit the bombed cities. The inter-departmental air war damage committee (Luftkriegsschädenausschuss) was based in his ministry, despite Party attempts to take over this responsibility. It issued regular bulletins of instruction (*LK-Mitteilungen*) to members of the committee, Gauleiters and the Party propaganda offices (*Reichspropagandaämter* or *RPÄ*). Goebbels issued a large number of instructions concerning the evacuation of the population and industry, the latter to have priority over all other measures. Repeated requests that Gauleiters refrain from taking their own uncoordinated measures and overloading the transport system appear to indicate that he was powerless to stop this practice. Himmler's contribution to overcoming bombing continued: the SS building brigades continued their work. The Party intensified measures to ensure protection against air raids; boys of 15 and over were drafted to work on anti-aircraft batteries.[55]

One Gauleiter commented that 'from 1942 to the end of the war my work had increasingly and, finally almost only, concerned defence from the enemy air war, activation of civilian air protection, [and] the mobilisation of all means . . . of assistance.'[56] The stepped-up bombing heightened the pressure on resources and personnel and lessened productivity. While the volume of consumer goods production had ostensibly decreased by only 12 per cent from the beginning of the war, it now barely met the needs of 10 per cent of the bombed. Speer advised Hitler that the effects of the bombing would require increased provision of household goods, which he planned to meet by increasing the amount of such goods produced in the occupied territories and by producing simplified standard types. Speer and Goebbels were concerned at the effects of the raids on production, but Goebbels believed that popular morale would continue to be good. German propaganda emphasised more and more the possibility of retaliation with new miracle weapons.

Just as it met the Stalingrad crisis with a flurry of measures designed to increase economic efficiency and productivity, the regime overcame the internal effects of the defection of Italy with policies designed to increase the political reliability of the home front and the military. By the end of the year Goebbels assured Hitler that in this war the home front would hold out to the last. Interest in a compromise peace grew, but leaders were not able to persuade Hitler to take action as they desired. This resulted in a certain degree of disillusionment for Goebbels.[57] Fewer new policies to ensure economic efficiency and free labour were introduced: the regime appeared to be still digesting the effects of the Ausschuss' measures. As the resources at their disposal diminished and the external pressures on the Reich grew, the leaders' disagreements about the allocation of labour and materials sharpened. They could only await 1944 with apprehension, since the regime no longer held the military initiative.

6

The Lull before the Storm
(January-June 1944)

Germany's military position continued to worsen in the first six months of 1944. This period marked the high point of Speer's success in increasing economic production; at the same time his policies came under sustained criticism for the first time. The influence of the ideological model increased, and the activities of the SS and the Party expanded.

In the East Soviet offensives during January and February 1944 cleared Leningrad and cut the German Sixth Army in the South in two. A further offensive in the Ukraine in March divided the German front, capturing considerable German equipment on the way, and pre-empted plans by Speer to bomb Soviet electricity works. By the end of March Soviet forces had reached Romania and had pushed the Germans out of most of the Ukraine. On 8 April attacks began on the remaining German forces in the Crimea, who surrendered by 12 May, with the loss of 80,000 men. In the fighting from Kursk to May 1944, some 41 German divisions had virtually been destroyed. The Soviet summer offensive began on 9 June against Finland and on 22 June against the Germans' Ukraine salient and White Russia. One week after the opening of the offensive, the German defensive system had been broken, with the loss of 350,000 men. Hitler still hoped to man a rear defence line where the Soviet advance could be stemmed, but Soviet attacks continued. By 1 July the Berezina was taken, marooning two corps of the German Fourth Army.[1]

The pace of the Allied bombing campaign against Germany was stepped up in January 1944. Allied forces launched raids aimed at the German air force industry and the fuel industry as well as German cities. The Luftwaffe was increasingly ineffective: its failure to protect the Reich discredited it. People in German cities, particularly those of the Ruhr, other industrial centres and Berlin, became accustomed to carrying out their daily life under bombing. The raids did not lead initially to a drop in morale: hostility was directed outwards against the enemy pilots. Because of the popular mood the leadership demanded development of weapons of retaliation. The public mood has been described as better than in 1943, because apathy and fatalism had become prevalent.[2]

The enemy bombing campaigns continued to require the diversion of staff and materials from other purposes to protect Germany's cities, maintain the bare necessities of life and uphold public morale. Bormann believed that greater use had to be made of purchases in occupied territories to replace destroyed goods. Between November 1943 and February 1944, for example, 11.7 million additional ration portions were distributed, while some 500,000 foreign workers were used to repair bomb damage. Defending the Reich from bombing diverted resources from other armaments production. By 1944 some 2 million Germans were employed in anti-aircraft defence. Thirty per cent of total gun output, 20 per cent of heavy ammunition and 50 per cent of electro-technical production were allocated to counter bombing. Production was also diverted to weapons of retaliation. The resources devoted to the V-1 and V-2 rockets were the equivalent of those to produce 24,000 fighter aircraft. Workers had to be redirected to secure transport connections. The air war increased tension between the various ministries and organisations because of their differing requirements. Speer opposed efforts by Gauleiters to build new headquarters secure from bombing because of the strain on resources. Such headquarters had to be built in existing buildings. While Speer supported the necessary air protection measures, he told Goebbels' State Secretary, Leopold Gutterer, that they should not reduce armaments production. He would not free uk German workers in the armaments industry to become air raid police.[3]

All civilian sources of authority were involved in overcoming the effects of bombing. Here the Party played an important role. It set up formations to counter damage and care for the population after air attacks. The responsibilities of Goebbels' inter-departmental bombing committee widened. Hitler instituted a Reich inspection of civil air war measures led by Goebbels to standardise practices and agreed to common measures it proposed. Gaus with considerable experience of air attack provided detailed advice to other areas.

The SS building brigades continued to be in demand. The German leadership undertook co-ordinated measures to overcome weakening of morale and to draw on the experience of those cities already bombed. These measures diverted labour, raw materials, consumer production and administrative resources. They prevented the breakdown of morale and avoided the break-downs of administration and failure to learn from experience which charac-terized the British response to bombing.[4]

The German position worsened dramatically when the Anglo-American forces landed in Normandy on 6 June. German forces were unable to dislodge the invaders, who landed a million men in France by the end of the first week in July. At the end of June, the Allied forces were still bottled up in Normandy. The opening of the second front weakened the Reich's ability to withstand pressure on its lines of defence in the East. The failure to defeat the invading force quickly depressed the popular mood. A brief upsurge in morale following the first use of V-1 rockets against Britain soon dissipated.[5]

Before the invasion, Germany's leaders had hoped that successful defeat of an invasion force might lead the Western Allies to withdraw from the conflict. This could give Germany a year or two's breathing space in the West. If not, Goebbels told his aides in April, Germany would have to find a way of ending the war with the Soviet Union.[6]

Goebbels continued his efforts to persuade Hitler to change German foreign policy. He was less and less influenced by Hitler's optimistic judgements of the situation, despite the two men's increased closeness in this period. In March 1944 he held discussions with Hitler on ending the war with the Soviet Union, discussions of which no record apparently survives in his diary entries. Semler's diary relates that Goebbels then prepared a 40-page memorandum which he sent to Hitler on 12 April. (This memorandum itself is not known to have survived.) The memorandum ruled out the possibility of military victory for Germany, because of the drain of the war on two fronts. Goebbels suggested that it was crucial to stop the war on one front as soon as possible. He played lip service to Hitler's desire for a separate peace with the Western powers by describing it as the preferable option. But he still believed that, because of his anti-British and anti-American attitudes, Stalin could be persuaded to change his policies more easily than the British or US leadership. Soundings could be made through the Japanese, and the Germans would have to make Stalin a definite offer.

Goebbels hoped to use territories still held as bargaining counters in any settlement. He proposed that Germany allocate Finland and North Norway to the Soviet sphere of influence; the Baltic states would be absorbed into Russia; Germany would surrender all Polish territory to the frontier of the

Warthegau. The future of Czechoslovakia was left open; Romania, Bulgaria and Greece would come into the Soviet sphere of influence. Goebbels believed that such an offer would be attractive to Stalin; Greece would give him a foothold in the Mediterranean, and it was far more than Molotov had demanded in Berlin in November 1940. The memorandum also suggested that Ribbentrop should not be entrusted with such an offer, but that Goebbels himself should undertake it.[7]

Like some other earlier proposals for a compromise peace, Goebbels' memorandum urged the bypassing of Ribbentrop. In part Goebbels judged Ribbentrop was so distrusted by the enemy that he would be ineffective as a negotiator. He also seems to have believed that Ribbentrop did not support a compromise peace and assumed that he was responsible for Hitler's inflexibility on this issue. This indicates suspicion and lack of communication among senior members of the leadership, and is another example of Goebbels' tendency to blame Hitler's inappropriate policies on bad advice. In fact Ribbentrop had also urged Hitler to make terms. As late as 1945 Goebbels refused to believe this, describing Ribbentrop as Hitler's 'evil genius, driving him on from one reckless adventure to the next.'[8] Ribbentrop's role as a member of the 'war party' in 1939 may have created in Goebbels a lasting prejudice against him.

Semler reports that Bormann buried the paper in his in-tray; he would not take the responsibility of forwarding the paper to Hitler because it advocated the betrayal of Germany's allies. Goebbels' response was that these allies had long ceased to feel any loyalty to Germany and that the slogan 'my country, right or wrong' should apply. When the paper was rediscovered Hitler asked to see it, but showed no annoyance at Bormann's action. Hitler's lack of concern suggests that he may have found Bormann's role as a barrier to new proposals useful. Goebbels hoped to hear of Hitler's response to the memorandum when he was called to the Obersalzberg on 5 June, but it was not mentioned. Hitler did tell Goebbels that he saw no hope of a compromise peace with Britain and stressed his support for Ribbentrop. Goebbels concluded Hitler was not ready to undertake any decisive action against Ribbentrop.[9] Hitler's hopes that the invasion in the West could be repulsed and the Western Allies thereby encouraged to withdraw from the war may have accounted in part for his lack of interest in Goebbels' suggestions.

The memorandum indicated that Goebbels retained his dual approach to ending the war: total war and pursuit of a compromise peace were complementary elements. The proposals are evidence of Goebbels' desperation at the position in which the regime found itself. While he was probably unrealistic in assuming that the Soviet Union would still be willing to negotiate a compromise peace, his proposals were more sensible than earlier German ones. He was willing to give up a considerable portion of Germany's conquests to save the regime. He was also right in assessing that the period before the second front opened was the last chance for the Germans to be able to bargain with the Soviet Union.

This issue demonstrates both the strength and weakness of Goebbels' position. Unlike Bormann, he felt free to put such ideas to Hitler, and such moves did not lead Hitler to suspect him of treason or defeatism. Nevertheless he could not get Hitler to agree to his proposals. Once again his attempts to salvage some future for the regime foundered on Hitler's reluctance to make a compromise peace.

The treatment of the memorandum also illustrates the negative power of Bormann's position—his ability to block or delay proposals rather than originate policy—and his unrealistic assessment of Germany's position. Goebbels explained his motives as follows: 'in the circle round Hitler, which is dominated by Bormann, the war situation is still regarded with irresponsible optimism.' They did not understand the importance of Goebbels' paper because only 'blind Party doctrine' got a hearing.[10] Bormann's views on the military situation can be seen not only in his treatment of Goebbels' memorandum. He also described a speech by Goebbels on the current situation as being of fundamental political significance. In this speech Goebbels ruled out surrender and claimed that despite the bombing campaigns, the resulting loss of production in no way threatened the war effort. He also maintained that the retreat on the Eastern front in 1943 was due to Italian treachery and continued that Germany had not lost operational freedom in the East, although the territory and raw materials lost was significant. Goebbels pointed to differences of opinion among the English elite about the war and compared Germany's situation to the Nazi position in December 1932. Bormann's comments indicate that these were the views he considered to be the correct ones to put to a Party audience. He may even have believed these analyses. His optimism is also seen in his consideration of proposals to increase the postwar birth rate.

Goebbels persisted in seeking support for his ideas on total war. He continued to gather influential members of the regime for discussions and supper on Wednesday nights. The so-called Wednesday Group included Speer, Funk, Ley, Milch, Sauckel, Backe, Friedrichs, Stuckart and Naumann. Semler described them as acknowledging Goebbels' authority without always agreeing with his ideas. Goebbels believed that they would prefer to work in a Cabinet under him rather than in the present conditions. He hoped to fill a position like that of Chancellor, to combine all offices in a government capable of action. His motives were a mixture of personal ambition, his clear conviction that a central authority was needed to give impetus and control to the war effort on the home front, and his frustration at what he perceived was the inactivity of the current system. This was another attempt to re-create the powers of 'deputy Chancellor' which Göring had possessed from 1939 to 1941. Goebbels saw the clique under Bormann in Hitler's headquarters as the main danger, since they profited from the current conditions. His loyalty to Hitler meant that there was no chance of the group forming an opposition. His political and psychological support for Hitler was such that he secretly organised a declaration of loyalty to Hitler by the German Field Marshals.[11]

It is not known what further total war policies Goebbels urged on Hitler in early 1944. From her work on the 1944 diaries, Fröhlich concludes 'in 1944 . . . he [Goebbels] became the most important promoter of the internal radicalising and totalising of the war.'[12] He supported Speer in his various moves of rationalisation. His persisting organisation and maintenance of the Wednesday Group indicates that he maintained his interest in a radicalisation of the war effort.

The other leaders took no action to encourage a compromise peace in this period, but the earlier efforts of Goebbels and others had shown that such moves enjoyed widespread support among the leadership. While members of the leadership did not explicitly criticise Hitler's military conduct of the war, they did not agree with his policy of a dogged defence of each captured territory and his refusal to compromise with the Soviet Union.

In public Himmler also maintained his optimism about the outcome of the war. He claimed the enemy had reached their maximum armaments output, but was much more conscious of Soviet military strength than in his earlier speeches. He reassured Party and military leaders about the strength of the home front in comparison to 1918. He had fulfilled his promise to Hitler at the beginning of the war that the German armed forces could face the outside world without fear of another stab in the back, because criminals and Communists were not free to undermine national security. The Germans would not have been able to withstand the Allied bomber offensive had Jews still lived in Germany, he claimed. His speeches suggest that he saw the maintenance of internal order as the main precondition of victory. Himmler drew parallels with the Nazi Party's problems in 1932. He contended that victory would go to the side whose nerve held.[13]

Himmler seemed to be hoping for a breakdown in the enemy coalition. His speeches drew attention to developments he saw as favourable—racial tension in the United States, strikes and the growth of Communist influence in Britain—but warned that these developments would not bear fruit immediately. The Germans would go through a difficult six to nine months but had to keep their nerve to win.[14]

Schellenberg had failed to persuade Himmler to begin peace negotiations. His efforts had led, however, to a wavering in Himmler's loyalties. Ohlendorf claimed at Nuremberg that, from this time on, Himmler and other SS leaders were toying with the idea of assassinating Hitler. Himmler began to comment more openly about the Final Solution in January 1944 speeches. This has been attributed to increasing psychological strain as he distanced himself from Hitler.[15]

Himmler did change his mind on another issue. In 1943 he was strongly opposed to the Vlasov movement, but as Germany's position in the East worsened, the SS also adopted a more flexible position. During the first half of 1944 Himmler was persuaded by Gunter d'Alquen, editor of the SS weekly *The Black Corps* (*Das Schwarze Korps*), to support Vlasov. Specifically he authorised an SS operation to increase the numbers of deserters from the Red Army using officers of the Vlasov group. His conversion to a more flexible policy came too late to have any practical political effect, since Germany had lost credibility by harsh occupation policies. It appears to have been a product of desperation rather than conviction or even opportunism. Himmler's other statements indicate that he was not persuaded of the need for milder policies. When the Generalkommissar for the Crimea, Frauenfeld, wrote a paper making extensive criticisms of previous German occupation policy and urging a more lenient and politically adroit policy, Himmler and Bormann agreed that a new occupation would have to find a different form from what Frauenfeld suggested.[16]

Another significant sign of Himmler's belated willingness to abandon ideology for the sake of victory was his negotiations with the Hungarian Jewish community. During 1944 an estimated 600,000 Jews, mainly Hungarian Jews, were exterminated. In April 1944 the SS offered to trade the lives of 1600 Jews in exchange for approximately 4 million Reichsmarks (RM). In May 1944, acting on Himmler's orders, Eichmann called on Joel Brand, the representative of a Hungarian Zionist relief committee, and offered to save Hungarian Jews in exchange for goods and war materials, including 10,000 trucks to go to the Waffen-SS on the Eastern front. Despite a lack of response from the Allies, a limited deal was struck in June 1944 when the Hungarian committee exchanged materiel and goods with a value of 2.5 million RM for the lives of 18,000 Jews.[17] Such moves were aimed at protecting Himmler's own position, encouraging a split in the enemy alliance and gaining war material for Germany.

Himmler's willingness to modify the extermination policy and his change of attitude toward Vlasov indicate that his view of the regime's prospects was more realistic than it had been in 1943 and that he was prepared to make important changes to protect his own position. No other leaders had raised the treatment of the Jews as part of any wider debate about how the war should be waged: either they accepted it as part of the 'German model of total war' or they did not feel free to question so central a policy. Only Himmler, whose responsibility it was, could make such a change. In early 1944 Himmler showed himself willing to abandon ideological policies which he had pursued at great economic and political cost to the war effort from 1941 to 1943. The change dramatically highlights both his comparative optimism about the war effort until 1944 and his new realism with the collapse of the German front in the East. In view of these changes, Himmler cannot be said to have had a coherent concept of total war, unlike Goebbels or Speer. From 1941 to 1943 he aimed at victory through implementation of National Socialist ideology as well as greater production and simplification. At this stage he was not willing to compromise on issues such as the treatment of the Eastern peoples where other leaders, particularly Goebbels, were prepared to be more flexible. Once he realised Germany's military position had deteriorated, Himmler was willing to dilute many of the policies he had previously implemented. He began to vacillate, one moment clinging to his old ideological pattern of total war and the next willing to abandon all these policies.

Bormann's optimistic view of the situation has already been noted; Speer had other preoccupations during this period. On 18 January 1944 he was hospitalised with a knee injury. His heavy workload in 1942 and 1943 may have contributed to the resulting medical complications. His hospitalisation and convalescence lasted until 8 May. Speer did not appoint a deputy but continued the work of his ministry from his sickbed, despite his physician SS-Gruppenführer Dr Gebhardt's protests that this would delay his recovery. Gebhardt was only successful in forbidding official visits from 8 to 20 February.[18]

During his illness, Speer sent four submissions to Hitler which appear to have been designed to strengthen his position and bring Sauckel under his control. In the first submission he proposed that Hitler increase the number of workers available to the armaments industry by greater Party intervention, using the Gauleiters and Sauckel. This could be achieved only if the Gauleiters and all other offices unconditionally obeyed all his specialist directives and if Sauckel regarded himself as an assistant to the armaments industry and did not seek to interfere in the use of the workers provided, which was Speer's responsibility. If Hitler agreed with this, he should sign a decree regulating the forms of collaboration with the Reich defence commissioners. Speer pointed out to Hitler that naturally he did not intend to opt for political activity either in the war or after the war. He saw his current employment purely as wartime employment and looked forward to taking up his tasks as an artist again. In this way he sought to reassure Hitler about extending his powers, just as Goebbels assured Hitler of his disinterested loyalty when making his foreign policy proposals.[19] By this submission Speer tried to overcome Party interference with his policies by incorporating the Party into armaments production, by giving it responsibility and bringing it under his control.

In a second submission Speer defended himself against charges that armaments was failing to meet its obligations to the front. He suggested that he make presentations in Berlin and in Hitler's headquarters on the armament industry's achievements from 1941 to 1943. His third submission also sought to reduce Sauckel's independence. Sauckel had made a speech in his own Gau of Thuringia urging workers to increase their productivity. By publishing the speech in all newspapers, Speer alleged, Sauckel was using it as a platform in his capacity as plenipotentiary for labour. He asked that Sauckel be instructed to seek Speer's permission before holding such meetings in future. In a fourth submission Speer asked in addition that all articles and announcements on armaments production be referred to his office for approval, and that he have the final say when and how often such publications occurred.[20] While Goebbels and Speer had co-operated in the past about armaments propaganda, this request could be expected to meet with Goebbels' opposition as well as Sauckel's. Speer's attempts to control the Gauleiters would also have increased their hostility had they become public. These proposals indicate Speer's unrealistic expectations of the extent of his powers.

Speer claimed that his ministry's smooth working during his illness showed that he did not need to worry about details but could concentrate on essentials. He did have to protect himself against intrigues in his ministry by Xavier Dorsch, his deputy in the Organisation Todt. Speer refused to resume some of his responsibilities and talked of resignation, because of what he believed was lack of support from Hitler. Field Marshal Milch intervened to secure a reconciliation between the two on 20 April. In a meeting on 24 April, Hitler declared that he agreed with all measures Speer had taken in the building industry and halted attempts to separate building from armaments. The result, according to the Speer Chronik, was that Speer's authority was strengthened. Speer moved generally to reassert his authority.[21]

Hitler did not respond to Speer's memoranda. Schmidt has suggested that Speer sent Hitler such frequent memoranda because he feared that lack of personal contact with Hitler would cost him power. But Hitler visited him three times during his illness and hinted that he was not influenced by any complaints the Gauleiters made against Speer. Speer's perception that he was being undermined contrasts strangely with the wide range of powers he had actually been granted by Hitler. Speer's position was still strong enough in May for him to disregard an order from Himmler as Interior Minister banning leave because of the increased threat of invasion.[22]

He may have felt that his power base was under threat because he and his policies came under greater criticism. The first half of 1944 was the last period in which German armaments production rose; thereafter loss of territory and labour, together with the effects of intensified bombing, made this impossible. On 1 January 1944 Speer was able to report to Hitler that he had met all the targets in the armaments programme set him in February 1942. But the fuel situation was already deteriorating.[23] For all the rises in production the new weapons were not having an effect on the battlefield.

Party intervention in the economy, especially by Gauleiters, grew. Speer considered this intervention unjustified. The Gau economic advisers moved to contest his control of labour allocation for armaments production in the Gaus. Speer was particularly critical of Gauleiters' tendencies to protect their own Gau labour forces and industries, but Fear's research suggests that this was an economically rational response on their part. In his study of the armaments industry in Schwaben, Fear found that Gaus were largely closed to labour transfers from other Gaus and that therefore 'it would be in the interests of the individual Gauleiters to block the transfer of labor outside their Gaus, . . . also in the interests of armaments production.'[24] On 3 February Speer was visited by Gerhard Klopfer, head of the state division of the Party Chancellery, to discuss the question of involving the Party in armaments tasks through the Gauleiters, particularly co-ordinating various middle-level armaments offices. Speer emphasised that the Gauleiters should not make any difficulties for the industrialists called on to co-operate. Speer's role in the allocation of resources caused tension. He protested against the use of armaments workers in work to restore transport connections after an air attack. He also encountered Party criticism because, against Hitler's wishes, a considerable number of German firms were forced to work on the 1 May holiday, particularly in mining, iron production and the fighter programme. Speer agreed to Goebbels' request, however, that the Propaganda Ministry be more strongly involved in all questions of war clothing, an indication that their informal alliance on the question of total war continued.

As competition for scarce resources intensified and economic production encountered increasing difficulties, Party suspicion of the self-responsibility of industry and non-Party industrialists grew. For the first time, suggestions were made that a change in the method of allocating raw materials and controlling industry might be more efficient. The dangers of corruption in the system were highlighted. The SS alleged that Speer's system of rings and committees allowed larger firms to build up their own economic position at the expense of their competitors. This did occur at times. The rings and committees also competed against one another for resources. The Speer ministry often lacked the expertise to enforce policies such as rationalisation of production, and those with the expertise gave their first loyalty to their firms. Ohlendorf claimed that Speer countenanced corruption, black marketeering and profiteering as incentives to industrialists. A SD report set out instances of corruption in the allocation of raw materials and uk positions and warned that corruption was 'one of the most conspicuous causes of the 1918 collapse.'[25] These allegations are difficult to substantiate: many firms are reluctant to allow access to their files of the period. Individuals involved in such activities would try to avoid leaving any evidence of them. In addition, Carroll has suggested that there was inefficiency and confusion in the armaments ministry. Gauleiter Eigruber of the Upper Danube encountered problems which provide further evidence of this. Although he and Speer had agreed on the necessary closures of firms, in each case the committees and rings sought to have the decisions reversed. Other misunderstandings arose from poor communications in Speer's ministry. Gauleiter Florian of Dusseldorf also pointed out that often the armaments industry committees and rings interfered in attempts to reallocate workers to urgent production. Speer's system did have the potential for waste of material and labour, continued peacetime production and corruption. Speer challenged attacks on men active in the industry committees and rings by speaking to the SD and sending a memorandum to Bormann on the matter in January. It is simultaneously a measure of Hitler's support and Speer's own influence that he was largely able to ensure that the system remained comparatively untouched.

Just as Speer suspected the Gauleiters' commitment to total war, so too the Gauleiters suspected his commitment, particularly where obtaining additional labour sources was concerned. This mutual suspicion was the product of a number of forces, including the competition for power intensified by the structure of the National Socialist political system and the lack of any recognised or accepted regulation of areas outside the individual responsibility of the leader. Party leaders, including Bormann, Ley and various Gauleiters, favoured greater Party involvement in examining uk positions and 'combing out' staff. They believed they could gain better results. In some Gaus, such as North Westphalia and Pomerania, Gauleiters were already involved in inspecting uk positions. Bormann predicted that Speer would respond by saying that the Party would have to take over responsibility for armaments, and Hitler would in consequence reject such moves. Bormann suspected Speer's claims that more workers could not be freed from the armaments industry. He believed Hitler's intervention was needed to force armaments, railways and the post to give up staff. In Bormann's opinion, Keitel's belief that this could be overcome by the involvement of the Gauleiters was completely false. Speer already disregarded the Gauleiters' opinions 'laughing.'[26] Current conditions could be altered only by Hitler's orders. Whatever Speer thought of his standing with Hitler, Bormann believed that Speer still had Hitler's confidence to such an extent that the Gauleiters could not intervene. He showed a wary respect for Speer's influence with Hitler.

The picture of the German economy which Speer advanced was one of the comparative efficiency of armaments and his ministry, because of the self-responsibility of industry, and the comparative inefficiency of the party and its attempts to interfere with the economy. In describing these conflicts after the war in terms of technical efficiency versus the Party, Speer oversimplified the disputes. Some Gauleiters, such as Goebbels and Hanke, seem to have been very active where total war was concerned. The success of the Ruhrstab showed that Gauleiters did not necessarily prevent successful work. In addition, there were reasons to be concerned at some of the results of the self-responsibility of industry. Hoffmann's earlier reports on conditions in the East indicated that industry could be as wasteful and corrupt with manpower as the administration or the party.[27] It too could pursue its own interests at the expense of the war effort.

Concerted Allied air attacks began to threaten the functioning of the German economy. In April and May 1944 Allied attacks were directed against oil fields in Romania and Hungary and on synthetic oil plants in Germany. At the end of May 1944, on Speer's suggestion, Hitler appointed Edmund Geilenberg, the former chairman of the main committee for munitions, as Reich commissioner for emergency measures to repair the damage to industry and war production. Geilenberg used 350,000 workers to overcome the damage to synthetic oil plants and began dispersal. Because fighter production fell as a result of increased bombing of air frame plants in January

and February 1944, Hitler agreed to set up the Fighter Staff (*Jägerstab*), led
by Karl Otto Saur, the head of the Armaments Ministry's technical office,
on 5 March. This appointment confirmed an earlier agreement between Speer
and Milch. Speer feared Saur's ambition and had wanted his friend, Gauleiter
Hanke, for the position; but Hitler overruled him and insisted on Saur's
appointment. By reorganising production and increasing working hours to
72 hours a week for men, the Fighter Staff raised production from an average
of 1100 machines in the preceding seven months to 1670 new fighters in
March alone. Milch attributed these rises to the loyalty of the German
workers. The Fighter Staff, in Speer's opinion, came too strongly under Air
Ministry influence during his illness. He took the reins back into his hands,
according to the Speer Chronik. By June 1944 Speer had gained control of
the air armaments industry.[28]

More targetted bombing forced the Armaments Ministry in February
1944 to begin the dispersal of armaments plants in the aircraft and other
industries. Speer had previously prevented dispersal except as a last resort
and had intervened to stop Gauleiters dispersing industry on their own
initiative. As Milward notes, Speer's approach was surprising in view of the
German awareness of the Ruhr's vulnerability to air attack and invasion. The
Ruhr was so central to German production that large-scale dispersal was not
possible, but Speer's attitude meant that the dispersal which took place was
neither well organised nor coherent. Milward suggests that 'more foresight
earlier in the war might have enabled Germany to maintain high levels of
war production for longer than she was able.'[29]

Speer continued his plans to extract more productive capacity from the
economy. He concentrated armaments production among fewer firms and
continued plans to transfer firms to more important production, a move he
and Goebbels had advocated for some time. Forced moves as part of a
transfer to armaments production proved to be very unpopular with German
workers; in 1944 a new policy, advocated by Kehrl, was gradually adopted.
Instead of physically moving the workers, armaments work was brought to
them in their normal workplace with 'surprisingly good results.'[30] By January firms transferred, including the entire confectionery and papermaking
industries, numbered 117,500. Resistance to the closure of two firms in the
cigarette industry was overcome with the help of Saxon Gauleiter
Mutschmann in March. In the same month, with Goebbels' approval, Speer
appointed Haegert from the Propaganda Ministry to cut back the production
of printed material. Beck's study of the German home front suggests that
production and supply of consumer goods was 'virtually suspended' by
1944.[31] Rationing offices were unable to replace clothes and goods for most

of those who were bombed; those replacements which could be found were of very poor quality.

On 26 January Speer informed Bormann that concentration of the war economy required an end to production unimportant to the war effort, transfer of firms to armaments production and severe rationalisation of remaining firms and production. He and Funk appointed Walter Rafelsberger, the deputy leader of the production office for consumer goods, to plan and suggest the necessary measures. Rafelsberger was appointed to rationalise and simplify the economic administration and accountancy, drawing on previous experience, and to make workers available for armaments. Bormann in turn requested that Speer advise him about Rafelsberger's exact tasks and specifically how Speer's measures would affect other offices. Speer replied that they would, but only with the head of the organisation involved. (Rafelsberger's commission continued until 30 September 1944, when Speer considered it to be superfluous in the light of the appointment of a plenipotentiary for total war.)[32]

The SS's economic activities continued to expand. Under Pohl's control, 150 different firms manufactured airplanes, grenades, small weapons and cartridges. Schieber, an official of Speer's ministry, argued that Himmler had decided on greater involvement in economic leadership and the buildup of firms as a financial foundation for various SS tasks. He believed SS opposition to the self-responsibility of industry was an important reason for this expansion, which was made possible by the SS's almost unlimited labour resources. Himmler claimed that the SS's prisoners contributed about 35 million hours of armaments production a month. If the armaments industry was not more successful in transferring concentration camp prisoners into its own firms, Schieber warned, it would lose them to the SS. Some evidence to support Schieber's analysis can be seen in Himmler's clash with Kehrl, the leader of Speer's planning office. Himmler took umbrage at Kehrl's criticisms of the extraordinarily small yield from the kok-saghyz harvest. (Himmler was Hitler's plenipotentiary for the rubber plant, *Taraxacum kok-saghyz*.) Himmler told Kehrl that he received his orders from Hitler, who alone was in a position to release him from it. Both Kehrl and Himmler had to obey Hitler. 'I personally am not ready to break this tradition of obedience.' He added that Kehrl's letter demonstrated 'a typically narrow big capitalist mentality' which feared undesirable competition for I.G. Farben's rubber substitute, Buna.[33]

Himmler took steps to ensure that the SS controlled production of armaments for its own forces. He decided that SS units needed to be armed with more medium and heavy mortars, and authorised Jüttner, the head of the SS Leadership Main Office, and Pohl to contact the Armaments Ministry so that such production could be transferred to a concentration camp. In this way the SS could retain a greater number of mortars for its troops. Himmler encouraged Pohl in his plans to expand the use of the Oranienburg brick-works for this production. He considered the matter to be very important and instructed Pohl to ensure he received the necessary powers from Saur. The foundry should be set up as quickly as possible 'with Russian-style improvisation.'[34] Pohl investigated the building of caves for use in armament production and the use of tunnels as storerooms. The SS was far more willing than Speer to build the underground factories Hitler wanted to use to avoid bombing.

Speer and Sauckel's disputes continued. Speer believed that labour was the area of armament production which failed most often. At the beginning of the year Sauckel had promised Hitler 4 million foreign workers, but the invasion of France ended any hope of increasing the use of foreign labour. This meant that for the first time the numbers in armaments employment decreased. On 31 May and again on 30 June Speer and Sauckel met to discuss the advantages and disadvantages of evacuating workers out of France. Sauckel favoured evacuation, while Speer wanted workers from the Sperr-Betriebe to be left in France. The question was not clarified in their 30 June meeting but was soon decided by the military course of the war. Hitler decided that in doubtful cases concerning the creation of new Sperr-Betriebe, the decision was to be left to Speer.[35]

Speer continued to support reducing the use of labour on the home front. He ordered his offices to give up at least 25 per cent of their male personnel to the armed forces or armaments without regard to age or fitness grading. He supported Backe's proposals to reduce numbers employed in agriculture by 15,000 to 25,000 people and suggested that further savings could be made. He continued to set his hopes on rationalising employment in business and the administration, but there were limits to the additional number of staff some organisations could give up. For example, the Reich Post Office (*Reichspost*) had sent 70 per cent of its male employees to the front even though its volume of work was two to three times greater than in 1938.[36]

Where did Speer believe additional labour could be found? He knew that both free and captive sources of labour were diminishing as the territory under German control decreased. He could hope to gain some workers from the closing down of unimportant production, and he planned to set up a reserve of armaments workers to meet the most urgent requirements. His ministry believed that an additional 2 million men and women could be employed by expanding outwork (*Heimarbeit*), lessening the incidence of illness and absenteeism, and making better use of foreign workers. Speer cited this as evidence that German reserves of workers were not exhausted. He tried to foster outwork despite opposition to it from both manufacturers and workers. The reduced supply of foreign workers led Speer to seek greater employment of concentration camp inmates from Himmler because of the latter's helpfulness on such issues. In particular he requested 7,500 prisoners for the OT's building in the Atlantic Wall and 10,000 prisoners for use in Upper Silesian chemical works, in addition to the 15,000 prisoners already used for tank production.[37]

There were no indications that Speer was actively seeking to change Hitler's mind on the question of female employment at this time, and no signs that he urged firms to take measures to encourage women to work. He told Sauckel—erroneously—that the percentage of women employed in Germany was considerably less than in Britain. Nonetheless, Speer did not attend part of a meeting with Hitler in April 1944 where Ley's proposal of equal pay for equal work was discussed. The wide wage differentials between men and women in industry discouraged female employment, particularly since women who took over men's jobs in the administration received male wages. De facto, with DAF support, some firms granted equal pay. Hitler had agreed to lengthen the labour service of some young women to meet Luftwaffe requirements for staff, irrespective of any resulting dangers to their health. But, as the British government had, he rejected the policy of equal pay, apart from in unspecified exceptional cases; otherwise the regime would set in motion measures it could not control. The post-war policy had to be that women left the factories and returned to the family. In the discussion Bormann echoed Hitler's views, and Ley found no support. The discussion did not really focus on the implications of the decision for wartime production or for encouraging more women into the workforce. A number of reasons influenced Hitler's decision. Granting women equal pay would have inflationary implications and would set an unwelcome precedent of breaking the freeze on wages. Hitler's decision avoided establishing an ideologically undesirable precedent rather than overcoming the present problem. He may have believed that compromise on ideological principles, whatever short-term advantages it presented, would undermine rather than secure final victory. In an attempt to take Hitler's attitudes into account, Speer was planning to transfer as much production as possible to work which could be done in the home.[38]

Without referring the proposal to Hitler, Bormann and Lammers altered an earlier attempt by Sauckel to broaden the categories of women who had to register for work. Sauckel proposed that the category should be extended to include women with children over the age of one who had a female relative living with them capable of caring for the children. After Bormann and Lammers intervened, the new rule applied to women with children over the age of two and with female relatives living with them aged between 18 and 70 who were not studying or employed. Lammers concluded that women should look after their own children below the age of two. Other leading figures were trying to increase women's employment: General Walter Model, commander of Army Group North, tried to win Himmler's support for measures to encourage more German women to work in agriculture, but Himmler did not appear to support these measures. No response is on file.[39]

Hitler introduced new policies to find additional men for the front. In January 1944 fathers of five to seven children lost their exemptions from call-up; in March even fathers of eight or more lost their exemptions. By mid-1944 about one half of all German men and over two thirds of those 18 to 45 years old were soldiers. In March Hitler put General von Unruh at Keitel's disposal to free more men from the Ersatzheer for the front, particularly kv soldiers from the class of 1897 and younger. Von Unruh was empowered to make various organisational simplifications to achieve this. Hitler appointed General Ziegler as his special deputy, successor to von Unruh, leading a commission to simplify the armed forces. Speer described Ziegler as 'an extraordinarily active, clear thinking front-line general.'[40] Six commissions were formed under Ziegler to simplify building, supply (weapons, munitions, equipment, lorries), armed forces' transport, feeding, clothing and administration. Göring and Speer had successfully requested that Hitler use industry to ensure that increased rationalisation of the armed forces took place behind the lines. Speer appointed the industrialists for the commission, placing great emphasis on choosing those whose judgement Hitler valued. Speer promised Goebbels that he would be able to equip all the soldiers being made free for the front as a result of these measures. Pohl, head of the SS administration and economy main office, for his part told Himmler that he did not expect much from the appointment of leading industrialists as chairmen. He predicted that this action would come to nothing, as General von Unruh's action had. Instead of the setting up of six commissions, Pohl preferred the appointment of an experienced, decisive administrative dictator possessing revolutionary momentum.

Ziegler's appointment suggests that von Unruh may have lost Hitler's support. It is not clear why this occurred, after Hitler had relied on him for so long. He may have fallen into disfavour because he had advocated the creation of a war ministry to administer all sections of the armed forces and the placement of all fighting units under a supreme commander.[41] Such a measure would have reduced Hitler's direct control over the armed forces.

The sixth commission—that for administration—was the first to meet. Industrialist Hellmuth Röhnert, a member of Speer's armaments council (*Rüstungsrat*), chaired it, with SS-Gruppenführer Frank as his deputy. In Pohl's judgement Frank largely succeeded in controlling this commission. At the meeting it was revealed that Ziegler intended to set up a war ministry equipped with full powers to unite the administration of all sections of the armed forces while putting all fighting units under a supreme commander, despite evidence that von Unruh's advocacy of similar ideas had been unsuccessful.[42]

Himmler was pleased with the commission's report, but objected to the proposal to unite the armed forces' administration. He favoured unification and co-ordination of regulations to ensure that they were the same but separate implementation. He continued to advocate administrative simplification and oppose internal disputes. Some of his attempts to enforce administrative simplification encountered difficulties. SS offices initially resisted his decision that they transfer responsibility for SS welfare (*Versorgung*) to the Labour Ministry, but it was enforced. Himmler also ordered the unification of the nine official SS gazettes (*Verordnungsblätter*) into one with effect from 1 January 1944. By August he had been advised that this was not possible.[43]

This period saw the high point of Speer's economically rational model of armaments production—production rose to unprecedented levels. Speer's advice to Gauleiter Meyer of North Westphalia provides a further example of his model. He told Meyer that the war had to be pursued to the utmost. All that mattered was how a region could help win the war, not what condition it would be left in at the end of the war.[44] Speer was seeking to counter the Gauleiters' attempts to pursue their own regional interests.

Emphasis on the ideological model of total war continued. Hitler and Bormann extended Party control over the NSFOs. Bormann created a section in the Party Chancellery to secure cooperation between the Party and the OKW's NS-Führungsstab, which had been set up in December 1943. He wanted work to begin quickly. The head of the OKW office, General Reinecke, described the relationship between the two offices as close.[45]

Hitler saw National Socialist leadership in the armed forces as decisive for the war effort, and Bormann agreed. He wanted a thorough 'partification'[46] of the armed forces. Officers had to be the fanatical representatives of the National Socialist state. Hitler himself was concerned at army opposition to the NSFOs. He claimed that his experience as an instruction officer (*Bildungsoffizier*) with the Reichswehr showed him that the opposition of a regiment or battalion commander could completely kill such a thing. He warned against NSFOs being used as a dumping ground for incapable officers. Bormann was also aware of the need to choose the correct workers. He proposed to supplement the work of the NSFOs by calling on the Gauleiters to help politicise the army by using Gau deputies (*Gaubeauftragten*) for armed forces' questions. He aimed for a common political and ideological orientation and an increase in political dynamism.

The Party Chancellery believed that NSFOs should follow Party guidelines. The Party had to suggest suitable people, provide educational material, activate members serving in the armed forces and make contact with NSFOs through the Gau deputies. Hitler ordered that the Party Chancellery was responsible for any tasks arising from NS-Führung and the views of Party offices were to be given to the Wehrmacht only with Bormann's agreement. Bormann had to agree to all personnel and technical measures concerning NSFOs. These measures indicate the growing power of Bormann and the Party and a marked weakening of the Wehrmacht's comparatively independent position. The attention paid to the NSFOs was a further expression of the view, which Bormann increasingly embodied, that political radicalism and Party control would lead to more effective military resistance. It derived from the belief that fanaticism and willpower could outweigh material strength. Political education was also intensified in the SS when Himmler appointed an inspector of ideological education for the SS.[47]

Bormann's power continued to expand. One Party Chancellery official described the SS and the Hitler Youth as the only organisations which did not follow Party Chancellery orders. His ability to restrict access to Hitler and prevent information from reaching Hitler, illustrated in his treatment of Goebbels' foreign policy memorandum, was an important source of this influence. Bormann's increasing authority led him to criticise attempts by the SD to take over the Party's role in judging the political reliability of state officials. He severely reprimanded Speer because his staff had stopped the building of air raid shelters for foreign missions. Hitler had deputised Bormann to tell Speer of his indignation. 'Orders of the Führer are to be carried out by every German and can in no case be annulled or stopped or checked without further ado.'[48]

The Party had continuing problems, particularly because it did not work with the zeal Hitler and Bormann judged necessary. Popular hostility to it continued and new measures were introduced to strengthen its morale and effectiveness: National Socialist family evenings (Sprechabende) were held by the local Party organisations, and repeated general instructions were issued on the need for members to serve as an example in fulfilling their war service and in strong nerves and bravery. In a speech to Gau- and Kreisleiters, Friedrichs noted that the series of blows experienced in 1943 had made some Party members weak and tired. The Sprechabende and general membership meetings had been successful in combating this.[49]

The Party filled an important role in combating the effects of the bombing. Serious demands were being placed on it, as seen in Bormann's circular on Party responsibilities in the event of an invasion; it suggests that he saw the Party exercising an increasing role in military matters. The Party had to prepare for possible paratroop attack and sabotage commandos and uprisings of foreign workers. Its most important practical task was to direct the mobilisation of all men in the home front in collaboration with the armed forces recruiting offices (*Wehrersatzdienststellen*). The local Party leader would command the total reserve of the German civilian work force. Party formations had to be prepared and capable of action if the alarm was given. To enable this, each man had only one mobilisation order for his employment outside the area. In directly affected Gaus, women might need to help in camouflage and planning. This would require careful organisational and psychological preparation, and the approval of the Party's leadership. The Wehrmacht and the police would be in charge of the evacuation of industry and agriculture and destruction of positions, while the Party's sole task would be to handle the possible evacuation of the German civilian population. These tasks would have justified the comparatively generous continued staffing of the Party organisations. The party had some 26,000 full-time employees in the Gaus, 10,000 in the various Party organisations and 342 in the Party Chancellery.[50]

The two views of total war ran parallel in this period. Action on total war concentrated as much on the ideological aspects of uniting the nation and ensuring it still had the will to fight as on further simplifying production and administration and devoting more resources to the war effort. While Himmler was wavering in his commitment to the ideological model, Bormann was taking an increasingly prominent role in this area. New measures of overall co-ordination of production were not introduced, and the existing policies of Speer's ministry came under growing criticism. There may have been a feeling that the measures taken in 1943 had to be given time to take effect; they may have been considered to be sufficient. Speer's illness meant the temporary removal of one of the more forceful and persistent advocates of total war. Goebbels' efforts to link total war and a compromise peace also failed, even though the period before the opening of the second front may have been the last chance for such a move. Despite Hitler's interest in such a peace in late 1943, there were no signs that any further action had been taken. The opening of the second front would change the regime's approach.

7

Hitler 'Sees Reason' (July 1944)

There could be no mistaking the seriousness of Germany's deteriorating position after June 1944. It prompted Speer and Goebbels to urge Hitler to adopt more radical measures, to secure more men for the armed forces as well as for production. In response Hitler appointed Goebbels plenipotentiary for total war and created a people's army, the *Volkssturm*.

Germany's position on the Eastern front declined dramatically from July to December 1944. In a few weeks in June and July, the Germans lost almost 50,000 square kilometres of territory. Soviet forces destroyed the German Army Group Centre in White Russia, causing the loss of some 400,000 men. Germany's allies, Romania and Finland, sought armistices with the USSR in August. Soviet forces opened an offensive against German forces in the Baltic states on 14 September. Advance Soviet units had reached German territory in East Prussia by August 1944 and were less than 400 miles from Berlin. Public morale continued to decline. Loss of the occupied areas worsened German rations.[1]

Germany's position on the Western front deteriorated rapidly in August and September 1944: the war was expected to be over by the end of the year. In late August 60,000 German troops were lost in the closing of the Normandy pocket. Paris was freed on 24 August, and by the beginning of September Montgomery's army had taken Brussels and Antwerp. Germany's western border areas of Eupen, Malmédy and Aachen were evacuated, and in September US forces reached German territory.[2]

The bombing campaign against Germany entered a new phase, as the strategic bombing offensive's effectiveness increased. The Luftwaffe was no longer capable of meeting any of the challenges it faced. Most significantly, since March 1944 Allied air forces adopted a plan to concentrate their attacks on the German railroad system and oil industry. The attacks on railroads successfully restricted the mobility of German forces and supplies. The new focus of attack had ominous implications for the German economy, with its dependence on rail transport to and from the Ruhr. There were serious losses of production in the Saar.[3]

Bombing spread to previously unaffected areas, and the strafing of civilians by fighter bombers in the west disrupted agricultural production. Overcoming the effects of bombing was 'a labour of Sisyphus.'[4] The costs of the air war can be seen from the example of the Firma Bosch in Wurttemberg which sustained an estimated 88 million RM damage. It was split into 213 offices in 102 locations, a move that cost 28 million RM. In Wurttemberg by July more room could be found for production only by closing other firms.

The military crisis led to greater political flexibility on the Eastern front. Himmler met Vlasov on 16 September and agreed to set up new Russian divisions, create a real Russian national army and stop derogatory propaganda about the Eastern peoples. Such moves came too late, since the population in the East was already back under Soviet control. In addition, the Propaganda Ministry was pleased to see its plans to arm Ukrainian partisans realised, but these efforts were undermined by Hitler's decision to appoint Koch as Reich commissar for Ostland. Because of Koch's harsh rule in the Ukraine, Taubert, a Propaganda Ministry official, described the decision with considerable understatement as a propaganda problem.[5]

Worried by the worsening German position, Goebbels met Hitler in Berchtesgaden on 21 June 1944. Assuring Hitler that he was no defeatist, he stressed the need for total war and reform of the armed forces, including their reduction behind the lines. Goebbels promised Hitler a further million men for the front by these means. In reply, Hitler criticised Göring for the failures of the Luftwaffe, praised Speer's achievements and told Goebbels that a further one million soldiers would be no use if they could not be equipped with weapons. He indicated his awareness that some generals opposed National Socialism but he still needed their skills. Hitler advised that the time was not yet ripe to call on the public for even greater exertions in the name of total war, but promised to return to these plans if the situation worsened. Goebbels was unconvinced by Hitler's arguments, evidence of the urgency with which Goebbels viewed the situation and of the strength of his views.[6]

There was general agreement among a wide range of leaders that more decisive policies needed to be adopted on the home front. Goebbels had prepared the groundwork with an article of 2 July 1944 in *Das Reich*, '*Führen wir einen totalen Krieg?*' Hitler agreed that Speer could discuss the possibilities of gaining more labour with a small circle—Himmler, Lammers, Keitel, Goebbels and Sauckel. (Bormann, interestingly, was omitted from the list.) At the official level, Klopfer of the Party Chancellery chaired a meeting with Naumann and Kritzinger of the Reich Chancellery, which agreed on radical measures to call up more workers. Bormann advised Gauleiters to adopt harsher measures and employ all workers in activities important to the war. Sauckel ordered men and women in the age groups encompassed in compulsory registration for labour (the *Meldepflicht*) to report to the labour offices again, if not already employed.[7]

The military crisis revived the alliance between Speer and Goebbels, who believed he had 'wonderful' co-operation with Speer.[8] The two men met on 10 July 1944 and agreed to send Hitler separate memoranda on total war to urge him to appoint a delegate with greater powers to introduce total war policies. There were considerable similarities between the proposals and even the phrasing of the resulting memoranda.

Speer wrote to Hitler on 12 July 1944, noting Hitler's belief that three to four months production of Germany's new, technically superior, weapons would overcome the military crisis. Germany needed to use its last reserves to achieve this production as well as make more soldiers available to the army. Speer believed that a total involvement of the German people in the war effort should begin immediately, but would take some months to be visibly effective. Additional workers had to be transferred to armaments before armaments workers could be exhorted to the highest productivity. The population would respond enthusiastically to the proclamation of total war, but it would have to be implemented, not merely proclaimed. If the regime did not act, German workers would reproach them for indecisiveness and might lose their energy.

Speer suggested that additional labour could be found for the home front. Completely contradicting the policy he had enforced until then, Speer claimed that 'of course' he thoroughly agreed with Sauckel that as many workers as possible had to be brought in from the occupied territories, and he supported Sauckel gaining the necessary powers to do so. Germany could not rely on foreign workers alone. He proposed that the army free 100,000 to 150,000 soldiers from the home front, to be replaced either by German women or Italian military internees; the railways should give up 30,000 workers; and armaments should give up more than the required 50,000, if suitable German replacements were available. Speer suggested specifically that additional German workers could be obtained as follows—some 300,000 to 400,000 female domestic servants, some 400,000 office cleaning women (one quarter to one third of all cleaners), some 30,000 women students of inessential subjects and the 100,000- to 150,000-man German air defence police (*Luftschutzpolizei*) who could be transferred as a body to armaments firms. More staff could be freed by simplifications in the Wehrmacht's administration and home offices. Speer claimed there were still reserves in the home front. The experience of bombed towns showed that life was continued despite the absence of many normal requirements of daily life. Everything inessential had to disappear.

For such measures to succeed, one man had to be given power over the entire economy and all ministries. Such a conscious break with Germany's bourgeois notions of everyday life had to be carried out in a revolutionary manner. Men from industry, the armed forces and administration were not suitable to carry out such measures: this was shown by the failure of the Dreier Ausschuss. Committees could be no longer relied on; power had to be given to an individual who had the courage and nerve to take risks.[9]

In a second letter dated 20 July 1944, Speer claimed that no one gave Hitler an overview of German labour reserves. In order to solve manpower problems, Hitler had to become more involved in this issue. Only radical measures would bring success.

Speer alleged that disproportionate numbers of staff were still used for unproductive maintenance of living standards and administration. He believed that staff could be saved by further administrative simplifications, which could be undertaken without disruption. In speeches he cited as evidence the example that people continued to pay their taxes once they were not collected and that takings in the underground and on trains had not diminished since the abolition of conductors. Speer claimed 1.4 million were still employed as household help, but this number includes workers in canteens and messes.[10] He provided Hitler with figures which suggested that the number of uk positions in armaments industries was small in comparison to other sectors of the economy.

Speer's figures are open to question and were strongly protested by officials. Lammers countered that there were only 1.5 million in administration in May 1942 and 420,000 in the Wehrmacht administration—a total figure of 1.92 million. The Reich Chancellery was still protesting suggestions that the administration had a surplus of staff in November 1944, stating that it had made 330,000 staff available to armaments. Rebentisch notes that

Sector	Total employed	uk positions	
Army armaments	1.94 m	81,000	of the class of 1910 and younger
Air armaments	2.33 m	97,000	of the class of 1910 and younger
Navy armaments	530,000	22,000	of the class of 1910 and younger
Mining	970,000	91,000	of the class of 1910 and younger
Iron industry	450,000	120,000	of the class of 1910 and younger
Administration, including armed forces administration	about 3 million		
Commerce	3.18 million		
Servants	1.45 million[11]		

of the remaining one million-odd male employees in the civil service, only 78,000 were younger than 43.[12]

Speer claimed there was some 7.4 million men available in the age group of 18 to 34 (classes 1910 to 1926), of whom 600,000 were wounded or missing and 588,000 were in uk positions. At least 4.3 million more men should therefore be available from this age group to the Wehrmacht, he estimated. He proposed a threefold process for delivering the classes of 1918 to 1926, approximately 3.6 million men, to the front. No replacements would be provided.[13]

Speer criticised the armed forces' use of staff as no more efficient than the civil service. Germany had 210 fighting divisions of 10.5 million men in the armed forces and Waffen-SS, while in 1917, excluding Austria, it had 230 divisions. If the average strength of an infantry division was taken as 11,000 men, and air force and navy were excluded, Germany only had 2.3 million men in fighting divisions. Speer attributed this to organisational mistakes; overestimation of the value of behind-the-lines organisation and 'the terrible German organisational habit' of creating as many independent units as possible.[14] He gave the example that supply, transport and health care were organised separately for each section of the armed forces. Additional soldiers for duties behind the lines had to be found by simplification of the Wehrmacht administration, rather than by calling up older armaments workers. To win the war, the Wehrmacht had to be organisationally simplified. Germany and Britain were too tradition bound, while the Americans and Russians improvised and simplified. The OKW itself did not have the strength to enforce such measures; an individual equipped with complete powers was needed.

In his letter to Hitler and in his speeches, Speer compared the German war effort unfavourably to that of World War I. In his 20 July letter to Hitler, he repeatedly compared the over-organised army of 1944 disparagingly to the more efficient army of World War I. Surprisingly, in view of the munitions crises of 1914-18, he believed that the supply of munitions to the front was better organised in World War I. Speaking to the Gauleiters, he made the following specific comparisons: the World War I Waffenamt had ten times fewer personnel than its 1944 equivalent; the proportion of German women working in industry was greater in 1914-18; and restrictions in many areas of the home front had been more incisive then. (Sauckel claimed, however, that the percentage of women employed in 1939 was greater than that in 1914.) In a surprisingly paradoxical argument, Speer claimed that because Germany had had so much time to prepare for World War II, it had created an excess of organisations which prevented the country from reaching 1917 levels of production in 1939-40.[15] His analysis of World War I is misleading. It was part of his rational, non-ideological and technocratic style that he was prepared to cite Walther Rathenau, a Jew, as a model. But his overall claims for the superior efficiency of German economic production in 1914-18 were unjustified. It is not clear whether he made such claims to goad his audience into action, or whether he believed them. If the latter, then his view of total war was too narrow. If production of some weapons was less than in 1914-18, the overall variety and complexity of weapons to be produced was greater, as were the other demands on the German economy. The increased technical requirements of warfare required greater numbers employed in weapons development and procurement. Above all there were good economic and political reasons not to restrict the home front as much as in World War I.

Speer repeatedly stressed in his speeches that the war was a technical war, and that only armaments, food and transport were important for the war effort. His model of total war, mirroring his own training and responsibilities, emphasised the efficient use of economic resources. If anything, it was too narrowly focussed on such considerations. Despite his calls for a proletarianisation of Germany,[16] there were reasons to maintain some inessential activities for the sake of morale, reasons which Speer seemed to disregard.

Speer's arguments to Hitler about the number of staff who were still available seem unrealistic and raise the question whether he was exaggerating the numbers to convince the Führer that such measures would bring results. The existence of large numbers behind the lines in the armed forces was not necessarily a sign of inefficient or wasteful military organisation.

Similarly his suggestion that all remaining 4.3 million men were available for call-up was over-simplified. Even men who had not classed as indispensable might not be easily replaced, or might not be fit enough to see action. Speer himself does not appear to have taken a prominent role in reducing the number of skilled jobs or 'deskilling' them. It was not necessarily clear whether women, largely industrially unskilled, could be trained quickly to take the place of skilled industrial workers, or easily transferred to areas of labour shortage. British experience suggested that, by the standards of the time, the number of women who could be classed as mobile was limited. 'The existence of a large reserve of transferable "unoccupied" women had proved a mirage: they were mainly . . . running households for other people.'[17] The regime could have used civilian conscription orders to force women to move from one region to another, as Salter implies. German experience had shown that the work force resented forced evacuations and transfers of men away from their families for the war effort, and productivity was far greater if they worked in their home regions. There can be little doubt that forced evacuations, particularly of married women, would have been counter-productive. Because of their family commitments and the attitudes of the period, women cleaners in Hamburg, for example, might not have been free to move to other areas of the Reich to work, unless the regime radically changed social expectations of women's roles. Speer does not appear to have considered these factors.

Goebbels wrote to Hitler on 18 July with a similar proposal for greater mobilisation of the home front. Describing enemy forces as completely superior in numbers and almost unreachable in materiel and technology, Goebbels nonetheless expressed his belief that this coalition would finally disintegrate. The question was whether Germany had enough bargaining counters at its disposal to take advantage of any crisis.[18]

Goebbels claimed that Germany had not yet exhausted its strength. The war leadership had asked too much of some and not enough of others. The von Unruh commission had not succeeded because it lacked the necessary powers. Goebbels lacked confidence in Germany's existing organisations. While he had unreserved trust in the Party, he explained, his trust in the armed forces was heavily shaken. He did not believe the Wehrmacht was capable of reforming itself. He implicitly criticised the National Socialist system of administration. In almost every area of public life three or four authorities governed next to each other, making difficulties for one another. His specific examples were competitors with the Propaganda Ministry—Rosenberg's Ostministerium and the foreign ministry.[19]

In civilian life, one person or organisation had to be given comprehensive powers, greater than already existing powers. This had to be done by an outsider from the Party or economic life; the policies should be carried out by the Party, which alone had the necessary initiative and improvisational talents. Hitler needed to appoint men with backbone and character, with clear authority, who would act without regard to people or offices. Goebbels warned Hitler against expecting too much from a committee. The Dreier Ausschuss' work had been a tragedy, since each decision had been discussed until only a shadow of the original remained.

The man Hitler appointed should draw up a plan to follow, a meeting of all concerned should be held and then each leader should proceed with his task. Goebbels proposed a looser control by Hitler's appointee than Speer. He suggested the appointee distribute guidelines, spark off the adoption of total war and oversee its implementation. Guidelines would be set up within which a Gauleiter could act, but the rest would be left to the Gauleiters' ability. If Hitler gave the Gauleiters this task, he suggested, they would vie with each other to fulfil it quickly. Despite Goebbels' private belief that the Party membership in general was not up to its wartime responsibilities, he gave the Party a position of prominence in his proposals. He seems to have decided to exploit for his own purposes Hitler's loyalty to his Party comrades, on which some of his earlier proposals had foundered. Such an appointment, Goebbels suggested, would make 50 new divisions available in three to four months and would give Speer additional workers to increase armaments production.[20]

Goebbels concluded by assuring Hitler he was not motivated by personal ambition but by concern for the Fatherland. He pointed out that he had always been Hitler's loyal and unswerving supporter. He warned that too often Germany took the necessary measures only when forced by the economy. A decision taken too late had no practical effect, as the example of the winter 1941 wool collection demonstrated. He told Hitler he and his family would not wish to live in a world that was not National Socialist. 'You know that my life belongs to you.'[21] Goebbels' letter contained more fulsome assurances of his loyalty and belief in total victory than Speer's, partly reflecting their different relationships and styles of dealing with Hitler. Goebbels' tone may also be the result of Hitler's rejection of his earlier proposals.

Goebbels' proposals, unavailable to researchers when Carroll's study was published, are sufficiently detailed to disprove her contention that where total war was concerned, he simply screeched for sacrifices.[22] He was less specific than Speer in identifying areas where staff could be freed, and his promises of manpower were less extravagant. Fifty new divisions (using Speer's staffing of 11,000 men a division) was a promise of 550,000 extra men, or (if the wartime level of 17,000 was adopted) 850,000 extra men; Speer promised an additional 4.3 million men from the classes 1910 to 1926, an additional 390 peacetime or 246 wartime divisions. The introduction of female military service was so radical a concept that it occurred to neither man as an alternative.

Both Speer and Goebbels criticised the Ausschuss' measures. A Reich Chancellery paper claimed, however, that the January 1943 Meldepflicht added 1,126,000 to the work force; a further 150,000 workers were freed by closing down industry; 400,000 more workers were transferred to more important areas of the economy by combing out actions. The Reich Chancellery could not provide numbers freed by individual Supreme Reich authorities (ORBs). This suggests that the Ausschuss did not or could not exercise oversight of these measures, thus vindicating some of Goebbels' criticisms in early 1943. The paper noted that Hitler himself had personally influenced the choice of measures.[23] So Speer and Goebbels' criticisms of the Ausschuss were also in effect criticisms of Hitler's lack of radicalism.

Speer and Goebbels both sought to persuade Hitler that further simplification was possible; Goebbels pointed to the way in which they managed without many offices after air raids. Both claimed that the reserves of the home front were not exhausted, but immediate measures needed to be taken. Both men suggested the war would be lost if their measures were not adopted and reassured Hitler that total war policies would obtain popular support.

Both men lacked an understanding of economic and social constraints on their proposed mobilisation, underestimating the political and social difficulties of finding and using the remaining reserves. Both suggested unrealistic numbers of men and women who could be transferred to the armed forces and armaments. These expectations were shared by others. Schmelter claimed in May 1944 that a further 1.8 million men could be found for the armed forces.[24] Goebbels' letter did not specify where staff might be saved and may have thereby been more politically adroit in not creating new enemies for the programme from the outset.

Goebbels' memorandum was a further attempt to create a co-ordinating body which could control and guide the government. It differed from his earlier suggestions in that it proposed one person rather than a committee or council. Longerich accordingly interprets it as an attempt to take over internal political leadership and resolve the succession. He sees Goebbels' powers, and his later methods of work as plenipotentiary for total war as 'the long desired realisation of pure National Socialist rule.'[25] Personal ambition played an important part in all Goebbels' moves, but his proposals must be seen in their wider context. His suggestion of a plenipotentiary came after his earlier unsuccessful attempts to establish other forms of co-ordination, including a revitalised cabinet or Reich Defence Council. Longerich's judgement therefore seems harsh.

Goebbels' paper differed from Speer's in setting his proposals against a wider political context, as seen in his foreign policy initiatives of 1944. His plan involved initiation of peace feelers, hopes of splitting the enemy alliance, as well as relying on the Party to implement armed forces' reform. Speer's proposals were not part of a comprehensive plan to maximise the regime's chances of surviving the war as Goebbels' were. Speer's proposals centred far more around his own ministry. They would allow Hitler to maintain the fronts until the (unspecified) new weapons, partly developed within Speer's own area of responsibility, could come into action and decide the war.

•   •   •

The unsuccessful assassination attempt against Hitler on 20 July gave him the impetus both to grant Goebbels' and Speer's requests for the appointment of a man with powers concerning total war and to strengthen the ideological aspect of total war. Goebbels was able to display his loyalty dramatically when he suppressed the conspiracy in Berlin. Two points are worth noting: the role Goebbels played in quashing the revolt, including the coolness and decisiveness he showed compared to Bormann and Himmler, and the presence among the conspirators of men with links to both Goebbels and Speer. Although Speer subsequently exaggerated the extent to which he was suspected of involvement in the plot, he did have links with some of the army conspirators and shared their criticisms of the conduct of the war. Goebbels' friends Berlin Police President von Helldorf and Field Marshal Rommel were also among the conspirators.[26] It was clear to all, except possibly Hitler and Bormann, that Germany's position was desperate. Criticism of the current conduct of the war was widespread among the leadership, but the critics were divided on whether to get rid of Hitler or not. Those too identified with the regime or too emotionally bound to Hitler tried to revitalise the war leadership without killing him.

After the defeat of the conspiracy, Goebbels travelled to Hitler's headquarters, where he seized the opportunity to urge total war policies on Hitler. This was the crisis Hitler had mentioned in their 21 June talk. Goebbels learnt that he was to be given the powers to supervise the mobilisation he had urged on Hitler. His persistence in putting his views to Hitler had finally been rewarded; Hitler had turned to his plans. Goebbels guaranteed Hitler that he would raise an army of one million men within three months, a pledge his staff thought excessively optimistic. He was aware that his appointment was a great and thankless task. He told his staff that he saw two possibilities— either peace negotiations, which he judged unlikely to be successful at that time, or a last effort to regain the military and political initiative. He claimed that, had he gained his new powers when he first sought them, the war would probably be over, 'but it takes a bomb under his arse to make Hitler see reason.'[27]

Goebbels' persistence in advocating total war may have influenced Hitler to appoint him. If Hitler still believed total war needed to be sold to a reluctant population and had to embody ideological mobilisation as well as economic reorganisation, then Goebbels as Propaganda Minister would be the logical choice. In addition, Goebbels had proved his loyalty during the assassination attempt: the appointment could serve to reward this loyalty. Timing may have also been a factor. Hitler received Goebbels' memorandum at a time when he was in the mood for radical policies.[28]

At a meeting called on 22 July to discuss questions touched on in Speer's submission to Hitler (presumably that of 12 July), leaders agreed on the need for total war measures to be organised by Goebbels. Berger described Speer's submission as having only a general orienting significance. Speer called for radical measures to be taken, while others present challenged his figures concerning the numbers remaining in the economy and claimed no more staff could be called up. Goebbels agreed that the administration no longer had substantial reserves of labour. It had to reduce its tasks rather than its manpower. Goebbels and Lammers adroitly steered discussion away from questions of detail. Giving an overview of what had already been accomplished, Lammers claimed that the Ausschuss had done everything possible with the means available. He proposed Goebbels to comb out the civilian and Himmler the military sector. Goebbels himself saw Himmler's role as involving a rigorous combing out of the home front and the étappe with the help of Keitel. He believed that implementation of Hitler's order of 27 November 1943, directing that fewer troops be kept behind the lines, would produce at least 500,000 additional soldiers.[29]

Goebbels stressed the importance of the psychological and symbolic effects of total war to the meeting. Reform of public life would have only an optical or symbolic character to some extent, but its effect, presumably on morale, should not be underestimated. Goebbels stressed the need for Party involvement along the lines of his letter to Hitler. The Party should secure the implementation of measures by middle- and lower-level authorities, while Lammers would draw up the necessary legal regulations. Bormann agreed that the powers granted by Hitler had to be clear and unmistakable, and the whole action carried through with *élan* and tempo. Longerich sees this meeting's decisions as reducing Goebbels' powers, because they involved other leaders in implementation and not Goebbels alone.[30] Goebbels does not appear to have seen his powers as lessened, and in practice, as will be seen in Chapter 8, they were not diminished.

Two decrees from Hitler on 25 July created the office of plenipotentiary for the total war effort (*Reichsbevollmächtigter für den totalen Kriegseinsatz*) and appointed Goebbels to the position. Maintaining the fiction of Göring's continuing authority over the economy, Hitler ordered Göring as chairman of the Ministerial Council for Reich Defence to adapt public life to the requirements of total war. The decree claimed Göring had suggested the appointment of a plenipotentiary, whose tasks were to ensure all public activity was in keeping with total war and did not divert workers from the armed forces or armaments; to inspect all the state organisations and all public establishments, institutions and firms aiming for completely rational use of workers and material; and to restrict less important tasks, simplify organisations and provide men for the army. He could require information from ORBs and give orders, in agreement with Lammers, Bormann and Himmler as plenipotentiary for administration. Bormann would ensure Party support for the measures.[31]

The decree extended to the occupied territories, but the Wehrmacht would be excluded. Hitler refused a Foreign Ministry request for exemption. He agreed with Lammers that the Reich, Presidential and Party Chancelleries did not have to report to Goebbels. Offices directly responsible to Hitler were also excluded in practice, despite Goebbels' attempts to overcome this. Lammers told Goebbels that this was no obstacle for fulfilling his task.[32] The protection of Hitler's building projects from cuts appears therefore to have continued.

Historians have disagreed about the extent of Goebbels' new powers. In practice they meant a weakening of Speer's position and a further loss of power for Göring. Longerich's views have been noted above; Rebentisch too suggests that while Goebbels had gained a great victory, he did not possess the internal powers he claimed, since his decrees had to gain the agreement of the Reich Chancellery, the Party Chancellery and Himmler as plenipotentiary for the administration. Historians agree that Goebbels' appointment did not diminish Hitler's power as ultimate supreme decision maker.[33]

Bormann and Himmler also gained additional powers. Hitler deputised Bormann to implement total war in the Party by closing offices and freeing workers. Bormann interpreted this to mean that the Party should be kept as small as possible, but not be restricted in its important political tasks. A large number of Party papers and all its research and planning work was stopped; and considerable, but unspecified, numbers freed in the DAF. In July 20,964 male Party functionaries of a total of 37,192 were still classified as uk.[34]

At the same time as Goebbels and Bormann were empowered to implement total war measures in the civilian sector and the Party respectively, Himmler was given similar powers over the armed forces. He was made commander of the Ersatzheer, which he considered overstaffed and intended to cut back. This appointment gave him an additional role in the economy in his capacity as chief of army armaments. He raised a further 500,000 troops for the front and founded 15 new divisions of new recruits, the people's grenadier (*Volksgrenadier*) divisions, which were more like a militia than normal army divisions.[35]

On 2 August Hitler deputised Himmler to inspect the organisation and administration of the armed forces and the Waffen-SS, OT and the police; to save manpower by simplifying them; and to shut down offices and transfer staff, with the agreement of the heads of the armed services. Hitler wanted fundamental reforms and radical measures to achieve the greatest concentration of men in the army. Himmler believed more men could be found for the front and ordered Pohl to begin work immediately. Reviewing past progress, Pohl considered that von Unruh's failure was 'obvious,' but Ziegler's commissions had achieved much.[36] He estimated that some 70,000 to 75,000 men would be freed if all Ziegler's recommendations were strictly implemented.

Himmler acquired Ziegler's responsibility for the simplification of Wehrmacht administration in October. Most of the commissions were dissolved, and Pohl suggested to Himmler that Ziegler's proposal to create a central office for all armed forces administration be abandoned. The current military situation made it unjustifiable. Himmler welcomed this transfer of responsibility and was pleased by the savings so far achieved. He instructed Pohl to make no concessions to the OKW but to proceed without any further inhibitions, since the population expected results from the SS. Pohl's office investigated the other proposals.[37]

Himmler lost these powers by 10 December 1944, when Hitler appointed Goebbels to inspect and comb out the armed forces. Goebbels gained powers to rationalise and simplify both civilian and military sectors. Goebbels' appointment suggests that Himmler had been ineffective in this position. Yet Goebbels' expectations of what he could achieve were unrealistic. In theory he believed that 8 million men could be freed, but recognised that he did not have the time to achieve such a reorganisation. He believed unrealistically that the ideal ratio was 90 per cent of the armed forces fighting and 10 per cent behind the lines. He erroneously believed this ratio applied in the Soviet armed forces. In practice he hoped to transfer a further million men to the front.[38]

Himmler's general attitude at the time is illustrated by his support for Frank's proposal that the General Government's civilian administration be wound up, both as a symbol of total war and because the Germans no longer held more than one fifth of the General Government's area. Himmler noted that Hitler might want to retain a skeleton organisation, as he had done with the Ostministerium, to avoid giving the impression of a political renunciation of the territories.[39]

One observer suggested that these appointments created a triumvirate of Bormann, Goebbels and Himmler. Bormann's position strengthened as Hitler's health failed, Hitler's concentration on the military situation grew and Lammers' contact with Hitler ceased after September 1944. The assassination attempt worsened Hitler's already deteriorating health. Goebbels told his former adjutant in 1945 that he should be glad he had not seen Hitler again, because 'the Hitler, in whom you once believed, has not existed for a long time.'[40] As Weber's model predicted, Hitler's charismatic authority could not withstand a series of failures. These failures not only undermined his popularity with the German population but also weakened his hold over the leaders and the Gauleiters. The plot against him slowed this process, but only temporarily.

Hitler's decision to grant wide-ranging powers to lesser leaders and to appoint Goebbels as plenipotentiary seems to have been prompted by the internal treachery revealed by the assassination attempt and his narrow escape from death. This, as much as the invasion, persuaded him that more radical action on total war was necessary. As had been the case in the 1941 winter crisis, Hitler's decision was also influenced by the increasing consensus among the leadership that more radical measures were needed. The leadership's reaction to the July 1944 assassination attempt provides further evidence of the origins of the dual German model of total war in the 1918 defeat and revolution. 'Perhaps for the first time in the history of the NSDAP' in a speech to the Gauleiters on 3 August 1944, Himmler blamed Germany's World War I defeat on the failings of the officer corps and general staff.[41] Himmler's comments on the Imperial Army indicate that National Socialist policies were based not only on the publicly mentioned, and privately believed, 'stab in the back' myth, but also on a private awareness of defeat's origins in the failings of Germany's elites in 1914-18.

The Party leadership reacted to the plot with an increase in radicalism and a closing of ranks. Like the Italian treachery of 1943, the plot provided an explanation for all the regime's setbacks and was followed by severe repression directed not only against the plotters and their families, but also against politicians of the pre-National Socialist era. The threat to their leader united the Party as it momentarily united the nation. While popular mood was still described as depressed or resigned, shock at the assassination attempt made the population receptive to the introduction of drastic measures. Reports suggested that the working class was more optimistic and more receptive of radical policies than other groups.[42]

The disloyalty of sections of the armed forces hastened and intensified the extension of Party control of them. As early as 13 July, the Propaganda Ministry proposed establishing a border guard of volunteer Party members in the eastern Gaus. On 22 September the Volkssturm, a militia of men between 16 to 60, was set up. Goebbels had anticipated that he would handle its personnel issues while SA commander Schepmann controlled military aspects. Instead Bormann persuaded Hitler that the Party, not the SA, be given the task. Himmler became the military commander and Bormann its political and organisational leader. Speer promised the Volkssturm all the weapons it needed. Bormann was closely involved in all details of the Volkssturm's creation. It was financed by the Party, and its territorial organisation corresponded to Gau boundaries, with no relation to German military districts.[43]

Bormann saw the Volkssturm as purely a Party matter. He saw the role given to the Gauleiters in organising the Volkssturm and building fortifications as a sign of Hitler's 'boundless trust' in them.[44] The Volkssturm was a manifestation of the hope that popular enthusiasm and the Party's revolutionary leadership could overcome material deficiencies and the failings of the professional army. It was to symbolise national unity and the participation of the whole nation in the war.

Hitler also ordered strengthened National Socialist leadership at the front, in the face of great difficulties for the NSFOs.[45] The development of the NSFOs and the Volkssturm strengthened another aspect of total war, the idea of the 'nation in arms,' substituting revolutionary loyalty and fervour for professional military expertise. This development was supported and led by Himmler and Bormann, with Goebbels playing the role of herald of the Volkssturm. This corresponded with their concepts of total war: Bormann and Himmler placed greater emphasis on the ideological model, while Goebbels' concept combined elements of the economically rational model and the ideological model.

Party involvement in military issues increased with its organisation of the frontier Gaus for building fortifications. Party leaders continued to exercise authority in an operational area: the military supreme commander could give orders on military matters to the Reich defence commissioner and civilian offices, while a civilian Reich defence commissioner would be appointed with executive powers. Party offices were instructed to continue their activity in operational zones. Despite its increased responsibilities, the Party continued to be a weak reed. Propaganda Ministry officials judged some 80 per cent of the 7 to 8 million Party members to be 'driftwood,' awaiting defeat.[46]

Party leaders favoured a more radical approach to waging war, but this radicalism did not extend to supporting Goebbels' plan to set up a women's armed forces auxiliary. Goebbels initially proposed a call-up of all women born in 1914 and later to work in smokescreen companies, barrage batteries and radar establishments. (Some contemporaries defined this as training to use weapons.) In October plans were 'pending' to call up women of the classes 1920 to 1924 for such an auxiliary,[47] and by the end of the month Goebbels had presented a draft decree for Hitler's signature making childless women of the classes 1914 and later liable for military service.

The Reich Chancellery expressed concern at the proposed decree's effects on morale and on other employment of women. It would call up some 600,000 women from each individual class, instead of the 300,000 to 400,000 it believed were needed. Reich Chancellery, Party Chancellery and the plenipotentiary for labour's officials agreed that it was more appropriate to use existing powers. Bormann and Sauckel agreed. In Bormann's view, publication of such a decree would lead to some public disquiet, and the decree would encompass many more women (he estimated 10 million) than were needed. Experience had shown that almost all women in these age groups were already employed in war work. Continuing to adopt a conservative position on women's roles, Lammers described himself as completely persuaded by Bormann. Bormann told Goebbels more rational use of labour by the Wehrmacht had to be the first priority. As long as men still occupied positions which could be handled by women, use of weapons by women had to be rejected. He conceded, however, that the Party and Frauenschaft should prepare the population for a far greater use of women, even with weapons in some cases. The Reichs Chancellery agreed with this position 'unreservedly.'[48]

Instead of Goebbels' proposal, a female auxiliary armed services corps (*Wehrmachthelferinnenkorps*) of 120,000 to 150,000 personnel was planned, either volunteers or women made available through total war measures. All women's auxiliaries were combined into one corps by February 1945.[49]

Contemporary perceptions of the role of women created opposition to Goebbels' plans; a more conservative solution was adopted than Goebbels intended. This reaction reflected a longer German tradition. 'The German pattern has been to resist the presence of women in the armed forces in anything but a marginal, preferably civilian, capacity.'[50] Nonetheless, women were used to build fortifications and trenches in border areas and to free men for the front, replacing them in previously male activities such as staffing floodlight batteries. Hitler had decided that women would not directly participate in Volkssturm training but the League of German Girls (*Bund deutscher Mädel* or *BDM*) and Frauenschaft could equip and clothe units.

· · ·

Germany's military decline gave added urgency to leaders' consideration of wider issues. Himmler acted to secure his position in any peace negotiations with the Western allies. He ordered an end to the extermination of the Jews in September-October 1944. (Over 100,000 Jews, however, still died in 1945.)[51] Himmler's decision may also reflect Hitler's waning authority.

Jockeying for increased powers and competition over the succession to Hitler undoubtedly motivated leaders who advocated total war. Once granted the increased powers he sought, Goebbels did not abandon his wider view of total war nor did he allow his work as plenipotentiary to stop him from urging it on Hitler. He still toyed with the idea of reviving the cabinet, with Himmler as war minister or a deputy chancellor: clear lines of authority were needed. The current system did not work unless Hitler concerned himself with the smooth course of its government machinery.[52]

Goebbels too continued to advocate a compromise peace. In September Japanese Ambassador Oshima approached him about an alliance among Japan, Germany and the Soviet Union. Goebbels was attracted by the idea but felt that Germany had little to offer the Soviet Union.[53]

In an undated letter to Hitler, written in September 1944, Goebbels noted that Germany had lost the line it hoped to hold in the East and had failed to repel the invasion. He pointed out that never in its history had Germany won a two-front war, and it could no longer do so in this war. The Quebec conference of Roosevelt and Churchill highlighted contradictions in the enemy coalition, despite attempts to conceal them. He speculated that the Western allies might be considering abandoning the formula of unconditional surrender, and Eden's journey to Quebec was to convey the Kremlin's protests at any such attempt. Stalin's attempts to secure his position in southeast Europe could lead to an irreparable conflict with the West: German diplomacy had to seize this opportunity.[54]

Although Goebbels believed peace with the West was more logical, and most suited Hitler's foreign policy aims, internal politics made it impossible for Western leaders. Stalin, on the other hand, had no such domestic constraints and could make decisions without taking public opinion into account. He had a cool realism which Churchill lacked and would be aware that he would eventually come into conflict with the Western powers.

Goebbels then reassured Hitler about possible objections to his plans. Japan would help bring about a German-Soviet understanding; the regime no longer needed to concern itself about its European allies, who had themselves surrendered; the people would be deeply satisfied. This would not be the victory they had dreamed of in 1941, but it would still be the greatest victory in German history.[55]

Hitler might dismiss this as Utopian, but it had to be tried, naturally with care and circumspection. Goebbels concluded that Ribbentrop was incapable of overseeing such a development. The Foreign Office was largely defeatist and corrupt, and could not work ardently for victory. Before criticising Ribbentrop, Goebbels disingenuously claimed that he had never criticised a colleague before when writing to Hitler, but in this case he considered it his duty. Other members of the leadership shared his opinion. A minister with intelligence, flexibility and tenacity was needed to follow Hitler's clear guidelines, deepen divisions among the enemy and clean up the foreign office. According to his staff, Goebbels aimed to become Foreign Minister. As in his memorandum on total war, Goebbels denied any personal ambition and referred to his plans to leave politics after the war. He had not discussed the issues with anyone else. He did not doubt that Hitler would lead them to victory, but presumed to provide his own advice, the result of countless lonely evenings.[56]

Nothing came of Goebbels' memorandum. In October he learned that Bormann had not submitted it to Hitler but only told him that the memorandum contained nothing new and that Goebbels wanted to be Foreign Minister. As a result Hitler greeted Goebbels curtly and told him these was no question of a change of minister. Goebbels was completely shattered.[57]

Bormann's decision not to pass on Goebbels' memorandum to Hitler was striking evidence of his influence, which was negative rather than positive. Bormann's successes were never victories 'in-depth.'[58] He was often not in a position to persuade Hitler to adopt a certain course of action, but he could stop others from presenting their points of view to Hitler. Tiessler suggested he did so particularly when he feared Hitler would agree with the view. In this case it seems unlikely that Hitler would have agreed with Goebbels' proposals. He had always rejected Goebbels' earlier proposals along similar lines, and he did reject his plan to replace von Ribbentrop.

The atmosphere in late 1944 was such that attempts to foresee difficulties could be seen as defeatism. Göring told his chief of staff in October that he did not dare to suggest peace negotiations for fear of losing Hitler's trust. Goebbels' increasing closeness to Hitler can be inferred from his letter's comparative plain frankness. It was an attempt to overcome 'the completely hazy, unreal atmosphere of mistaken ideas in the Führer's headquarters.'[59] Goebbels' realism was, of course, limited by his commitment to Hitler and to the regime. Due to his standing, he could make these proposals with little fear of Hitler's reaction or of being accused of defeatism, but he was unable to move Hitler further to adopt the plan he outlined. Once again Goebbels tried to complement his domestic total war proposals with a foreign policy which aimed to salvage the regime. While this was based on a rational assessment of the regime's interests, it came too late. The psychological moment of Soviet receptiveness to German offers, if it ever existed, had long since passed, as victory was clearly in sight for Germany's enemies. Goebbels refused to recognise that Hitler was incapable of accepting such policies, and continued to believe that he could persuade him by constant repetition of his arguments. In 1943 Hitler told Ribbentrop that if he made peace with Russia he would not be able to help himself; he would attack Russia again the next day.

Goebbels continued to argue for a compromise peace without an apparent response from Hitler. These efforts were too late, as Goebbels was aware.[60] He had gained the powers he wanted to orient the home front completely to the war effort, but Germany was too obviously at the end of its tether to tempt an enemy to a compromise peace.

Hitler responded to the threat on his life by finally granting Goebbels the powers to implement total war which he had sought for at least a year and a half, but Hitler also gave more power to Himmler and Bormann. Goebbels still did not have an unrestricted right to make the necessary changes. Hitler effectively divided some of his powers among them. All three men could be seen as advocates of a more radical approach to the conduct of the war. Goebbels threw himself into his work as plenipotentiary with urgency,[61] telling testimony to his assessment of the regime's prospects.

8

Men versus Weapons: Goebbels as Plenipotentiary for Total War

As plenipotentiary for total war Goebbels was granted wide powers to adapt German life to the requirements of total war, powers he exercised until the end of the war. He undertook extensive simplifications of life on the home front and increasingly called up uk staff. The second half of 1944 was marked by growing tension between his attempts to meet the armed forces' manpower needs and Speer's claims for manpower for production. Both were necessary for continuation of the war; neither demand could be met effectively; and the resulting disputes illustrated the over-optimism of both Goebbels' and Speer's promises of additional staff to Hitler in July 1944.

Goebbels' new powers were exercised against the background of continued deterioration of the military situation. The Allies had hoped to by-pass Germany's prepared defences by seizing Arnhem in an air and ground attack and then advancing into Germany via the Netherlands. The failure of this operation allowed the Germans time to consolidate their defences on their western borders. Hitler gave Field Marshal von Rundstedt the task of holding the remainder of the Siegfried line and of planning an offensive in the Ardennes to recapture Antwerp in December 1944. The offensive, launched on 16 December, had faltered by the end of the month; after initial successes the Germans had to return to the defensive. In the East Soviet forces advanced into the Baltic states in October, isolating the remaining forces of Army Group North for the remainder of the war. The German economy came under increasing strain from bombing of marshalling yards and the canal system in September 1944 and stepped up bombing in the Ruhr in October. This required the diversion of considerable resources to repairs.[1]

The effects of increased bombing meant armaments production began to decline. With Hitler's agreement Speer adopted policies to concentrate armaments production on priority programmes, creating an armaments staff (*Rüstungstab*).[2] Speer's armaments policy in late 1944 aimed at short-term results. In a conference with Hitler on 20 August, Speer proposed, and Hitler agreed, that industrial planning should concentrate on the next nine months. Both men agreed that Germany was in a fight for its survival. Speer created armaments sub-commissions to co-ordinate the actions of the Gauleiters. By September he had to take drastic steps to overcome the coal crisis and other problems of production. On 6 September he ordered that all completed weapons should be shipped away to the armed forces; raw materials holdings, except coal, were reduced to two weeks' supply; stocks of components were reduced to eight days. The aim of all these measures was to produce the maximum number of completed armaments to the front. Speer called on elasticity of supply to carry the economy through the coal emergency, a 'wildly unrealistic' gamble for survival.[3]

As plenipotentiary for total war, Goebbels introduced as immediate measures: a ban on sham work (Scheinarbeit) after 15 August, with employees and employers subject to punishment; a decree by Sauckel raising the upper age limit for obligatory labour duty for women from 45 to 50 years; reduction of the postal service to one service a day and none on Sundays; simplification of railway control measures and replacement of men by women where possible; closing university and specialist schools; simplifying questionnaires, card systems, the tax system and the legal system. On 23 August Hitler agreed to the extension of the upper age limit for women's labour duty to 55. By the end of August a 60-hour week was introduced for men and a 48-hour week for women and the young. This had little effect on productivity.[4]

Goebbels sought public response to his policies. He aimed to mobilise public enthusiasm for the campaign by use of a special field post box, '*Feldpost-Nr. 08 000 Totaler Krieg*,' for suggestions. Both the Armaments Ministry and the Propaganda Ministry had already set up similar schemes, which allowed the public to feel they were influencing the government and gave them an outlet for their criticisms. Over 50,000 suggestions were received. A 1944 analysis claimed that they were of a 'unanimous radicalism.'[5] The contributors wanted still further simplifications, reduction of luxuries and increased employment of women. The letters mainly suggested creation of a commissar-style system and other increased Party influence in the armed forces, and a system of economic commissars or plenipotentiaries to oversee total war in the economy. In apparent vindication of Goebbels' assessment of public opinion, the main contributors were soldiers, workers and the middle classes while officers, professionals and the nobility barely contributed. Letters of complaint comprised 17 per cent but the overwhelming number of letters showed an honourable concern about the future, the ministry reported. The number of contributions decreased after a high point in August 1944. By 24 January 1945 Propaganda Ministry staff could note that they had received 109,832 suggestions. They felt the system gave them information about previously inaccessible institutions and presumably also thereby a means of finding new areas where labour could be saved. Despite support for the measures taken, public morale continued to decline.

Goebbels continued to call for the leadership to ensure that its style of life, that of their relatives and public life in general, was in keeping with total war. Some measures were taken to improve the optics of war, to remove suspicions that the leadership was not serious about total war, such as a ban on accepting hunting invitations, but they were undermined by other measures which attracted public criticism such as the introduction of a new uniform for political leaders.[6]

Goebbels quickly set up an administrative structure with a staff of 50 to support his activities. The planning committee (*Planungsausschuss*) was to undertake overall organisation of measures to be taken, to provide ideas for individual acts to 'totalise' public life and to inspect all suggestions coming from the population for their practicality. Led by Werner Naumann, the state secretary of the Propaganda Ministry, it would prepare proposals, note objections and document the expected saving of workers. The executive committee (*Exekutivausschuss*), led by Gauleiter Paul Wegener, in connection with the responsible offices, had to implement those planning committee suggestions to which Goebbels agreed. The committees would have advisory members from the offices of Lammers, Bormann, Himmler both as Reichsführer-SS and Interior Minister, Speer, Funk, Sauckel, the DAF and von Unruh. Hans Faust, a regional council chairman (*Regierungspräsident*), with good connections to the Reich Chancellery and the Party Chancellery, was General Secretary of the two committees, responsible for general co-ordination of business, including reports to Hitler, weekly presentation of estimated and actual results, and informing the public. The committees worked quickly and unbureaucratically.[7]

Goebbels planned that the department heads and Gauleiters would implement all measures themselves, and he would intervene directly only if particular difficulties had to be overcome. The executive committee would send deputies into Gaus to help carry out measures. Only 20 people would be employed by these two committees. Any substantial measures would be placed before Hitler in a submission via Bormann.[8]

Goebbels intended to increase the Gauleiters' involvement in armaments. Notifying Party leaders of Goebbels' appointment, Bormann told them that the seriousness of the situation required quick and judicious treatment. He formed a special staff for the total war effort. Goebbels' measures increased the involvement of the Gauleiters in the armaments economy. He planned a decree to involve the Gauleiters more specifically in his work. Bormann agreed with Goebbels' attempt to use the Gauleiters' initiative, but wondered if his proposed decree would serve this purpose. It would grant them lesser powers than they already had as Reich defence commissioners. An alteration of the ministerial council decree (*Ministerratsverordnung*) was all that was necessary to expand their authority to railways, post and finance administration. It was also necessary for Gauleiters to intervene more strongly into the inspection of the numbers of uk positions, especially in armaments by appointing Gau and Kreis commissions. These commissions had the right to inspect all firms, including armaments and army firms, and to make recommendations for more purposeful employment. Speer agreed with the view that their tasks were to deal with optical cases of abuse of uk positions and to make new workers available to armaments. Speer conceded that some Gauleiters co-operated successfully with armaments in these commissions.[9]

Gauleiters had responsibility for total war issues which impinged on other Gaus. Bormann opposed attempts by ORBs to supervise measures in detail, since this restricted the flexibility of middle-level officials, firms and Gauleiters. He and Goebbels had agreed to check any irregular and hasty measures by individual Gaus. For this reason their decree asked Gauleiters to act within ORB guidelines, which had to be broad and allow for independent decisions. Bormann also opposed Speer's proposals that Gauleiters become the chairmen of armaments commissions. Speer had suggested to Hitler in September that the Gauleiters should have responsibilities in armaments. In Bormann's view this would signify so strong a subordination to the Armaments Ministry that the Party's initiative in armaments would be completely crippled. The Party's influence was greatest everywhere it could develop its initiative most fully vis-à-vis the state.[10]

In practice Goebbels increasingly served as a source of information to and from the Gauleiters and as a 'court of appeal' for them. They approached him for assistance in solving problems they had with the central administration, sought reassurance and guidance from him on the policies they should follow and on the regime's future. Late in 1944 Goebbels had instituted radio conferences with all Gauleiters, speaking to them about the political and military situation. (Gauleiters continued to seek advice and support from him into 1945.)[11] The manner in which they turned to Goebbels reflects his higher profile but also suggests that neither Hitler nor Bormann were fulfilling this role. Bormann either chose not to act in this manner or did not do so adequately. Possibly he was more concerned to secure his position with Hitler and meet Hitler's needs than represent the Gauleiters' interests.

Hitler created new divisions to be staffed by men freed through total war measures. This meant that they could meet only one third of the losses of existing divisions. Under pressure from Hitler Goebbels had to find the men to fill these positions. He and Speer had both assured Hitler in July 1944 that these men were available. Goebbels saw his task as transferring recently trained, and still uk, kv men to front service and replacing these workers in the armaments industry. In contrast to Speer's calculations in his July 1944 memorandum to Hitler, Goebbels discovered in practice that fit men could be found in large numbers only in uk armaments positions. The Wehrmacht demanded in both August and September 150,000 trained uk soldiers, a further 100,000 untrained soldiers in September, and 200,000 untrained soldiers a month from October to December. In contrast to this demand for around a million soldiers, there were only some 1.5 million uk positions as a reserve; Wehrmacht requirements could be met only if the numbers of uk men could be reduced by 66 per cent.[12]

Goebbels kept Hitler continuously informed by submissions which requested his permission, even for measures in the Propaganda Ministry. In a submission to Hitler in early August 1944, Goebbels envisaged a decree forbidding any uk positions for the classes of 1914 and later outside the armaments industry. Only the personal approval of the Gauleiter would allow such positions to continue. The overwhelming majority of kv men still available were in armaments, and agreement would have to be reached with Speer to exchange them. Speer had ordered that all uk men from the class of 1918 and later be given up to the Wehrmacht, thereby freeing some 47,000 men. He was also prepared to give up all kv men from the classes of 1910 and later still employed in firms in less important industries, such as textiles. Replacements would come from ministries and sectors of the economy which agreed to give up approximately 810,000 positions as follows:

Ministry/Area	Staff Numbers
Education	250,000
Justice	28,000
Post	100,000
Tourism	40,000
Cultural life	60,000
KDF troop entertainment programmes*	12,000
Agriculture	120,000
Foreign domestic servants	200,000

* *Kraft durch Freude*—Strength through Joy—a German Labour Front recreation programme.

These numbers were not guaranteed, Goebbels advised Hitler, but gave an approximate picture of how extensively workers would be freed.[13]

Workers would be given up in order of priority: first, those who could be spared without great public sacrifices, by closing lotteries and statistical offices and by simplifying questionnaires. In a second category more serious cuts had to be made—culture, films and theatres. A final category included those firms and organisations which had to exist as long as possible for economic reasons or reasons of morale, and which would be restricted or stopped only in extreme emergency, such as breweries, cakebaking and transport. Goebbels and Sauckel had agreed that the labour offices were to be placed more strongly than ever under Party influence so the 'improvisational skill of the National Socialist movement' could be used.[14] A further 850,000 workers could be saved, according to the submission, by extensive restriction of educational courses so that only disciplines important to the war effort continued, by restriction of various law courts and closure of up to 75 per cent of the Reich cultural chamber (*Reichskulturkammer*.)

Goebbels proposed extensive restrictions to the film industry, publishing and the cultural sector in general, including the simplification of tickets, reducing staff in cinemas, restriction of film studios, closing down all but one daily paper in all cities except Munich and Berlin, and restricting armed forces and specialist publications. Outwork would be energetically encouraged. These rigorous measures only resulted in the saving of an estimated 5000 staff from the feature film industry, an indication of how tight the labour situation already was.[15]

In a further submission Goebbels noted that the cultural sector had previously been completely exempted from call-up measures, a principle which would have to be abandoned. He wanted to pre-empt any criticisms that his area was not making the best use of its staff, he told Hitler. He therefore planned to free 140,000 artists, closing theatres, orchestras, art training schools and art exhibitions for six months. The most gifted artists would still be exempted; and all others would be employed so as not to harm their future ability to carry on their profession. Publication of literature would be restricted to standard ideological works, school books, scientific and technical works, and publications relating to armaments. Newspaper publication was to be extensively restricted. The result of the printing restrictions would be to free 14,000 workers and compensate for the loss of Finnish paper production. (Finland left the war in August 1944.) As a result of these restrictions, Haegert estimated that 145,000 staff were freed from the cultural sector.[16]

Despite these restrictions, the film director Veit Harlan claimed that Goebbels withdrew 187,000 soldiers and 4000 sailors from active duty for the film *Kolberg* in mid-1944. (Harlan's claims have been widely used by historians, but I have been unable to find any additional confirmation of them.) Whether these figures are exaggerated or not, Goebbels was being inconsistent, even if the propaganda importance he attached to the film's message of holding out against the enemy and the parallels it drew between the Volkssturm and the 1813 war of liberation against the French is taken into account. He may have believed that the film would help overcome the growing defeatism and crisis of confidence in the leadership.[17]

Goebbels also proposed to save large numbers from the post office. On 11 August a meeting under the chairmanship of Ministerialdirigent Haegert from the Propaganda Ministry discussed the release of postal workers. In keeping with Ohnesorge's commitment to the war effort, the proposed measures were extensive, freeing mainly unskilled or semi-skilled female workers. The Post Ministry's two-stage plan involved making 50,000 workers free in stage one and 75,000 to 100,000 workers in stage two. In Haegert's own view the measures envisaged in stage two came close to shutting down postal services. In stage one handling of printed materials, business matters and samples, would stop; the forwarding of small parcels would be restricted; quotas would be set on the forwarding of packets by individual post offices; registered mail would be limited to letters to and from officials; postal deliveries on Sunday would end and where possible there would be only one delivery a day; long-distance phone calls other than for business reasons would be restricted, as would telegrams with prepaid answer forms. Those attending the meeting pointed out legal difficulties in stopping private registered mail and were concerned that the proposed savings all made life more difficult for the population. Instead they suggested ending the issue of separate stamps and postmarks.[18]

Hitler's response, Bormann advised Goebbels, had been to ask if, in each case, the results really justified the dislocation. Hitler objected to the harshness of many of the proposals and believed that care had to be taken lest the measures weaken morale. He therefore wondered whether the ban on sending of small parcels was necessary and also had some objections to the plan to stop private telegrams for distances under 150 kilometres. In some circumstances this might mean that people could not be advised of a death in the family. Simultaneously Bormann told Ohnesorge that Hitler wanted the halving of parcel mail not interpreted too strictly. He also pointed out to Goebbels and Ohnesorge that they had proceeded without seeking the permission of all the necessary officials. Goebbels proposed to meet Hitler's objections by allowing small parcels up to 1000 grams and making the proposed quotas on the parcel post milder. Private telegrams would continue in local areas in case of death or accidents. Soldiers would also be allowed to continue to receive their hometown papers, a proposal Goebbels had previously opposed.[19]

Various undated press releases indicated additional measures which Goebbels took after 17 August and before 19 September: most appear to have been introduced in the space of two weeks. One such press release announced the immediate dissolution of the Prussian Finance Ministry, some 18 months after this was first suggested. (Bormann had obviously not been successful in overcoming Hitler's opposition to the measure in June 1943.) It also listed the restriction of educational facilities and publications to those directly necessary for the war effort, and reported that by replacements and use of female workers the German Red Cross had been able to free tens of thousands of workers. Another communiqué announced the simplification of taxes and foreshadowed further restrictions on commercial life. German commerce had employed some 3.4 million men at the beginning of the war; these numbers had been reduced by 45 per cent and would be reduced further. Even those firms whose production was judged necessary for the war would be inspected. Firms occupied with fashion accessories, toys, flowers, zoological articles, perfume, confectionery, jewels, furs and so on were to be closed completely. Staff unsuited to armaments were to be employed in artisanal work, the building industry and firms meeting the needs of bombing victims. The employment of domestic servants was reviewed once more; servants were allowed only in households with three children under 14. The new rules would free some 300,000 to 400,000 domestic servants. Sauckel agreed to release 200,000 Ukrainian women, some employed as servants and some working in canteens, for armaments. By 23 August Sauckel had raised the age for women to register for employment to 55; but of the 500,000-odd women who registered who were suitable for employment, only 265,000 were allocated jobs. Most women were tied to their homes.[20]

After 11 August there was a general ban on leave; business and the administration were working a minimum 60-hour working week. Local offices and administrative organisations were further simplified. Some offices suffered considerable reduction of staff. For example, 42 per cent of the employees of the Reich health office were let go. The post office had by now made over 250,000 men free, and the railways gave up 57,904 workers in the course of Goebbels' first call-ups. In October Goebbels ordered an end to all planning activities for developments after 1 October 1945. He continued to introduce further economies in his own ministry and to reduce uk positions in areas under his control. Goebbels appointed Dr Hayler, the State Secretary of the Economics Ministry, to prepare suggestions and make the necessary investigations to simplify the economic administration.[21] This task was similar to that with which Speer and Funk had entrusted Rafelsberger in 1943.

Goebbels had introduced a wide range of measures, some which freed staff and others which introduced a further austerity and functionalism into German life, which focussed on the optics of total war. A survey of the first three months of the total war measures, apparently prepared by an official of the Armaments Ministry, claimed that they had a great effect. Longer working hours made more workers available while ensuring that the same amount of work was done. Decrees simplifying salaries and pay and banning leave freed staff as well. At the same time various measures had been taken which made life easier for those employed, including keeping offices, shops and doctor's surgeries open later. It concluded that 'an enormous regrouping of workers has occurred in favour of the Wehrmacht and armaments.'[22] The report did not, however, give specific numbers of staff freed, and it is difficult to reconstruct from the surviving material how great the numbers actually freed were.

How effective were Goebbels' measures? Some historians have been very critical. Rebentisch argues that Goebbels' policies were action for its own sake. He is particularly critical, calling the programme a 'failure which did not alter the outcome of the war, at best delayed . . . the defeat for a few weeks.'[23] From the leadership's point of view, this was, of course, better than nothing. Orlow has suggested that Goebbels' Achilles heel was his reliance on the Gauleiters for implementation of his proposals and claimed, on the evidence of von Oven's diaries, that the total war proposals had come to a standstill by September. Additional measures were taken after this period, and Goebbels also proceeded to inspect the armed forces' use of staff. Simplifications and freeing of staff continued during and after September. The only evidence Orlow provides of Party sabotage is that Bormann exempted Party leaders from being allocated to armaments work and that the Party Chancellery did not treat decrees as binding until they had Bormann's counter-signature. In general he argues that the Gauleiters continued to lack the will to impose hardships on the people.[24]

A final answer to the question of how effective Goebbels' measures were requires further widespread local studies. The local histories which were consulted give no indication that these decrees were being circumvented or that the Gauleiters were reluctant to impose hardships on the people. They depict, rather, a life increasingly oriented towards bare essentials. Reliance on the Gauleiters did lead to unevenness in the implementation of the measures.[25] Goebbels realised the weaknesses of the Party and the difficulties of controlling the Gauleiters in 1943; he gave them a role at least in part because his attempts to circumvent them had failed. He recognised that they might pose problems. But the main problem with the Gauleiters was their excessive zeal to implement the policies.

Semler observed that there was a considerable waste of manpower in the course of Goebbels' simplifications. Some staff freed found other administrative positions, while not all measures filtered down to the lower levels: Goebbels could not see beyond the numbers of staff released. Many armaments firms hesitated to give up their qualified staff and take up the replacements they were offered. The exchanges of staff did lead to breaches of production. Closures initially created considerable unemployment as staff were freed before they could be taken on by the armaments industry. The RAD leader, Hierl, believed this unemployment would continue because Speer refused to free uk men in armaments and equally refused to take up the new staff, presumably because this would weaken his stand against giving up existing staff. While there clearly was waste in the process of the closures, the unemployment Hierl highlighted indicates that the measures Goebbels ordered were adopted, but that there was a delay before the staff freed were absorbed by the armaments industry. The 'time lag' was not evidence of lack of action but of lack of planning and co-ordination of the measures. Similar unemployment arose when inessential activity was stopped in Britain.[26]

Salter has noted that by the time Goebbels was appointed, it was doubtful whether any fundamental reorganisation of labour policy was possible. It is difficult to assess how effective Goebbels' policies were and whether there were untapped labour resources. This difficulty arises partly because of the lack of reliable figures on the effects of his policies. There was some disagreement about the number of men encompassed in all the plans under way to gain staff. Goebbels fulfilled his promise to Hitler to send one million men to the front, albeit in five months and not in the three months he promised. Overall approximately one million men, previously uk, were sent to the front from August to December 1944. But from August to October 1944, however, German losses were 1,189,000 killed and wounded.[27] So these measures could not even maintain the numbers of the German armed forces, let alone create a reservoir of new staff.

When Goebbels began to implement the measures he had urged on Hitler for over a year, he did not find large numbers of fit men evading military service on the home front. Instead he was soon forced to call up uk men in armaments. This suggests that most of the men remaining in the economy without uk positions were not capable of military service, a suggestion borne out by the age structure of remaining male workers in administration. Some 70 per cent of men employed by the Justice Ministry were 50 years old or more. Figures prepared by the General Armed Forces Office of the OKW (Allgemeines Wehrmachtsamt or AWA), however, provide evidence for the continued belief that there were still more labour reserves to be exploited. Figures taken from the 1939 census suggested there were still 13,535,000 German men available for employment inside Germany on 30 September 1944. Of these some 7.4 million were of fitness gradings suitable for service, and 6.5 million of these men (87.84 per cent) were in uk positions. Of the 22,857,000 German women aged between 15 and 50, some 12,645,000 were employed (55.32 per cent of the women of this age group). Over 2 million women over 50 were also still employed. The total number of women in employment, however, was only 271,000 more in September 1944 than in May 1939. The percentage of women in the work force had risen from 37 to 47 per cent, but this increase mainly came from foreign workers. From 1939 to mid-1941, the report suggested, the employment of German women constantly declined, and then only gradually increased again later. 'Despite all the measures of the GBA' by the end of September 1944 only 500,000 women had been mobilised; 230,000 replaced older women leaving the workforce, and 270,000 were a net addition.[28] (Others had presumably moved in and out of the work force.)

Before the war foreign workers had been 0.8 per cent of the work force; by September 1944 they were 16.8 per cent of the work force, or 20.8 per cent if POWs were included. Agriculture relied heavily on foreigners (23 per cent) and women (59 per cent). The local female labour force in industry was much less. There were only 849,500 fewer German men employed in industry in September 1944 than May 1939; about half the German male industrial workforce in September 1944 occupied uk positions (2,657,800 out of 4,710,700). While 761,900 more women were employed in industry than in 1939, only 4500 of these were German. From 1 June 1943 to 31 May 1944, 102,600 German women left industry, while 52,300 were added as a result of the third extension of the Meldepflicht.[29]

The report also found that the reduction of staff in the administrative sector was less than expected; it was only 17 per cent less than in 1939. German men were now 46 per cent of those employed, compared with 68 per cent in 1939. Female employees had grown to 343,900, of whom 327,300 (95.17 per cent) were German. The AWA assumed, without providing corroborating evidence, that more women could still be employed in administration, armaments and the armed forces. The armaments sector, which included civilian employees of armaments, police and workers of the Speer ministry, employed 112 per cent more staff than in 1939, 47 per cent more men and 484,400 additional German men. Female employees of the Wehrmacht had increased by 468 per cent in total, of whom 506,900 out of 535,500 (94.65 per cent) were German. The police, who employed 110 per cent more German men than in 1939, still employed an 'astonishingly low' number of women.[30]

The AWA's claims that there were still potentially large reservoirs of German men and women who could be used for the war effort are problematic. The figures were drawn from the 1939 census and updated by reference to Labour Ministry records. In practice, however, Goebbels found that there were fewer fit men even in armaments than the AWA's figures would suggest. He either could not find or could not release most of the 7.4 million men still listed as fit for service.

Goebbels appears to have successfully ended any remaining less important economic activity, aided by the sense of urgency induced by the invasion and the attempt on Hitler's life. His reductions and simplifications seem to have pared German life on the home front down to the essentials and to have freed staff. Yet he was not able to free the numbers which both he and Speer believed possible in July 1944. The reservoir of staff they believed existed proved elusive.

If there was still a reservoir of fit Germans, then the AWA's figures suggest this was to be found in the female population, a group that German leaders had found difficult to use extensively. Other German statistical authorities disagreed with this assessment, with one suggesting that the mobilisation of women had largely been carried out. Here too Goebbels and

Speer had exaggerated expectations. Women's distribution in the work force made it difficult to increase their employment, especially in industry. Forty per cent of women in paid employment and 83.5 per cent of *mithelfende Familienangehoerigen*, family members helping in family businesses, were in German agriculture, from which they could not be spared. With the help of foreign labour, in wartime women handled most agricultural work. The reorganisation and modernisation of agriculture was in itself a massive task which could not have been undertaken in wartime. The category of domestic servants, which is often given as an example of German lack of seriousness about women's employment, is misleading. Of the 1.36 million domestic servants, an unknown number were effectively agricultural workers on farms. In other cases domestic servants freed women to continue small family businesses.[31]

Historians have disagreed about the extent to which the German government was able to make effective use of its labour force. While Overy and Siegel suggest that it did, Recker disagrees. Many historians have agreed with Speer's claims that Germany made insufficient use of women in the work force. These arguments rely on implicit and/or explicit comparison with the mobilisation of other countries, particularly the United Kingdom. Such studies emphasise the increase in the percentage of women employed. The proportion of women 14 and over in paid employment in Britain rose from 27 per cent in 1939 to 37 per cent in 1944; in the United States it rose from 26 per cent in 1939 to 32 per cent in 1944. In contrast, the German percentage of women employed only increased by one per cent during the war. However, Overy has pointed out that a greater percentage of women was employed than in either Britain or the United States. In Germany 47 per cent of women were employed, and German women were 51.1 per cent of the German civilian work force in 1944.[32] The percentage of women employed was only slightly less than in the Soviet Union, where there was a different ideology on the role of women and a historical pattern of greater tradition of women in heavy industry and the armed forces existed. Soviet women made up 53 per cent of the civilian labour force in 1942. Historically the percentage of German women in employment has been high. But the higher German figures partly reflect a different method of recording employment. Unlike other countries, the German census listed family members helping in family businesses as employed. These family members, predominantly women, were often not paid and were not counted as employed in the British census, for example. In both societies women's traditional role and domestic skills could be expected to become more important in wartime.

German figures and subsequent historical studies also give little indication of the situation of women not in paid employment. Some of them were engaged in voluntary work under the auspices of the Frauenschaft, the National Socialist welfare organisation (*Nationalsozialistische Volkswohlfahrt* or *NSV*) and the Red Cross, which helped the war effort: for example, women volunteers were used to adapt materials donated in the 1941 winter clothing campaign for use at the front. The overall number of volunteers is difficult to assess. The results of bombing also increased the demands on, and the need for, women's domestic skills. Women up to the age of 25 were largely involved in various forms of compulsory service, such as in the Reich labour service (Reichsarbeitsdienst or RAD), which were not statistically classified as employment; in practice this was a form of conscription equivalent to that experienced by women of the same age group in Britain. Bormann claimed the experience of earlier call-ups showed that women in these age groups were almost all employed in war work. Women aged 25 to 34 were mainly married with children; so the main untapped group was women over 35, an age where their productivity in armaments decreased.[33]

In addition, the rate of employment of German women was already so high that attempts to employ still more workers were hampered by invisible social and cultural barriers, a form of 'glass ceiling'—obstacles due to contemporary perceptions of the roles of women, their child rearing responsibilities, and so on. To employ more women might require a head-on assault on these beliefs. These perceptions were barriers both for the leadership and the population as a whole, and were not as apparent in those countries where fewer women had been employed in peacetime. Because comparatively few women had previously been employed, their employment could be raised substantially without encountering such barriers. This raises the question why there was so strong an impression in Germany among sections of the leadership and the population that insufficient numbers of women were employed. The lack of any dramatic visible increase in female employment may account for some of these perceptions. Class resentments, hostility to the regime and the distrust created by an atomised, totalitarian society also played a part, as can be seen in the continued popular belief, despite the statistical evidence, that it was overwhelmingly privileged women who were slacking.

•   •   •

Goebbels' attempts to reorganise the economy met opposition from the SS and resistance from Speer. Some of Himmler's advisers wanted the SS to take over Goebbels' recently acquired powers. The wartime Chief of the SS Main Office, Berger, suggested to Werner Naumann in August that there were no more labour reserves in Germany, except for women not in paid employment. The need for soldiers and military equipment had to be met through an increase in efficiency per hour and head. Rather than maintain the existing system of rings, armaments inspectors and various other layers of responsibility, a new productivity organisation of firms had to be set up, whose task would be to inspect all work processes from planning to dispatch and to judge the productive capacity of firms. This could be carried out only by technicians. Payments linked to productivity should be introduced. Berger proposed the establishment of a central office led by Himmler or a representative to liaise closely with Goebbels. Naumann's response is unrecorded but Goebbels probably opposed the proposals. Nothing further appears to have come of them. Separately, Ohlendorf unsuccessfully approached Speer with a proposal to create a super ministry, including food, agriculture, the economy, labour and armaments, with Speer as minister and Ohlendorf as secretary-general.[34] These moves may reflect SS hostility to the extent of Goebbels' new powers, or a belief that such powers would be better exercised by the SS.

Paradoxically, Goebbels' greatest opposition came from Speer, his ally in urging total war measures on Hitler. Indeed, Speer claimed to have urged Goebbels' appointment to Hitler because he believed he was 'the best man to put across austerity measures on the home front.'[35] Like Bormann Speer's initial response to Goebbels' appointment was positive. He reportedly promised Goebbels that he could equip 100 new divisions. He saw the total war policies as giving the armaments industry a one-off possibility to gain 1.3 million people: they had to take as many people as possible to build a cushion of staff for armaments against later call-ups. Speer noted that members of his ministry were often in a position to see possibilities of simplification in the economy and army which could not always be seen by other organisations. He therefore ordered Armaments Ministry officials to make personally at least one suggestion of organisational change to save workers by 10 August. In response to Speer's call, his ministry prepared suggestions in August to win additional workers. Proposals included the transfer of 30 per cent, or 450,000, of workers employed in domestic service to armaments; another combing-out action of the civilian sector; the dissolution of the RAD and transfer of its personnel to the Wehrmacht and armaments; employment of all female students (except those studying medicine, chemistry and technical subjects) and the current female matriculation-year students in armaments; an intensified drive to ensure evacuated women were employed; introduction of restrictions in public life so that unbombed towns operated under the same restrictions as bombed towns; only one daily postal delivery; immediate employment of men in air defence for armaments; no more tram conductors; combing out and restriction of customs; and other restrictions. Many of these measures were adopted by Goebbels. He wanted to reduce government administrative work overall by 30 per cent: the staff of the administration of the Armaments Ministry, its outside offices and the administration of firms involved in armaments production after 1 November were reduced by the same percentage. Goebbels in turn undertook that the firms' administrative work would be reduced by this amount.

Speer planned his own programmes to secure building workers. In August he set up a minimum building programme to secure all production necessary for the war, transport connections and fortifications works. About 60 per cent of current building capacity was required for its fulfilment. His decree of 28 June expressly stopped all building tasks not in this programme. The OT was too busy to pursue the shutting down of forbidden building tasks, and Speer asked Wegener of the Exekutivausschuss to use the Party to ensure that all building workers and equipment were used for the minimum building programme.[36]

He also used the total war simplifications to gain extra staff. In August Speer approached Goebbels with the request that the tens of thousands of theatre and film tradesmen released by his total war measures be employed in armaments. The need for workers led Speer to intervene with Goebbels concerning Sauckel's ban on the employment of Hungarian Jewish prisoners in Thuringia. This might lead to other Gauleiters introducing a similar ban. Of course, Speer told Goebbels, the employment of Jewish prisoners was also against his convictions, but under current conditions they had to resort to such an emergency measure. He therefore asked Goebbels to influence Sauckel to withdraw the ban.[37] Goebbels' response is not on record.

Speer set up his own programmes to free staff. He told Keitel on 11 August that he had four such programmes under way and could not, therefore, make 150,000 trained kv men of the 1901 class and later available to the armed forces in August from armaments. First, he would probably make the classes of 1918 to 1926 available from armaments. This would make declining coal production unavoidable. He would suggest to Hitler that this be accompanied by the four fighting forces also freeing men from the classes 1918 and younger for the front. Secondly, he would probably free from the armaments administration those of the classes 1910 to 1926 who were kv and not employed in technical positions; thirdly, he would probably make the classes of 1910 to 1926 available from less important production, such as textiles and glass. Fourthly, he was calling for industry leaders to give up uk positions voluntarily and would introduce a further exchange action with the commander of the replacement army. He stressed that Hitler had told him that at the moment the production of weapons, tanks and planes was more important than calling up men in uk positions, a view Guderian shared.[38]

In advice to Gauleiters on 11 August, Goebbels supported Speer's call to industry leaders to give the age groups 1918 to 1926 up voluntarily from armaments. He completely agreed with Speer that production of important weapons and armaments was at least as important as soldiers; Gauleiters were to avoid placing firm leaders under any kind of moral pressure to give up more uk positions. Firm leaders would decide how many workers were to be given up only when replacement workers actually arrived. In no cases were workers to be given up on the promise of replacements, and influence on the head of the firm was only to follow in agreement with the armaments offices.[39]

Speer protested at the refusal of Gauleiters to exempt armaments employees from the building of fortifications and digging of trenches, which Hitler had ordered on 1 September. He asked Bormann for a decision by Hitler whether securing the borders or equipping troops with weapons was more important. If these workers were not returned to the firms in eight days, then he would not accept responsibility for the consequences. The Gauleiters had to maintain production completely until the last minute. Speer experienced a partial victory when Bormann ordered their return on 20 September.[40]

But Goebbels came under pressure from Hitler to find more soldiers; this in turn led to greater demands on armaments. On 17 August, Goebbels had to advise Gauleiters that Hitler needed to create new fighting divisions from 165,000 kv men from the class of 1897 and later. Quotas were allocated for each defence district (*Wehrkreis*) and Gau to be completed by 1 September. Goebbels called on the Gauleiters to report any difficulties, but he hoped that simplifying measures would free sufficient men and women to exchange for the men to be given up. The quotas Goebbels set were needed to allow him to fulfil his commitments to Hitler. By the end of August Speer complained to Goebbels that the majority of Gauleiters were not keeping to the policy that staff should be given up voluntarily. Instead they were setting firms such high quotas that disruptions of production resulted. For example, in Hamburg a quota of 3400 men was set; in Schleswig-Holstein, 16,123; in Main-Franken, 50 per cent of all kv. Speer asked Goebbels to stress once again the voluntary nature of these quotas. His complaints suggest in fact that instead of being reluctant, as Orlow states, the Gauleiters were, as Goebbels predicted in his July 1944 memorandum, proving eager to vie with each other to deliver the most men for the armed forces. Armaments officers at the middle level experienced pressure from Gauleiters whose ambitions for the provisions of soldiers had been awakened.[41]

This issue led Speer to ask Klein, an official in Goebbels' office, on 1 September whether Goebbels wanted the quotas in the Gaus to be filled in every case. Klein confirmed that this was his impression, but all kinds of difficulties had arisen. Everywhere the heads of firms had declared their willingness to give up staff but were then not willing to sign the necessary written declarations. Where disruption in armaments production occurred, the men would be called back or replaced. On the whole the armaments industry would hardly need to be involved for September and October. Klein estimated that some 40 to 50 per cent of kv workers, or about 150,000 men, had been given up by the armaments industry. During the discussion Speer reiterated his opinion that call-ups could follow only with the written agreement of the head of the firm; Goebbels agreed with him on this, he claimed. Klein pointed out that in order to provide the promised 30 new divisions to the front, eventually some 60 per cent of uk positions in armaments would have to go.[42]

Speer and Goebbels clashed heatedly in a meeting about the calling up of uk positions from armaments at this time, and Goebbels forced Speer to deliver his share of a 300,000-man quota for call-up. This marked a significant breach between the two men. Goebbels complained afterwards of the reactionary nature of the armaments industry and commented that he would no longer defend Speer. In turn Speer appealed to Hitler to overturn the decision. Hitler called Goebbels to his headquarters. Both men expected Hitler to back Speer. Instead, Hitler and Bormann took Goebbels' side completely. Hitler decided he wanted both weapons and soldiers. By 1 September Goebbels had provided 300,000 men; Hitler decided he wanted a further 450,000 later that month.[43]

Speer now launched a series of protests at the repercussions of these policies. On 4 September he wrote to Goebbels noting that when Goebbels' position was created, they had agreed on the need to carry out the necessary measures together. Instead of calling up only kv men of the class of 1910 and later, as they agreed, he found that men from the classes of 1898 to 1905 had also been called up. Instead of the agreement that armaments and Party offices together would approach the firm leaders, in numerous Gaus Party offices had approached firm leaders on their own; in almost all cases psychological pressure had been placed on firm leaders to fill quotas. He refused to take responsibility for any resulting breaches in production. Speer warned that they would soon have more soldiers than weapons.[44]

On 5 September 1944 Speer told the Gauleiters that he would not accept responsibility for breaks in production due to the call-ups. He advised the armaments inspectors that the guidelines he and Goebbels set down were still in force and the call up of those uk positions given up would be carried out. It was the duty of the armaments office to resolve any disruption of outputs by finding replacements and transfers from other production. On 8 September this was followed by a telegram to all Gauleiters from Speer, Goebbels and Bormann, noting that the quotas called on for 1 September from Gaus by Hitler had been met, but various irreplaceable workers had been called up. These exceptional cases were to be inspected and to be resolved judiciously. This applied not only to production of weapons and materiel but also to the coal, mining, chemical and iron industries. Drawing on the reports of the chairmen of the armaments commission, the Gauleiters were to report the probable effects of the call-up on armaments. The Gau and Kreis commissions had to seek to prevent any breaks in production by producing replacements or returning those who were called up. If there was no agreement, then the decision of Goebbels, Speer and Bormann was to be sought. The telegram suggests that some of Speer's earlier complaints had been justified. The order stated that Hitler wanted both more soldiers and more weapons; this required a close and trusting collaboration between all responsible offices. It thus also placed a difficult choice before the Gauleiters. It concluded by calling on all Gauleiters to support securing all production important to the war.[45]

From this period on Speer was engaged in a continuing battle with Goebbels over the latter's plans to call up armaments workers. Goebbels' demands were a response to the German need for troops, due in part to the deteriorating military situation and heavy losses. From the beginning of the Normandy invasion to September 1944, the German armies in the west lost some 600,000 men. Goebbels was also responding to Hitler's demands: Speer as well as Goebbels had led Hitler to believe that he could make these demands without disrupting production. The Speer Chronik recorded that where Speer had previously fought for workers with Sauckel, he now struggled with Goebbels, who did not take armaments requirements into account. Goebbels had 'valuable allies' in Bormann and Keitel.[46] Bormann lacked any sympathy for Speer and believed that armaments, and surprisingly, railways and the post never made available the numbers requested. In September Speer told Goebbels that he was fundamentally prepared to make available all workers still expendable. He wanted to wait until the effects of previous call-ups were apparent, and suggested no further call-ups for the August quotas after 20 September to allow him to gain an overview of the overall numbers of those liable for military service (*Wehrpflichtigen*) in armaments. There were many troops on the Western front who did not have any weapons; there was no sense in providing more troops if they could not be completely equipped with heavy weapons. 'In this war, which is a technical war, a "levée en masse" is not decisive.'[47] Here Speer was directly jibing at Goebbels' plans for a levée en masse. These conflicts led to 'tension and irritation' on both sides.[48]

In July 1944 Speer had claimed that all men born between 1918 and 1926 could be called up without replacements, and suggested to Hitler that some 4.3 million men in the economy could be drawn on for the armed forces; in practice he objected to all Goebbels' attempts to reduce the staff at his disposal. Other leaders tended to ignore Speer's complaints and attribute them to a desire to protect his own power base. The lack of specific detail in his protests did not help his case. Rather than give evidence, he tried to rely on assertion and generalisation, and failed to convince. He would complain that skilled workers were being called up and valuable production affected, but his complaints were usually general, and he did not provide chapter and verse to back up his claims. Perhaps because he had been able to go his own way for so long as a result of Hitler's backing, he had not developed and 'sold' to other members of the leadership the concept of the technical requirements of armaments production. He had supported the Reich Industry Group's plans for Umschulung, the training of unskilled workers to take on skilled work, but he does not seem to have taken active steps to expand this programme or persuade other leaders of its usefulness. Instead he had concentrated on protecting those skilled workers he had rather than reducing his reliance on them. One of Speer's concerns was protecting his own area of responsibility and his power base. This may have been one motive for his later attempts to ensure that abandoned factories were disabled rather than destroyed; and it certainly motivated his consistent resistance in this period to attempts to reduce the staff at his disposal. He asked Goebbels to ensure that women employed in the armaments industry were exempted from any call-ups. He did not believe that the work of the Reich patent office could be dispensed with during the war, and therefore asked that its tasks be restricted to those of particular importance to the war. He requested that Goebbels abandon plans to form a committee to examine tax levying systems, since attempts to simplify this were already under way in the Economics Ministry and his own ministry.[49]

In a letter to Hitler of 20 September, Speer defended his ministry against allegations by Bormann and Goebbels that it was dominated by people hostile to the Party and by reactionary economic leaders. These comments may derive from Goebbels' criticisms earlier that month. It was significant that such allegations re-emerged at this time. They may have been prompted by indications that industry was beginning to prepare for the post-war world and by the frustrations of the Nazi Party seeing its own authority disappearing with the regime. In fact, 'contrary to Party suspicions, Speer's relationship with industry was deteriorating.'[50] He now faced open disobedience of his orders and less co-operation from industry leaders who were no longer willing to exert themselves for the regime. Speer pointed out that he had set up the self-responsibility of industry system on Hitler's advice and claimed that he saw his task as seeking to prevent any conflict between that system and the Party. Hitler handed the letter to Bormann, who told Speer he was subordinate to Goebbels. Speer was able, nonetheless, to obtain a notice from Hitler commending German industry leaders for the increase in production in August and stating that the self-responsibility of industry had once again proved itself to be the best. Speer claimed that this would normally have represented a victory for him but that Hitler's authority in the Party was waning, 'the first clear signs of disintegration.'[51] Bormann advised Gauleiters that there were ways around a decree from Hitler ordering Gau economic advisers not to interfere in the process of armaments production. This was further evidence that Hitler's charismatic authority was being steadily weakened by military failure.

Speer continued to lose support on issues related to the call-up of staff for the armed forces. Hitler was advised by Goebbels' Planungsausschuss that Himmler and Keitel had ordered the release of 250,000 kv men as the September quota of the military replacement plan (*Wehrersatzplan*). Armaments, which still had some 1.2 million men in the classes of 1901 and later, had to give up 100,000. Speer had recognised that the distribution was correct but would agree only if Hitler ordered that the armaments economy had to free the men without regard to any production consequences. Asked by Bormann, Keitel, Himmler and Klein of the Planungsausschuss, leading industrialists believed they could bear the required demands. Speer also did not get the support he expected from industrialists at a meeting in late August. Most considered that the giving up of uk positions was acceptable and were more concerned that the inclusion of the Party meant they faced dual lines of command. Speer also reprimanded Gauleiters who assumed that because their armaments industry could give up workers, the rest of the Reich could.[52]

Since Speer would not agree with the call-up of 250,000 kv men, Bormann, Speer and Klein asked the Gauleiters' opinions. The overwhelming majority of Gauleiters, predictably, declared that armaments could still give up kv workers. Hitler was asked for his view. Speer's own submission argued that the proposed call-ups would damage armaments, since the current call-up action had not yet finished and he needed some three to four months before a new action could be contemplated. Men in uk positions could be called up again after 25 October, because by then the new staff would be trained in their work. Each premature call-up lessened the possibility of training new workers. By 25 October armaments could make 60,000 men free for the call up, of whom 5000 students and 16,000 men from the armed forces working on a ticket-of-leave system—*Rüstungsurlauber*—could come some 14 days earlier. Some further 40,000 uk workers could be called on 15 November.[53]

On 1 October Bormann, who had become increasingly involved in the termination of uk positions, claimed that armaments firms were not satisfactorily absorbing those workers newly available as a result of the various total war measures. This could either be because they were saturated with staff or because of a false estimate of the call-ups from the armaments industry in the next months. Janssen suggests that this confusion arose because Goebbels and Bormann calculated the number of staff received by armaments on the basis of the targets set, while Speer and the armaments industry calculated on the basis of the numbers which actually arrived. The industry leaders had to face the possibility that by the end of the year, with the exception of a few irreplaceable workers, they would lose all kv men from the classes 1906 and younger. A number of measures were necessary to overcome any bottlenecks—the firms had to train workers as soon as possible; workers who could not immediately be employed should be given a standby certificate (*Bereitstellungsschein*).[54] In this dispute the Gauleiters' failure to support Speer was not surprising; the industrialists' failure to support him was both surprising and damaging. If Goebbels' call-up measures undoubtedly did disrupt production at times, some of Speer's claims about the effects may also have been exaggerated.

On his return from a journey in the West, Speer learnt that Hitler agreed, reportedly at Bormann's instigation, that the 60,000 uk workers were to be given up on 14 and not 25 October. Speer objected and repeated that he could not be held responsible if the call-ups could not be carried out. Speer also turned to Guderian and Göring in his efforts to have this decision overturned. Since 20 July, he argued, he had given up 50,000 men voluntarily, 150,000 men through Goebbels' action largely without his agreement, a further

60,000 men at Hitler's orders and a planned further 80,000 men in November—a total of 340,000 in uk positions. These would lead to severe consequences for production. Speer also objected to Hitler that his decision was extraordinarily serious and drastic. He had already pointed out on 26 September and 2 October that he could no longer take responsibility for unrestricted implementation of armaments policy if these measures were carried out. The proposed changes would interrupt production. He again asked Hitler to decide which was more important—soldiers or weapons. Goebbels later blamed Speer for delaying the freeing of such workers and thereby weakening the front at critical times.[55]

Despite Speer's complaints that production was being endangered, in November Hitler placed several programmes under total protection from call-up—shipyards, anti-aircraft, munitions, infantry and fighter production. But Speer lost ground on other issues. In the same month he had to agree to the co-responsibility of Gauleiters and Gau economic advisers in the production of armaments.[56]

Speer also had to defend himself against charges he was not using labour effectively. The Berlin Gau alleged that the armaments sector was not using workers becoming available—only 4000 of the 120,000 people freed in Berlin through total war measures had been employed. Speer countered by pointing out that since the beginning of measures for total war, armaments production had employed 30,000 in Berlin, 4000 of whom came from the Meldepflicht action (women 45 to 50). The rest came from other measures—closing theatres, putting restrictions on various authorities. That week 3000 were employed from the Meldepflicht action, 6000 from other total war measures. A further 42,000 workers could be expected in Berlin: 10,000 from cutting back on government authorities and other total war measures, 24,000 from the 30 per cent restriction of administration of armaments firms, 3000 from the combing out of domestic servants, 5000 from students and schools. These would continuously become available in the next eight weeks. Once they had lost their previous jobs they would be transferred to the armaments industry within 24 hours.[57]

Speer was following a restrictive policy on the evacuation of industry. In making arrangements for the fate of industry in areas under threat of enemy occupation, he ordered that only the most urgent production be evacuated. He wanted only those industries having more than 50 per cent of the total Reich production in the affected area to be evacuated.[58] When in 1945 Speer opposed the 'scorched earth' policies of Hitler and claimed that the war was lost once key industrial border areas were lost, his own earlier decisions partly added to the speed of the German collapse. Germany's economic vulnerability because of the concentration of industry in the Ruhr and Silesia was well known. Speer's concentration on short-term gains prevented any repetition by Germany, however small scale, of the Soviet evacuation of industry in 1941.

Some of the alleged disruption of armaments production may have been due to factors other than the call-ups of uk staff. German armaments production began to decline unevenly in this period, with munitions production being among the first to drop off in September 1944. Milward has suggested that Goebbels' call-ups of skilled workers was one reason; others were shortages of raw materials caused by bombing, losses of territory and Speer and Hitler's more frequent disagreements on policy. More recently, Mierzejewski's research suggests that bombing of transportation links in the Ruhr in September and October was beginning to undermine the Reich economy. 'By late October 1944 the bombing of marshalling yards and the cutting of the Ruhr waterways had caused a severe reduction in Germany's coal supplies, substantially reduced iron and steel output, forced a slight contraction of armaments production but not of key weapons, and gravely hindered the exchange of goods within the economy and the delivery of weapons to the Wehrmacht.'[59] Only those at the highest levels of the economic ministries were aware of the developing crisis.

Speer objected to Goebbels' policies as plenipotentiary strongly and frequently, but this very frequency demonstrated the extent to which he was losing ground. By October Speer described his position as extremely weak. He was criticised for the losses of production due to his earlier decisions to transfer production to France and other occupied territories. Speer claimed that armaments production was usually higher than American production. His claims for German production, particularly of aircraft, were not believed since—because of the transport problems—there were no signs of this production arriving at the front. (His claims were exaggerated.) Reports that large industrial firms were already transferring to peacetime production also did not help his position. Bormann clearly suspected Speer's future plans and described him as seeking to take away the few remaining responsibilities of the Economics Ministry. Bormann saw Speer as allying himself with Göring against Goebbels and himself. Goebbels noted that Bormann, Himmler and all the Gauleiters opposed Speer. Homze claims that Bormann and Goebbels opposed Speer's desire to divide the Reich into seven or eight armaments commands staffed by businessmen under Speer.[60]

Speer and Goebbels had been long-standing allies in their moves to adopt total war. Speer had urged that Goebbels be given such powers and that staff should be cut back ruthlessly, but once Goebbels made use of these powers he objected. Indeed he claimed after the war that Goebbels came out openly as his enemy after the appointment.[61] Speer had much less success in defending his position against Goebbels in his role as plenipotentiary than against any other earlier moves to reduce staff or interfere in production. In fact, Speer's relations with Hitler seem to have worsened once he fell out with Goebbels and no longer had the latter's protection or support. This raises the interesting question of whether Goebbels' support had been important for Speer's earlier position of strength. Alternatively Goebbels' abilities may now have been more important to Hitler than Speer's. Hitler may have felt that Goebbels' skills as a propagandist were needed to mobilise the population and convince them of the need for increasingly harsh measures.

Some of the clashes between Speer and Goebbels were inevitable: both more weapons and more soldiers were needed. Speer later wrote that Hitler sought to mediate between him and Goebbels by first deciding in favour of one and then the other. Hitler could not decide since he wanted, and needed, both. Pressures on the two men came partly as a result of the exaggerated expectations they themselves had created. Speer's frequent assurances that he could supply weapons for the various new levies contributed to Goebbels' demands. In view of these promises, Speer's later objections were assumed to reflect a desire to keep staff in his own area rather than actual conditions. Despite the justification for at least some of his objections, Speer was also defending the basis of his power—factories and the men and women staffing them—from reduction in size. The armaments industry had previously gained staff when other offices lost theirs.[62] In 1944 it too had to lose staff, and Speer accepted this unwillingly.

Goebbels achieved greater simplifications and rationalisations. His task was made easier by the shock of the invasion and the attempt on Hitler's life, making the need for such measures obvious to even the most recalcitrant or obtuse. Earlier rounds of simplification, and the effects of bombing, made later more drastic simplifications possible. But at the same time the problems facing the various Gaus became more diverse, and implementing a unified policy became more and more difficult. Industry was preparing for a non-National Socialist future, which did not help the cause of increasing arms production. The regime's response to the attempt on Hitler's life had been to seek to mobilise the entire nation. Two means had been used for this— Goebbels was employed to mobilise the forces of the economy and labour while Bormann and Himmler were to mobilise the 'nation in arms' in the Volkssturm. The latter concept came to predominate in the regime's last four months of existence in 1945.

9

'A Nation in Arms'? (1945)

In the first few months of 1945, efforts were made to mobilise the entire German nation to resist the invaders. Policies were still pursued to win more men for the battlefield, to convey more workers to the armaments factories and to maintain armaments production as long as possible. These measures could no longer win the war, but they did prolong the life of the regime and therefore of some of its leaders. Even at this late stage there was disagreement about the policies to be adopted, but an overall trend of radicalisation can be detected. Hitler's authority weakened and disintegrated under the impact of impending defeat and his reluctance to intervene in day-to-day administration.

The Germans' Ardennes offensive had stopped by the end of December 1944, and its failure had removed any last hopes of staving off defeat. At the beginning of January 1945, the Germans still held most of their gains from this offensive, and Speer claimed that Hitler and Bormann were still optimistic about the outcome of the war. On 12 January a new Soviet offensive began in the East; despite fierce German resistance, Soviet forces reached the Oder and Neisse rivers by the beginning of February. What little civilian life remained was decisively interrupted to send all men possible to the front. In the west the Germans were defending the Rhine; on 7 March an American unit crossed the Rhine at Remagen and American forces headed for central Germany. As Allied troops approached, anti-fascist groups prepared to take over from the Nazis in some cities and towns. Soviet armies began their final attack on Berlin on 16 April. By 22 April fierce street fighting was taking place in the capital. Hitler committed suicide on 30 April, and his successor as President, Admiral Dönitz, surrendered on 7 May. At the time of Germany's surrender, German forces still held isolated pockets in northern and southern Germany.[1]

Before final defeat, some National Socialists had still hoped for a salvation by secret weapons. Speer disingenuously disclaimed responsibility for this propaganda. Others still hoped for an improvement in Germany's position by diplomatic and political means, perhaps through a collapse of the enemy alliance. Attempts were made to contact both Britain and the Soviet Union for peace negotiations, but the regime had nothing to offer its enemies. Goebbels and Himmler still hoped changes in the German leadership would help the regime's chances. They agreed on the need to dismiss Göring and Ribbentrop, but Himmler could not see how Hitler could be persuaded to do this. Goebbels was toying with a reconstruction of the cabinet with himself as Chancellor and Foreign Minister, Himmler as head of the armed forces and Bormann as minister for the Party. The SS continued to try to make military use of Vlasov and his supporters. Himmler considered, too late, that the Vlasov movement was of great importance to Germany.[2]

Himmler himself had been unsuccessfully used by Hitler as a military commander. Hitler had appointed him commander of the Army Group Weichsel (Vistula) on 21 January 1945, to close gaps existing in the Eastern front between the Army Groups A and Centre, to prevent a breakthrough of the enemy in the direction of Danzig and Posen, to secure the deployment of new workers and to organise national defence behind the whole Eastern front. Hitler's trust in Himmler may have prompted this appointment. Himmler described this as 'perhaps the most difficult task of my life up to now,' and his life as 'at present unpleasant.'[3] He had earlier unsuccessfully commanded the Army Group Upper Rhine and proved ill-suited to his new position. He had to be replaced by General Heinrici on 22 March: this weakened Himmler's overall position. He had also been succeeded as head of army armaments by General Buhle in January 1945, because his deputy, SS-Obergruppenführer Jüttner, kept interfering with the system of self-responsibility of industry. When Hitler heard of this, he had Himmler removed. Speer commented that the atmosphere of general indifference in Hitler's headquarters was such that this did not excite much interest.

From the beginning of 1945 intensified bombing made all aspects of administration and defence more difficult and further depressed public morale, particularly in the west. The leaders recognised these effects of the air war but were powerless to prevent them, a refrain which is constant in

Goebbels' *Final Entries*. The SD, on the whole, judged the popular attitude to be particularly good. 'This time the home front cannot be accused of a collapse.'[4] Despite depressed morale and signs of dissolution in the armed forces, they kept fighting and the population remained obedient, partly bound to the regime by fear of the advancing Soviet forces and of their likely treatment by the enemy. RPÄ reports suggested that the working class was the most in favour of radical measures to pursue the war. The regime's control over the population faltered only at the end of the war, in April, when there were some protests at food shortages and some local attempts to organise surrenders.

Germany's rapid military decline created new demands on the leadership and the bureaucracy. Millions of refugees fled the advancing Soviet forces. The need to reconquer lost territory, withstand new attacks, cope with the influx of refugees from border territories and protect the population complicated the pursuit of administration and other policies in 1945. Central co-ordination of the administration became more and more difficult: Rebentisch has suggested that Bormann, for example, increased his instructions to the Party at the same time as they became harder to implement.[5] Gaus and regions faced differing problems and pressures, and the capacity and will to implement central directives varied greatly. Nonetheless, despite the progressive disintegration of the country, the apparatus of government and military defence continued, more or less effectively and with bureaucratic rationality, until the end.

Meetings of the state secretaries were held in Berlin to co-ordinate administrative matters and respond to the problems of the refugees. This co-ordination was particularly necessary in the light of the increasing geographic dispersal of the leaders and evacuation of ministries. In January schools in Gaus designated to receive refugees were closed to make room for them. Only political schools were excepted. The state secretaries planned to withdraw the classes of 1929 and 1930 from areas threatened by the enemy, and to collect the class of 1929 in training camps. Speer promised to use all means to maintain railway travel. Two million workers were to be used, and thousands of men continuously stationed in the junctions to re-create shunting or marshalling stations. It was agreed that the priority for transport was first operational transport for the armed forces, including fuel, second coal, third food, fourth armaments and fifth refugees. Hitler was to uphold this order so that the Gauleiters, who independently often put refugees first, were bound by this. An attempt by Gauleiter Hofer of the Tyrol to seek exemption from the evacuations was rejected by Himmler, who pointed out that the need of other areas of the Reich was much greater.[6]

The leadership initially followed a restrictive policy on the evacuation of civilians and organisations, probably to stop panic and defeatism. In February Lammers issued a decree banning the evacuation of central offices from Berlin without Hitler's approval. This ban was subsequently extended to middle and lower offices. Goebbels also favoured a policy where the removal of Wehrmacht and civilian offices from the East occurred only with express approval. The capital was not to be seen as threatened, because 'the Oder position must be held under all circumstances,' Bormann advised in February.[7] By then the prospect of evacuating a million people to the east of the Rhine was also investigated. On 23 March Hitler agreed to evacuate the population 10 to 20 kilometres behind the battle area of Army Group West. The first priority was to move 14- to 17-year-olds and all those available for military service. He ordered areas whose occupation by the enemy was anticipated to be evacuated; he made it the duty of the Gauleiters to secure this. Although seemingly impossible, the rescue of citizens had to be coped with, Bormann advised. In practice these instructions were increasingly ignored because they could not be followed.

As late as 18 April the question of evacuations from Berlin was still being discussed at a meeting of state secretaries. They suggested to Hitler that some 500,000 women and children could still be evacuated to Mecklenburg. It was also decided that the suggestion of setting up a Reich fortress Tyrol (*Reichsfestung Tyrol*), as suggested by its Gauleiter Hofer, would have a purpose only if the feeding of the troops and inhabitants was secured. The Armaments Ministry was to inspect the area with a view to setting up production for infantry munitions and anti-tank weapons (*Panzerfäuste*).[8]

More men were urgently needed by the armed forces and the armaments industry. As a result pressures on labour continued in 1945. In January Berger still proposed to Himmler creating a central office to govern the total employment of German men, which would have decentralised offices so that in every area there was both a defence and work office. Berger supported Speer's claim that weapons rather than men were needed. In January 1945, despite Speer's objections, Hitler decided that from January to March 80,000 uk men would be called up a month. Goebbels inspected Luftwaffe installations and proposed far-reaching reductions in the size of the Luftwaffe, while Himmler ordered all available SS leaders report to the army or the Waffen-SS. On 1 February Bormann issued a circular on legal sanctions to ensure inspections of the armed forces, Waffen-SS and police in the home front. He pointed to a 26 January decree on securing the front which threatened the strongest punishment if such inspections were sabotaged. In April, the armed forces' replacement office (*Wehrersatzamt*) concluded that, from 3 January to 27 March, a total of 330,632 men had been provided to the armed forces as a result of Goebbels' call-ups, the widened call-ups of armaments workers, and calling up of the classes 1884 to 1896 and 1926 to 1928.[9]

The disputes about priority for troops or industrial production grew even more heated as pressure on limited staff became greater. In January Speer was still protecting armaments firms from attempts by Gauleiters to call up those liable for military service of the classes 1900 and earlier to relieve youths of the class of 1928 helping in anti-aircraft batteries. This measure had not been discussed with Speer, who had to oppose it. He could not agree to give up staff over and above the special call-up programme under way on Hitler's orders (*SE Vi-Aktion*). He asked Goebbels only to order the removal of staff from the war economy once it had been discussed with him and his armaments offices. In February he told Goebbels that he could not meet his request to make a further 20,000 kv men free from the OT to the army. The OT had already given up some 25,000 men to the front and had only 55,000 kv men liable for military service of the classes 1901 and later left, of whom 15,000 were being given up in the SE Vi-Aktion. A further 10,500 were already in the army or Volkssturm in the Eastern Gaus. He only had 30,000 remaining, of whom many were building fortifications and could not be freed, according to Bormann. On the same day Speer took issue with Goebbels' assumption that the armaments sector had fulfilled only one third of its January rate for call-up action.[10]

In October 1944 Hitler had ordered the creation of the Front-OT, 25,000 young fit members of the OT used for building tasks. They could not be given up and they should therefore be left out of his rate in future calculations of quotas, Speer contended. Himmler inspected the organisation and administrative basis of the OT to suggest measures to free men for the front. The first result suggested that some 20,000 men could be saved.[11]

Speer again defended himself again from allegations that the Armaments Ministry had not been willing to give up staff in a meeting with Naumann in February. They agreed that the ministry had fulfilled its duty and call-up itself was a matter for the armed forces' recruiting offices (Wehrersatzdienststellen). They differed on the question of whether Volkssturm men should be seizable. In a subsequent circular Bormann advised the Gauleiters that call-ups from armaments had in all circumstances to be carried out with the agreement of the armaments offices. A letter from Bormann, Goebbels and Speer to the Gauleiters on 31 January noted that Hitler had ordered the raising of 240,000 kv men from the armaments industry of the classes 1901 and later, but had also particularly protected emergency weapons programmes from these measures. Gauleiters were asked to co-operate to implement both orders. The armaments offices on their own responsibility would name those to fulfil the quota. The Gau and Kreis commissions were to support the recruiting offices and postpone call-up if possible.[12]

The need for more troops was pressing. The old and the young were called up: men aged up to 59 (class of 1886) and 6000 16-year-olds (class of 1929). Desertion increased and was one sign of disintegration in the armed forces. Bormann pointed out that while the regime offered 15-year-olds and women to strengthen the front, some 500,000 to 600,000 soldiers were in the Reich on leave passes given out too easily. This problem had to be tackled with particular severity. Bormann responded by issuing an order in March which made every citizen responsible for seizing deserters and called for deserters to be eradicated ruthlessly. Scattered Wehrmacht personnel who had lost contact with their units were also to be seized quickly. Keitel issued an attached order to restrict travel and leave for members of the Wehrmacht. This problem also concerned other members of the leadership.[13]

The situation was so desperate that Hitler agreed to set up a women's battalion 'on probation.'[14] The women should be trained as soon as possible in connection with the Reichsfrauenführung. If this women's battalion proved itself, then others would be set up immediately. Hitler expected a decided repercussion on male attitudes and morale. This plan and others for female participation in the Wehrmacht were never realised. Hitler also agreed to equip women with hand weapons for personal protection. Yet his attitude to increased use of women in the armed forces wavered. Despite his plans to train a women's battalion, in March he decided the first priority was securing the protection of women employed by the armed forces. Army group commanders had to evacuate in good time all women not directly necessary for maintaining action readiness. In general, with the exception of the volunteer flak batteries, women could not be called on to work firing weapons in battle. Those who conveyed orders to the fighting troops or serviced equipment were to be treated as combatants. On the other hand women aged up to 55 were used to build fortifications and dig trenches in some areas and were used in the 'Werewolf' resistance and other Party-organised measures of resistance.

Bormann sought to ensure greater Party control over military policy and decisions. The Gauleiters were responsible for constructing fortifications and defensive lines, which were built up with great effort, particularly the Westwall and those in the Eastern Gaus. Yet they were quickly overrun and contributed little or nothing to defence. The manpower to occupy the positions was not available in the East. Hitler therefore decided that in future all resources would be used at the focal points to build positions to the necessary depth. All available units and weapons were to be employed only in these defence lines. It was the Gauleiters' task to motivate those building the fortifications and to do everything to place the newly built positions into a condition capable of defence. Speer had earlier recommended use of the Party to ensure supply of materials in the front line.[15]

Even greater reliance was placed on the employment of ideological indoctrination as a means of strengthening resistance and attaining victory. The surviving Party Chancellery files of this period indicate that considerable attention was paid to greater use of the NSFOs. Yet there was still concern from Himmler and the Party Chancellery that they should not seem like political commissars. In March Bormann made political activation and fanaticising the troops the most urgent task of troop leaders. He wanted German propaganda considerably strengthened. The Wehrmacht had to speak to the people frequently. A Party Chancellery official, Noack, suggested that NSFOs fall back on the proven propaganda methods of the Kampfzeit.[16]

On 10 April Walkenhorst, a Party Chancellery official, reported that National Socialist leadership work in the armed forces had come to a complete stop because Hitler's order of 13 March had been held up. This order granted Bormann a decisive influence in political leadership in the Wehrmacht, dissolved General Reinecke's National Socialist leadership staff and replaced it by a National Socialist leadership staff led by Bormann. Party Chancellery officials considered General Reinecke to have failed and wanted to be able to give fundamental orders about political education and leadership to the Wehrmacht. Bormann himself suggested a direct role for the Party Chancellery in February. He rejected a suggestion that Reinecke be replaced by General von Hauenschild, and commented that Himmler could not take it over since Hitler opposed giving Himmler more tasks.[17]

These plans came to nothing because various opposing, but unidentified, streams in Hitler's headquarters—presumably the military staff—proved stronger than the Party Chancellery. A decree by Hitler authorising the change drawn up on 13 March had still not been signed by 29 March. The result was an uneasy interregnum in which Reinecke no longer had responsibility yet the Party Chancellery could not act as the centre of command. Bormann's response to calls by his officials to clarify matters was to 'let the matter be.'[18] In view of the various enemy breakthroughs, it would be foolish for them to occupy themselves with organisational changes. All men should now be in action. The change in Bormann's attitude from February to late

March suggests that at first in February he may not have fully faced the seriousness of Germany's situation.

In the eyes of the leadership, Party leaders had a crucial role in areas under military threat. Party leaders were urged to carry out their orders with determination and to ensure they were obeyed quickly and without contradiction by offices under them. Bormann also pointed to their duty to provide higher offices with a clear knowledge of the situation. The closest collaboration between the Party and Wehrmacht was necessary to lift the people to the final struggle. Bormann concluded that, as in 'the struggle and time of need that was 1932,' the Party had to be the 'unbreakable backbone and the engine of our war leadership which drives everything forwards.'[19]

Bormann told Gauleiters that Hitler expected them to master the situation in their Gaus 'with lightning speed and utmost hardness.'[20] All political leaders who had led the population back in refugee treks were given until 20 February to report to the responsible Kreis office. If not they would be treated as deserters. In February Bormann reminded Party leaders that the current situation required exemplary leadership and unconditional trust. Hitler expected that every Party leader place his personal ego in the background and live for his leadership tasks. All who abandoned others for their families, sought to distance themselves from the Party or did not fight to the last were to be expelled from the NSDAP. In March Bormann repeated his call for Party leaders to conduct themselves so that their 'courage and energy' gave an example to Party comrades.[21] Political leaders had to fight or fall in their Gaus. They were not directed to stay behind to direct resistance. These instructions illustrated Bormann's and Hitler's unpreparedness to contemplate behind-the-lines resistance; repeated with threats of punishment, they were prompted by increasing evidence that while the administration and armed forces may have possessed the discipline to keep at their posts as the situation worsened, the Party leadership, particularly at the level of Gauleiters, did not. The highest levels of the leadership were aware of this and apparently had no explanation for it. The Party as well as the armed forces had 'crumbled.'[22] Goebbels commented, 'in the great days they [old fighters and their wives] ... played popular leader and mother of the country, but now they long to be back in their cheese shops or plumbing establishments.'[23]

The failure of Party and civilian offices, particularly in the East, to withstand the 'evacuation psychosis,' which allegedly led to many areas being evacuated without being defended, led to a proposal to use political leaders in endangered western and eastern Gaus to mobilise and employ all manpower and materiel for resistance. Bormann accepted these suggestions and sent NSFOs to weak areas of the front to shore up resistance. Berger was critical of this policy. He suggested that Himmler be informed that with the current mood at the front, such political commanders in Party uniform would be killed. (Bormann refused to believe in the increasing public hostility to the Party.) The policy also involved sending Party leaders to army personnel offices and the offices of military district commanders, but it proved to be unsuccessful. In practice the SS and not the Party increasingly fulfilled the role of ensuring that resistance continued under all conditions. Himmler pointed out to a Higher SS and Police Leader that he would have SS leaders shot for failures in this regard.[24]

Previously Germany's leaders had not devoted attention to preparing for resistance behind the lines; it seemed defeatist to anticipate such an eventuality. Waging total war now required consideration of such issues. Earlier reluctance to contemplate such policies meant that the outcome of planning at this stage was not particularly successful. In January 1945 a Kreisleiter Dotzler prepared suggestions for the creation of a resistance movement in the Eastern territories occupied by the Bolsheviks. Bormann considered the paper worth reading and passed it to Himmler. Himmler considered that some unspecified suggestions by Dotzler were practicable and instructed SS-Obergruppenführer Prützmann, leader of the Werewolf resistance organisation, to discuss his special task with Bormann. Although Dotzler hoped to encourage sabotage behind the lines, the OKW was aware that Germans behind Soviet lines did not resist. A paper on conditions behind the lines stated that the only sabotage, and the greatest help to German fighters behind the lines came from Poles.[25]

The war situation forced the Germans to exhaust all possibilities to reduce enemy strength, Bormann told Party leaders in March. This could be achieved by striking at the enemy's supply lines, destroying camps and communication links, and reporting military developments behind enemy lines. Only determined and courageous men and women were suitable for these tactics. The Gauleiters were to deputise reliable Party activists to select people for these tasks and to report their names to the responsible HSSPF with the catchword 'Werewolf.' The enemy had to be taught that it had no weapon against the secret war of the Werewolf, Bormann claimed.[26]

The extent to which the Werewolf organisation, which was intended to fight a guerilla war behind enemy lines, seriously functioned as such is doubtful. Goebbels certainly hoped it would encourage resistance among the German population itself and devoted considerable effort to guiding its activities so that it was led with 'spirit and enthusiasm.'[27] Goebbels also wanted to radicalise the conduct of the war further by withdrawing from the

Geneva Convention, but Hitler was persuaded by Keitel, Himmler, Bormann and Speer not to agree. Goebbels' comment on Speer's and Bormann's attitude was that it was 'semi-bourgeois. Their thinking may be revolutionary but they do not act that way.'[28]

The Volkssturm had not been trained to engage in partisan warfare, even though Himmler had pointed out the need for such training in 1944. Use of the Volkssturm continued to be urged, as a military means of gaining additional troops, as a response to perceived defeatism of regular army officers and as a political means of making the struggle more all-encompassing. All men participated in the Volkssturm in case of a threat close to home. Until then they were not to be withdrawn from important civilian activities. Volkssturm units were to be employed in the face of a direct enemy threat, rather than used as an additional reserve to be exhausted. In particular the Volkssturm was not intended to interfere with the production of the emergency armaments programme (*Rüstungsnotprogramm*). The call-up of specialists employed in the armaments emergency programme could only follow by arrangement with the chairman of the armaments commissions. But it did create considerable difficulties for production.[29]

In practice there were a number of difficulties in making effective use of the Volkssturm. Despite Speer's promises, the Volkssturm was short of weapons and this was a key problem. This meant that units not immediately in action had all their weapons except the Panzerfaust taken from them. Inadequate training in the use of weapons and poor selection of officers rendered the Volkssturm militarily ineffective in some areas. There was some justification to Party claims that the army did not understand how to use the Volkssturm in a people's war: Major General Kissel believed that it should be used only where the Wehrmacht units were too weak. A reluctance to admit that training in guerilla warfare tactics might be necessary, because it admitted the possibility of defeat, helped contribute to the Volkssturm's problems.[30]

The Volkssturm was also hampered by a lack of public support. Germany did have the experience of the war of liberation of 1813 as an apparent model of a popular uprising against an invader, and the leadership attempted to use this to encourage the population. But both the German military and civilians saw fighting as a task for professional armies. The public's lack of support reflected the absence of a commitment to the idea of the citizen soldier or the partisan fighter. Instead citizens saw waging war as the business of the professional military and use of the Volkssturm as militarily pointless. These attitudes in themselves lessened its effectiveness. They are also reflected in more recent German studies of the Volkssturm. The Volkssturm is more readily judged as militarily futile than either the British Home Guard or the Soviet partisans.[31]

A combination of the effects of bombing and the fear of Soviet occupation in the east meant that the Volkssturm fought considerably better in the east than the west. The Volkssturm's younger members were more committed to their tasks than the older men. The effects of the bombing were largely responsible for the absence of serious resistance in the west once the formal military and governmental apparatus had been removed, as members of the leadership recognised. The regime's reluctance to make use of women in a military capacity prevented it from exploiting some committed supporters who were willing to fight.[32]

War weariness helped to dash the hopes placed on the Volkssturm. Instances of corruption and a 'sauve qui peut' mentality among Party leaders, who often failed to participate in Volkssturm service and training, lessened the chances of calls to a nation in arms being successful. Because of its role in the creation and organisation of the Volkssturm, the Party itself must share responsibility for these failings. Bormann appears to have emphasised political education and reliability at the expense of its military role.

The Volkssturm, the hopes Goebbels and Himmler pinned on a defence of Berlin similar to the defence of Moscow in 1941[33] and attempts to set up partisan movements proved to be of only limited success. The Party's approach appears to have been modelled on its experiences of the struggle for power in the Kampfzeit. Agitation, political education and holding firm were seen as the basis of successful resistance rather than planning to set up an underground network if conquered or making serious preparations for guerilla warfare. Some members of the leadership looked at the Soviet Union's recovery from its losses in 1941 and believed that similar measures could work in Germany. But unlike the Communist Party of the Soviet Union, neither the Nazi Party cadres nor the army had the necessary background in theory or practice to organise such a defence.

• • •

Armaments production in January 1945 was still higher than the yearly average for 1943, although production had completely collapsed in some areas of the Reich. Berlin had become the Reich's armaments centre. Territorial losses and raw material shortages were adversely affecting production. Stepped-up Allied bombing campaigns against transportation routes and waterways increased pressure on rail links in the Ruhr from November 1944 to January 1945. Speer had to set aside large numbers of workers to repair rail links. The results were large drops in hard coal production (down 40 per cent in November and December 1944 and 48 per cent in January 1945), drops in armaments production and an inability to transport what was produced. By February rail traffic and economic production in the Ruhr had collapsed. Speer's efforts to counter these problems were hampered by some business leaders' hoarding of resources for the post-war period. In other areas the co-operation of workers and management maintained improvised production to the end.[34]

Speer continuously advised Hitler of the consequences of the losses of German territory for the economy and armaments production. In January he pointed out that the Russian advance endangered the rail line from Oppeln to Gotenhafen. Disruption of this line would endanger sea travel in the Baltic, the armaments industry and rail transport. By the end of January Speer warned that if Upper Silesia was lost, Germany would lose its one remaining source of coal. The remaining coal supply capacity would be only 26 per cent of that of January 1944, and the loss of crude steel capacity would mean that only some 175,000 tonnes of munitions could be produced. Speer concluded that the German armaments industry would then not be in a position to meet the requirements of the front in munitions, weapons and tanks. (Copies of this memorandum went to Hitler, Guderian, Ganzenmüller and Bormann.)[35]

In a paper of 15 March, discussing the economic situation of March-April 1945, Speer began by noting that the economic collapse of the Reich would be effected more quickly since the loss of Upper Silesia. He emphasised that in four to eight weeks they could count on the final collapse of the German economy. In this paper Speer asserted that the German people had done their duty and could not be blamed for the loss of the war. He suggested a number of measures to help the population, such as distribution of stocks of clothing and other consumer goods, and measures to secure German agricultural production. More importantly Speer suggested that no destruction of industry, energy or transport should occur if battle was carried further into the Reich; even the previous paralysing of firms had to end if reconquest was not possible. Instead on 20 March Hitler issued his 'scorched earth' order that all important installations and objects in Reich territory which the enemy could use to continue the fight were to be destroyed.[36]

In September 1944 Speer had wanted production to continue until the last possible moment and factories to be disabled by removal of key parts rather than destroyed. His attitude later changed. Speer wrote to the Army General Staff in the middle of March stating that operationally important street bridges could be destroyed only on the OKW's express order; others which were not operationally important should be dismantled only. In April, at Speer's suggestion, Hitler ordered that operationally important bridge building works had to be destroyed so that the enemy could not use them. The strongest punishments would be imposed if the measures were not obeyed. All other works were to be destroyed only if the Reich defence commissioners and the responsible offices of the Transport and Armaments Ministries ascertained the suspension of their production or the impossibility of evacuation. All other means of transport were to be paralysed. Speer ordered firms which were not evacuated to continue production to the last day.[37]

Stating that he was one of his few colleagues ever to tell him his views openly and honestly, Speer wrote to Hitler on 29 March, claiming that he had believed that the war might change in Germany's favour until 18 March. Until then he hoped that not only the new weapons and planes but also their fanatical belief in the future would enable the people and leadership to make the last sacrifice. But by the end of March Speer felt that the war was lost. He could not, however, believe in their success, if at the same time they were destroying the foundation of the people's life. He pointed out that he had achieved much for Germany. 'Without my work the war would perhaps have been lost in 1942-3.'[38] He had not mastered his task as a specialist but with an artist's qualities. Speer now claimed that in the days of victory in 1940 the leadership had been too lax and lost a year of precious time through comfort and indolence. He had firmly expected that Hitler would agree with the proposals in his paper of 15 March, but Hitler's comments indicated he believed the people were lost if the war was lost. The future belonged to the stronger Eastern peoples, Hitler had told him. He had been 'deeply shocked' by these words and saw the destruction order as the first step to carry out these views.[39]

Speer proceeded to take steps to thwart Hitler's scorched earth order. Speer's actions in the last few months of the regime, in particular this well-known disobedience, may be seen in part as a preparation for life in a Germany after National Socialism. Preservation of industrial property served the interests of the country, of the industrialists and might also serve the interests of Germany's conquerors. The decrease in Hitler's authority made evading his orders less dangerous than it had once been. Indeed Orlow suggests that the scorched earth order broke the spell of Hitler's charisma: the ideal of preservation of the nation was stronger than Hitler's authority. Even Goebbels opposed the policy. Speer was assisted by Gauleiters Hoffmann, Schlessmann and Kaufmann, by the Reich commissioner for the Netherlands, Seyss-Inquart; by Ohlendorf and by Bormann's deputy, Klopfer. Only three Gauleiters (Grohé, Florian and Meyer) refused to cooperate with his sabotage of Hitler's orders, and only a few Gauleiters, such as Hanke, Goebbels and Stürtz of Brandenburg, continued the struggle fanatically. Speer would, in any case, have been aware that the effects of Hitler's scorched earth policy could not have been as catastrophic as he suggested.[40] Discussion of the policy has relied heavily on Speer's perspective. Just as in historians' judgement of the futility of the Volkssturm's resistance, judgement of Hitler's scorched order has been harsher than judgement of Stalin's similar orders.

The final month of the regime brought increased pressure on all its leaders, pressure to decide their own fate. At the same time the prize of so many rivalries—the leadership—seemed nearer than ever. Bormann had wanted Hitler to leave Berlin for Bavaria while there was still time but decided to stay with Hitler, the source of his authority, in the capital. At the same time, his actions show an intensified desire to oust his rivals. Here he was assisted by the efforts of Göring and Himmler to assume Hitler's authority: Göring believed that Hitler was sealed off in Berlin and Himmler was persuaded by the group surrounding him—principally Schellenberg, his masseur Kersten, Berger and Rudolf Brandt, the deputy chief of Himmler's personal staff—to begin negotiations with representatives of the World Jewish Congress and Count Bernadotte to free Jewish and other concentration camp victims. The publicity given to Himmler's abortive attempt to negotiate with Eisenhower led to Hitler to dismiss him from the Party. He also ordered Göring's arrest for attempting to take over the leadership of the Reich. After Hitler's death Bormann clearly hoped to be able to exercise a role in the government of Hitler's successor Doenitz—he had a favourable opinion of Doenitz's political reliability.[41] But Bormann was killed while attempting to make his way to Flensburg. Himmler too still saw himself as a potential figure in Doenitz' government. Because of the support he initially gave Doenitz and the forces still at his disposal, he could only slowly be eased out of any position. It is possible that Himmler did not realise the outside world's view of him and had not anticipated an end to his political activities or his life.

Goebbels and Speer, the two leaders who can be said to have been more clear sighted about the war, proved also to be more clear-sighted about their own futures. While Goebbels had hoped to the end for a breakdown of the enemy alliance, he had been preparing himself for years for defeat. To him this had meant suicide and the deaths of his entire family; he did not share the illusions of Göring, Himmler or Speer that there might be a place for him in a Germany after National Socialism. He took refuge in the consolations of philosophy and in the perfection of the myth of National Socialism.

Appointed Chancellor by Hitler, Goebbels enjoyed a last day of authority in Berlin and a last triumph over Bormann in that his authority rather than Bormann's survived Hitler's death.[42]

Speer succeeded in making the transition to the Flensburg government as Minister of Economics and Production, even when Doenitz dropped other leading National Socialists. After editing the files of his ministerial office to remove incriminating documents, he presented himself to his interrogators as an apolitical technocrat. He may have hoped unrealistically to be able to pursue his career as a minister,[43] but he had realistically assessed his ability to distance himself from the regime he had once hoped to lead.

Increasingly in 1945 the leadership urged the population and the Party to stand firm, to resist with fanaticism and radicalism. Exhortations became all the more vehement as the regime's own ability to influence events decreased. The gradual capture of various areas of Germany diminished the effectiveness of any central government orders. The demands may therefore be seen as an attempt to overcome feelings of powerlessness. They also reflect the last despairing hope that some miracle weapon, extraordinary effort or enemy dissension could prevent defeat. Attempts to create a nation in arms by means of the Volkssturm under Party leadership failed, despite the regime's increasing verbal and actual radicalism in pursuit of the war effort. The process of political radicalisation, which intensified in 1945, was the strongest expression of an emphasis which began to emerge from 1943 on and which originated in the National Socialist analysis of World War I, the importance of ideology in overcoming the odds. Goebbels' willingness to contemplate abandoning the Geneva Convention on the treatment of prisoners of war and Hitler's decision to set up a women's battalion were signs of the leadership's recognition of the desperation and seriousness of the situation.

—

Conclusion

Looking back on the war effort in 1945, Goebbels and Speer believed that Germany's leaders had been insufficiently committed to waging a total war and had not organised the home front effectively for the war effort. They attributed this to failings of leadership, lack of support for total war among the leadership, lack of central authority and Hitler's unwillingness to take the necessary steps. Many historians have subsequently agreed with them. Despite their claims, however, this study has shown that the National Socialist regime itself sought to follow policies of total war. Further evidence has been found to substantiate the interpretation advanced by Overy: that there was agreement on the need for total war among the leadership and attempts were made to implement it.

In the 1930s the regime had planned and organised the economy and German society for wars against major powers in such a manner that by the late 1930s the economy could be described as a 'wartime economy in peace.' Consumer production and living conditions for the average German were already being cut back. Hitler was willing to delegate large areas of power and responsibility to successive leaders, particularly Göring and Speer, to control economic production. As the war progressed Hitler demonstrated a willingness to respond to military crises by adopting policies which sought to squeeze still more out of the German economy. He responded to the resulting military crisis of 1941-2 by appointing General von Unruh to find additional manpower for the armed forces, ordering the government and

Party to simplify their staffing and responsibilities, and agreeing to Todt's proposals to control armaments production. These measures, and the clear path he ensured for Speer after his appointment, showed that Hitler was willing to adopt measures to reorganise the home front, increasingly orienting it to the demands of war. After Stalingrad Hitler set in motion requirements for men and women to report for labour duty, businesses in inessential areas to be closed and further restrictions of numbers in, and functions of, government.

National Socialist leaders generally agreed on the need for total war policies. Examination of the concepts of total war and policies of Bormann, Goebbels, Himmler and Speer suggests there was more agreement in principle on the measures needed than Goebbels or Speer realised. The leaders agreed that more rationalisation and simplification was necessary and that fewer people should be employed in areas other than armaments and the armed forces.

Their concepts of total war extended beyond the simplification of life on the home front and the devotion of all available resources to the war effort to ideas of a levée en masse, a revolutionary war and mobilisation of the people under the leadership of the Party or the SS. The main emphasis of the leaders' debates on total war was on the social and labour prerequisites of mobilising for total war—freeing labour, simplifying the administration and economy, abolishing anything inessential. While the provision and allocation of raw materials and the conduct of the military campaigns are equally aspects of total war, they did not usually form part of the debate or the policies put forward. On the whole the leaders seem to have agreed with Hitler that Speer's allocation of raw materials was efficient; they did not dare openly criticise the conduct of the war, although they were increasingly critical in private. For some of the leaders, support for a compromise peace also arose from concern at the military conduct of the war and its results. As early as 1943 Guderian had found that both Goebbels and Himmler agreed that Hitler should no longer command the army in the East.[1] Their pursuit of plans for a compromise peace can be seen as an implicit criticism of, and proposal to alter, the overall conduct of the war.

While there were differences in emphasis among the four men studied, none can be said to have been against total war. For Bormann and Himmler, and to a lesser extent for Goebbels, total war carried implications of a levée en masse which sought to use popular enthusiasm to overcome deficiencies of material. For Bormann and Himmler victory was to be achieved by the pursuit of ideological goals. For Goebbels in addition there was a revolutionary style to his policies of total war which sought to harness class antagonisms to reduce social privilege.

Conflict arose from differences of perception and of priority among the measures to be taken. Some disagreements derived from different interests, particularly the institutional perspectives of the various leaders. All four men could defend themselves against cuts in their own staff numbers by pointing to the importance of their organisations for the pursuit of the war effort. It is not surprising to find the head of the Party Chancellery advocating a greater role for the Party or to find Speer, a minister dependent on the support of industry for the success of his policies, advocating a more economic and less ideological approach.

One problem for members of the leadership was that to find a role for the Party in their plans of total war meant increasing Bormann's power. Speer's opposition to the interference of the Party in his ministry and his attempt to exclude the Party from a role in the economy was therefore based on an unrealistic assessment of power relationships. Goebbels on the other hand resigned himself to the inevitable and by 1944 came to an agreement with Bormann. He recognised that the Party's involvement was necessary although he did not have a high opinion of the capacities of most of his party colleagues.

While Speer criticised the Gauleiters as an obstacle to more efficient policies, he did not suggest that the 'self-responsibility of industry' created similar problems. Just as the SS's responsibility for concentration camps and the extermination of the Jews went unquestioned by these leaders, so, on the whole, did the efficiency of industry. Although there were suggestions of corruption and inefficiency in industry, the only opposition to Speer's methods came from Party circles, including Bormann and Sauckel. The study has shown that Speer achieved high production and quick results by relentless pursuit of his own interest vis-à-vis other leaders and institutions and flexible exploitation of existing methods and conditions, but often at the cost of long-term production. Perhaps because the results of his system so bolstered his position, Speer opposed any policies which required a temporary drop in production. Accordingly, he opposed bringing foreign labour into Germany rather than keeping them at home, dispersing factories and stocks of raw materials, and using underground factories. Speer bought his immediate successes, therefore, at the expense of reducing the regime's long-term options and at the cost of bringing German resistance to an end sooner than might otherwise have been the case.

If there was one area which might have been scrutinised further by the leadership, it was the self-responsibility of industry, but such scrutiny and criticism developed only slowly and without a strong political campaign along these lines. The fact that Speer's system appeared to be delivering increased production muted criticism. Hitler's admiration for successful entrepreneurs, the Party's own middle-class support and Speer's ability, if attacked, to call on Hitler's approval of his policy may have made some reluctant to criticise. These obstacles were less likely to affect Goebbels or Bormann, both of whom exercised at least a verbal radicalism. In Goebbels' case this radicalism went further. One of the attractions of total war for him appears to have been that it allowed scope for an anti-bourgeois animus and social levelling.

The absence of criticisms of the self-responsibility of industry until late 1944 suggest that Speer's success in increasing production, his alliance with Goebbels on the issue of total war, his capacity for self-advertisement and his emphasis on the 'technical' nature of his task discouraged criticism. As long as Speer's system of industrial self-responsibility produced results, he enjoyed Hitler's protection. The failure of this production to affect the course of the war weakened his position by mid-1944, and the Party gained an increased influence in the economy. This influence had positive as well as negative effects. At times Speer was inclined to overlook practical or political considerations for the sake of pursuing short-term production increases.

Some tensions between members of the regime arose because of their differing concepts of total war. Total war is usually defined as the complete orientation of the resources of a nation to the war effort; it encompasses a rational use of economic and productive resources, aiming at the total defeat of the enemy, and involving the civilian population of the combatant countries as well as its fighting forces. To fight such a war, the enthusiasm of the population as a whole has to be maintained. Most historians who have assessed Germany's preparations for total war have used a model of it as economic rationality—the optimum use of resources, labour and production to further the nation's war aims—and have tended to underestimate the political and economic need for apparently inessential production.

The National Socialist model of total war also had an important ideological component, specifically influenced by the lesson National Socialists drew from Germany's experience in World War I. This led them to emphasise various ideological and psychological measures designed to maintain the unity of the home front, including adequate feeding of the population, establishing a national sense of community (Volksgemeinschaft), and an emphasis on the importance of propaganda and on the ideological education of the armed forces. The absence of scrutiny in the area of industrial self-responsibility and the delays and ambivalence about the employment of women can also be attributed in part to their being among the 'unlearned lessons of World War I.' The leadership wanted to prevent a repetition of the revolution of 1918. Anti-Semitism was 'justified' by the 'lessons' they drew from World War I, and in this analysis the extermination of the Jews was seen as a 'contribution' to the war effort. It is important to bear in mind that divergence from an economically rational model of total war was often intended as a contribution to it, according to this 'German doctrine of total war.'

There could be tensions between the ideological and technical needs of the models of total war. The ideological requirements of this policy often conflicted with the requirements of economic rationality; pursuit of these ideological goals did not necessarily illustrate opposition to total war but rather a different understanding of what it involved.

The deteriorating military situation reinforced the belief that a lack of ideological commitment and reliability on the part of the armed forces contributed to German defeats. The fall of Mussolini and the surrender of Italy revived memories of 1918 and led to extensive measures to mobilise the population and armed forces ideologically. For the regime this was as much part of total war as labour policy.

These issues and Hitler's continuing preoccupation with the military situation increased Bormann's influence. He ensured that the Party Chancellery increased its role in the ideological education of the armed forces and sought to steady the Party members. Of all of the leaders Bormann appears to have been the least radical in his approach to economic issues; he was also the most optimistic about the military situation, and perhaps not coincidentally he was the one who had the best opportunities to reflect and/or influence Hitler's views.

Both Speer and Goebbels were willing to make political concessions within certain limits for a more effective war effort, such as Goebbels' campaign for better treatment of Eastern workers. Goebbels' attitude toward total war can be described as socially radical but not always ideological. He was prepared to set aside or by-pass most elements of National Socialist ideology to win the war or achieve a satisfactory peace settlement. His informal alliance with Speer was aided by the fact that the latter shared a similar approach. Speer's view of total war was overwhelmingly one of economic rationality—maximising production by reducing living standards, saving material and increasing productivity, which meant inter alia that his powers increased.

Such compromises stopped at the regime's Jewish policy. These policies were not questioned in the name of total war, except by Himmler after 1944.

Initially a firm advocate of the pursuit of ideological goals as a means of achieving victory, Himmler later showed a willingness to abandon all such considerations. Hitler on the other hand was not willing to set aside ideological goals for short-term gains after 1941.

This study has shown that Hitler's approval was central to the success of total war measures. It found further evidence for Rebentisch's conclusion that Hitler was the central source of power for all structures of the political system, and that, whatever power he delegated to others, he retained the right to decide and the possibility of influence.[2] Those second-level members of the regime who sought to pursue such policies in the absence of his agreement were easily blocked. This is illustrated by the fate of Goebbels' total war policies. Blocked in 1942-3, he was considerably more effective in getting the measures he wanted adopted in late 1944 once he won Hitler's support. In addition, those leaders who favoured or opposed various plans demonstrated by their own actions that they considered Hitler's agreement of paramount importance to their success. This is not to say that considerable scope did not exist for the leaders to pursue lines of policy in their own areas of responsibility and vis-à-vis members of the leadership with lesser access to Hitler. The extent to which Himmler was able to dabble with plans for a separate peace and links with the resistance indicates the freedom of action enjoyed by those Hitler trusted. As defeat followed defeat, Hitler's charismatic authority began to weaken and be undermined. From mid-1944 on, secondary leaders' scope for independent action and willingness to ignore Hitler's orders increased, as was seen in Chapters 8 and 9.

The study supports an interpretation of the National Socialist political system which accords neither with the strictly monocratic nor the polycratic model, but suggests a combination of the two. The leaders were hampered by the absence of institutional forms of cooperation; competition for resources and attention occupied the various organisations and leaders; nonetheless Hitler's role remained crucial. Leaders were dependent on Hitler's agreement to get measures outside their own narrow areas of responsibility adopted. Goebbels' failure in 1943 to achieve change by seeking support among the secondary group of leaders is a case in point. Hitler, on the other hand, seemed more likely to make important decisions when a consensus emerged among the second-level leadership, such as on the need for policy changes in armaments at the end of 1941.

While the book has shown instances where Bormann influenced Hitler's decisions, at other times he clearly reflected Hitler's views and/or was powerless to influence them. While Bormann exerted considerable influence, particularly in 1944-45, to call him an *éminence grise* is perhaps an exaggeration. His importance was more as a blocking rather than an initiating force. By using the Party he could interfere with, and prevent the success of, the policies of other leaders; it was more difficult for him to seek to pursue a positive course himself.

The power given to the Gauleiters as direct agents of Hitler could on occasion be an obstacle to any uniform implementation of total war policies. The extent to which German resources were used efficiently and rationally in pursuit of the war effort therefore varied from Gau to Gau, as the central leadership sometimes acknowledged. A further detailed study of various Gaus is needed to understand differences in implementation. One possible explanation for the differences was varying wartime experiences. In many Gaus the effects of bombing reinforced the need for urgent measures and simplifications; indeed bombing helped make these policies more severe. In Gaus which were further east (whose records are less accessible), in central Germany and in agricultural areas the immediate impact of the war was less, and therefore perhaps also the need for some total war measures may have seemed less urgent.[3] Further studies of the armaments industry are needed to explore Fear's suggestion that the Gaus developed regional armaments economies.[4] Whatever their personal commitment to total war, the Gauleiters impeded the introduction of uniform measures. Speer, however, exaggerated the irrationality of the Gauleiters' attitudes and their lack of support for total war. He was prone to see opposition to his own policies and the extension of his own powers as implying opposition to total war.

Some difficulties arose out from Hitler's attitudes. While there is considerable evidence that Hitler was not always consistent on individual policies, there is very little to support the argument that he did not want a state organised for 'total war.' What he understood by 'total war' was less radical than the models of Speer or Goebbels, the last of whom was influenced by the model of Soviet mobilisation. The most notable anomaly in Hitler's view was the question of more extensive employment of women. (Senior civil servants also had conservative views on this issue.)

Hitler's attitude can be described as ambivalent, and this in turn may reflect what Speer described as his reluctance to face unpleasant realities.[5] Speer pointed out that in 1939 Hitler spoke and acted as if he were planning a long-drawn-out war which would involve a bid for world domination. At the same time he refused to restrict his building projects. Much the same pattern can be seen in Hitler's response to arguments about total war. In early 1943 Goebbels could get him to agree to these measures, but he was not prepared to draw all the necessary conclusions about the policies to be followed. Because of Hitler's central importance to the exercise of authority in the Reich, his vacillation on individual policies, such as the abolition of the Prussian Finance Ministry, held up other leaders' proposals and made it appear that other members of the regime shared his doubts.

On the other hand, Hitler's caution can also be justified at times or understood as stemming from a lack of interest in the puritanism of total war. He saw no point to imposing constraint for the sake of constraint and was more alive to the political sensitivities of an issue. There is evidence that Hitler was attentive to the 'cosmetic' effect of reductions in consumer goods. In early 1943 particularly he showed himself susceptible to arguments in favour of altering measures, such as the compulsory employment of women or the closure of hairdressing salons, out of concern for morale. But in these cases he believed that the same results for the war economy could be achieved by other means—use of foreign labour and a stop to the production of hairdressing materials and equipment respectively. Hitler's attitude seems to have derived from a belief that the measures already agreed to would be sufficient rather than a lack of interest in waging a total war. As Germany's position worsened in 1943 and 1944, Hitler overcame his reluctance to employ women more widely. He intervened occasionally to ensure that the measures took popular interests into account, but the extent to which he affected the impact of these measures can be exaggerated.

Tim Mason has argued that fear of a return of the revolutionary uprisings of 1918 hampered the regime's ability to ask the population to make sacrifices and therefore meant it could not organise the home front for total war. This interpretation has been widely challenged. This study has shown that the leaders studied on the whole did not consider this an obstacle. Goebbels, Speer and Himmler in particular were confident that they did not need to fear a collapse of the home front. In many ways the government's policies, both positive and negative, encouraging and punitive, were designed to remove the danger of such unrest[6] and aimed to correct the mistakes of World War I. Some of this concern was also economically rational. The privations suffered by the German population during World War I had weakened the war effort, and there were both economic and political reasons to avoid them. In another sense, however, the model of 1918 and of World War I in general was a distraction. As long as the German soldiers and home front were loyal,[7] members of the leadership could sometimes blind themselves to the seriousness of other problems.

Mason has described Hitler's comments that workers were his most loyal supporters as 'conversion fantasies.'[8] These may have been fantasies, but they were widespread among the leadership. It was confidence that the lessons of 1918 had been learnt and that the population could be relied upon which led members of the leadership such as Himmler, Speer and Goebbels to consider that more radical measures could be adopted. The representative of the SD at a meeting of the State Secretaries in 1945 commented that this time the reproach of failing the soldiers could not be made to the home front.[9] There is of course no means of knowing conclusively if their confidence was justified, except to point to the fact that the population, as a whole, continued to work and fight as long as the state apparatus existed.

The 'fear of 1918' did influence the responses of Hitler, and to a lesser extent Bormann, but not exclusively. Hitler was not totally confident of the ability of the German population to withstand the rigours of war. His response reflected his own preconceptions rather than any close knowledge of conditions of the home front; those leaders who had a greater opportunity to assess popular morale were more optimistic about the population's being able to bear a greater burden. In fact, evidence suggests that the living standard of the civilian population was progressively reduced, even if the starvation of World War I did not recur. In practice the regime asked considerable sacrifices from the population. Local and oral histories indicate that total war measures had a marked effect on life on the home front: there was neither an abundance of consumer goods nor of unnecessary business or economic production.[10] Bombing reduced Germans to the bare minimum required to continue life.[11]

Another misleading model for National Socialist leaders was the experience of their party's rise to power, particularly the period from 1930 to 1933. To a certain extent the National Socialist leadership applied the tactics of their seizure of power in 1933 to waging war. This led to a disproportionate hopes being placed on willpower, fanaticism and propaganda as means of winning the war, as highlighted in their conceptions of the NSFOs and the Volkssturm. The continued hopes of finding a way out by splitting the enemy alliance also derived in part from the National Socialist experience of coming to power by splitting their conservative opponents and playing on the threat of the left wing in 1932-3.

The German war effort was hampered from the beginning by the long-term effects of the restrictions of the Treaty of Versailles. Much initial rearmament had to be devoted to making up for these bans and limitations. Although by 1941 Germany had access to or control over the economies of most European states, the haste with which Hitler sought to achieve his international goals ensured that there was insufficient time to develop a completely integrated European economy serving the war effort. By 1942 when Germany was at war with the United States, the Soviet Union and the

British Empire, 'neither thorough planning of production nor the timely mobilisation of every last potential reserve could have saved Germany.'[12]

Problems in the German organisation of the home front did not arise from lack of nerve or energy or commitment to total war on the part of the four leaders examined. They arose because of problems of organisation, lack of co-ordination and follow-up, and conflicting priorities. To say that the regime and the leadership were committed to total war is not to say that there was not inefficiency, overlapping, disorganisation and confusion in the economy. This was compounded by regionalism, as exemplified in the role of the Gauleiters; and in this respect Germany was less favoured than the more centralised British and Soviet administrations.

Other obstacles stemmed from the difficulties of implementation and co-ordination. While individual ministries had set up internal checks on the implementation of their programmes and policies, this co-ordination of the home front was much more difficult to establish between ministries. For example, in 1944 Lammers did not know how many staff members individual ministries had freed in 1943. An overview of implementation was never adequately achieved, particularly for the period 1944-5. Even where checks and balances existed, the leaders' suspicion and mutual distrust prevented their relying on them.

Administrative difficulties arose in the implementation of the various policies which were agreed on in the period 1941 to 1945, particularly because of the lack of any reliable method of co-ordination and control. The fact that the Gauleiters could report directly to Hitler made it difficult for secondary leaders to control them. Various attempts were made in the period studied to provide this coordination: the Dreier Ausschuss, Goebbels' abortive attempt to get Göring to exercise his powers, Goebbels' plans for a National Socialist 'senate' and the Reichsbevollmächtigter für den totalen Kriegseinsatz. The powers Hitler gave initially to Göring and later to Speer suggest that there was no theoretical obstacle to the creation of such a coordinating body. Neither man, however, seemed able to set up an apparatus to enforce his powers. Here Bormann's role was increasingly crucial. In seeking to protect his own control over the Party, he obstructed other attempts to control the Gauleiters.

Other constraints on decision making existed. Members of the regime were aware of a lack of popular support for the war; some of them, such as Goebbels, had shared it. They were conscious of a lack of national self-confidence, a brittleness among the population as a whole. This was a constraint on their demands on the population and heightened the effects of Allied bombing.

Additional restrictions on the leadership from 1942 on were cumulatively the economic and psychological impact of the air war and the worsening military situation. These factors hampered the leadership's room to manoeuvre in a variety of ways. Allied bombing campaigns and the needs of a population in a long war meant that a certain level of civilian production had to be maintained to allow for the replacement of lost goods. The air war also made necessary expenditure and production to maintain morale. Germany's occupation of other European territories required men to be committed behind the lines in administration and control of these countries.[13]

As the military situation worsened, the regime progressively lost territory, raw materials and sources of labour. Decisions to allocate war resources became more and more difficult, and intensified competition between the various ministries and organisations. In 1944 and 1945 the choices the regime had to make were not between what was necessary for the war effort and what was inessential but between two policies both necessary for the continuation of the war.

Speer and Goebbels had expected too much from total war. In 1944 they delivered almost one million extra men to the front and had maintained production under increasingly difficult conditions, even when the production could not be used. The regime had succeeded in keeping part of Goebbels' promise of 1938—the 'stab in the back' of 1918 was not repeated. Speer's and Goebbels' criticisms of the existing war effort were a mixture of personal ambition, lack of realism and desperation. Some of Speer's complaints about the regime's failings where total war was concerned may also be attributed to his desire to curry favour with post-war interrogators. For the greater part of his ministerial life Speer had had support from Hitler for the expansion of his powers such as few other ministers received; his complaints that he did not receive even more power suggest unrealistic expectations. Speer and Goebbels had exaggerated hopes regarding the amount of production and labour which could still be squeezed out of the economy. They were insufficiently aware of the geographic and social restrictions on gaining more workers.

The regime did not have the resources to fulfil all the demands it had to meet yet it had to fulfil these demands to survive. This explains both the urgency with which Goebbels and Speer in particular pursued the cause of more efficient organisation of German society for the war effort and why they were disappointed. They were expecting more than was possible to be achieved because they knew more was needed for the regime to survive.

Total war was part of a wider plan for Goebbels. Partly because his own position as Propaganda Minister required him to have an overview of the situation, Goebbels put forward policies aimed at strengthening not only his position but that of the regime. From the beginning of the war Goebbels considered a 'positive' war aim necessary. Soon after the beginning of the campaign against the USSR, he was persuaded of the need for better treatment of the peoples of the Soviet Union to make military success easier. He came to develop his proposals for total war on the home front as part of an overall effort to better Germany's political position. In 1944 he twice sought by means of a formal memorandum to persuade Hitler to treat for peace. While no similar formal memoranda survive for 1943, his diary entries indicate that then too he was seeking to persuade Hitler to take this step. The compartmentalisation of the system of government, the absence of formal cabinet meetings and the way in which other forms of consultation had atrophied meant that Goebbels seems to have been unaware of the efforts made by Todt and Fromm to convince Hitler of the need for a compromise peace and by some of Himmler's subordinates, particularly Schellenberg, to negotiate a peace with Himmler's halfhearted support. There could therefore be no means of combining these efforts.

Goebbels' criticisms of the regime's failure to adopt total war policies in part reflect despair at his failure to persuade Hitler to adopt his wider strategy. For Goebbels total war was a means to an end, not an end in itself: it was a means to ensure the survival of the regime. In order to do this, like Stalin, he was willing to make promises to the German people and to others that he had no intention of keeping. He had developed a coherent although implicit policy which aimed both to meet the social and labour needs for intensifying the war effort and to counter Hitler's political and military conduct of the war. The nature of the regime, however, meant that such a policy needed Hitler's support for its adoption, and this it never gained in full. The adoption of the total war policies Goebbels sought would have made the cost of victory higher for the enemy powers; thus he hoped it would be a means of persuading them to the conference table. If this was not successful, then at least the life of the regime, and his own life, would be prolonged. The urgency he felt about total war was in many ways an urgency about saving the regime. Himmler came to share these concerns but was also unable to persuade Hitler. Ultimately, unlike Goebbels or Speer, Himmler chose to pursue a compromise peace separately.

With the exception of Bormann, who echoed Hitler's ideas, as early as 1942 there was a common perception among the leadership that the war needed to be ended quickly. Goebbels, Speer and other members of the leadership were all prepared to forgo the regime's total ideological goals for the sake of its survival. Even Himmler, who had pursued most radically the total destruction of Germany's enemies, intended to settle for less and by 1944 was willing to abandon principles he had earlier pursued at the expense of Germany's needs for labour and political support. But without Hitler's support their moves were in vain. Speer suggested after the war that Hitler's lack of interest in such proposals was a reflection of his greater realism. He knew that with the implementation of the 'Final Solution' there was no way out.[14] Goebbels was trying to win Hitler's support for a policy of realism and compromise. This was the very opposite of the all-or-nothing approach Hitler had adopted since Barbarossa.

APPENDICES

Table A.1

German Ranks

Civil Service Ranks

Reichsminister	Minister
Staatssekretär-StS.	Administrative head of the ministry
Unterstaatssekretär-UStS.	Head of a department (Abteilung)
Ministerialdirektor-MinDir.	Head of an Unterabteilung (subdivision),
Ministerialdirigent-MinDirig.	Amt (office) or Amtsgruppe
Ministerialrat-MinRat.	Head of a Referat (section)
Oberregierungsrat-ORR.	
Regierungsrat-RR.	
Referent	Usually an expert; prepared first drafts of most legislation

SS and Army Ranks

SS	German Army	US Army
Reichsführer-RFSS	Generalfeldmarschall-Gfm.	General of the Army
Oberst-Gruppenführer-ObstGruf.	Generaloberst-Genobst.	General
Obergruppenführer-OGruf.	General der Infanterie, Artillerie,etc.—Gen. d. Inf., Gen. d. Art., etc.	Lieutenant General
Gruppenführer-Gruf.	Generalleutnant-Glt.	Major General
Brigadeführer-Bgf. or Brif	Generalmajor-Genmaj.	Brigadier-General
Oberführer-Obf.	No equivalent rank	No equivalent rank
Standartenführer-Staf.	Oberst-Obst.	Colonel
Obersturmbannführer-OStubaf.	Oberstleutnant-Obstlt.	Lieutenant-colonel
Sturmbannführer-Stubaf.	Major-Maj.	Major
Hauptsturmbannführer-HStuf.	Hauptmann-Hptm.	Captain
Obersturmführer-Ostuf.	Oberleutnant-Olt.	First lieutenant
Untersturmführer-UStuf.	Leutnant-Lt.	Second lieutenant

Adapted from Raul Hillberg, *The Destruction of the European Jews*, vol. 3 (revised and definitive edition, New York, 1985), pp. 1197-8.

Table A.2

Military Expenditure, State Expenditure and National Income in Germany 1938-44 (billion RM)

Year	Military Expenditure	State Expenditure	National Income
1938/39	17.2	39.4	98
1939/40	38.0	58.0	109
1940/41	55.9	80.0	120
1941/42	72.3	100.5	125
1942/43	86.2	124.0[*]	134
1943/44	99.4	130.0[*]	130

[*]Figures based on revenue from occupied Europe and Germany together.
Taken from R. J. Overy, *Goering the 'Iron Man'* (London, 1984), p. 95.

Table A.3

Distribution of Labour in Germany 1939-44 (millions)

Date	German Civilian Labour Force			Foreign Labour and POWs	Armed Forces	Total Lost	Active Strength
	Men	Women	Total				
01/05/39	24.5	14.6	39.1	0.3	1.4	—	1.4
31/05/40	20.4	14.4	34.8	1.2	5.7	0.1	5.6
31/05/41	19.0	14.1	33.1	3.0	7.4	0.2	7.2
31/05/42	16.9	14.4	31.3	4.2	9.4	0.8	8.6
31/05/43	15.5	14.8	30.3	6.3	11.2	1.7	9.5
31/05/44	14.2	14.8	29.0	7.1	12.4	3.3	9.1
30/09/44	13.5	14.9	28.4	7.5	13.0	3.9	9.1

Taken from R. J. Overy, *Goering the 'Iron Man'* (London, 1984), p. 148.

Table A.4

Index of German Armaments Finished Production
(*Endfertigung*)*

Quantities: January/February 1942 = 100

Month	1942	1943	1944	1945
January	103	182	241	227
February	97	207	231	175
March	129	216	270	145
April	133	215	274	
May	135	232	285	
June	144	226	297	
July	153	229	322	
August	153	224	297	
September	155	234	301	
October	154	242	273	
November	165	231	268	
December	181	222	263	
Average	**142**	**222**	**276**	

* According to the calculations of the Planungsamt.

Taken from Dr. Rolf Wagenführ, *Die deutsche Industrie im Kriege 1939-1945* (Berlin, 1963), pp. 66, 114.

Table A.5

Male and Female Civilian Foreign Workers
According to Country of Origin, 30 September 1944

Nationality	Men	Women	Total	Women as % of workers	Men and women as % of civilian foreign workers
Belgium	170,058	29,379	199,437	14.7	3.4
France	603,767	42,654	646,421	6.6	10.8
Italy	265,030	22,317	287,347	7.7	4.8
Yugoslavia and Croatia	294,222	30,768	324,954	9.5	1.6
Netherlands	233,591	20,953	254,544	8.2	4.3
Slovakia	20,857	16,693	37,550	44.4	0.6
Hungary	17,206	7,057	24,263	3.0	0.4
Soviet Union	1,062,507	1,112,137	2,174,644	51.1	36.4
Poland	1,115,321	586,091	1,701,412	34.4	18.5
TOTAL	3,986,306	1,990,367	5,976,673	33.3	100.0

Taken from Ulrich Herbert: *Fremdarbeiter*, Bonn 1985, 1986. Copyright © 1991 by Verlag J.H.W. Dietz Nachf. Bonn

---

Table A.6

Oberkommando der Wehrmacht List of uk Positions of the 1897-1925 Age groups as at 4 December 1942

Armaments sector	1,279,419
Agriculture	647,657
Railways	500,155
Industrial war economy outside armaments	461,353
Coal mining	328,933
Administration (excluding police, rail, post and transport)	254,056
Police	252,897
Liberal professions and others	241,826
Food supply (excluding agriculture)	189,290
Organisation Todt	165,541
Post	103,807
Mineral oil firms	86,476
Forestry and wood products	83,953
Others, each area under 80,000	683,607
Total	**5,278,970**

Taken from Dieter Rebentisch, *Führerstaat und Verwaltung im Zweiten Weltkrieg: Verfassungsentwicklung und Verwaltungspolitik 1939-1945* (Stuttgart, 1989), p. 477.

Table A.7

Index of Consumer Goods Production 1939-41

(1928 = 100)

Year	Consumer Goods	Consumer Goods per Head	Consumer Goods of Elastic Demand	Consumer Goods of Elastic Demand per Head
1939	127	103	127	103
1940	118	91	112	86
1941	119	86	108	78

Taken from Willi A. Boelcke, *Die deutsche Wirtschaft 1930-1945: Interna des Reichswirtschaftsministeriums* (Dusseldorf, 1983), p. 254.

Table A.8

Total Production of Consumer Goods in 1943 and 1944

in millions of pieces (for public and civilian use)

	1943	1944	Total
frying-pans	1,150	1,218	2,368
buckets	10,350	10,357	20,707
cooking-pots	20,200	13,620	33,820
blankets	30,500	23,000	32,800
leather street shoes	54,000	26,640	80,640
bedsteads	1,091	1,900	2,991
linen- and clothing-cupboards	410	265	675

Taken from Willi A. Boelcke, *Die deutsche Wirtschaft 1930-1945: Interna des Reichswirtschafts-ministeriums* (Dusseldorf, 1983), p. 326.

Table A.9

Tank Production in 1944

Germany	17,800
Soviet Union	29,000
Britain	5,000
United States	17,500
(United States in 1943)	29,500

Taken from Paul Kennedy, *The Rise and Fall of the Great Powers: Economic Change and Military Conflict from 1500 to 2000* (Random House, New York, 1987 and HarperCollins, London, 1987), p. 353.

Table A.10

Armaments Production of the Powers, 1940-43

(billions of 1944 dollars)

Nation	1940	1941	1943
Britain	3.5	6.5	11.1
USSR	(5.0)*	8.5	13.9
USA	(1.5)	4.5	37.5
Total Allied Combatants	3.5	19.5	62.5
Germany	6.0	6.0	13.8
Japan	(1.0)	2.0	4.5
Italy	0.75	1.0	—
Total Axis Combatants	6.75	9.0	18.3

* Figures in parentheses indicate combatants not yet formally at war.

Taken from Paul Kennedy, *The Rise and Fall of the Great Powers: Economic Change and Military Conflict from 1500 to 2000* (Random House, New York, 1987 and HarperCollins, London, 1987), p. 355.

NOTE ON SOURCES

The main sources used for this study were the Bundesarchiv file holdings in Koblenz of the Propaganda Ministry (R 55); the Reichspropagandaleitung (NS 18); Goebbels' diaries (NL 118); the Reich Ministry of Munitions and War Production (R 3), particularly its ministerial office; the Party Chancellery files (NS 6), augmented by the Institut für Zeitgeschichte's reconstruction of these files; and the files of the Reichsführer-SS's personal staff (NS 19) and the Reich Chancellery (R 43 II). The files of the Reich Chancellery are among the most comprehensive sources for the activities of the Dreier Ausschuss and those of the plenipotentiary for total war.

Most research was completed by 1988, but some supplementary research was undertaken in 1989 and 1990. Files of the Statistisches Reichsamt (R 24), Reichsfrauenführung (NS 44), Reichspostministerium (R 48), Reichswirtschaftskammer (R 11), Labour Ministry (R 41), Deutsche Arbeitsfront (NS 5 I), Reichswirtschaftsministerium (R 7) and the Reichsgruppe Industrie (R 12 I) were consulted in the Bundesarchiv. Files from the Landesarchiv Berlin, the Geheimes Preussisches Staatsarchiv Berlin-Dahlem and the Bayrisches Hauptstaatsarchiv in Munich were also used. My investigation of the secondary literature was substantially finished by early 1988; only particularly noteworthy subsequent studies have been included.

The reports on the state of public opinion compiled by the Sicherheitsdienst (SD) were drawn on in their published form, *Meldungen aus dem Reich*. Memoirs and interviews held by the Institut für Zeitgeschichte and the records of the trial of the major war criminals at Nuremberg were used. The files of the armed forces, particularly those of the OKW and its Wehrwirtschaftsrüstungsamt, were examined at the Bundesarchiv Militärarchiv in Freiburg. In view of Keitel's position on the Dreier Ausschuss, I examined these files and his private papers (N 54), in the expectation that he also may have followed an independent policy or sought to promote a 'design' for total war, but found no evidence that this was the case.

The private papers of Speer and the memoirs of Goebbels' state secretary, Werner Naumann, are not yet available. The Propaganda Ministry files were for the most part destroyed in 1945 and survive only in a fragmented state; some files were held in the archives of the former German Democratic Republic in Potsdam. Unfortunately, I was not granted permission to use these files, nor to consult the files of the Berlin Document Center. The Armaments Ministry files, while extensive, were edited by Speer at the end of the war, as was the Chronik or office diary of Speer's activities.

Goebbels' wartime diaries exaggerate his importance and effectiveness, but are still valuable as a reflection on the events at the time, rather than a post-war apologia. The major part of these diaries first became available in the 1970s, and consequently they have not been used by many historians of the period. Publication has begun of a scholarly edition of these diaries, and has reached July 1941. I was permitted to consult unpublished diaries for the period 1941 to 1943 in the Bundesarchiv; the 1944 diary entries were not available for examination. Some idea of their contents can be gained from Dr Elke Fröhlich's article, 'Hitler und Goebbels im Krisenjahr 1944.'

In addition, despite the extensive German archival holdings, there are gaps in the records. Hitler's personal archives, such as they were, were destroyed in 1945; the Goebbels diaries for the wartime period are incomplete and, as mentioned, are not yet available for 1944; Todt's papers have not survived to any great extent. The fragmented state of the Party Chancellery files means that the extent to which Bormann influenced Hitler's views or merely reflected them is still not clear.

Citation of documents has been reduced to the minimum, and the method of citation simplified as far as possible. Usually when one document is cited, there are several more references which support the point. Scholars wishing to explore these are referred to my doctoral thesis, 'Mobilizing for Total War: The National Socialist Leadership and Social and Labour Prerequisites for Intensifying the German War Effort, 1941-1945,' submitted to the Australian National University in Canberra in June 1988, where more comprehensive and detailed references are set out.

ABBREVIATIONS AND GERMAN TERMS USED IN NOTES

Allgemeines Heeresamt—general army office.

Andreyev, *Vlasov*—Catherine Andreyev, *Vlasov and the Russian Liberation Movement: Soviet Reality and Émigré Theories* (Cambridge, 1987).

Arbeitseinsatz—mobilisation of labour.

Aron, *Century of Total War*—Raymond Aron, *The Century of Total War* (Boston, 1966.)

av.—arbeitsverwendungsfähig—fit for work, capable of work in staffs, offices and units and garrison battalions.

av. H.—arbeitsverwendungsfähig Heimat—fit for work, capable of work in staffs, offices and units and garrison battalions on the home front.

AWA—Allgemeines Wehrmachtsamt—General armed forces office.

BA—Bundesarchiv—German Federal Archives, Koblenz.

Baird, *Nazi War Propaganda*—Jay W. Baird, *The Mythical World of Nazi War Propaganda, 1939-1945* (Minneapolis, Minn., 1974.)

Bajohr, *Hälfte der Fabrik*—Stefan Bajohr, Die Hälfte der Fabrik: Geschichte der Frauenarbeit in Deutschland 1914 bis 1945 (Marburg, 1979).

BA MA—Bundesarchiv Militärarchiv—German Federal Military Archives, Freiburg.

Beck, *Under the Bombs*—Earl R. Beck, *Under the Bombs: The German Home Front 1942-1945* (Lexington, 1986).

Boberach (ed.), *Meldungen aus dem Reich*—Heinz Boberach (ed.) *Meldungen aus dem Reich 1938-1945: Die geheimen Lageberichte des Sicherheitsdienstes der SS* (Herrsching, 1984).

Boelcke, *deutsche Wirtschaft*—Willi A. Boelcke, *Die deutsche Wirtschaft 1930-1945: Interna des Reichswirtschaftsministeriums* (Dusseldorf, 1983).

Boelcke (ed.), *Hitlers Konferenzen*—Willi A. Boelcke (ed.), Deutschlands Rüstung im Zweiten Weltkrieg: Hitlers Konferenzen mit Albert Speer 1942-1945 (Frankfurt, 1969).

Boelcke (ed.), *Secret Conferences*—Willi A. Boelcke (ed.), The Secret Conferences of Dr Goebbels October 1939-March 1943 (London, 1967).

Bond, *War and Society in Europe, 1870-1970*—Brian Bond, *War and Society in Europe, 1870-1970* (London, 1984).

Borsdorf and Jamin (eds.), *Überleben im Krieg*—Ulrich Borsdorf and Mathilde Jamin (eds.), *Überleben im Krieg. Kriegserfahrungen in einer Industrieregion 1939-1945* (Hamburg, 1989).

Bracher, *Zeitgeschichtliche Kontroversen*—Karl Dietrich Bracher, *Zeitgeschichtliche Kontroversen: Um Faschismus, Totalitarismus, Demokratie* (Munich, 1976).

Bracher et al. (eds.), *Nationalsozialistische Diktatur*—Karl Dietrich Bracher, Manfred Funke, and Hans-Adolf Jacobsen (eds.), *Nationalsozialistische Diktatur 1933-1945: eine Bilanz* (Dusseldorf, 1983).

Bramsted, *Goebbels and National Socialist Propaganda*—E. K. Bramsted, *Goebbels and National Socialist Propaganda 1925-1945* (East Lansing, Mich., 1965).

Broszat, *The Hitler State*—Martin Broszat, *The Hitler State* (London, 1981).

Broszat et al. (eds), *Bayern in der NS-Zeit*—Martin Broszat, Elke Fröhlich, and Falk Wiesemann (eds.), *Bayern in der NS-Zeit: soziale Lage und politisches Verhalten der Bevölkerung im Spiegel vertraulicher Berichte* (Munich, 1977).

Broszat et al. (eds.), *Von Stalingrad zur Währungsreform*—Martin Broszat, Klaus-Dietmar Henke, and Hans Woller, (eds.), *Von Stalingrad zur Währungsreform: zur Sozialgeschichte des Umbruchs in Deutschland* (Munich, 1989).

Burchardt, 'Impact of the War Economy on the Civilian Population,' in Deist (ed.), *German Military in the Age of Total War*—Lothar Burchardt, 'The Impact of the War Economy on the Civilian Population of Germany during the First and Second World Wars,' in Wilhelm Deist (ed.), *The German Military in the Age of Total War* (Leamington Spa, 1985).

Burin, 'Bureaucracy and National Socialism,' in Merton et al., eds., *Reader in Bureaucracy*—F. S. Burin, 'Bureaucracy and National Socialism: A Reconsideration of Weberian Theory,' in R. K. Merton, A. P. Gray, B. Hockey and H. C. Selvin (eds.), *Reader in Bureaucracy* (New York, 1952).

Calvocoressi, *Total War*, I—Peter Calvocoressi, Guy Wint and John Pritchard *Total War: The Causes and Courses of the Second World War*, Peter Calvocoressi, *Volume I: The Western Hemisphere* (second edition, London, 1989).

Carr, *Arms, Autarky and Aggression*—William Carr, *Arms, Autarky and Aggression: A Study in German Foreign Policy 1933-1939* (London, 1972).

Carroll, *Design for Total War*—Berenice A. Carroll, *Design for Total War: Arms and Economics in the Third Reich* (The Hague, 1968).

Chef. H.L.—*Chef Heeresleitung*—head of the army leadership.

Chef. H. Rüst u. BdE—*Chef Heeresrüstung und Befehlshaber des Ersatzheeres*—head of army armaments and commander of the Replacement Army.

Clark, *Barbarossa*—Alan Clark, *Barbarossa: The Russian-German Conflict 1941-45* (Harmondsworth, 1966).

Conot, *Nuremberg*—Robert E. Conot, *Justice at Nuremberg* (New York, 1983).

DAF—*Deutsche Arbeitsfront*—German Labour Front.

Dallin, *German Rule in Russia*—Alexander Dallin, *German Rule in Russia 1941-1945: A Study of Occupation Policies* (second edition, London, 1981).

Deist (ed.), *German Military in the Age of Total War*—Wilhelm Deist (ed.), *The German Military in the Age of Total War* (Leamington Spa, 1985).

Deist, 'Überlegungen,' in Michalka (ed.), *Der Zweite Weltkrieg*—Wilhelm Deist, 'Überlegungen zur "widerwilligen Loyalität" der Deutschen bei Kriegsbeginn,' in Wolfgang Michalka (ed.), *Der Zweite Weltkrieg: Analysen, Grundzüge, Forschungsbilanz* (Munich, 1989).

Abbreviations and German Terms Used in Notes 215

Deist, *Wehrmacht and Rearmament*—Wilhelm Deist, *The Wehrmacht and German Rearmament* (London, 1981).

Dietrich, *Hitler*—Otto Dietrich, *The Hitler I Knew* (London, 1957).

Dreier Ausschuss—Committee of Three.

DRZW—Militärgeschichtliches Forschungsamt, *Das Deutsche Reich und der Zweite Weltkrieg*, volumes 1—5/1 (Stuttgart, 1979-88).

Erickson, *Road to Berlin*—John Erickson, *The Road to Berlin: Stalin's War with Germany*, vol. 2, (London, 1985).

Ersatzheer—Replacement Army.

Fanning, 'German War Economy in 1941'—William Jeffress Fanning Jr., 'The German War Economy in 1941: A Study of Germany's Material and Manpower Problems in Relation to the Overall Military Effort' (Texas Christian University Ph.D. thesis, 1983).

Feldman, *Army, Industry and Labor*—Gerald D. Feldman, *Army, Industry and Labor in Germany, 1914-1918* (Princeton, N. J., 1966).

Fest, *Face of the Third Reich*—Joachim C. Fest, *The Face of the Third Reich* (Harmondsworth, 1972).

Fleischhauer, *Chance des Sonderfriedens*—Ingeborg Fleischhauer, *Die Chance des Sonderfriedens: Deutschsowjetische Geheimgespräche 1941-1945* (Berlin, 1986).

Förster, 'German Army and Policies of Genocide,' in Hirschfeld (ed.), *Policies of Genocide*—Jürgen Förster, 'The German Army and the Policies of Genocide,' in Gerhard Hirschfeld (ed.), *The Policies of Genocide: Jews and Soviet Prisoners of War in Nazi Germany* (London, 1986).

Frauenschaft—Women's League of the NSDAP.

Fredborg, *Behind the Steel Wall*—Arvid Fredborg, *Behind the Steel Wall* (London, 1944).

Fröhlich, 'Hitler und Goebbels im Krisenjahr 1944'—Elke Fröhlich, 'Hitler und Goebbels im Krisenjahr 1944. Aus den Tagebüchern des Reichspropagandaministers' *Vierteljahrshefte für Zeitgeschichte*, vol. 38, 1990.

Fröhlich (ed.), *Tagebücher von Joseph Goebbels*, 4—Elke Fröhlich on behalf of the Institut für Zeitgeschichte and in association with the Bundesarchiv (ed.), *Die Tagebücher von Joseph Goebbels Sämtliche Fragmente Teil I Aufzeichnungen 1924-1941, Band 4 1.1.1940-8.7.1941* (Munich, 1987).

Führerhauptquartier—main Führer headquarters.

Führerinformation—literally Führer information, submission.

Gau—region, the main territorial division of the NSDAP.

Gauleiter—Nazi Party functionary responsible for administration in a province or federal state.

GBA—Generalbevollmächtigter für den Arbeitseinsatz—General plenipotentiary for employment.

GBK or *GBTK—Generalbevollmächtigter für den Totalen Krieg* or *Generalbevollmächtigter für den Totalen Kriegseinsatz*—General plenipotentiary for total war.

GBV—Generalbevollmächtigter für die Reichsverwaltung—General plenipotentiary for Reich administration, Interior Minister.

GenGouv—Generalgouvernement—General Government, administration of unannexed sections of central occupied Poland.

Gerth, 'Nazi Party,' in Merton et al., eds., *Reader in Bureaucracy*—H. Gerth, 'The Nazi Party: Its Leadership and Composition,' (1940) in R. K. Merton, A. P. Gray, B. Hockey and H. C. Selvin (eds.), *Reader in Bureaucracy* (New York, 1952).

Gestapo—Geheime Staatspolizei—Secret State Police.

Geyer, 'German Strategy in the Age of Machine Warfare,' in Paret (ed.), *Makers of Modern Strategy*—Michael Geyer, 'German Strategy in the Age of Machine Warfare, 1914-1945,' in Peter Paret (ed.), *Makers of Modern Strategy from Machiavelli to the Nuclear Age* (Princeton, N. J., 1986).

gv.H.—garnisonsverwendungsfähig Heimat—capable of serving in a garrison on the home front.

Gliederungen—Formations or divisions; the collective name for paramilitary groups and other sections, including the Hitler Youth.

Hans Mommsen, 'Hitlers Stellung,' in Hirschfeld and Kettenacker, eds., *"Führer State,"*—Hans Mommsen, 'Hitlers Stellung im nationalsozialistischen Herrschaftssystem,' in Gerhard Hirschfeld and Lothar Kettenacker (eds.), *The "Führer State": Myth and Reality. Studies on the Structure and Politics of the Third Reich* (Stuttgart, 1981).

Hancock and Gowing, *British War Economy*—W. K. Hancock and M. M. Gowing, *British War Economy* (London, 1949).

Hauptamt—Main Office.

Heiber, *Goebbels*—Helmut Heiber, *Joseph Goebbels* (second edition, Munich, 1974).

Heiber (ed.), *Goebbels-Reden*, 2—Helmut Heiber (ed.), *Goebbels-Reden Band 2, 1939-1945* (Dusseldorf, 1972).

Herbert, *Fremdarbeiter*—Ulrich Herbert, *Fremdarbeiter: Politik und Praxis des "Ausländer-Einsatzes" in der Kriegswirtschaft des Dritten Reiches* (Berlin, 1985).

Herbst, *Totale Krieg*—Ludolf Herbst, *Der Totale Krieg und die Ordnung der Wirtschaft. Die Kriegswirtschaft im Spannungsfeld von Politik, Ideologie und Propaganda 1939-1945* (Stuttgart, 1982).

Heyl, 'The Construction of the *Westwall*, 1938'—J. D. Heyl, 'The Construction of the *Westwall*, 1938: An Examplar for National Socialist Policymaking,' *Central European History*, vol. 14, 1981.

Hirschfeld and Kettenacker, eds., *"Führer State,"*—Gerhard Hirschfeld and Lothar Kettenacker (eds.), *The "Führer State": Myth and Reality. Studies on the Structure and Politics of the Third Reich* (Stuttgart, 1981).

Hitler, *Mein Kampf*—Adolf Hitler, *Mein Kampf* (first published 1925 and 1927, Boston, 1943).

Hoheitsträger—'bearer of sovereignty'; title given to territorial chiefs in the Nazi Party's political organisation.

Homze, *Foreign Labor*—Edward Homze, *Foreign Labor in Nazi Germany* (Princeton, N. J., 1967).

HSSPF—Höhere SS- und Polizei Führer—Higher SS and Police Leaders.

HWaA—Heereswaffenamt—army weapons office.

IfZ—Institut für Zeitgeschichte, Munich.

IfZ APK—Institut für Zeitgeschichte, *Akten der Parteikanzlei Teil I* (Munich, 1983-1985).

Irving, *Göring*—David Irving, *Göring: A Biography* (New York, 1989).

Jacobsen, 'Krieg in Weltanschauung und Praxis,' in Bracher et al. (eds.), *Nationalsozialistische Diktatur*—Hans-Adolf Jacobsen, 'Krieg in Weltanschauung und Praxis des Nationalsozialismus (1919-1945),' in Karl Dietrich Bracher, Manfred Funke, and Hans-Adolf Jacobsen (eds.), *Nationalsozialistische Diktatur 1933-1945: eine Bilanz* (Dusseldorf, 1983).

Janssen, *Ministerium Speer*—Gregor Janssen, *Das Ministerium Speer: Deutschlands Rüstung im Krieg* (Frankfurt, 1968).

Jordan, *Erlebt und Erlitten*—Rudolf Jordan, *Erlebt und Erlitten: Weg eines Gauleiters von München bis Moskau* (Leoni am Starnberger See, 1971).

Jukes, *Hitler's Stalingrad Decisions*—Geoffrey Jukes, *Hitler's Stalingrad Decisions* (Berkeley, Calif., 1985).

Kampfzeit—literally period of struggle, period before the NSDAP came to power.

KDF—Kraft durch Freude—Strength through Joy, a DAF programme for worker recreation.

Kehrl, *Krisenmanager*—Hans Kehrl, *Krisenmanager im Dritten Reich. 6 Jahre Frieden 6 Jahre Krieg Errinerungen* (Dusseldorf, 1973).

Kempner, *Dritte Reich im Kreuzverhör*—Kempner, *Das Dritte Reich im Kreuzverhör: aus den Vernehmungsprotokollen des Anklagers* (Dusseldorf, 1984).

Kennedy, *Rise and Fall of the Great Powers*—Paul Kennedy, *The Rise and Fall of the Great Powers: Economic Change and Military Conflict from 1500 to 2000* (New York, 1987).

Kershaw, *'Hitler Myth'*—Ian Kershaw, *The 'Hitler Myth': Image and Reality in the Third Reich* (Oxford, 1989).

Kershaw, *Nazi Dictatorship*—Ian Kershaw, *The Nazi Dictatorship: Problems and Perspectives of Interpretation*, (second edition, London, 1989).

Kirwin, 'Allied Bombing and Nazi Domestic Propaganda'—Gerald Kirwin, 'Allied Bombing and Nazi Domestic Propaganda,' *European History Quarterly*, vol. 15, 1985.

Kitchen, *Silent Dictatorship*—Martin Kitchen, *The Silent Dictatorship: The Politics of the German High Command under Hindenburg and Ludendorff, 1916-1918* (London, 1976).

Klein, *Germany's Economic Preparations*—Burton H. Klein, *Germany's Economic Preparations for War* (Cambridge, Mass., 1959).

Kocka, *Facing Total War*—Jürgen Kocka, *Facing Total War: German Society 1914-1918* (Leamington Spa, 1984).

Koonz, *Mothers of the Fatherland*—Claudia Koonz, *Mothers of the Fatherland: Women, the Family and Nazi Politics* (London, 1987).

Kreisleiter—district party leader.

kv.—kriegsverwendungsfähig—fit for active service.

Lochner (ed.), *Goebbels Diaries*—Louis P. Lochner (ed.), *The Goebbels Diaries 1942-1943* (Garden City, N. Y., 1948).

Lochner, *What about Germany?*—Louis P. Lochner, *What about Germany?* (London, 1943).

Longerich, 'Joseph Goebbels und der totale Krieg'—Peter Longerich, 'Joseph Goebbels und der totale Krieg: eine unbekannte Denkschrift des Propagandaministers vom 18. Juli 1944,' *Vierteljahrhefte für Zeitgeschichte*, vol. 35, 1987.

Lothar Burchardt, 'Impact of the War Economy on the Civilian Population,' in Deist (ed)., *German Military in the Age of Total War*—Lothar Burchardt, 'The Impact of the War Economy on the Civilian Population of Germany during the First and Second World Wars,' in Wilhelm Deist (ed.), *The German Military in the Age of Total War* (Leamington Spa, 1985).

Lothar Kettenacker, 'Sozialpsychologische Aspekte der Führer-Herrschaft' in Hirschfeld and Kettenacker, (eds.), *"Führer State"*—Lothar Kettenacker, 'Sozialpsychologische Aspekte der Führer-Herrschaft,' in Gerhard Hirschfeld and Lothar Kettenacker (eds.), *The "Führer State": Myth and Reality. Studies on the Structure and Politics of the Third Reich* (Stuttgart, 1981).

Luftkriegsschädenausschuss—air war damage committee.

MA—*Bayerischen Staatskanzlei*—designation for files of Bavarian State Chancellery.

Mammach, *Volkssturm*—Klaus Mammach, *Der Volkssturm: Das letzte Aufgebot 1944/45* (Cologne, 1981).

Manvell and Fraenkel, *Goebbels*—Roger Manvell and Heinrich Fraenkel, *Doctor Goebbels* (revised edition, London, 1968).

Marrus, *Holocaust in History*—Michael R. Marrus, *The Holocaust in History* (London, 1987).

Mason, *Arbeiterklasse und Volksgemeinschaft*—Tim Mason, *Arbeiterklasse und Volksgemeinschaft. Dokumente und Materialen zur deutscher Arbeiterpolitik 1936-1939* (Opladen, 1975).

Mason, 'Intention and Explanation,' in Hirschfeld and Kettenacker, (eds.), *"Führer State"*—Tim Mason, 'Intention and Explanation: A Current Controversy about the Interpretation of National Socialism,' in Gerhard Hirschfeld and Lothar Kettenacker (eds.), *The "Führer State": Myth and Reality. Studies on the Structure and Politics of the Third Reich* (Stuttgart, 1981).

Mason, 'The Legacy of 1918 for National Socialism,' in Nicholls and Matthias (eds.), *German Democracy and the Triumph of Hitler*—Tim Mason, 'The Legacy of 1918 for National Socialism,' in Anthony Nicholls and Erich Matthias (eds.), *German Democracy and the Triumph of Hitler—Essays in Recent German History* (London, 1971).

Mason, 'Zum Frauenarbeit im NS-Staat'—Tim Mason, 'Zur Frauenarbeit im NS-Staat,' *Archiv für Sozialgeschichte*, vol. 19, 1979.

McNeill, *Pursuit of Power*—William H. McNeill, *The Pursuit of Power: Technology, Armed Force, and Society since A.D. 1000* (Oxford, 1983).

Meissner, *Magda Goebbels*—Hans-Otto Meissner, *Magda Goebbels: A Biography* (London, 1980).

Merton et al., eds., *Reader in Bureaucracy*—R. K. Merton, A. P. Gray, B. Hockey and H. C. Selvin (eds)., *Reader in Bureaucracy* (New York, 1952).

Mierzejewski, *Collapse of the German War Economy*—Alfred C. Mierzejewski, *The Collapse of the German War Economy, 1944-1945: Allied Air Power and the German National Railway* (Chapel Hill, N.C., 1988).

Milward, *German Economy*—Alan S. Milward, *The German Economy at War* (London, 1967).

Milward, *War, Economy and Society*—Alan S. Milward, *War, Economy and Society 1939-1945* (Berkeley, Calif., 1977).

Ministerratsverordnung—ministerial council decree.

MInn—*Staatsministerium des Innern*—designation for files of the Bavarian State Ministry of the Interior.

Mollin, *Montankonzerne und "Drittes Reich"*—Gerhard Mollin, *Montankonzerne und "Drittes Reich" : Der Gegensatz zwischen Monopolindustrie und Befehlswirtschaft in der deutschen Rüstung und Expansion 1936-1944* (Göttingen, 1988).

Müller, 'Die Mobilisierung der deutschen Wirtschaft,' *DRZW*, 5/1—Rolf-Dieter Müller, 'Die Mobilisierung der deutschen Wirtschaft für Hitlers Kriegsführung,' in Militärgeschichtliches Forschungsamt, *Das Deutsche Reich und der Zweite Weltkrieg*, vol. 5/1, *Kriegsverwaltung, Wirtschaft und personelle Ressourcen: 1939-1941* (Stuttgart, 1988).

Murray, *Luftwaffe*—Williamson Murray, *Luftwaffe* (Baltimore, 1985).

Murray, *The Path to Ruin*—Williamson Murray, *The Change in the European Balance of Power, 1938-1939: The Path to Ruin* (Princeton, N.J., 1984).

NL 118—*Nachlass Goebbels*—designation of the files of the personal papers of Joseph Goebbels.

NS 5 I—*Deutsche Arbeitsfront*—designation of the files of the German Labour Front.

NS 6—*Parteikanzlei der NSDAP*—designation of files of the NSDAP Party Chancellery.

NS 10—*Adjutantur des Führers*—designation of the files of the Führer's adjutants.

NS 18—*Reichspropagandaleitung*—designation of the files of the National Socialist Reich propaganda office.

NS 19—*Persönlicher Stab Reichsführer-SS*—designation for the files of the personal staff of the Reichsführer-SS.

NS 31—*SS Hauptamt*—designation for files of the SS Main Office.

NS 34—*SS Personal Hauptamt*—designation for the files of the SS personnel main office.

NS 37—*Hauptamt für Volkswohlfahrt, Nationalsozialistische Volkswohlfahrt*—designation of the files of the main office for popular welfare, National Socialist People's Welfare.

NS 44—*Reichsfrauenführung*—designation of the files of the National Socialist Reich women's leadership.

NSDAP—*Nationalsozialistische Deutsche Arbeiterpartei*—National Socialist (Nazi) German Workers' Party.

NSFO—*Nationalsozialistischer Führungsoffizier*—National Socialist leadership officer in the armed forces.

NSKK—Nationalsozialistisches Kraftfahrer-Korps—National Socialist Automobile Corps.

NS-Reichskriegerbund—National Socialist war veterans' league.

NSV—Nationalsozialistische Volkswohlfahrt—National Socialist welfare organisation.

OKH—Oberkommando des Heeres—Supreme Command of the Army.

OKL—Oberkommando der Luftwaffe—Supreme Command of the Air Force.

OKM—Oberkommando der Marine—Supreme Command of the Navy.

OKW—Oberkommando der Wehrmacht—Supreme Command of the armed forces.

ORBs—Oberste Reichsbehörden—Supreme Reich authorities.

Orlow, *Nazi Party*, II—Dietrich Orlow, *The History of the Nazi Party*: Vol. II *1933-1945* (Newton Abbot, 1973).

Ostministerium, or RMO—Reichsministerium für die besetzten Ostgebiete—Reich ministry for the occupied Eastern territories.

OT—Organisation Todt—building organisation involving state building administration and private firms.

Overy, '"Blitzkriegwirtschaft"?'—R. J. Overy, '"Blitzkriegwirtschaft"?' Finanzpolitik, Lebensstandard und Arbeitseinsatz in Deutschland 1939-1942,' *Vierteljahrshefte für Zeitgeschichte*, vol. 36, 1988.

Overy, 'Germany, "Domestic Crisis" and War'—R. J. Overy, 'Germany, "Domestic Crisis" and War,' *Past and Present*, Nr. 116, August 1987.

Overy, *Goering*—R. J. Overy, *Goering the 'Iron Man'* (London, 1984).

Overy, 'Hitler's War and the German Economy'—R. J. Overy, 'Hitler's War and the German Economy: A Reinterpretation,' *The Economic History Review*, vol. 35, 1982.

Overy, 'Hitler's War Plans and the German Economy,' in Boyce and Robertson, (eds)., *Paths to War*—Richard Overy, 'Hitler's War Plans and the German Economy,' in Robert Boyce and Esmonde M. Robertson (eds)., *Paths to War: New Essays on the Origins of the Second World War* (London, 1989).

Overy, *Air War*—R. J. Overy, *The Air War 1939-1945* (London, 1980).

Persönlicher Stab Reichsführer SS—Personal Staff of the Reichsführer of the SS.

PO—Politische Organisation—political organisation; cadre for mobilizing NSDAP political activists.

R 3—*Reichsministerium für Rüstung und Kriegsproduktion*—designation for the files of the Reich Ministry of Armaments and War Production.

R 7—*Reichswirtschaftsministerium*—designation for the files of the Reich Economics Ministry.

R 11—*Reichswirtschaftskammer*—designation for the files of the Reich Economics Chamber.

R 12 I—*Reichsgruppe Industrie*—designation for the files of the Reich Industry Group.

R 24—*Statistisches Reichsamt*—designation for the files of the Statistical Reich Office.

R 26—*der Beauftragte für den Vierjahresplan*—designation for the files of the plenipotentiary for the four year plan.

R 41—*Reichsarbeitsministerium*—designation for the files of the Labour Ministry.

R 43 II—*Reichskanzlei*—designation of Reich Chancellery files.

R 48—*Reichspostministerium*—designation for the files of the Reich Post Ministry.

R 55—*Reichsministerium für Volksaufklärung und Propaganda*—designation of files of the Ministry for Popular Enlightenment and Propaganda.

RAD—*Reichsarbeitsdienst*—Reich Labour Service.

RD 75—designation for Statistisches Reichsamt publications.

Rebentisch, *Führerstaat und Verwaltung*—Dieter Rebentisch, *Führerstaat und Verwaltung im Zweiten Weltkrieg: Verfassungsentwicklung und Verwaltungspolitik 1939-1945* (Stuttgart, 1989).

Recker, *Nationalsozialistische Sozialpolitik*—Marie-Luise Recker, *Nationalsozialistische Sozialpolitik im Zweiten Weltkrieg* (Munich, 1975).

Reichspostdirektionen—Reich post management offices.

Reichsbevollmächtigter für den totalen Krieg—Reich plenipotentiary for total war.

Reimann, *Goebbels*—Viktor Reimann, *The Man Who Created Hitler: Joseph Goebbels* (London, 1977).

Rep. 312—designation for the files of the von Unruh commission.

RFSS—*Reichsführer-SS*—Reich SS Leader.

RH 2—*Oberkommando des Heeres (OKH)/Generalstab des Heeres*—designation for the files of the army supreme command/ army general staff.

RH 8 I—*Oberkommando des Heeres (OKH)/Heereswaffenamt*—designation for the files of the army supreme command/ army weapons office.

RH 15—*Oberkommando des Heeres (OKH)/Allgemeines Heeresamt*—designation for the files of the army supreme command/ general army office.

RK—*Reichskommissar*—Reich commissioner; title of a Nazi chief of civilian administration in the occupied areas of Europe.

RKFDV—*Reichskommissar für die Festigung Deutschen Volkstums*—Reich Commissioner for the Strengthening of Germandom.

RL 2—*Generalstab der Luftwaffe*—designation for the files of general staff of the air force.

RL 2 I—*Chef des Generalstabes*—designation for the files of head of the general staff of the air force.

RL 3—*Generalluftzeugmeister*—designation for the files of the head of air force supplies.

RM—*Reichsmark*—German unit of currency.

RPÄ—*Reichspropagandaämter*—Reich propaganda offices.

RPL—*Reichspropagandaleitung*—propaganda leadership; NSDAP propaganda office.

Rupp, *Mobilizing Women*—Leila J. Rupp, *Mobilizing Women for War: German and American Propaganda, 1939-1945* (Princeton, N.J., 1978).

Rupp, 'Women, Class and Mobilization in Nazi Germany'—Leila J. Rupp, 'Women, Class, and Mobilization in Nazi Germany,' *Science and Society*, vol. 43, 1979.

RW 4—*Oberkommando der Wehrmacht (OKW)/Wehrmachtführungsstab*—designation for the files of the supreme command of the armed forces/ armed forces leadership staff.

RW 6—*Oberkommando der Wehrmacht (OKW)/Allgemeines Wehrmachtamt*— designation for the files of the supreme command of the armed forces/ general armed forces office.

RW 19—*Oberkommando der Wehrmacht (OKW)/ Wehrwirtschafts- und Rüstungsamt*— designation for the files of the supreme command of the armed forces/ war economy and armaments office.

Ryan, *Last Battle*—Cornelius Ryan, *The Last Battle* (London, 1968).

SA—Sturmabteilungen—Storm troopers.

Salter, 'Mobilisation of German Labour'—Stephen Salter, 'The Mobilisation of German Labour, 1939-1945. A Contribution to the History of the Working Class in the Third Reich,' (unpublished D. Phil. thesis, Oxford, 1983).

Sauer, *Württemberg*—Paul Sauer, *Württemberg in der Zeit des Nationalsozialismus* (Ulm, 1975).

S-Betriebe—Sperr-Betriebe—blocked firms, in the occupied territories whose employees were protected from transport to Germany.

Scheinarbeit—illusory employment, nominal employment designed to prevent the employee from being called on for actual labour.

Schellenberg, *Labyrinth*—Walter Schellenberg, *The Labyrinth: Memoirs of Walter Schellenberg* (New York, 1956).

Schlüsselkräfte—key workers, protected from call up because of their importance to the war effort.

Schmidt, *Speer Myth*—Matthias Schmidt, *Albert Speer—The End of a Myth* (London, 1985).

Schupetta, *Frauen- und Ausländererwerbstätigkeit*—Ingrid Schupetta, *Frauen- und Ausländererwerbstätigkeit in Deutschland von 1939 bis 1945* (Cologne, 1983).

SD—Sicherheitsdienst—Security Service, SS secret intelligence unit.

SE—Sondererziehung—special call-up programme, known as SE I, etc.

Seidler, *"Deutscher Volkssturm"*—Franz W. Seidler, *"Deutscher Volkssturm" : Das letzte Aufgebot 1944/45* (Munich, 1989).

Semmler, *Goebbels*—Rudolf Semmler, *Goebbels—the man next to Hitler* (Ohio State University reprint, 1982 of London, 1947 edition).

Speer Chronik—office journal compiled in Albert Speer's office recording his official activities.

Speer, *Slave State*—Albert Speer, *The Slave State: Heinrich Himmler's Masterplan for SS Supremacy* (London, 1981).

Speer, *Spandau*—Albert Speer, *Spandau: The Secret Diaries* (London, 1978).

Speer, *Third Reich*—Albert Speer, *Inside the Third Reich* (London, 1970).

SS—Schutzstaffel—Guard squadrons.

SS-Führungshauptamt—SS Leadership Main Office.

Statistisches Reichsamt—Reich office of statistics.

Steinert, *Hitler's War and the Germans*—Marlis Steinert, *Hitler's War and the Germans: Public Mood and Attitude during the Second World War* (Ohio, 1977).

Stephenson, '"Emancipation" and its Problems'—Jill Stephenson, '"Emancipation" and its Problems: War and Society in Württemberg 1939-45,' *European History Quarterly*, vol. 17, 1987.

Stolper, *German Economy*—Gustav Stolper, Karl Häuser and Knut Borchardt, *The German Economy 1870 to the Present* (second edition, London, 1967).

Summerfield, *Women Workers in the Second World War*—Penny Summerfield, *Women Workers in the Second World War: Production and Patriarchy in Conflict* (second edition, London, 1989).

Sywottek, *Mobilmachung*—Jutta Sywottek, *Mobilmachung für den totalen Krieg: Die propagandistische Vorbereitung der deutschen Bevölkerung auf den Zweiten Weltkrieg* (Opladen, 1976).

Thomas, *Geschichte*—Georg Thomas, *Geschichte der deutschen Wehr- und Rüstungswirtschaft (1918-1943/45)* (Boppard am Rhein, 1966).

Tidl, *Die Frau im Nationalsozialismus*—Georg Tidl, *Die Frau im Nationalsozialismus* (Vienna, 1984).

Tiessler, 'Licht und Schatten,' IfZ ED 158—Walter Tiessler, 'Licht und Schatten oder Schonungslose Wahrheit (1922-1945),' IfZ ED 158.

TMWC—*Trial of the Major War Criminals Before the International Military Tribunal, Nuremberg, 14 November 1945-1 October 1946* (reprint, New York, 1971).

Trevor-Roper (ed.), *Bormann Letters*—Hugh Trevor-Roper (ed.), *The Bormann Letters: The Private Correspondence Between Martin Bormann and His Wife from January 1943 to April 1945* (London, 1954).

Trevor-Roper (ed.), *Final Entries*—Hugh Trevor-Roper (ed.), *Final Entries: The Diaries of Joseph Goebbels* (New York, 1978).

Trevor-Roper, *Last Days*—Hugh Trevor-Roper, *The Last Days of Hitler* (revised edition, London, 1965).

Tuten, 'Germany and the World Wars', in Goldman (ed.), *Female Soldiers*—Jeff M. Tuten, 'Germany and the World Wars', in Nancy Loring Goldman (ed.), *Female Soldiers—Combatants or Noncombatants? Historical and Contemporary Perspectives* (Westport, Conn., 1982).

uk—*unabkömmlich*—indispensable workers.

Verordnungsblätter—literally decree paper; gazette.

Volkssturm—'People's Storm'; militia organisation.

von Gersdorff, *Frauen im Kriegsdienst*—Ursula von Gersdorff, *Frauen im Kriegsdienst, 1914-1945* (Stuttgart, 1969).

von Lang, *Bormann*—Jochen von Lang, *Bormann the Man Who Manipulated Hitler* (London, 1979).

von Oven, *Finale Furioso*—Wilfred von Oven, *Finale Furioso: Mit Goebbels bis zum Ende* (first published 1948-50, Tübingen, 1974).

VWHA—*Verwaltungs- und Wirtschafts-Hauptamt*—Main Office for Administration and the Economy of the SS.

WaA—*Waffenamt*—Weapons Office.

Weber, 'Sociology of Charismatic Authority,' in Gerth and Mills (eds.), *From Max Weber*—Max Weber, 'The Sociology of Charismatic Authority,' in H. H. Gerth and C. Wright Mills (eds.), *From Max Weber: Essays in Sociology* (new edition, New York, 1973).

Wehrhilfsdienst—armed forces' auxiliary service.

Wehrmachtssanitätswesens—armed forces' medical service.

Wehrersatzdienststellen—armed forces' recruiting offices.

Wehrersatzplan—armed forces' replacement plan.

Wehrwirtschaft—defence economy.

Wehrpflichtige—those liable for military service.

Weinberg, *World in Balance*—Gerhard Weinberg, *World in the Balance: Behind the Scenes of World War II* (Hanover, 1981).

Werner, 'Belastungen der deutschen Arbeiterschaft in der zweiten Kriegshälfte,' in Borsdorf and Jamin (eds.), *Überleben im Krieg*—Wolfgang Franz Werner, 'Belastungen der deutschen Arbeiterschaft in der zweiten Kriegshälfte,' in Ulrich Borsdorf and Mathilde Jamin (eds.), *Überleben im Krieg. Kriegserfahrungen in einer Industrieregion 1939-1945* (Hamburg, 1989).

Werner, *'Bleib übrig!'*—Wolfgang Werner, *'Bleib übrig!' Deutsche Arbeiter in der nationalsozialistischen Kriegswirtschaft* (Dusseldorf, 1983).

WFSt.—Wehrmachtsführungsstab—armed forces' leadership staff.

Winkler, 'Frauenarbeit versus Frauenideologie'—Dörte Winkler, 'Frauenarbeit versus Frauenideologie: Probleme der weiblichen Erwerbstätigkeit in Deutschland 1930-45,' *Archiv für Sozialgeschichte*, vol. 17, 1977.

WiRüAmt—Wehrwirtschafts- und Rüstungsamt—war economy and armaments office.

W. Mommsen, *Age of Bureaucracy*—W. J. Mommsen, *The Age of Bureaucracy: Perspectives on the Sociology of Max Weber* (Oxford, 1974).

Wright, 'Army of Despair'—Burton Wright III, 'Army of Despair: The German Volkssturm 1944-1945' (Florida State University, Ph.D. thesis, 1982).

WVHA—Wirtschafts- und Verwaltungs-Hauptamt—Main Office for Economy and Administration in the SS (reorganisation of VWHA).

Zilbert, *Speer and Nazi Ministry of Arms*—Edward R. Zilbert, *Albert Speer and the Nazi Ministry of Arms: Economic Institutions and Industrial Production in the German War Economy* (East Brunswick, N.J., 1981).

NOTES

In each chapter books and articles will be cited in full at their first citation; citations then follow the abbreviated format as set out in the list of abbreviations. Documents are cited by giving the author's name and position, date of writing or delivery, the title or heading of the document, the abbreviation for the archive, the overall number or abbreviation given to the files of that organisation or ministry by the archive, and finally the specific file number. These abbreviations are set out in Abbreviations and German Terms Used in Notes.

Introduction

1. Entry, 9 March 1945, Hugh Trevor-Roper (ed.), *Final Entries 1945: The Diaries of Joseph Goebbels* (New York, 1978), p. 88. Goebbels' views: entry, 4 March 1945, *ibid.*, p. 41; entry, 7 March 1945, *ibid.*, p. 71. Speer's views: Speer to Hitler, 29 March 1945, BA R 3/1538, p. 2; notes typed by Speer after the war, probably at Nuremberg, 'AH/III/Blatt 13,' BA R 3/1626, p. 8. Reasons advanced in Speer's memoirs: Albert Speer, *Inside the Third Reich* (London, 1970)—Hitler's fear of unrest, p. 214; Hitler's reluctance to face reality about enemy capacity and to relinquish his building projects, pp. 165, 168, 181; excessive bureaucratisation, p. 213; the failure to employ women, pp. 220-1.

2. Studies include Berenice A. Carroll, *Design for Total War: Arms and Economics in the Third Reich* (The Hague, 1968); Alan S. Milward, *War, Economy and Society 1939-1945* (Berkeley, Calif., 1977); Alan S. Milward, *The German Economy at War* (London, 1967); William Jeffress Fanning Jr., 'The German War Economy in 1941: A Study of Germany's Material and Manpower Problems in Relation to the Overall Military Effort' (Texas Christian University Ph.D. thesis, 1983); Edward R. Zilbert, *Albert Speer and the Nazi Ministry of Arms: Economic Institutions and Industrial Production in the German War Economy* (East Brunswick, N. J., 1981); Gregor Janssen, *Das Ministerium Speer: Deutschlands Rüstung im Krieg* (Frankfurt, 1968); Jutta Sywottek, *Mobilmachung für den totalen Krieg: Die propagandistische Vorbereitung der deutschen Bevölkerung auf den Zweiten Weltkrieg* (Opladen, 1976); Ludolf Herbst, *Der Totale Krieg und die Ordnung der Wirtschaft. Die Kriegswirtschaft im Spannungsfeld von Politik, Ideologie und Propaganda 1939-1945* (Stuttgart, 1982). National Socialist propaganda: Jay W. Baird, *The Mythical World of Nazi War Propaganda, 1939-1945* (Minneapolis, Minn., 1974); E. K. Bramsted, *Goebbels and National Socialist Propaganda 1925-1945* (East Lansing, Mich., 1965). Historians argue the regime mobilised reluctantly: Carroll, *Design for Total War*, p. 93; Milward, *German Economy*, pp. 6, 8-16; Herbst, *Totale Krieg*, pp. 174-5; Zilbert, *Speer and Nazi Ministry of Arms*, pp. 228-31. Study of Armaments Ministry: Janssen, *Ministerium Speer*. Studies of Economics Ministry: Herbst, *Totale Krieg;* Willi A. Boelcke, *Die deutsche*

Wirtschaft 1930-1945: Interna des Reichswirtschaftsministeriums (Dusseldorf, 1983). OKW's economics and armaments office: Carroll, *Design for Total War*. Railways: Alfred C. Mierzejewski, *The Collapse of the German War Economy, 1944-1945: Allied Air Power and the German National Railway* (Chapel Hill, N.C., 1988).

3. Carroll, *Design for Total War*, p. 9.

4. Bormann's displacement of Hess: Dietrich Orlow, *The History of the Nazi Party: vol. II, 1933-1945* (Newton Abbot, 1973), pp. 75-62. Bormann becomes head of the Party Chancellery: Speer, *Third Reich*, p. 175. Hitler content to let Bormann handle most matters: Otto Dietrich, *The Hitler I Knew* (London, 1957), pp. 196-7. Bormann's admiration for Hitler: his letters to Gerda Bormann of 16 January 1943, 16 February 1943 and 6 July 1943, H. R. Trevor-Roper (ed.), *The Bormann Letters: The Private Correspondence Between Martin Bormann and His Wife from January 1943 to April 1945* (London, 1954), pp. 2, 6, 12. Bormann's position as one of co-ordination: Hans Mommsen, 'Hitlers Stellung im nationalsozialistischen Herrschaftssystem,' in Gerhard Hirschfeld and Lothar Kettenacker (eds.), *The "Führer State": Myth and Reality. Studies on the Structure and Politics of the Third Reich* (Stuttgart, 1981), p. 50. Sources of Bormann's power: Jochen von Lang, *Bormann the Man Who Manipulated Hitler* (London, 1979), p. 270; Walter Tiessler, 'Licht und Schatten oder Schonungslose Wahrheit (1922-1945),' IfZ ED 158, p. 176. Bormann's ability to influence decisions: Walter Schellenberg, *The Labyrinth: Memoirs of Walter Schellenberg* (New York, 1956), p. 317. Bormann's power not recognised: Speer, *Third Reich*, p. 87. For suggestions that Bormann controlled Hitler: von Lang, *Bormann*, p. 220; Speer, *Third Reich*, p. 253. The opposite view is advanced by Hugh Trevor-Roper, *The Last Days of Hitler* (revised edition, London, 1965), p. 89; and most recently Dieter Rebentisch, *Führerstaat und Verwaltung im Zweiten Weltkrieg: Verfassungsentwicklung und Verwaltungspolitik 1939-1945* (Stuttgart, 1989), p. 412. Christa Schroeder's view: Christa Schroeder, *Er war mein Chef: Aus dem Nachlass der Sekretärin von Adolf Hitler* (Munich, 1985), p. 32. Lammers' view: Rebentisch, *Führerstaat und Verwaltung*, p. 412. Speer's views of Bormann: Speer, *Third Reich*, pp. 95, 122, 253.

5. Goebbels' positions: Roger Manvell and Heinrich Fraenkel, *Doctor Goebbels* (revised edition, London, 1968), pp. 69, 83, 112. Goebbels' view of his task: 'Reichsminister Goebbels über die Aufgaben seines Ministeriums,' 16 March 1933, Wolff's Telegraphisches Büro, BA R43II/149, col. 1, p. 2. Goebbels' control and direction of propaganda: Baird, *Nazi War Propaganda*, pp. 16-19, 23-35. Characterisation of Goebbels: interrogation of Meissner, 31 August 1945, IfZ MA 1300/2, frame 0531. Baarova affair strains Hitler's friendship: Dietrich, *Hitler*, p. 238. Goebbels' position strengthened in wartime: Martin Broszat, *The Hitler State* (London, 1981), p. 313. Goebbels' membership of Hitler's inner circle: Speer, *Third Reich*, pp. 120, 123-6. Goebbels' commitment to Hitler: Goebbels to Hitler, 20 April 1944, p. 6; Goebbels to Hitler, Christmas 1943, BA NL 118/106, pp. 1-5.

6. Hitler certain of Goebbels' and Himmler's loyalty: Dietrich, *Hitler*, pp. 114-15. Himmler's loyalty to Hitler: Felix Kersten, *The Kersten Memoirs 1940-1945* (London, 1956), pp. 152, 298-301. Positions held by Himmler: Roger Manvell and Heinrich Fraenkel, *Heinrich Himmler* (second edition, London, 1969), pp. 29, 63. A summary of the expansion of SS power is provided by Broszat, *Hitler State*, pp.

270-6. Himmler's world view: Joachim C. Fest, *The Face of the Third Reich* (Harmondsworth, 1972), pp. 171-90.

7. Quoted in David Irving, *The Rise and Fall of the Luftwaffe: The Life of Luftwaffe Marshal Erhard Milch* (London, 1973), p. 332. Speer's career in the 1930s: Matthias Schmidt, *Albert Speer—The End of a Myth* (London, 1985), pp. 33, 38-46. Speer's close links to Hitler and his ability to prosper in the National Socialist system: *ibid.*, pp. 41-3, 50-2; testimony of Otto Ohlendorf, 3 January 1946, *Trial of the Major War Criminals Before the International Military Tribunal, Nuremberg, 14 November 1945-1 October 1946* (reprint, New York, 1971), vol. 4, pp. 343-4. Historians' views: Trevor-Roper, *Last Days*, pp. 120-2; Fest, *Face of the Third Reich*, pp. 298-314.

8. Peter Longerich, 'Joseph Goebbels und der totale Krieg: eine unbekannte Denkschrift des Propagandaministers vom 18. Juli 1944,' *Vierteljahrshefte für Zeitgeschichte*, vol. 35, 1987, pp. 289-314; Herbst, *Totale Krieg*, p. 197.

9. For an introduction to the historical debate on monocracy versus polycracy: Ian Kershaw, *The Nazi Dictatorship: Problems and Perspectives of Interpretation*, (second edition, London, 1989), chapter 4. Conflict arises because Hitler governs by divide and rule: Dietrich, *Hitler*, p. 119. The system was based on Hitler's personal authority: Karl Dietrich Bracher, 'Tradition und Revolution im Nationalsozialismus,' and 'Probleme und Perspektiven der Hitler-Interpretationen,' both in *Zeitgeschichtliche Kontroversen: Um Faschismus, Totalitarismus, Demokratie* (Munich, 1976), pp. 65, 85; Andreas Hillgruber, 'Tendenzen, Ergebnisse und Perspektiven der gegenwärtigen Hitler-Forschung,' *Historische Zeitschrift*, vol. 266 (1978), p. 612, note 35.

10. Hitler's power arose out of political and institutional divisions: Tim Mason, 'Intention and Explanation: A Current Controversy about the Interpretation of National Socialism,' in Hirschfeld and Kettenacker (eds.), *"Führer State,"* p. 25; Broszat, *Hitler State*, p. 359. Reasons for the regime's sudden and extreme decisions: Mason, 'Intention and Explanation,' in Hirschfeld and Kettenacker (eds.), *"Führer State,"* pp. 25, 27. Radicalisation of policy: Hans Mommsen, 'Hitlers Stellung,' in *ibid.*, pp. 50-6, 61. Hitler's style of working: *ibid.*, p. 59; Mason, 'Intention and Explanation,' in *ibid.*, p. 33; Orlow, *Nazi Party*, II, p. 9. Historians' differing views on autonomy: Walther Hofer, 'Fifty Years On: Historians and the Third Reich,' *Journal of Contemporary History*, vol. 21 (1986), pp. 228-9; Broszat, *Hitler State*, pp. 278-9.

11. H. Gerth, 'The Nazi Party: Its Leadership and Composition' (1940), in R. K. Merton, A. P. Gray, B. Hockey and H. C. Selvin (eds.), *Reader in Bureaucracy* (New York, 1952), p. 102. Other recent works using charismatic authority: Ian Kershaw, *The 'Hitler Myth': Image and Reality in the Third Reich* (Oxford, 1989), pp. 8-9; Gerhard Mollin, *Montankonzerne und "Drittes Reich": Der Gegensatz zwischen Monopolindustrie und Befehlswirtschaft in der deutschen Rüstung und Expansion 1936-1944* (Göttingen, 1988), pp. 24-5. Theories of charismatic leadership: Max Weber, 'The Sociology of Charismatic Authority,' in H. H. Gerth and C. Wright Mills (eds.), *From Max Weber: Essays in Sociology* (new edition, New York, 1973), pp. 247, 262; W. J. Mommsen, *The Age of Bureaucracy: Perspectives on the Sociology of Max Weber* (Oxford, 1974), pp. 73, 78-80, 102; F. S. Burin, 'Bureaucracy and National Socialism: A Reconsideration of Weberian Theory,' in Merton et al. (eds.), *Reader in Bureaucracy*, pp. 36, 38; Gerth, 'Nazi Party,' in

ibid., p. 100. Hitler's followers willing to subject themselves unconditionally to his leadership: Burin, 'Bureaucracy and National Socialism,' in *ibid.*, pp. 33-47; Lothar Kettenacker, 'Sozialpsychologische Aspekte der Führer-Herrschaft,' in Hirschfeld and Kettenacker (eds.), *"Führer State"*, p. 129. Consequences of Hitler's charismatic authority: Gerth, 'Nazi Party,' in Merton et al. (eds.), *Reader in Bureaucracy*, pp. 100-113.

12.   Orlow, *Nazi Party*, II, p. 7.

13.   Third Reich both monolithic and pluralistic: Karl Dietrich Bracher, 'Der umstrittene Totalitarismus: Erfahrung und Aktualität,' *Zeitgeschichtliche Kontroversen*, p. 47. Polycracy reigned among the secondary leaders: H. Mommsen, 'Hitlers Stellung,' in Hirschfeld and Kettenacker (eds.), *"Führer State,"* p. 45; Wolfgang Horn, 'Zur Geschichte und Struktur des Nationalsozialismus und der NSDAP,' *Neue Politische Literatur*, vol. 18, 1973, p. 206; W. Mommsen, *Age of Bureaucracy*, p. 78. Hitler could be influenced but not directed: Rebentisch, *Führerstaat und Verwaltung*, pp. 414. Nature of Hitler's rule that decisions not final: *ibid.*, p. 411. Interpretation of Hitler's orders by secondary leaders: see Bormann's response to Hitler's decree shutting down building on the Obersalzberg: entry for 5-6 June 1943, Willi A. Boelcke (ed.), *Deutschlands Rüstung im Zweiten Weltkrieg: Hitlers Konferenzen mit Albert Speer 1942-1945* (Frankfurt, 1969), p. 72, and Martin Bormann to Gerda Bormann, 8-9 September 1944, Trevor-Roper (ed.), *Bormann Letters*, pp. 103-4.

14.   Instability of charismatic authority: W. Mommsen, *Age of Bureaucracy*, pp. 79-83; Max Weber, 'The Routinization of Charisma,' in Merton et al. (eds.), *Reader in Bureaucracy*, pp. 92-100; Weber, 'Sociology of Charismatic Authority,' in Gerth and Mills (eds.), *From Max Weber*, p. 248. Irrational charisma and rational bureaucracy: Mollin, *Montankonzerne und "Drittes Reich,"* p. 278. Tension between bureaucracy and party leadership: E. N. Peterson, 'The Bureaucracy and the Nazi Party,' *Review of Politics*, vol. 28, 1966, pp. 178, 186, 190-2. Power of Gauleiters: Orlow, *Nazi Party*, II, pp. 11, 33-52; Zilbert, *Speer and Ministry of Arms*, pp. 43-4.

15.   Broszat, *Hitler State*, p. xiv. Broszat recognises Hitler's charismatic authority: *ibid.*, pp. x-xii. Organisational conflict in a bureaucratic system: M. H. Halperin, *Bureaucratic Politics and Foreign Policy* (Washington, 1974), pp. 219, 232, 245. Murray has pointed out: Williamson Murray, *The Change in the European Balance of Power, 1938-1939: The Path to Ruin* (Princeton, N. J., 1984), pp. 23, 26-7. Hitler saw conflict as a substitute for checks and balances: Carroll, *Design for Total War*, pp. 121 note 29, 271-2 note 10. Conflict as a means of seeking optimum performance: Michael Geyer, 'German Strategy in the Age of Machine Warfare, 1914-1945,' in Peter Paret (ed.), *Makers of Modern Strategy from Machiavelli to the Nuclear Age* (Princeton, N. J., 1986), p. 586.

16.   Mierzejewski, *Collapse of the German War Economy*, p. 6.

17.   Charles W. Sydnor, Jr., *Soldiers of Destruction: The SS Death's Head Division, 1933-1945* (Princeton, N. J., 1977), p. 346.

18.   W. K. Hancock and M. M. Gowing, *British War Economy* (London, 1949), pp. 10-11. Importance of industrial capacity: William H. McNeill, *The Pursuit of Power: Technology, Armed Force, and Society since A.D. 1000* (Oxford, 1983), pp. 242-3; Raymond Aron, *The Century of Total War* (Boston, 1966), p. 19; Brian

Bond, *War and Society in Europe, 1870-1970* (London, 1984), pp. 24, 27. Constraints on organisation of modern economy: Hancock and Gowing, *British War Economy*, pp. 20, 491-2.

19. Carroll, *Design for Total War*, p. 9. The nation in arms: Michael Howard, *War in European History* (revised edition, Oxford, 1979), pp. 80-1; McNeill, *Pursuit of Power*, p. 192. Use of ideology and political indoctrination in French revolutionary wars: Geoffrey Best, *War and Society in Revolutionary Europe, 1770-1870* (London, 1982), pp. 75, 77-8, 87, 93-5, 96-7; John A. Lynn, *The Bayonets of the Republic: Motivation and Tactics in the Army of Revolutionary France, 1791-94* (Urbana, Ill., 1984), pp. 67, 77-87, 106-8, 124-62.

20. Herbst, *Totale Krieg*, p. 100-1.

Chapter 1

1. Quoted, entry, 26 September 1938, William Shirer, *Berlin Diary: The Journal of a Foreign Correspondent 1934-1941* (London, 1942), pp. 118-19.

2. Goebbels to Hitler, Christmas 1943, BA NL 118/106, p. 2.

3. William H. McNeill, *The Pursuit of Power: Technology, Armed Force, and Society since A.D. 1000* (Oxford, 1983), pp. 309, 317-18, 321-2, 330-1, 335-6; Raymond Aron, *The Century of Total War* (Boston, 1966), p. 19; Brian Bond, *War and Society in Europe, 1870-1970* (London, 1984), pp. 101, 106, 148; John U. Nef, *War and Human Progress: An Essay on the Rise of Industrial Civilization* (Cambridge, Mass., 1952), pp. 331, 335.

4. Aim of armed forces' demands: Michael Geyer, 'German Strategy in the Age of Machine Warfare, 1914-1945,' in Peter Paret (ed.), *Makers of Modern Strategy from Machiavelli to the Nuclear Age* (Princeton, N. J., 1986), p. 544. Hindenburg Programme divorced from economic reality: Gerald D. Feldman, *Army, Industry and Labor in Germany, 1914-1918* (Princeton, N. J., 1966), pp. 150, 153-4, 272-3; Martin Kitchen, *The Silent Dictatorship: The Politics of the German High Command under Hindenburg and Ludendorff, 1916-1918* (London, 1976), p. 274. Military attempt to command labour: Feldman, *Army, Industry and Labor*, pp. 33-4, 117, 172-3; Kitchen, *Silent Dictatorship*, pp. 69-75. Uncontrolled profitmaking: Feldman, *Army, Industry and Labor*, pp. 63, 157-8. Lack of economic planning for a long war and poor co-ordination of production: McNeill, *Pursuit of Power*, pp. 323, 328. German economic failure in the misallocation of resources: W. K. Hancock and M. M. Gowing, *British War Economy* (London, 1949), p. 19. Inadequacy of food supply: Lothar Burchardt, 'The Impact of the War Economy on the Civilian Population of Germany during the First and Second World Wars,' in Wilhelm Deist (ed.), *The German Military in the Age of Total War* (Leamington Spa, 1985), pp. 41-4, 46. Food shortages: Jürgen Kocka, *Facing Total War: German Society 1914-1918* (Leamington Spa, 1984), pp. 24-6. Problems in German agriculture: Gerd Hardach, *The First World War 1914-1918* (Harmondsworth, 1987), pp. 112-16.

5. Ludolf Herbst, *Der Totale Krieg und die Ordnung der Wirtschaft. Die Kriegswirtschaft im Spannungsfeld von Politik, Ideologie und Propaganda 1939-1945* (Stuttgart, 1982), pp. 39, 180. Belief that the German home front had not been as reliable: *ibid.*, p. 42. Emphasis on propaganda and ideological mobilisation by

Ludendorff and Tirpitz: Geyer, 'German Strategy in the Age of Machine Warfare,' in Paret (ed.), *Makers of Modern Strategy*, pp. 544-5, 548. Schmitt's concept of total war: Herbst, *Totale Krieg*, p. 36; Jutta Sywottek, *Mobilmachung für den totalen Krieg: Die propagandistische Vorbereitung der deutschen Bevölkerung auf den Zweiten Weltkrieg* (Opladen, 1976), p. 19. Jünger's view of the next war: Wolfram Wette, 'From Kellogg to Hitler (1928-1933). German Public Opinion Concerning the Rejection or Glorification of War,' in Deist (ed.), *German Military in the Age of Total War*, pp. 81-8. Ludendorff called for a total orientation of the state for waging war: Geyer, 'German Strategy in the Age of Machine Warfare,' in Paret (ed.), *Makers of Modern Strategy*, p. 538. Ludendorff envisaged Germany in the next war: Herbst, *Totale Krieg*, p. 38. Ludendorff proposes a military command structure: *ibid.*, p. 43. Ludendorff on excluding Jews: *ibid.*, pp. 45, 49.

6.   Adolf Hitler, *Mein Kampf* (first published 1925 and 1927, Boston, 1943), p. 327. His arguments on the role of the Jews: *ibid.*, pp. 167-9, 192-7.

7.   Hitler sees need for process of regeneration: Göring's testimony, 13 March 1946, *Trial of the Major War Criminals before the International Military Tribunal, Nuremberg, 14 November 1945-1 October 1946* (Official Text, English edition, reprint of 1947-9 edition, New York, 1971), vol. 9, p. 238; Hitler's speech: 23 November 1939, Document 789-PS, *TMWC*, vol. 26, pp. 328-9. A major theme of inter-war studies was the importance of propaganda: Wolfram Wette, 'Ideologien, Propaganda und Innenpolitik als Voraussetzungen der Kriegspolitik des Dritten Reiches,' Militärgeschichtliches Forschungsamt, *Das Deutsche Reich und der Zweite Weltkrieg* (Stuttgart, 1979), vol. 1, p. 122. British propaganda had undermined Germany at home: Hitler, *Mein Kampf*, pp. 181-9. Better propaganda would have prevented defeat in 1918: 'Das Wesen der nationalsozialistischen Propaganda. Vortrag von Reichsminister Dr Goebbels vor dem Nationalpolitischen Lehrgang der Wehrmacht, gehalten am 21. Januar 1937,' BA R 55/1338, p. 23. Sywottek, *Mobilmachung*, sets out the organisations with responsibility for propaganda at pp. 23-41. Armed forces' attempts to gain overall control of propaganda unsuccessful: draft, L Ia Pr., 26 August 1938, 'Vortrag. Die Vorbereitende Zusammenarbeit von Wehrmacht und Propaganda im Krieg,' BA MA RW 4/ v. 238, pp. 1-3.

8.   Ludendorff pioneers ideological education: Erich Ludendorff, *My War Memories 1914-1918*, vol. 2 (third edition, London), pp. 460-2. Ideological education responsibility of the armed forces: guidelines in the order of the Army Oberbefehlshaber, pp. 1-7, attached to Bormann, 21 December 1940, 'Rundschreiben an alle Reichsleiter und Gauleiter!,' BA NS 6/332. Soldiers could not be apolitical: 'Wesen und Grundbegriffe des Nationalsozialismus. (Vortrag des Reichsministers Dr. Goebbels in mehreren Standorten der Wehrmacht),' BA MA RW 6/ v. 158, pp. 14-15. Hitler rules out party militia: Klaus-Jürgen Müller, 'Deutsche Militär-Elite in der Vorgeschichte des Zweiten Weltkrieges,' in Martin Broszat and Klaus Schwabe (eds.), *Die deutschen Eliten und der Weg in den Zweiten Weltkrieg* (Munich, 1989), p. 262.

9.   The regime's response affected by Germany's World War I experiences: Herbst, *Totale Krieg*, pp. 42-73. Social conflict of the second Reich: 'Das Wesen der nationalsozialistischen Propaganda. Vortrag von Reichsminister Dr. Goebbels vor dem Nationalpolitischen Lehrgang der Wehrmacht, gehalten am 21. Januar 1937,'

BA R 55/1338, pp. 20, 22. Hitler emphasised workers being fully part of the nation: Hitler, *Mein Kampf*, pp. 182-8.

10. Government concern for food supply: Goebbels' speech, 23 February 1944, 'Die politische und militärische Lage,' BA NS 19/1870, pp. 4-5; J. E. Farquharson, *The Plough and the Swastika: The NSDAP and Agriculture in Germany 1928-1945* (London, 1976), pp. 222-8, 242. Popular morale in World War I: Kocka, *Facing Total War*, pp. 48-9. The regime's political and social strategy: R. J. Overy, 'Germany, "Domestic Crisis" and War,' *Past and Present*, No. 116, August 1987, pp. 159-60. Public judged war progress: Wolfgang Franz Werner, 'Belastungen der deutschen Arbeiterschaft in der zweiten Kriegshälfte,' in Ulrich Borsdorf and Mathilde Jamin (eds.), *Überleben im Krieg. Kriegserfahrungen in einer Industrieregion 1939-1945* (Hamburg, 1989), p. 33.

11. Hitler, *Mein Kampf*, p. 151. Germany's enemies superior from the start: *ibid.*, p. 229. German victory in 1917: *ibid.*, pp. 194-5.

12. Mason's argument: Tim Mason, 'The Legacy of 1918 for National Socialism,' in Anthony Nicholls and Erich Matthias (eds.), *German Democracy and the Triumph of Hitler—Essays in Recent German History* (London, 1971), pp. 215-39. Speer recalled Hitler's concern: Albert Speer, *Inside the Third Reich* (London, 1970), p. 214. Few specific cases where it affected wartime policymaking: Mason, 'The Legacy of 1918 for National Socialism,' in Nicholls and Matthias (eds.), *German Democracy and the Triumph of Hitler*, pp. 228-9; Tim Mason, *Arbeiterklasse und Volksgemeinschaft. Dokumente und Materialen zur deutscher Arbeiterpolitik 1936-1939* (Opladen, 1975), pp. 154-8.

13. Alfred C. Mierzejewski, *The Collapse of the German War Economy, 1944-1945: Allied Air Power and the German National Railway* (Chapel Hill, N. C., 1988), p. 29. Germany lacks other raw materials needed: Williamson Murray, *The Change in the European Balance of Power, 1938-1939: The Path to Ruin* (Princeton, N. J., 1984), p. 4. Dependence of German industry on coal and location: Mierzejewski, *Collapse of the German War Economy*, pp. 22, 29. No long war without Ruhr: WaA to Wehrmachts-Amt, May 1934, 'Die Rüstungslage Deutschlands, wie sie sich augenblicklich und vorraussichtlich in den nächsten Jahren im Falle eines Krieges darstellt,' BA MA RH 8 I/ v. 957, pp. 7-9, 16. Waffen Amt recommends evacuation: *ibid.*, p. 33.

14. Military develop concept of defence-based economy: Rolf-Dieter Müller, 'Die Mobilisierung der deutschen Wirtschaft für Hitlers Kriegsführung,' in Militärgeschichtliches Forschungsamt, *Das Deutsche Reich und der Zweite Weltkrieg*, vol. 5/1, *Kriegsverwaltung, Wirtschaft und personelle Ressourcen: 1939-1941* (Stuttgart, 1988), p. 351; Richard Overy, 'Hitler's War Plans and the German Economy,' in Robert Boyce and Esmonde M. Robertson (eds.), *Paths to War: New Essays on the Origins of the Second World War* (London, 1989), p. 97. Banse's argument: Ewald Banse, *Wehrwissenschaft. Einführung in eine neue nationale Wissenschaft* (Leipzig, 1933), pp. 24-7. Hitler's awareness of these issues: Murray, *The Path to Ruin*, chapter 1; Overy, 'Hitler's War Plans and the German Economy,' in Boyce and Robertson (eds.), *Paths to War*, p. 98.

15. Rearmament from 1933 to 1936: *ibid.*, pp. 99-101; Willi A. Boelcke, *Die deutsche Wirtschaft 1930-1945: Interna des Reichswirtschaftsministeriums* (Dusseldorf, 1983), pp. 149-55. 1936 armaments programme: table in Wilhelm Deist, *The Wehrmacht and German Rearmament* (London, 1981), p. 52. A more detailed

study of the process of rearmament is contained in Wilhelm Deist, 'Die Aufrüstung der Wehrmacht,' *DRZW*, 1, pp. 400-532.

16. Significance of the Four Year Plan: R. J. Overy, *The Nazi Economic Recovery 1932-1938* (London, 1982), p. 61. A detailed study of German economic preparations for war is provided by Hans-Erich Volkmann, 'Die NS-Wirtschaft im Vorbereitung des Krieges,' *DRZW*, 1, especially pp. 208-316, 349-68. Hitler and the Four Year Plan: Deist, *Wehrmacht and Rearmament*, pp. 51-3, 105. On the organisation of the Four Year Plan: R. J. Overy, *Goering the 'Iron Man'* (London, 1984), pp. 57-62. Göring's statement: R. J. Overy, 'Hitler's War and the German Economy: A Reinterpretation,' *The Economic History Review*, vol. 35, 1982, pp. 278-9. Artificial raw materials: Gustav Stolper, Karl Häuser and Knut Borchardt, *The German Economy 1870 to the Present* (second edition, London, 1967), p. 136. Increases in raw materials production: Volkmann, 'Die NS-Wirtschaft im Vorbereitung des Krieges,' *DRZW*, 1, pp. 353-4. 1938 *Schnellplan*: Murray, *The Path to Ruin*, pp. 24-5.

17. Control of armaments economy passes from military: Overy, 'Hitler's War Plans and the German Economy,' in Boyce and Robertson (eds.), *Paths to War*, p. 106. Military programme concentrated on immediate needs: Deist, *Wehrmacht and Rearmament*, p. 111. Hitler's directions: Overy, 'Hitler's War Plans and the German Economy,' in Boyce and Robertson (eds.), *Paths to War*, pp. 111-12. Problems of co-ordination in armed forces' expansion: Deist, *Wehrmacht and Rearmament*, pp. 91-2; Document Keitel-11, 29 March 1946, *TMWC*, vol. 40, p. 370. The Wirüamt: William Jeffress Fanning Jr., 'The German War Economy in 1941: A Study of Germany's Material and Manpower Problems in Relation to the Overall Military Effort' (Texas Christian University Ph.D. thesis, 1983), pp. 14-15. Thomas's opposition: Berenice A. Carroll, *Design for Total War: Arms and Economics in the Third Reich* (The Hague, 1968), pp. 49, 191-2. In practice little difference: Müller, 'Die Mobilisierung der deutschen Wirtschaft,' *DRZW*, 5/1, p. 358.

18. Economics Ministry: Müller, 'Die Mobilisierung der deutschen Wirtschaft,' *DRZW*, 5/1, pp. 353-5; Boelcke, *deutsche Wirtschaft*, pp. 185-9, 226-7.

19. Not an effective steering organisation: Müller, 'Die Mobilisierung der deutschen Wirtschaft,' *DRZW*, 5/1, pp. 366, 414-15. Göring hampered: Overy, *Goering*, p. 100.

20. 1938 spending figures: Murray, *The Path to Ruin*, p. 20. Decline in consumption: Overy, 'Germany, "Domestic Crisis" and War,' p. 153. Falls in investment: Overy, *Goering*, pp. 60, 83. German consumption patterns low: Overy, 'Hitler's War Plans and the German Economy,' in Boyce and Robertson (eds.), *Paths to War*, p. 111.

21. Shortages and rationing: Deist, *Wehrmacht and Rearmament*, p. 87. Use of Austrian and Czech reserves: William Carr, *Arms, Autarky and Aggression: A Study in German Foreign Policy, 1933-1939* (London, 1972), p. 86. On the economic incorporation of Austria and Czechoslovakia, see Volkmann, 'Die NS-Wirtschaft im Vorbereitung des Krieges,' *DRZW*, 1, pp. 323-335. Germany's economic position at outbreak of war: Stolper, *German Economy*, p. 159. Effect of foreign exchange shortages: Murray, *The Path to Ruin*, pp. 15-17.

22. Army and air force in 1939: Deist, *Wehrmacht and Rearmament*, pp. 89-91. Navy armament: Carr, *Arms, Autarky and Aggression*, p. 113. 'Z plan': Overy, 'Hitler's War Plans and the German Economy,' in Boyce and Robertson (eds.), *Paths to*

War, p. 110. Continued large-scale production planned: Overy, 'Hitler's War and the German Economy,' p. 281. German mobilisation plans: Müller, 'Die Mobilisierung der deutschen Wirtschaft,' *DRZW*, 5/1, p. 358.

23. Munitions low: Paul Kennedy, *The Rise and Fall of the Great Powers: Economic Change and Military Conflict from 1500 to 2000* (New York, 1987), p. 307. German and British aircraft production rates: Alan S. Milward, *The German Economy at War* (London, 1967), p. 6. Motorisation of army in 1939: Carr, *Arms, Autarky and Aggression*, pp. 120-2. Economic preparations incomplete: Overy, *Goering*, pp. 89, 98; Boelcke, *deutsche Wirtschaft*, pp. 246-7.

24. Burton H. Klein, *Germany's Economic Preparations for War* (Cambridge, Mass., 1959), p. 76. Influence of United States Strategic Bombing Survey (USSBS): R. J. Overy, '"Blitzkriegwirtschaft"? Finanzpolitik, Lebensstandard und Arbeitseinsatz in Deutschland 1939-1942,' *Vierteljahrshefte für Zeitgeschichte*, vol. 36, 1988, pp. 379-80. Klein suggested that higher level of arms production could be achieved: Klein, *Germany's Economic Preparations*, p. 21. Klein's arguments about rise of production and consumption: *ibid.*, p. 13. The government avoided greater economic effort: *ibid.*, p. 79.

25. Milward, *German Economy*, p. 7. Armament in width and armament in depth: *ibid.*, p. 6.

26. *Ibid.* German economy in Blitzkrieg period: *ibid*, p. 28. Carroll argues: Carroll, *Design for Total War*, pp. 230-1.

27. Blitzkrieg interpretation still finds support among historians: most notably Hans-Erich Volkmann, 'Die NS-Wirtschaft im Vorbereitung des Krieges,' *DRZW*, 1, pp. 208-369; Carr, *Arms, Autarky and Aggression*, pp. 59, 75; Stolper, *German Economy*, pp. 161-3; Fanning, 'German War Economy in 1941,' pp. 9, 10, 23-40; Burchardt, 'Impact of the War Economy on the Civilian Population,' in Deist (ed.), *German Military in the Age of Total War*, pp. 62-3; Bernhard R. Kroener, 'Squaring the Circle. Blitzkrieg Strategy and Manpower Shortage, 1939-1942,' in *ibid.*, pp. 284-5. The *Wehrwirtschaft*: Herbst, *Totale Krieg*, pp. 96-8. Delay in transition: *ibid.*, p. 108; Hans Kehrl, *Krisenmanager im Dritten Reich. 6 Jahre Frieden 6 Jahre Krieg Errinerungen* (Dusseldorf, 1973), pp. 202, 214-5.

28. Mason shares belief on government fear of public reaction: Mason, *Arbeiterklasse und Volksgemeinschaft*, pp. 119-37. War the only way to avoid workers' hostility: *ibid.*, pp. 120-3. Economic overheating forced the regime to go to war: Timothy W. Mason, 'Innere Krise und Angriffskrieg 1938/1939,' in Friedrich Forstmeier and Hans-Erich Volkmann (eds.), *Wirtschaft und Rüstung am Vorabend des Zweiten Weltkrieges* (second edition, Dusseldorf, 1981) pp. 158-88. On this debate see also Jost Dülffer, 'Der Beginn des Krieges 1939: Hitler, die innere Krise und das Mächtesystem,' in Karl Dietrich Bracher, Manfred Funke and Hans-Adolf Jacobsen (eds.), *Nationalsozialistische Diktatur 1933-1945: eine Bilanz* (Dusseldorf, 1983), pp. 317-44. Historians who argue that Mason has over-esti-mated the extent of working-class hostility to the regime and the extent of the economic over-heating of 1938-9: Overy, 'Germany, "Domestic Crisis" and War,' pp. 138-68; Overy, *Goering*, pp. 49-50, 89; Klaus Hildebrand, *The Third Reich* (London, 1984), pp. 133-5; Richard Bessel, 'Living with the Nazis: Some Recent Writing on the Social History of the Third Reich,' *European History Quarterly*, vol. 14, 1984, pp. 212-13; Johnpeter Horst Grill, 'Local and Regional Studies on National Socialism: A Review,' *Journal of Contemporary History*, vol. 21, 1986,

pp. 273-4, 277; Dörte Winkler, 'Frauenarbeit versus Frauenideologie: Probleme der weiblichen Erwerbstätigkeit in Deutschland 1930-45,' *Archiv für Sozialgeschichte*, vol. 17, 1977, p. 111. Salter's argument: Stephen Salter, 'The Mobilisation of German Labour, 1939-1945. A Contribution to the History of the Working Class in the Third Reich,' (unpublished D. Phil. thesis, Oxford, 1983), p. 309.

29. Arguments that Hitler did not require highest concentration: Mason, *Arbeiterklasse und Volksgemeinschaft*, p. 103. Mason on working-class consumption: *ibid.*, p. 115. Anecdotal evidence of contemporaries: Louis P. Lochner, *What about Germany?* (London, 1943), pp. 142-3, 258-61; Bernt Engelmann, *In Hitler's Germany: Daily Life in the Third Reich* (New York, 1986), pp. 147-8.

30. Other historians who follow total war: Müller, 'Die Mobilisierung der deutschen Wirtschaft,' *DRZW*, 5/1, pp. 387, 390-1; Mierzejewski, *Collapse of the German War Economy*, p. xiii; Boelcke, *deutsche Wirtschaft*, pp. 247-8. Overy's alternative model: Overy, 'Hitler's War and the German Economy,' p. 274. Hitler's long-term plans: Overy, 'Hitler's War Plans and the German Economy,' in Boyce and Robertson (eds.), *Paths to War*, p. 107. Plans for rearmament not complete in 1939: Overy, *Goering*, p. 89; see also pp. 98, 102. Conversion of economy began in 1939: *ibid.*, pp. 95-102. Decline in consumption: *ibid.*, pp. 78, 95-7.

31. Regime did seek to mobilise all necessary resources: Overy, *Goering*, p. 139. Overy sees bureaucratic competition and lack of central control: *ibid.*, pp. 154-8. Unwillingness of industrialists to co-operate: Overy, 'Hitler's War and the German Economy,' pp. 279-80. Hitler's lack of understanding of the economy: *ibid.*, p. 275. The regime's administrative inefficiency: Overy, *Goering*, p. 148. High German standards of armaments production: Overy, 'Hitler's War and the German Economy,' p. 286. Women employed to a far greater extent: R. J. Overy, 'The Audit of War,' *Times Literary Supplement*, No. 4332, 11 April 1986, p. 393; R. J. Overy, '"Blitzkriegwirtschaft"?,' pp. 425-32.

32. Murray, *The Path to Ruin*, p. 27. German armaments effort at a higher level: *ibid.*, p. 19. Economy limited by reliance on imports: *ibid.*, pp. 10, 14-15. Murray's criticism of the Blitzkrieg economy: *ibid.* pp. 12-13, 17, 37. He argues strongly against any links between the regime's economic and military strategies. 1941 steel production: *ibid.*, pp. 13-14.

33. Extensive plans for economic mobilisation: Ursula von Gersdorff, *Frauen im Kriegsdienst, 1914-1945* (Stuttgart, 1969), pp. 48-51; Georg Thomas, *Geschichte der deutschen Wehr- und Rüstungswirtschaft (1918-1943/45)* (Boppard am Rhein, 1966), pp. 153-7. On lack of implementation of plans: *ibid.*, pp. 153-60, 167-8. Hitler believed Britain and France would not seriously pursue war: Albert Speer, *Inside the Third Reich* (London, 1970), p. 165.

34. Goering's positions and the Ministerial Council: Dieter Rebentisch, *Führerstaat und Verwaltung im Zweiten Weltkrieg: Verfassungsentwicklung und Verwaltungspolitik 1939-1945* (Stuttgart, 1989), pp. 117-32. Kehrl's view: Kehrl, *Krisenmanager*, pp. 215-16.

35. Gauleiters as defence commissioners: Carroll, *Design for Total War*, pp. 206-7. Their powers: Rebentisch, *Führerstaat und Verwaltung*, pp. 132-4, 138. Todt: Speer, *Third Reich*, pp. 193-4; J. D. Heyl, 'The Construction of the *Westwall*, 1938: An Examplar for National Socialist Policymaking,' *Central European History*, vol. 14, 1981, pp. 66-7. Todt as Inspector-General: Thomas, *Geschichte*, p. 239.

'Combing-out' commissions: Salter, 'Mobilisation of German Labour,' pp. 27, 40, 46. Numbers freed: *ibid.*, pp. 40, 46. Todt's appointment: Edward R. Zilbert, *Albert Speer and the Nazi Ministry of Arms: Economic Institutions and Industrial Production in the German War Economy* (East Brunswick, N. J., 1981), p. 88. Todt introduces industrial self-responsibility: Carroll, *Design for Total War*, pp. 222-3. Todt breaks with command economy: Müller, 'Die Mobilisierung der deutschen Wirtschaft,' *DRZW*, 5/1, p. 485.

36. Leadership's attitude to war: Speer, *Third Reich*, pp. 162-3. Göring's opposition to war: David Irving, *Göring: A Biography* (New York, 1989), pp. 254, 261. Goebbels' view: Hans-Otto Meissner, *Magda Goebbels: A Biography* (London, 1980), p. 206.

37. Helmut Krausnick, quoted in Wilhelm Deist, 'Überlegungen zur "widerwilligen Loyalität" der Deutschen bei Kriegsbeginn,' in Wolfgang Michalka (ed.), *Der Zweite Weltkrieg: Analysen, Grundzüge, Forschungsbilanz* (Munich, 1989), p. 225. Unpopularity of the war: Marlis G. Steinert, *Hitler's War and the Germans: Public Mood and Attitude during the Second World War* (Ohio, 1977), p. 50. Morale influenced by memories of World War I: Deist, 'Überlegungen,' in Michalka (ed.), *Der Zweite Weltkrieg*, pp. 225-6. The effect of food supply problems on morale: 'Meldungen aus dem Reich (Nr. 242),' 1 December 1941, and 'Meldungen . . . (Nr. 270),' 23 February 1942, in Heinz Boberach (ed.) *Meldungen aus dem Reich 1938-1945: Die geheimen Lageberichte des Sicherheitsdienstes der SS* (Herrsching, 1984), vols. 8 and 9, pp. 3043, 3504 respectively. Problems with morale in 1939-40: Jay W. Baird, *The Mythical World of Nazi War Propaganda, 1939-1945* (Minneapolis, Minn., 1965), pp. 73-4. High point of morale 1940: Ian Kershaw, *The 'Hitler Myth': Image and Reality in the Third Reich* (Oxford, 1989), pp. 155-6.

38. Planning hampered by Hitler's changing priorities: Thomas, *Geschichte*, pp. 169-70, 233-5. Hitler stressed the need for flexibility: *ibid.*, p. 204. Hitler continued his building projects: Speer, *Third Reich*, pp. 168, 176-7, 180-1, 186.

39. Restriction of economy and administration began: Göring and Lammers, 'Verordnung zur Vereinfachung der Haushaltsführung in Reich und Ländern im Rechnungsjahr 1941 Vom 12 Februar 1941,' BA R 43 II/760a, pp. 1-2. War economy decree: Müller, 'Die Mobilisierung der deutschen Wirtschaft,' *DRZW*, 5/1, pp. 375-9, 382. Opposition to decree: Wolfgang Werner, *'Bleib übrig!' Deutsche Arbeiter in der nationalsozialistischen Kriegswirtschaft* (Dusseldorf, 1983), pp. 34-41. Disagreement about workers' opposition: Mason, *Arbeiterklasse und Volksgemeinschaft*, pp. 154-8, and Salter, 'Mobilisation of German Labour,' pp. 122-3, 193-5, argue symptom of wider opposition; Bernhard R. Kroener, 'Der Kampf um den "Sparstoff Mensch": Forschungskontroversen über die Mobilisierung der deutschen Kriegswirtschaft 1939-1942', in Michalka (ed.), *Der Zweite Weltkrieg*, p. 407, argues workers willing to bear burdens.

40. Clothes rationing introduced in November 1939: Willi A. Boelcke (ed.), *The Secret Conferences of Dr Goebbels October 1939-March 1943* (London, 1967), p. 4. Food rationing: Werner, *'Bleib übrig!,'* p. 52. Closure of small businesses: Herbst, *Totale Krieg*, pp. 120, 122; Boelcke, *deutsche Wirtschaft*, pp. 249-50. Restructuring by closures: Carroll, *Design for Total War*, p. 204; Overy, *Goering*, pp. 96-7, 139-40. Raw materials withheld: Carroll, *Design for Total War*, p. 205. Contemporary

observers on consumer goods' shortages: Fanning, 'German War Economy in 1941,' pp. 163-4.

41. Demographic problems: Bernhard R. Kroener, 'Die personellen Ressourcen des Dritten Reiches im Spannungsfeld zwischen Wehrmacht, Bürokratie und Kriegswirtschaft 1939-1942,' *DRZW*, 5/1, pp. 726, 728. Full employment in Germany: Stolper, *German Economy*, p. 137. Germans had no slack to take up: Rolf-Dieter Müller, 'Von der Wirtschaftsallianz zum Kolonialen Ausbeutungskrieg,' *DRZW*, 4, p. 158. Germans called up a higher proportion: Alan S. Milward, *War, Economy and Society 1939-1945* (Berkeley, Calif., 1977), p. 216. Foreign workers already employed: Ulrich Herbert, *Fremdarbeiter: Politik und Praxis des "Ausländer-Einsatzes" in der Kriegswirtschaft des Dritten Reiches* (Berlin, 1985), p. 58. On *Umschulung* policy: 'Ausführungsvorschriften zur Anordnung über die zusätzliche Ausbildung von Fachkräften vom 14. Januar 1939 (Deutscher Reichsanzeiger vom 16. Januar 1939 Nr. 13),' BA R 11/1226, other papers on this file and on R 11/1225, R 11/1227. Effectiveness of *Umschulung* hard to trace: a start has been made by Salter, 'Mobilisation of German Labour,' pp. 58-60. For the pre-war period, see John Gillingham, 'The "Deproletarianization" of German Society: Vocational Training in the Third Reich,' *Journal of Social History*, vol. 19, 1986, pp. 423-32.

42. National Socialist ideology: Leila J. Rupp, *Mobilizing Women for War: German and American Propaganda, 1939-1945* (Princeton, N. J., 1978), pp. 15-17. Percentage of women employed: Klein, *Germany's Economic Preparations*, p. 68. Koonz's figure: Claudia Koonz, *Mothers of the Fatherland: Women, the Family and Nazi Politics* (London, 1987), note 47, p. 471. Women predominate in agriculture and family businesses: Ingrid Schupetta, *Frauen- und Ausländererwerbstätigkeit in Deutschland von 1939 bis 1945* (Cologne, 1983), pp. 57-8. International employment rates: *ibid.*, p. 47. I am grateful to my colleague, Dr Marian Aveling, History Department, Monash University, for advice that some other countries did not count unpaid family assistants as employed.

43. Women's jobs reduce their interest in the work force: Mason, *Arbeiterklasse und Volksgemeinschaft*, pp. 143-4. Increased birth rate: Koonz, *Mothers of the Fatherland*, p. 186 and note 20, p. 469. Most women could find employment: Schupetta, *Frauen- und Ausländererwerbstätigkeit*, pp. 36-7. Women reluctant to volunteer for fear of coming into labour registration system: Rupp, *Mobilizing Women*, p. 111.

44. World War I support low: Burchardt, 'Impact of the War Economy on the Civilian Population,' in Deist (ed.), *German Military in the Age of Total War*, pp. 56, 59. A new generous rate: Schupetta, *Frauen- und Ausländererwerbstätigkeit*, pp. 44-5. Rate designed to overcome World War I problems: Overy, ' "Blitzkriegwirtschaft"?,' p. 405. Labour Ministry warnings: submission to Reichs Labour Minister, 2 February 1939, 'Verordnung über Kriegsfamilienunterhalt,' p. 2; and Wiedemann? signature, 19 May 1939, BA R 41/161, p. 3. The one group excepted: Jill Stephenson, ' "Emancipation" and Its Problems: War and Society in Württemberg 1939-45,' *European History Quarterly*, vol. 17, 1987, p. 354. At least 300,000 women left the work force: Thomas, *Geschichte*, p. 239. Efforts made to get women to return to work force: Göring to Reichsarbeitsminister, 20 June 1941, 'Wiedereinsatz von Frauen, die ihre Berufstätigkeit nach Kriegsbeginn aufgaben,' pp. 1-4; Dr Suren, Interior Ministry, to Göring, BA R 43 II/652, pp. 1-2. Göring

rejects decree: Marotzke to Kritzinger, 4 June 1940, BA R 43 II/652. Party publicity drive: Rudolf Hess, 16 March 1941, 'Anordnung A10/41,' Institut für Zeitgeschichte, *Akten der Parteikanzlei Teil I* (Munich, 1983-1985), 101 09332-5. On the campaign: BA R 43 II/652; and on the failure of these efforts: von Gersdorff, *Frauen im Kriegsdienst*, pp. 52-3.

45. Many women would rather accept reductions in their family support than work: 'Meldungen . . . (Nr. 224),' 29 September 1941, Boberach (ed.), *Meldungen aus dem Reich*, vol. 8, p. 2821. Men often the strongest opponents: Michael Zimmermann, 'Ausbruchshoffnungen Junge Bergleute in den dreissiger Jahren,' in Lutz Niethammer (ed.), *"Die Jahre weiss man nicht, wo man die heute hinsetzen soll." Faschismus-Erfahrungen im Ruhr-Gebiet: Lebensgeschichte und Sozialkultur im Ruhrgebiet 1930 bis 1960*, Band 1 (second edition, Bonn, 1986), pp. 126-7. Thomas' suggestions: Thomas, 30 March 1940, 'Fraueneinsatz im Kriege,' BA MA RW 19/317, pp. 1-2. Lack of particular awareness of need to encompass women: papers on BA R 11/1225 and R 11/1227. Firms do not make sufficient use of training for women: Salter, 'Mobilisation of German Labour,' pp. 58-60. Labour service for young women: Rita Thalmann, *Frausein im Dritten Reich* (Frankfurt, 1987), pp. 162, 173.

46. Labour policy: Edward Homze, *Foreign Labor in Nazi Germany* (Princeton, N. J., 1967), chapters 2 and 3. Number of foreign workers employed: report, 15 July 1941, 'Der Arbeitseinsatz im Deutschen Reich im Mai und Juni 1941 (Auszug aus den Textberichten der Landesarbeitsämter),' BA R 41/146, pp. 2-3. Men released from armed forces: Fanning, 'German War Economy in 1941,' p. 157. Civilian conscription programme: Salter, 'Mobilisation of German Labour,' pp. 13-16.

47. Müller, 'Die Mobilisierung der deutschen Wirtschaft,' *DRZW*, 5/1, p. 412.

48. *Ibid.*, p. 522. Müller's argument: *ibid.*, pp. 349-689.

49. Problems of German statistics: Fanning, 'German War Economy in 1941,' pp. 69-70; Carroll, *Design for Total War*, pp. 262-7.

50. Klein influenced by lack of central control: Klein, *Germany's Economic Preparations*, pp. 37-8. Civilian consumption the same proportion of GNP in 1940 as in 1937: Carroll, *Design for Total War*, p. 229. Consumer production reduced by one third per head of the civilian population (74 per cent of 1938-9): Rolf Wagenführ, *Die Deutsche Industrie im Kriege 1939-1945* (second edition, Berlin, 1963), p. 28. On the resulting shortages: 'Meldungen . . . (Nr. 223),' 25 September 1941, Boberach (ed.), *Meldungen aus dem Reich*, vol. 8, p. 2797; Lochner, *What About Germany?* pp. 142-3, 258-61. On the overall reductions of consumer production and consumption: Overy, *Goering*, pp. 95-8. Large percentage of consumer goods used by armed forces: Steinert, *Hitler's War and the Germans*, p. 93. Absence of a sharp shift: Marie-Luise Recker, *Nationalsozialistische Sozialpolitik im Zweiten Weltkrieg* (Munich, 1975), p. 291.

51. Rolf-Dieter Müller, 'Das Scheitern der wirtschaftlichen "Blitzkriegstrategie",' *DRZW*, 4, p. 936. Proportion of work force engaged on direct military orders: Overy, *Goering*, p. 140. Blocks to growth of war production: Müller, 'Von der Wirtschaftsallianz zum Kolonialen Ausbeutungskrieg,' *DRZW*, 4, pp. 158-60.

52. German exploitation of conquered territories: Hans Umbreit, 'Auf dem Weg zur Kontinentalherrschaft,' *DRZW*, 5/1, pp. 210-64. Germany drew on the economies of neutral countries: Bond, *War and Society in Europe, 1870-1970*, p. 193.

Conquered territories a great addition: Milward, *War, Economy and Society*, p. 137; France the most profitable: *ibid.*, pp. 137-45. Problems with exploitation of conquered territories: Fanning, 'German War Economy in 1941', pp. 112, 125. Fanning differs from Milward in suggesting that German efforts to use the French economy met with failure on the whole: *ibid.*, p. 117. Germany lacked the resources for a war of such a scale: Geyer, 'German Strategy in the Age of Machine Warfare,' in Paret (ed.), *Makers of Modern Strategy*, pp. 578-9. Tension between need for foreign labour and optimum use of economies of occupied territories: Fanning, 'German War Economy in 1941,' p. 194; Overy, *Goering*, p. 141.

Chapter 2

1. Initial Russian campaign: Peter Calvocoressi, Guy Wint and John Pritchard *Total War: The Causes and Courses of the Second World War*, Peter Calvocoressi, *Volume I: The Western Hemisphere* (second edition, London, 1989), pp. 190-7. Early propaganda: E. K. Bramsted, *Goebbels and National Socialist Propaganda 1925-1945* (East Lansing, Mich., 1965), pp. 244-5.

2. Quoted in Alan Clark, *Barbarossa: the Russian-German Conflict 1941-45* (Harmondsworth, 1966), p. 70. Hitler's view of Russia: Adolf Hitler, *Mein Kampf* (first published 1925 and 1927, Boston, 1943), pp. 649, 654-5. Himmler's views on the USSR: Himmler, speech at Gauleitertagung, 28 November 1940, BA NS 19/4007, pp. 18-19. Hitler's use of race to judge military strength: Michael Geyer, 'German Strategy in the Age of Machine Warfare, 1914-1945,' in Peter Paret (ed.), *Makers of Modern Strategy from Machiavelli to the Nuclear Age* (Princeton, N. J., 1986), p. 582.

3. A 1939 paper: OKH, 28 January 1939, 'Kurze Übersicht über die sowjet-russische Wehrmacht,' BA MA RW 4/ v. 317, p. 6. Cautious assessments ignored: Walter Schellenberg, *The Labyrinth: Memoirs of Walter Schellenberg* (New York, 1956), pp. 190-3.

4. War against USSR lost from the start: Earl F. Ziemke, 'Germany and World War II: The Official History?,' *Central European History*, vol. 5, 1982, pp. 406-7, has suggested that this is the argument of the Militärgeschichtliches Forschungsamt in *Das Deutsche Reich und der Zweite Weltkrieg*. It is implied by Manfred Messerschmidt, 'Einleitung,' *Das Deutsche Reich und der Zweite Weltkrieg* (Stuttgart, 1979-88), vol. 4, p. xviii. Lack of clear objectives and planning: Albert Seaton, *The German Army 1933-45* (London, 1983), pp. 162-6. Disputes among commanders: Geyer, 'German Strategy in the Age of Machine Warfare,' in Paret (ed.), *Makers of Modern Strategy*, pp. 588-90. Hitler told Goebbels: entry, 30 November 1941, BA NL 118/36, pp. 27, 29. Hitler may have recognised failure but did not alter his strategy: Jürgen Förster, 'Das Unternehmung "Barbarossa"—eine historische Ortsbestimmung,' *DRZW*, 4, p. 1086. Hitler Army Supreme Commander: Ernst Klink, 'Heer und Kriegsmarine,' *ibid.*, 4, p. 613.

5. Historians on decision to declare war on USA: Gerhard Weinberg, 'Germany's Declaration of War on the United States: A New Look,' in Gerhard Weinberg, *World in the Balance: Behind the Scenes of World War II* (Hanover, 1981), pp. 75-95; a different interpretation is advanced by Andreas Hillgruber, 'Die weltpolitischen Entscheidungen vom 22. Juni 1941 bis 11. Dezember 1941,' in K. D. Bracher, Manfred Funke and Hans-Adolf Jacobsen (eds.),

Nationalsozialistische Diktatur 1933-1945: eine Bilanz (Dusseldorf, 1983), pp. 459-60. This interpretation based on Enrico Syring, 'Hitlers Kriegserklärung an Amerika vom 11. Dezember 1941,' in Wolfgang Michalka (ed.), *Der Zweite Weltkrieg: Analysen, Grundzüge, Forschungsbilanz* (Munich, 1989), pp. 683-96.

6. Schellenberg, *Labyrinth*, pp. 199-200. Goebbels' only concern the psychological effect: entry, 13 September 1941, BA NL 118/26, p. 10. Göring largely responsible: R. J. Overy, *Goering the 'Iron Man,'* (London, 1984), pp. 105-6. More accurate views not believed: interrogation of Ambassador Karl Ritter, 1 November 1947, Robert W. Kempner, *Das Dritte Reich im Kreuzverhör: aus den Vernehmungsprotokollen des Anklagers* (Dusseldorf, 1984), p. 246.

7. Intensification of ideological side of the war: Hans-Adolf Jacobsen, 'Krieg in Weltanschauung und Praxis des Nationalsozialismus (1919-1945),' in Bracher et al. (eds.), *Nationalsozialistische Diktatur*, p. 436. Ideological war and war of annihilation: Jürgen Förster, 'The German Army and the Policies of Genocide,' in Gerhard Hirschfeld (ed.), *The Policies of Genocide: Jews and Soviet Prisoners of War in Nazi Germany* (London, 1986), p. 15. Begins with Commissar Order: Jürgen Förster, 'VII. Das Unternehmen "Barbarossa" als Eroberungs- und Vernichtungskrieg,' *DRZW*, 4, pp. 435-40. Deaths of Soviet POWs: Joachim Hoffmann, 'II. Die Kriegführung aus der Sicht der Sowjetunion' and Müller, 'Das Scheitern der wirtschaftlichen "Blitzkriegstrategie,' *DRZW*, 4, pp. 727-31, 993-4, especially 1015-20. Numbers who died: Förster, 'German Army and Policies of Genocide,' in Hirschfeld (ed.), *Policies of Genocide*, p. 21.

8. Neglect of planning for political appeals: Robert Gibbons, 'Dokumentation: Allgemeine Richtlinien für die politische und wirtschaftliche Verwaltung der besetzten Ostgebiete,' *Vierteljahrshefte für Zeitgeschichte*, vol. 25, 1977, pp. 252-77. Skillful attempt to win support: Alexander Dallin, *German Rule in Russia 1941-1945: A Study of Occupation Policies* (second edition, London, 1981) pp. 44-59, 65.

9. Bräutigam, Ostministerium, to Reich Commissioner for Ostland, 18 December 1941, Document 3666-PS, *Trial of the Major War Criminals Before the International Military Tribunal, Nuremberg, 14 November 1945-1 October 1946* (reprint, New York, 1971), vol. 32, p. 437. Jews killed in 1941: Michael R. Marrus, *The Holocaust in History* (London, 1987), p. 55. Economic costs of Final Solution: Ian Kershaw, *The Nazi Dictatorship: Problems and Perspectives of Interpretation*, (second edition, London, 1989), pp. 58-9. Final Solution strengthening the war effort: 'Rede des Reichsführers-SS auf der Ordensburg Sonthofen am 5. Mai 1944,' BA NS19/4013, p. 28. Objections of armed forces: 'Telefonat Amtschef-GFM Keitel Anfang September 1942,' 12 September 1942, BA MA RW 19/186; von Gienanth, Wehrkreisbefehlshaber im Generalgouvernement, to OKW, 18 September 1942, BA NS 19/352.

10. Geyer, 'German Strategy in the Age of Machine Warfare,' in Paret (ed.), *Makers of Modern Strategy*, p. 580. Historians' debate on origins of the Final Solution: Kershaw, *Nazi Dictatorship*, pp. 98-105.

11. Entry, 30 May 1942, BA NL 118/46, p. 44.

12. Entry, 11 January 1942, BA NL 118/37, p. 25. Goebbels' early confidence: entry, 14 October 1941, BA NL 118/32, pp. 12-13. He did not believe campaign would be over in November: entry, 15 October 1941, *ibid.*, pp. 11-12. Goebbels' anger at Dietrich's announcement: entry, 11 October 1941, BA NL 118/32, pp. 5, 7-8.

Goebbels' suggestions for winter clothing campaign in August 1941: entry, 28 August 1941, Rudolf Semmler, *Goebbels—the man next to Hitler* (Ohio State University reprint, 1982 of London, 1947 edition, published posthumously), pp. 50-1. Semler's name is incorrectly spelled as Semmler throughout the book. Propaganda results of Dietrich's claims, see Bramsted, *Goebbels and National Socialist Propaganda*, pp. 246-7. Effects of the winter clothing appeal: *ibid.*, pp. 247-50.

13.   Germans had misjudged Soviet military potential: entry, 16 September 1941, BA NL 118/26, p. 23. Soviets had reserves to mobilise: entry, 2 August 1941, Willi A. Boelcke (ed.), *The Secret Conferences of Dr Goebbels October 1939-March 1943* (London, 1967), pp. 179-80. Goebbels sensed difficulties: Müller, 'Die Mobilisierung der deutschen Wirtschaft,' *DRZW*, 5/1, p. 598. Goebbels' sympathy with the Soviet Union in the 1920s: entries, 7 and 9 July 1924, Elke Fröhlich (ed.), *Die Tagebücher von Joseph Goebbels Sämtliche Fragmente, Teil 1 Aufzeichnungen 1924-1941 Band 1 27.6.1924—31.12.1930* (Munich, 1987), pp. 35, 38. Goebbels' task to prepare people for another winter of war: entries, 29 August 1941, BA NL 118/23, pp. 15-16; 11 September 1941, BA NL 118/26, pp. 15-16, 19. More realism in reporting: Jay W. Baird, *The Mythical World of Nazi War Propaganda, 1939-1945* (Minneapolis, Minn., 1974), pp. 168-9.

14.   He was asked by experts on Russia to put these views to Hitler: quotation, entry, 4 September 1941, Semmler, *Goebbels*, p. 51; see also entries, 29 September, 4 October and 11 October 1941, *ibid.*, pp. 52-3, 56 respectively; entries, 29 January 1942, 11 February 1942, 25 April 1942 and 22 May 1942, Louis P. Lochner (ed.), *The Goebbels Diaries 1942-1943* (Garden City, N. Y., 1948), pp. 55, 77, 185 and 225. Goebbels raises treatment of Soviet peoples: Walter Tiessler, 'Licht und Schatten oder schonungslose Wahrheit (1922-1945),' IfZ ED 158, p. 158. Goebbels raised treatment of Russian POWs with Hitler: entry, 30 November 1941, BA NL 118/36, pp. 43-5. Hitler told him not to interfere: Tiessler, 'Licht und Schatten,' IfZ ED 158, p. 158. Goebbels used subordinates: Baird, *Nazi War Propaganda*, pp. 161-4. Goebbels' poor relations with Rosenberg: Dallin, *German Rule in Russia*, p. 43.

15.   Dr Walter Rohland Interrogation by Mr. Pannson, 16 October 1945, 'Einstellung von Todt und Speer zum Kriege,' IfZ ED 99 Speer Interviews Band 9, p. 2. Todt's earlier optimism: 'Chronik der Dienststellen des Generalbauinspektors für die Reichshauptstadt 1941,' BA R3/1735, p. 44. Todt concluded after visit to Eastern Front: Albert Speer, *Inside the Third Reich* (London, 1970), p. 185.

16.   Rohland Interrogation, 16 October 1945, IfZ ED 99 Speer Interviews Band 9, p. 2. Todt told Hitler: Gregor Janssen, *Das Ministerium Speer. Deutschlands Rüstung im Krieg* (Berlin, 1968), p. 33. Todt and Rohland's presentations: Rohland Interrogation, 16 October 1945, IfZ ED 99 Speer Interviews Band 9, p. 2. Todt's further efforts: Janssen, *Ministerium Speer*, p. 33.

17.   Jürgen Förster, 'The Dynamics of Volksgemeinschaft: The Effectiveness of the German Military Establishment in the Second World War,' in Allan R. Millett and Williamson Murray (eds.) *Military Effectiveness: Volume III: The Second World War* (Boston, 1988), p. 213. Hitler reportedly rejected a Soviet peace offer: Nicolaus von Below, *Als Hitlers Adjutant 1937-45* (Mainz, 1980), p. 299.

18.   Hitler continued to change priorities: Hitler order, 14 July 1941, Document 074-C, *TMWC*, vol. 34, pp. 298-302. Lack of a clear overview: Müller, 'Von der

Wirtschaftsallianz zum Kolonialen Ausbeutungskrieg,' *DRZW*, 4, pp. 181-9. Todt
becomes Inspector-General: Edward R. Zilbert, *Albert Speer and the Nazi Ministry
of Arms: Economic Institutions and Industrial Production in the German War
Economy* (East Brunswick, N. J., 1981), p. 93. Hitler's order of September 1941
and continuing disputes: Müller, 'Mobilisierung der deutschen Wirtschaft,'
DRZW, 5/1, pp. 596-7, 610-11.

19.   Growing awareness of crisis: *ibid.*, pp. 608, 627. Hitler rejects Goebbels' and Ley's
moves: *ibid.*, pp. 668-70. Hitler agrees to extend industrial self-responsibility:
Hitler decree, 3 December 1941, 'Vereinfachung und Leistungssteigerung unserer
Rüstungsproduktion,' BA NS 19/3513, pp. 1-6. Alan S. Milward, *The German
Economy at War* (London, 1967), pp. 60-8, sets out the workings of the committee
system. Hitler prefers to rely on industrialists: Müller, 'Von der Wirtschaftsallianz
zum Kolonialen Ausbeutungskrieg,' *DRZW*, 4, p. 119. Todt introduced price-fix-
ing system: Milward, *German Economy*, pp. 69-70. Previous system: Stephen
Salter, 'The Mobilisation of German Labour, 1939-1945. A Contribution to the
History of the Working Class in the Third Reich,' (unpublished D. Phil. thesis,
Oxford, 1983), pp. 133-4. Appointment of Zangen: Berenice A. Carroll, *Design
for Total War: Arms and Economics in the Third Reich* (The Hague, 1968), p. 231.
This initiative seems to have foundered after Todt's death. Todt's final talks with
Hitler: Müller, 'Mobilisierung der deutschen Wirtschaft,' *DRZW*, 5/1, p. 676.

20.   Alfred C. Mierzejewski, *The Collapse of the German War Economy, 1944-1945:
Allied Air Power and the German National Railway* (Chapel Hill, N.C., 1988), p.
9. Milward's view: Milward, *German Economy*, pp. 57, 71. Müller's assessment:
Müller, 'Mobilisierung der deutschen Wirtschaft,' *DRZW*, 5/1, pp. 639, 683-8.

21.   Speer, *Third Reich*, p. 202. Speer's appointment: Milward, *German Economy*, pp.
74-7. Hitler had already agreed to expand Todt's powers: *ibid.*, p. 70. Failure of
attempts to extend power at Speer's expense; 'CHRONIK der Dienststellen des
Reichsministers Albert Speer 1942,' BA R 3/1736, p. 11. Speer had over 12
meetings with Hitler from February to May 1942: *ibid.*, pp. 7-42. Hitler's support:
Speer, *Third Reich*, pp. 199-202. Hitler's ruling in Speer-Rosenberg dispute:
Janssen, *Ministerium Speer*, p. 47.

22.   Hitler's advice on industry: Müller, 'Mobilisierung der deutschen Wirtschaft,'
DRZW, 5/1, p. 680. Speer argued bureaucracy death of improvisation: Janssen,
Ministerium Speer, p. 47. Central Planning: Milward, *German Economy*, p. 83.
Wirüamt subordinated: Speer Chronik, May 1942, BA R 3/1736, pp. 34, 37.
Thomas soon frozen out by Speer: Georg Thomas, *Geschichte der deutschen Wehr-
und Rüstungswirtschaft (1918-1943/45)* (Boppard am Rhein, 1966), pp. 310-14,
352-3.

23.   German losses: Albert Seaton, *The Russo-German War 1941-45* (London, 1971),
p. 228. Hitler ordered: 'Erlass des Führers über die weitere Vereinfachung der
Verwaltung. Vom 25. Januar 1942,' BA R 43 II/353, pp. 1-3. Reports of such
measures: undated report, 'Übersicht über den wesentlicheren seit dem 1.1.1942
ergangenen, die allgemeine und innere Verwaltung entlastenden I. Ver-
einfachungsmassnahmen, II. Stillegungsmassnahmen, anderer Ressorts,' BA R 43
II/657, pp. 1-42.

24.   Goebbels began to reduce Propaganda Ministry staff: Leiter A to Abt. Pers., 20
January 1942, 'Ersatz für an die Wehrmacht abzugebende Angehörige des Hauses
durch Frauen,' BA R 55/988, pp. 1-2. Result: leader of the personnel section,

submission to the Minister, 30 April 1942, 'Fraueneinsatz,' BA R 55/18, pp. 1-4. Reporting to Hitler: Goebbels to Hitler, March 1942, 'Über den Fraueneinsatz im Reichsministerium für Volksaufklärung und Propaganda,' BA R 55/18, pp. 1-2. Other measures of simplification: Schmidt-Leonhardt to section heads, 16 January 1942, BA R 55/414. Hitler refuses Goebbels' plan: entry, 20 January 1942, BA NL 118/38, pp. 57-8.

25. 'Rede des Reichsführer-SS bei der SS-Gruppenführertagung in Posen am 4. Oktober 1943,' BA NS 19/4010, p. 3. Goebbels' plan and Göring's intervention: Ludolf Herbst, *Der Totale Krieg und die Ordnung der Wirtschaft. Die Kriegswirtschaft im Spannungsfeld von Politik, Ideologie und Propaganda 1939-1945* (Stuttgart, 1982), p. 198. Goebbels' diaries suggest: entries, 13 and 15 January 1942, BA NL 118/37, pp. 22 and pp. 18-19, 23 respectively. Hitler rejected his plan: entry, 20 January 1942, BA NL 118/38, pp. 54-5. Hitler orders use of Soviet POWs: Ulrich Herbert, *Fremdarbeiter: Politik und Praxis des "Ausländer-Einsatzes" in der Kriegswirtschaft des Dritten Reiches* (Berlin, 1985), p. 141. Soviet POW deaths: Christian Streit, 'Sowjetische Kriegsgefangene—Massendeportationen—Zwangsarbeiter,' in Michalka (ed.), *Zweite Weltkrieg*, p. 747.

26. Quoted in Clark, *Barbarossa*, p. 241. Hitler sees military situation positively: entry, 30 May 1942, BA NL 118/46, pp. 24, 29. Stalingrad: Clark, *Barbarossa*, p. 261.

27. Entry, 28 July 1942, Boelcke (ed.), *Secret Conferences*, p. 264. Goebbels considered US claims exaggerated: entry, 19 December 1942, Lochner (ed.), *Goebbels Diaries*, p. 251. Those who believed the US was superior: untitled unsigned report on the comments in November 1942 by Speer's economic adviser, Professor Hettlage, 7 November 1942, BA NS 19/2063, p. 3.

28. Morale vulnerable: Ian Kershaw, *The 'Hitler Myth': Image and Reality in the Third Reich* (Oxford, 1989), p. 186. Food supply and quality of goods worsening: Wolfgang Werner, *'Bleib übrig!' Deutsche Arbeiter in der nationalsozialistischen Kriegswirtschaft* (Dusseldorf, 1983), pp. 194-5, 203, 213-14. Hitler's powers over justice: 'Chronik der Daten und Ereignisse: Das "Dritte Reich",' in Martin Broszat and Norbert Frey (eds.), *Ploetz Das Dritte Reich: Ursprünge, Ereignisse, Wirkungen* (Würzburg, 1983), pp. 132. Thierack's appointment: *ibid.*, p. 133.

29. Goebbels linked struggle against Jews with war effort: entry, 28 May 1942, BA NL 118/46, pp. 29-30. Hitler gave Speer the task: entry, 20/21/22 September 1942, Willi A. Boelcke (ed.), *Deutschlands Rüstung im Zweiten Weltkrieg: Hitlers Konferenzen mit Albert Speer 1942-1945* (Frankfurt, 1969), p. 189. Goebbels' comment on Jews: entry, 30 May 1942, BA NL 118/46, pp. 39-41.

30. Himmler's war an ideological war: speech to the leadership corps of the SS Division Das Reich, 19 June 1942, BA NS 19/2571, pp. 3-4; 'Der Reichsführer-SS zu den Ersatzmannschaften für die Kampfgruppe Nord am Sonntag, dem 13. Juli 1941, im Stettin,' BA NS 19/4008, pp. 2-3. Numbers of Jews killed: Marrus, *Holocaust in History*, p. 55.

31. Himmler's speech to the leadership of the SS Division *Das Reich*, 19 June 1942, BA NS 19/2571, p. 1. Himmler warned it would be no easy fight: 'Rede des Reichsführer-SS am 16. September 1942 in der Feldkommandostelle vor der Teilnehmern an der SS- und Polizeiführer-Tagung, einberufen von SS-Obergruppenführer Prützmann, Höhere SS-und Polizeiführer Russland-Süd,' BA

NS 19/4009, pp. 1-2. Himmler considered Schellenberg overestimated Soviets: Schellenberg, *Labyrinth*, p. 310.

32. Schellenberg's March plan: Schellenberg, *Labyrinth*, pp. 254-6. Soviet offer: Nikita Khrushchev, 'Double-bluffing the Little Corporal,' *The Australian*, 25 September 1990, p. 13.

33. Schellenberg's proposal: Schellenberg, *Labyrinth*, pp. 299-301; Himmler's response, pp. 308-18. Fleischhauer argues that Himmler rejected Russian peace offers in summer 1942 and claims he only became interested in a compromise peace after Stalingrad: Ingeborg Fleischhauer, *Die Chance des Sonderfriedens: Deutschsowjetische Geheimgespräche 1941-1945* (Berlin, 1986), pp. 93-4, 114. Himmler advises Ribbentrop and Hitler: Schellenberg, *Labyrinth*, pp. 323, 329-30. Hitler rejects Japanese offers: *ibid.*, p. 256. Italian suggestions: Geoffrey Jukes, *Hitler's Stalingrad Decisions* (Berkeley, Calif., 1985), p. 183. Fromm urges Hitler: Bernhard R. Kroener, 'Die personelle Ressourcen des Dritten Reiches,' *DRZW*, 5/1, p. 1000. Rommel proposes withdrawing from North Africa: Jukes, *Hitler's Stalingrad Decisions*, pp. 109-110, 147, 182.

34. Entry, 28 July 1942, Boelcke (ed.), *Secret Conferences*, p. 264. Goebbels was not interested in a compromise peace earlier: entry, 6 March 1942, Lochner (ed.), *Goebbels Diaries*, p. 113.

35. Armaments production: Milward, *German Economy*, pp. 70, 100. Speer re-allocates resources: Mierzejewski, *Collapse of the German War Economy*, pp. 17, 19. Milward has suggested that Speer's opposition to Hitler's attempts to revert to a Blitzkrieg economy in this period caused him to begin to lose Hitler's favour, but he provides no evidence for this: Milward, *German Economy*, p. 88. There are no signs of such a loss of favour in late 1942.

36. Speech to Gauleiters in February 1942: Speer Chronik, February 1942, BA R 3/1736, pp. 15, 27. All Gauleiters made defence commissioners: Carroll, *Design for Total War*, p. 207.

37. Labour shortages expand SS role: Schieber, Rüstungslieferungsamt, Armaments Ministry, to Oberstleutnant Garelly, Heereswaffenamt IV, 19 June 1942, BA MA RH 8 I/v. 1020. SS use of prisoners: Falk Pingel, 'Die KZ-Häftlinge zwischen Vernichtung und NS-Arbeitseinsatz,' in Michalka (ed.), *Zweite Weltkrieg*, pp. 784-97. Actual work force of prisoners: Alan S. Milward, *War, Economy and Society 1939-1945* (Berkeley, Calif., 1977), p. 227. Himmler's plans for SS arms production: Himmler to Pohl, 7 July 1942, BA NS 19/1542. Speer's agreement: Pohl to Himmler, 16 September 1942, 'a) Rüstungsarbeiten. b) Bombenschäden,' BA NS 19/14, pp. 1-3. On the further course of these plans, and their failure: Albert Speer, *The Slave State: Heinrich Himmler's Masterplan for SS Supremacy* (London, 1981), pp. 21-5.

38. Testimony of Hoess, 15 April 1946, *TMWC*, vol. 11, p. 403. Speer sees SS production as obstacle: Speer, *Slave State*, *passim*. Himmler sees SS economic production as contribution: *ibid.*, pp. 48-9. Himmler tries to remove ethnic Germans: Himmler to Göring, 7 September 1942, pp. 1-2, and letter of same date to Sauckel, BA NS 19/3597. Sauckel and Göring refuse: Sauckel to Himmler, 26 October 1942, 'Ausgliederung der volksdeutschen Arbeiter aus dem Arbeitsprozess in Reich,' and Keitel to Himmler, 3 December 1942, BA NS 19/3597, pp. 1-3.

39. German losses: entry, 28 July 1942, in Boelcke (ed.), *Secret Conferences*, p. 247. Appointment of Sauckel: Speer, paper of 24 August 1945, 'Zur Vorgeschichte des Generalbevollmächtigte für den Arbeitseinsatz,' IfZ ED 99 Speer Interviews Band 9, pp. 1-2. Previous labour problems: 'Interrogation 3 Juli 1945,' IfZ ED 99 Speer Interviews Band 13, p. 1. Speer's friendship with Hanke: Speer, *Third Reich*, pp. 21, 24, 145. Speer's preference for Hanke in the position: Speer, paper of 24 August 1945, 'Zur Vorgeschichte des Generalbevollmächtigte für den Arbeitseinsatz,' IfZ ED 99 Speer Interviews Band 9, pp. 1-2. Sauckel effective: 'Interrogation 3 Juli 1945,' (interrogation of Speer), IfZ ED 99 Speer Interviews Band 13, pp. 2-3. Sauckel appoints Gauleiters: Edward Homze, *Foreign Labor in Nazi Germany* (Princeton, N. J., 1967), p. 115. Sauckel's figures: 'Bericht über dem Arbeitseinsatz im Jahre 1942,' 23 December 1942, BA R 41/280, pp. 7-8. Sauckel's figures possibly exaggerated: Janssen, *Ministerium Speer*, p. 85.

40. Boelcke (ed.), *Secret Conferences*, p. 247. Von Unruh's own reports: von Unruh, 13 August 1942, 'Bericht Nr. 3,' pp. 1-11; 'Bericht Nr. 7,' pp. 1-11; and other reports on BA NS 6/794, pp. 1-11. German firms moving staff: Hoffmann to Bormann, 9 August 1942, report about Warsaw, 'Bericht Nr. 1,' BA NS 6/795, p. 13; Hoffmann to Bormann, 27 August 1942, 'Bericht Nr. 4 Distrikt Krakau,' *ibid.*, p. 3. It gave no exemptions: Hoffmann to Bormann, 7 July 1942, 'Bericht Nr. 12,' 'Generalkommissariat Nikolajew und Schlussbericht,' *ibid.*, p. 7. It was able to reduce the staffs of the Reichskommissariats Ukraine and Shitomir: Hoffmann to Bormann, 5 June 1942, 'Bericht Nr. 6 Ukraine,' *ibid.*, p. 7; Hoffmann to Bormann, 7 June 1942, 'Bericht Nr. 7 Generalkommissariat Shitomir,' *ibid.*, p. 3. The civilian staff of the Kiev Generalkommissariat was reduced: Hoffmann to Bormann, 10 June 1942, 'Bericht Nr. 8 Generalkommissar Kiew,' *ibid.*, p. 5. Hoffmann estimated total number saved: Hoffmann to Bormann, 20 August 1942, 'Bericht Nr. 3 Krakau,' *ibid.*, pp. 8-9; Hoffmann to Bormann, 13 September 1942, 'Bericht Nr. 6 Galizien,' *ibid.*, p. 8; . Hoffmann warned: *ibid.*, p. 7.

41. Bormann, 11 December 1942, 'Rundschreiben Nr. 195/42,' BA NS 6/338, pp. 1, 3. Von Unruh's tasks: *ibid.*, pp. 1-3. Inspections in the economy: Bormann, 12 December 1942, 'Rundschreiben Nr. 189/42,' *ibid.*, p. 2.

42. Mussehl, quoted in Dieter Rebentisch, *Führerstaat und Verwaltung im Zweiten Weltkrieg: Verfassungsentwicklung und Verwaltungspolitik 1939-1945* (Stuttgart, 1989), p. 472.

43. Arvid Fredborg, *Behind the Steel Wall* (London, 1944), pp. 177-8. Ohnesorge's attitude compared to other officials: Rebentisch, *Führerstaat und Verwaltung*, pp. 472-3. Official savings claimed and Fredborg's estimate: Fredborg, *Behind the Steel Wall*, p. 178. Reliance on men called back from retirement: see papers on LAB Pr. Br. Rep. 57 Acc. Nr. 1501 Nr. 1227/2.

44. Hitler and OKW decrees: entry, 28 July 1942, Boelcke (ed.), *Secret Conferences*, p. 247. Keitel's order: Keitel order, 10 December 1942, 'Personaleinsatz in der Wehrmacht-Austausch vom minderkriegsbrauchbaren Soldaten und Weltkriegsteilnehmern gegen uk-gestellte kv-Wehrpflichtige jüngerer Geburtsjahrgänge,' BA MA RW 4/v. 473, pp. 1-4.

45. Foreign workers: Alan S. Milward, *War, Economy and Society*, p. 225. Do not satisfy need for labour: signature, 8 July 1942, 'Vermerk für Herrn Reichsminister Speer,' 'Arbeitseinsatz b.d. Fa. Friedrich Krupp AG., Essen,' BA R 41/228a, p. 2. Use of POWs expanded: signature, Armaments Ministry to Dr Timm, 9 June 1942,

BA R 41/172, pp. 1-2. Speer had to rely more on concentration camp labour: Speer Chronik, September and October 1942, BA R 3/1736, pp. 72, 83. Goebbels' early support for women's employment: entries, 14 February 1941, 12 March 1941 and 21 March 1941, Elke Fröhlich, on behalf of the Institut für Zeitgeschichte and in association with the Bundesarchiv, (ed.), *Die Tagebücher von Joseph Goebbels Sämtliche Fragmente Teil I Aufzeichnungen 1924-1941, Band 4 1.1.1940-8.7.1941* (Munich, 1987), pp. 503, 535, 546. Ley and Goebbels try unsuccessfully for compulsory registration: Bormann to Lammers, 25 September 1941, 'Frauen-Dienstpflicht,' BA R 43 II/652. Women's employment would be most successful: leader of the personnel section, submission to the Minister, 21 January 1942, BA R 55/18, pp. 1-7. Propaganda campaign prepared: Tiessler, submission to Goebbels, 26 August 1941, BA NS 18/659.

46. Himmler agreed to issue a general order: Brandt, Personal Referat of the Reichsführer-SS, to Berger, 3 June 1942, BA NS 19/1963, pp. 1-2. Berger's draft: Berger to Himmler, 18 May 1942, BA NS 19/1963, pp. 1-2. Himmler's order: Brandt to Berger, 3 June 1942, *ibid.*, pp. 1-2.

47. Elberding, 24 November 1942, 'Vermerk für Pg. Tiessler,' 'Arbeitseinsatz der Frau. Ihre Vorlage vom 6.11.1942,' BA NS 18/638, pp. 1-2. On the wider problems raised by Frauenschaft leaders: Berger to Himmler, 2 April 1942, 'Besprechung mit Vertreterinnen des Reichsfrauenführung,' BA NS 19/1963, pp. 1-5. Göring's opposition may have reflected Hitler's views: Overy, *Goering*, p. 84. Hitler ordered recruitment of 400,000 to 500,000 Ukrainian women as household servants: unsigned report, 4 September 1942, Document 025-RS, *TMWC*, vol. 25, pp. 84-5. Ultimately some 100,000 women were employed in this capacity: Herbert, *Fremdarbeiter*, note 262, p. 407. Herbert indicates the figures of 500,000 women put forward by Speer are incorrect: Speer, *Third Reich*, p. 221. Homze claims only 15,000 women were recruited: Homze, *Foreign Labor*, pp. 140-1.

48. Employment of women in SS: Reichsführer-SS, 30 November 1942, 'Richtlinien für die Betreuung der in Bereich der SS und Polizei eingesetzten deutschen Frauen insbesondere in den Gebieten ausserhalb der Reichsgrenze,' BA NS 19/3324, pp. 1-3. Divided leadership a reason for Hitler's attitude: Marianne Lehker, *Frauen im Nationalsozialismus: wie aus Opfern Handlänger der Täter wurden—eine nötige Trauerarbeit* (Frankfurt, 1984), p. 63. Goebbels believed propaganda would avert a 1918 uprising: entry, 27 November 1943, Lochner (ed.), *Goebbels Diaries*, p. 533.

49. 'Der Reichsführer-SS vor den Oberabschnittsführern und Hauptamtschefs im Haus der Flieger in Berlin am 9. Juni 1942,' BA NS 19/4009, p. 7. Use of concentration camps expanded: Martin Broszat, 'The Concentration Camps 1933-1945,' in Helmut Krausnick, Hans Buchheim, Martin Broszat and Hans-Adolf Jacobsen, *The Anatomy of the SS-State* (London, 1968), p. 483. Himmler willing to use the SS to develop new weapons: Himmler to Jüttner, 17 April 1942, BA NS 19/1947, pp. 1-2. High priority on freeing more men: 'Der Reichsführer-SS vor den Oberabschnittsführern und Hauptamtschefs im Haus der Flieger in Berlin am 9. Juni 1942,' BA NS 19/4009, pp. 6-8.

50. Himmler, speech in Berlin, 9 June 1942, BA NS 19/4009, p. 12. Himmler favours administrative simplicity: Himmler to Interior Ministry State Secretary Stuckart, 4 March 1942, BA NS 19/2393. Himmler's measures of simplification and decentralisation: Himmler to Daluege and Heydrich, 7 February 1942, BA NS

19/300, pp. 1-2. Himmler calls on SS leadership to reduce infighting: Himmler, speech to the leadership corps of the SS Division, Das Reich, 19 June 1942, BA NS 19/2571, p. 7; speech of 9 June 1942, BA NS 19/4009, pp. 11-12. Those who over-indulged to be punished: Himmler, speech in Berlin, 9 June 1942, BA NS 19/4009, p. 13. Those who made gains to be eradicated: Himmler, speech to the leadership corps of the SS Division, Das Reich, 19 June 1942, BA NS 19/2571, p. 7.

51. Some restrictions on administrative procedures: Bormann, 9 October 1941, 'Rundschreiben Nr. 119/41,' BA NS 6/335, pp. 1-3; Bormann, 28 January 1942, 'Rundschreiben Nr. 14/42,' BA NS 6/337, pp. 1-3. Number of uk party leaders: Dietrich Orlow, *The History of the Nazi Party: vol. II 1933-1945* (Newton Abbot, 1973), p. 341. At the end of 1942 the numbers employed: *ibid.*, p. 408. Hoffmann's reports propose party expansion: Hoffmann to Bormann, 7 July 1942, 'Bericht Nr. 12 Generalkommissariat Nikolajew und Schlussbericht,' pp. 19-20; 'Bericht Nr. 11,' 'Dnepropetorowsk,' all in BA NS 6/795, p. 7.

52. Goebbels optimistic about Stalingrad: entry, 19 October 1942, Boelcke (ed.), *Secret Conferences*, p. 288. Haegert's commission and proposals: Haegert to Goebbels, 15 October 1942, 'Aufhebung von Uk-Stellungen,' Haegert to Goebbels, 21 October 1942, 'Sonderauftrag. Teilergebnis im Hause,' BA R 55/324, pp. 5-7; and Dr Gerber, Abteilung Haushalt, 30 October 1942, 'Vermerk,' BA R 55/414. The nine organisations were *Deutsche Ausländerdienst, Bund zur Pflege persönlicher Freundschaften mit Ausländern, Deutsches Musikinstitut für Ausländer, International Rat zur Förderung der Sing- und Sprechkunst, Dienststelle des Reichskommissars für die Internationalen Ausstellungen, Radio-Union, Auslandsstelle für Musik, Ausslandsstelle für Theater* and *Reichsbund der deutschen Freilicht- und Volksschauspiele.* Haegert also scrutinised workers employed by the Reichsmesseamt: unsigned paper, 27 November 1942, 'Stellungnahme des Reichsmesseamts zur Frage einer weiteren Einschränkung von Arbeitskräften,' BA R 55/935, pp. 1-4. Closures Goebbels agreed to: head of Section S to head Section H, 28 November 1942, BA R 55/414. Removal of uk positions in Propaganda Ministry: undated paper, Abteilung RV, 'Reichsministerium für Volksaufklärung und Propaganda,' BA R 55/324, p. 2.

53. Goebbels proposed at beginning of war: unsigned, 'Gedanken zum Kriegsbeginn 1939,' BA NS 10/37, pp. 2-4, 18. The paper is undated and unsigned but is found in the Propaganda Ministry section of the Adjutantur des Führer files. Its style and contents suggest that it was Goebbels' work. Goebbels believed population could be relied on: entries, 1 February 1942 and 20 March 1942, Lochner (ed.), *Goebbels Diaries*, pp. 64, 132-4. He was probably basing this view on public morale as reported by SD reports; 'Anlage,' to 'Meldungen ... (Nr. 263),' 26 February 1942, in Heinz Boberach (ed.) *Meldungen aus dem Reich 1938-1945: Die geheimen Lageberichte des Sicherheitsdienstes der SS* (Herrsching, 1984), vol. 9, pp. 3391. Each citizen must feel they contribute: entry, 22 September 1941, BA NL 118/27, p. 19. Black market inevitable consequence: entry, 22 October 1941, BA NL 118/33, pp. 18-19. 1930 and 1932 crises as models: conference, 10 November 1942, Boelcke (ed.), *Secret Conferences*, p. 296; entry, 14 December 1942, Lochner (ed.), *Goebbels Diaries*, p. 243. Admired Soviet war effort: entry, 20 March 1942, *ibid.*, p. 136. Goebbels planning closer contact with Gauleiters: entry, 12 December 1942, *ibid.*, p. 240. Goebbels approaches Hitler for more radical

action: Müller, 'Die Mobilisierung der deutschen Wirtschaft,' *DRZW*, 5/1, pp. 669-70. Goebbels claimed Hitler agreed with his proposals: entry, 20 March 1942, Lochner (ed.), *Goebbels Diaries*, p. 134; opposition from bureaucracy: entry, 19 March 1942, *ibid.*, p. 129.

54. Himmler's suggestions: Himmler to SS-Gruppenführer Martin, 9 September 1942; Himmler to Daluege, 9 October 1942, pp. 2-3, 5-6; Himmler to Pohl, 9 September 1942, and Himmler to Speer, 9 September 1942, BA NS 19/14. Bombing absorbs resources: Hitler, 2 December 1942, 'Verfügung V 23/42,' BA NS 6/78, p. 1. A certain level of consumer production: Gustav Stolper, Karl Häuser and Knut Borchardt, *The German Economy 1870 to the Present* (second edition, London, 1967), pp. 167-8. Goebbels and Kehrl on ration cards: Hans Kehrl, *Krisenmanager im Dritten Reich. 6 Jahre Frieden 6 Jahre Krieg Errinerungen* (Dusseldorf, 1973), pp. 269-71. Shortages and rationing of metal items: Earl R. Beck, *Under the Bombs: The German Home Front 1942-1945* (Lexington, Mass., 1986), pp. 23-4. Civilian population overestimates effectiveness of bombing: Gerald Kirwin, 'Allied Bombing and Nazi Domestic Propaganda,' *European History Quarterly*, vol. 15, 1985, p. 354. For the effects of bombing on morale: Elke Fröhlich, 'Teil VII Stimmung und Verhalten der Bevölkerung unter den Bedingungen des Krieges. B. Berichte des Sicherheitsdienstes 1940-1944,' in Martin Broszat, Elke Fröhlich and Falk Wiesemann (eds.), *Bayern in der NS-Zeit: soziale Lage und politisches Verhalten der Bevölkerung im Spiegel vertraulicher Berichte* (Munich, 1977), p. 595. Hitler's decree on morale: 'Erlass des Führers über die Lebenshaltung führender Persönlichkeiten. Vom 21. März 1942,' Institut für Zeitgeschichte, *Akten der Parteikanzlei Teil I* (Munich, 1983-1985), 101 00506. Other steps taken: Dr Stuckart, Interior Ministry to the Reichsstatthalter, July 1942, BA R 55/7; Bormann telex to Lammers, 2 June 1942, IfZ *APK*, 101 04586; Keitel to OKH-Gen QU, 20 July 1942, and Himmler Fernschreiben to Streckenbach, 16 August 1942, BA NS 19/350.

55. Goebbels' speech, 23 February 1944, 'Die politische und militärische Lage,' BA NS 19/1870, p. 5. Goebbels' proposals: unsigned (from the context Tiessler), 23 November 1942, 'Vorlage,' 'Fahrt des Ministers durch die luftgefährdeten Gebiete,' BA NS 18/511a, pp. 1-2. Friedrichs' views reported: Elderling?, 22 December 1942, 'Vermerk für Pg. Tiessler,' *ibid.*, pp. 1-2. Responsibility for introducing immediate measures where the Gau's own resources were insufficient: Goebbels to all Gauleiters, 28 April 1942, IfZ *APK*, 103 06794. Establishment of *Luftkriegsschädenausschuss*: entry, 16 January 1943, BA NL 118/50, p. 13.

56. From June 1941 Hitler spent most of his time at his headquarters at Rastenburg, East Prussia; from July to November 1942 he was at Winniza: John Toland, *Adolf Hitler* (New York, 1976), pp. 924, 978. Himmler's headquarters: Elisabeth Kinder, 'Die Persönliche Stab Reichsführer-SS. Geschichte, Aufgaben und Überlieferung,' in Heinz Boberach and Hans Booms (eds.), *Aus der Arbeit des Bundesarchivs: Beiträge zum Archivwesen, zur Quellenkunde und Zeitgeschichte* (Boppard am Rhein, 1978), p. 392.

57. Goebbels' attempts to warn Hitler dismissed: entry, 16 February 1945, Semmler, *Goebbels*, p. 181.

58. Entry, 29 March 1941, Fröhlich (ed.), *Tagebücher von Joseph Goebbels*, 4, p. 557.

59. Entry, 7 January 1943, BA NL 118/51, pp. 14-15.

Chapter 3

1. Hitler still hoped Stalingrad could be relieved: Albert Speer, *Inside the Third Reich* (London, 1970), p. 248. True seriousness of situation not grasped: Geoffrey Jukes, *Hitler's Stalingrad Decisions* (Berkeley, Calif., 1985), pp. 245-8. Course of the battle: Peter Calvocoressi, Guy Wint and John Pritchard, *Total War: The Causes and Courses of the Second World War*, Peter Calvocoressi, *Volume I: The Western Hemisphere* (second edition, London, 1989), pp. 493-500.

2. Geoffrey Jukes, *Kursk: The Clash of Armour* (London, 1969), p. 152.

3. Early propaganda had been optimistic: Jay W. Baird, *The Mythical World of Nazi War Propaganda, 1939-1945* (Minneapolis, Minn., 1974), pp. 176-8. German public not kept informed: *ibid.*, p. 179. Propaganda treatment of Stalingrad in January 1943: E. K. Bramsted, *Goebbels and National Socialist Propaganda 1925-1945* (East Lansing, Mich., 1965), pp. 261-2. Shock to German morale: Ian Kershaw, *The 'Hitler Myth': Image and Reality in the Third Reich* (Oxford, 1989), pp. 192-4. Themes of total war for total victory: Baird, *Nazi War Propaganda*, p. 194. Goebbels' disapproval of Hitler's decision: entries, 7 and 12 January 1943, BA NL 118/51, pp. 17-18 and p. 16 respectively. Hitler's reluctance to meet with party leaders: Dietrich Orlow, *The History of the Nazi Party: vol. II 1933-1945* (Newton Abbot, 1973), p. 412.

4. Increasing attempts to improve treatment of Eastern peoples: entry, 10 January 1943, BA NL 118/51, pp. 17-18; Berger to Himmler, 14 January 1943, 'Berichte über die Lage in den besetzten Ostgebieten,' BA NS 19/3758, pp. 1-4. Schellenberg's proposals: Walter Schellenberg, *The Labyrinth: Memoirs of Walter Schellenberg* (New York, 1956), pp. 275-6.

5. Alexander Dallin, *German Rule in Russia 1941-1945: A Study of Occupation Policies* (second edition, London, 1981), p. 177. Goebbels dismayed: entry, 4 April 1943, BA NL 118/54, pp. 3-4.

6. Brandt to Berger, 20 February 1943, 'Behandlung der europäischen Völker,' BA NS 19/279. Goebbels' proclamation: Goebbels to Reichsleiters and others, 15 February 1943, 'Behandlung der europäischen Völker,' BA NS 19/279, pp. 1-5. In March 1943 he opposed attempts to stop the distribution of a SS pamphlet: Dallin, *German Rule in Russia*, note p. 181.

7. Goebbels' hopes for Vlasov: entry, 5 April 1943, BA NL 118/54, p. 4. Himmler noted: Catherine Andreyev, *Vlasov and the Russian Liberation Movement: Soviet Reality and Émigré Theories* (Cambridge, 1987), p. 50. Vlasov's advice ignored: *ibid.*, pp. 47-50. Goebbels' awareness of Hitler's lack of interest: entry, 17 January 1943, BA NL 118/50, pp. 9-11. Hitler may have decided against Goebbels: Dieter Rebentisch, *Führerstaat und Verwaltung im Zweiten Weltkrieg: Verfassungsentwicklung und Verwaltungspolitik 1939-1945* (Stuttgart, 1989), p. 321.

8. Further Japanese efforts: Schellenberg, *Labyrinth*, p. 256. Hitler forbids Ribbentrop to speak of negotiations: Fritz Hesse, *Das Vorspiel zum Kriege: Englandberichte und Erlebnisse eines Tatzeugen 1935-1945* (Leoni am Starnberger See, 1979), pp. 268-9. Fleischhauer claims that Goebbels was able to persuade Hitler to take up Russian peace soundings after Stalingrad but that negotiations faltered when the Russians demanded the partition of the Ukraine and a large part of the Baltic: Ingeborg Fleischhauer, *Die Chance des Sonderfriedens: Deutschsowjetische Geheimgespräche 1941-1945* (Berlin, 1986), pp. 115-19.

Weinberg argues that Germany could have had a separate peace but for Hitler's desire to keep the Ukraine: Weinberg, 'World War II: The Allies, 1941-1945,' in Gerhard Weinberg, *World in the Balance: Behind the Scenes of World War II* (Hanover, 1981), p. 43. Unconditional surrender discouraging: Willi A. Boelcke (ed.), *The Secret Conferences of Dr Goebbels October 1939-March 1943* (London, 1967), p. 323.

9. Berger to Himmler, 10 February 1943, 'Weltanschauliche Schulung der Truppe,' BA NS 19/281, p. 1. Criticism of army's lack of radicalism: entries, 9 March and 10 May 1943, Louis P. Lochner (ed.), *The Goebbels Diaries 1942-1943* (Garden City, N. Y., 1948), pp. 280, 368. Waffen-SS ideological education increased: Berger to Brandt, 12 May 1942; Berger to Jüttner, 13 May 1942, BA NS 19/1616. Himmler introduces more ideological training: Himmler, 24 February 1943, 'SS-Befehl,' BA NS 19/281, pp. 1-2.

10. Göring's views: Ministerialrat Dr Gönnert to Sauckel, 23 February 1943, BA R 41/229 and 'Besprechung Reichsmarschall 15.-17. (einschl.) II. 43 Reichsm. Polit. und Mil. Lage,' BA MA RL 2 I/22, pp. 25-7. Leaders suggest closure or takeover of rival organisations: Berger to Himmler, 9 January 1943, 'Vortrag Stabschef Lutze u. Reichsorganisationsleiter Dr Ley,' BA NS 19/2679.

11. Rebentisch, *Führerstaat und Verwaltung*, p. 497. Goebbels' December 1942 memorandum: Boelcke (ed.), *Secret Conferences*, p. xix; Ludolf Herbst, *Der Totale Krieg und die Ordnung der Wirtschaft. Die Kriegswirtschaft im Spannungsfeld von Politik, Ideologie und Propaganda 1939-1945* (Stuttgart, 1982), pp. 199-200. His discussions with Bormann: entry, 28 December 1942, Rudolf Semmler, *Goebbels—the man next to Hitler* (Ohio State University reprint, 1982 of London, 1947 edition), pp. 62-3. Some indication of Goebbels' proposals can be gained from Berndt, head of the propaganda section, to Goebbels, 31 December 1942, 'Massnahmen zum totalen Kriegseinsatz der Heimat,' BA Rep. 312 Nr. 12 Heft 4, pp. 1-10. Goebbels' proposals: entry, 3 January 1943, BA NL 118/51, pp. 16-17. Measures needed included the punishment of saboteurs and the need to supplement exhortation by laws and decrees, entry, 7 January 1943, BA NL 118/51, pp. 13-14.

12. Meeting chaired by Lammers: Speer Chronik, January 1943, BA R 3/1737, p. 2.

13. Bormann, 27 January 1943, 'Rundschreiben Nr. 12/43,' BA NS 6/340, p. 2. Decree: 'Erlass des Führers über den umfassenden Einsatz von Männern und Frauen für die Aufgaben der Reichsverteidigung vom 13. Januar 1943,' 13 January 1943, BA NS 6/340, pp. 1-5. Members of religious orders exempted: Bormann, 19 February 1943, 'Rundschreiben Nr. 32/43,' BA NS 6/340, pp. 1-2. Bormann on purpose of decree: Bormann, 27 January 1943, 'Rundschreiben Nr. 12/43,' BA NS 6/340, pp. 1-2. Work fell to Lammers: Rebentisch, *Führerstaat und Verwaltung*, pp. 334, 480.   •

14. Preliminary work by the Reich Chancellery staff: undated paper, 'Vereinfachung und Stillegung der Verwaltung,' BA R 43 II/654a, pp. 1-2. Subsequent submission: paper signed F., 2 February 1943, 'Durchführung des Führererlasses vom 13. Januar 1943 auf dem Gebiete der Verwaltung,' *ibid.*, pp. 1-5.

15. Unsigned paper, 5 February 1943, BA R 43 II/662, pp. 1-10.

16. Measures underway by 22 February: unsigned paper, 23 February 1943, 'Freimachung von Arbeitskräften,' BA R 43 II/654a, pp. 1-5. Measures in occupied

territories: Fernschreiben Koerner to Reichsprotector in Bohemia and Moravia, and others, 4 February 1943, BA R 41/228. Reports of various ministries: Justice Minister Thierack to Lammers, 14 January 1943, BA R 43 II/681a, pp. 1-2; von Unruh to Foreign Ministry, 13 February 1943, BA R 43 II/681b, pp. 1-2. Post Ministry's savings: Mussehl to Dr Killy, 29 January 1943, BA R 43 II/281b, p. 4. Symbolic measures taken: Schnellbrief from Meissner to the Oberste Reichs Behörden, 17 February 1943, 'Einschränkung der Verleihung von Orden und Ehrenzeichen während des Krieges,' BA Rep. 312 Nr. 2, pp. 1-2.

17. Entry, 17 January 1943, BA NL 118/51, p. 19. Goebbels worried by insufficient progress, the result of a committee: entry, 17 January 1943, BA NL 118/50, pp. 17-18. Goebbels' discussion with Bormann: entry, 18 January 1943, BA NL 118/51 p. 16.

18. Entry, 23 January 1943, BA NL 118/50, pp. 43-6.

19. Goebbels' disappointment at not being made a member of the Ausschuss: entries, 18 January and 26 January 1943, Semmler, *Goebbels*, pp. 66, 68. As late as 5 January Goebbels expected to be a member: entry, 5 January 1943, Willi A. Boelcke (ed.), *Wollt Ihr den totalen Krieg? Die geheimen Goebbels-Konferenzen 1939-43* (Stuttgart, 1989), p. 318. Goebbels' description of Lammers: entry, 20 January 1943, Semmler, *Goebbels*, p. 66. Goebbels' sense of urgency: entry, 9 January 1943, BA NL 118/51, pp. 35-6. His comparisons to the USSR: entry, 16 January 1943, BA NL 118/50, p. 9.

20. Historians who give credit to Goebbels: Marie-Luise Recker, *Nationalsozialistische Sozialpolitik im Zweiten Weltkrieg* (Munich, 1975), p. 179. See also note 19 Chapter 4. Rebentisch's argument: Rebentisch, *Führerstaat und Verwaltung*, pp. 475, 496-7.

21. Hitler did not want Goebbels to join the Ausschuss: entry, 23 January 1943, BA NL 118/50, pp. 43-6. Goebbels referred to it as the Vierer Ausschuss: entry, 26 January 1943, BA NL 118/51, p. 22.

22. Lammers and Bormann outmanoeuvred him: entry, 25 July 1944, Wilfred von Oven, *Finale Furioso: Mit Goebbels bis zum Ende* (first published 1948-50, Tübingen, 1974), pp. 432-3. All members based at Hitler's headquarters: Herbst, *Totale Krieg*, pp. 208-9. Berger's interpretation: Berger to Himmler, 29 January 1943, BA NS 19/2687, pp. 1-2.

23. Entry, 16 January 1943, BA NL 118/50, p. 12.

24. Fernschreiben Tiessler to Friedrichs, 22 January 1943, 'Meldung Nr. 55,' 'Meldepflicht von Maennern und Frauen,' BA NS 18/638, p. 3. Complete draft text is on pp. 2-3. Resistance to labour duty for women: entry, 26 January 1943, BA NL 118/51, p. 23. Party Chancellery alterations: Fernschreiben Tiessler to Witt, 25 January 1943, BA NS 18/638, pp. 1-3. Employment of women in day care centres: Tiessler, 19 March 1943, 'Vorlage für den Herrn Minister,' 'Betreuung der Haushalt und Kinder von dienstverpflichteten Frauen,' BA NS 18/462, pp. 1-2.

25. Use of employment of wives of prominent Party members: Tiessler, 27 February 1943, 'Vorlage,' 'Arbeitseinsatz von Frauen prominenter Parteigenossen,' BA NS 18/736. Goebbels' private lifestyle: Hans-Otto Meissner, *Magda Goebbels: A Biography* (London, 1980), pp. 207, 224-6; entry, 13 January 1941, Semmler, *Goebbels*, p. 16; entry, 19 June 1943, von Oven, *Finale Furioso*, pp. 37-9.

Employment of Magda Goebbels: Helmut Heiber, *Joseph Goebbels* (second edition, Munich, 1974), pp. 320-1.

26. Entry, 27 January 1943, BA NL 118/51, pp. 23-4. Women's labour service to allow two regiments: entry, 27 January 1943, BA NL 118/51, p. 21. Lammers had persuaded Hitler: entry, 27 January 1943, BA NL 118/51, pp. 23-4.

27. Speer, *Third Reich*, p. 256. Hitler rejected attempts by Sauckel and Goebbels: submission to Lammers, 25 January 1943, pp. 1-2 and a note by Lammers on pp. 2-3 of the same document, BA R 43 II/654.

28. British guidelines: W. K. Hancock and M. M. Gowing, *British War Economy* (London, 1949), p. 458.

29. Lammers' own account suggests: note by Lammers, 26 January 1943, Institut für Zeitgeschichte, *Akten der Parteikanzlei Teil I* (Munich, 1983-1985), 101 09428-9. Secondary leaders divided: Recker, *Nationalsozialistische Sozialpolitik*, p. 183. Hitler changes age limits: Rebentisch, *Führerstaat und Verwaltung*, p. 478. Goebbels had earlier claimed: entry, 23 January 1943, BA NL 118/50, p. 33.

30. Goebbels' differences with Hitler: entry, 9 March 1943, Lochner (ed.), *Goebbels Diaries*, pp. 283-4; Speer, *Third Reich*, p. 258 and note on p. 543. Hitler called on the Gauleiters: entry, 8 February 1943, BA NL 118/52, pp. 15, 42-3, 63.

31. Goebbels sees Gauleiters as unaware: entry, 8 February 1943, BA NL 118/52, p. 15. Gauleiters a crucial level of power: entry, 26 January 1943, BA NL 118/51, p. 26.

32. Bormann at a meeting of the Ausschuss: entry, 29 January 1943, BA NL 118/51, p. 16. Goebbels' claim at earlier meeting: Rebentisch, *Führerstaat und Verwaltung*, p. 488. Hitler's views are quoted in Bormann, 5 July 1943, 'Rundschreiben Nr. 99/43,' BA NS 6/342, p. 2. Loss of employment: Rebentisch, *Führerstaat und Verwaltung*, p. 489.

33. The decree and how it affected the party: Bormann, 12 January 1943, 'Anordnung A1/43 g,' BA NS 6/344, pp. 1-3; Speer to Betriebsführer der deutschen Rüstungswirtschaft, 19 December 1942, BA R 41/282, pp. 1-2.

34. Principles of von Unruh's work: Von Unruh to Meissner, 18 January 1943, BA Rep. 312 Nr. 2, p. 1. Lammers offered him nine employees without replacement: Lammers to von Unruh, 5 February 1943, BA Rep. 312 Nr. 1, p. 1. Savings in Ostministerium: F., 2 February 1943, 'Durchführung des Führererlasses . . .,' pp. 1-5, and unsigned paper, 5 February 1943, '1) Vermerk,' BA R 43 II/654a. Presidential Chancellery workers freed: von Unruh to Meissner, 18 January 1943, BA Hauptarchiv Rep. 312 Nr. 2, pp. 1-2. Education staff freed: von Unruh to Rust, Minister of Education, 22 February 1943, BA Rep. 312 Nr. 14 Heft 2, pp. 1-7. Savings contained in the commission's files: von Unruh to Labour Ministry, 13 February 1943, pp. 1-2; von Unruh to Interior Minister, 11 February 1943, pp. 1-6; von Unruh to Economics Minister, 13 February 1943, BA R 43 II/681b, pp. 1-2.

35. Speer Chronik, January 1943, R 3/1737, p. 5. Goebbels believed von Unruh not capable of inspecting armed forces rigorously: entry, 6 February 1943, BA NL 118/52, p. 22. Goebbels' clash with von Unruh: With to Himmler, 11 February 1943, 'Zusammenstoss zwischen Herrn General von Unruh und den Reichsminister für Volksaufklärung und Propaganda,' BA NS 19/2685, pp. 1-2. The literature shows some confusion about numbers involved. The figure 2400 for the Propaganda Ministry's quota is mentioned in signature, OKW to Propaganda Ministry,

5 February 1943, BA R 55/324. Propaganda Ministry subsequently pointed out: signature, letter to OKW Allgemeines Heeresamt, 8 February 1943, 'Rekruteneinstellung Februar 1943 für das Heer, 2. Rate,' BA R 55/324. Performing arts to be exempted: Olbricht OKW to W.KdoI-XIII and others, 12 February 1943, 'Einberufung UK-Gestellter,' BA R 55/324, pp. 1-2. Hitler banned closure of theatres, etc.: entry, 14 February 1943, BA NL 118/52, p. 29. Number of men in protected sectors: Titel to Minister, 9 February 1943, BA R 55/324, pp. 1-2.

36.   Non-artistic staff to be voluntarily freed in protected sectors: Titel to Minister, 9 February 1943, *ibid.*, pp. 1-2. Already combed out: signature, letter to OKW Allgemeines Heeresamt, 8 February 1943, *ibid.*

37.   Bormann's circular on von Unruh: Bormann, 12 January 1943, 'Rundschreiben Nr. 3/43g,' BA NS 6/344, p. 2. Von Unruh's principles: von Unruh to OKW, 6 January 1943, IfZ *APK*, 107 01135.

38.   Von Unruh criticised by Reich Chancellery: Rebentisch, *Führerstaat und Verwaltung*, pp. 472-3. Goebbels unpersuaded by Sauckel: entry, 13 January 1943, BA NL 118/51, pp. 17-18.

39.   The various measures restricting administrative tasks and use of material: entry, 23 January 1943, *ibid.*, p. 22; Gutterer to Reichsstatthalter and others, 8 February 1943, 'Verleihung von Kunstpreisen,' BA R 55/698, pp. 1-2. Goebbels discussed with Esser and proposed use of Amann: entry, 28 January 1943, BA NL 118/51, p. 20.

40.   Bormann suspends six organisations: Bormann, 12 February 1943, 'Rundschreiben Nr. 24/43,' BA NS 6/340, p. 1. A further organisation dissolved: Hitler, 3 March 1943, 'Verfügung,' IfZ *APK*, 103 04543; Bormann, 1 March 1943, 'Rundschreiben Nr. 35/43,' BA NS 6/340, pp. 1-2. Bormann used these simplifications: Orlow, *Nazi Party*, II, pp. 408-9.

41.   Bormann, 2 February 1943, 'Rundschreiben Nr. 17/43,' BA NS 6/340 p. 2. Restrictions on leave: Bormann, 20 January 1943, 'Anordnung A2/43,' BA NS 6/340. This measure introduced despite Bormann's opposition: Walter Tiessler, 'Licht und Schatten oder Schonungslose Wahrheit (1922-1945),' IfZ ED 158, p. 152. Gauleiters to read Hitler's appeal: Bormann, 25 January 1943, 'Rundschreiben Nr. 6/43gRs,' BA NS 6/344, pp. 1-2.

42.   Himmler, draft decree, January 1943, 'Erfassung aller Kriegsverwendungsfähigen SS-Führer,' BA NS 19/2092. Himmler ordered the responsible SS and Police Leaders: Funkspruch Himmler to Higher SS and Police Leaders (HSSPF) Ukraine Kiev and Russia Centre, 13 February 1943, BA NS 19/2844. 30,000 possible workers left behind: SS-Brigadeführer Zimmermann, 17 February 1943, 'Aktennotiz über meine Besprechung mit dem Generalquartiermeister, Generalleutnant Wagner, am 17.2.43,' BA NS 19/808, pp. 1-2. Various decisions on minor issues: Himmler Fernschreiben to Ohlendorf, 23 January 1943, NS 19/3787; Backe to Himmler, 10 February 1943, 'Sonderregelungen für Diplomaten,' pp. 1-2; Himmler to Backe, 20 February 1943, BA NS 19/280. Himmler persisted in his attempts to have ethnic Germans made available: Himmler to Sauckel, 12 January 1943, 'Ausgliederung der volksdeutschen Arbeiter aus dem Arbeitsprozess im Reich,' BA NS 19/3597, pp. 1-2; Sauckel to Himmler, 17 February 1943, *ibid.*, pp. 1-2.

43.   Numbers of Jews exterminated: Michael R. Marrus, *The Holocaust in History* (London, 1987), p. 55-6. Himmler planned to expand SS armaments factories in

the General Government: Himmler to Pohl, 11 February 1943, BA NS 19/2648. Himmler ordered HSSPF: Himmler to RSSHA, 15 January 1943, BA NS19/1542. Large transports of Jews from Berlin: Kurt J. Ball-Kaduri, 'Berlin wird judenfrei: die Juden in Berlin in den Jahren 1942/1943,' *Jahrbuch für die Geschichte Mittel- und Ostdeutschlands*, vol. 22, 1973, p. 207-8. Hitler and Goebbels agreed on Jews: entry, 23 January 1943, BA NL 118/51, pp. 73-5.

44. Speer Chronik, February 1943, R 3/1737, p. 19. Speer supported measures to simplify the administration: *ibid*. In his capacity as Generalbauinspektor, Speer put an end to the few planning activities still under way for the rebuilding of Berlin: *ibid*., p. 21. On licensing for building: Speer Chronik, January 1943, and on the lengthened working hours: Speer Chronik, February 1943, *ibid*., pp. 4-5 and p. 19 respectively.

45. He wanted to use improvisation: entry, 28 January 1943, BA NL 118/51, pp. 25-6. Atmosphere of crisis needed: entry, 29 January 1943, *ibid*., pp. 16-17.

46. He believed Speer obtaining everything possible from the armaments industry: entry, 5 February 1943, BA NL 118/52, pp. 31-2. Had Speer's full support in radicalising conduct of war: *ibid*., p. 30. The right psychological moment for more drastic measures: entries, 13 and 28 January 1943, BA NL 118/51, pp. 18-19 and 23-4 respectively. Goebbels plans to use public opinion as an ally: entry, 28 January 1943, *ibid*., p. 27.

Chapter 4

1. Military developments on Eastern front: Peter Calvocoressi, Guy Wint and John Pritchard, *Total War: The Causes and Courses of the Second World War*, Peter Calvocoressi, *Volume I: The Western Hemisphere* (second edition, London, 1989), p. 500. North African campaign: *ibid*., pp. 387-91. Bombing: Williamson Murray, *Luftwaffe* (Baltimore, 1985), pp. 161-2.

2. Popular morale: Earl R. Beck, *Under the Bombs: The German Home Front 1942-1945* (Lexington, 1986), pp. 47-9, 55-6. Propaganda losing credibility: Michael Balfour, *Propaganda in War 1939-1945: Organisations, Policies and Publics in Britain and Germany* (London, 1979), pp. 336-8.

3. Helmut Heiber, *Joseph Goebbels* (second edition, Munich, 1974), p. 292; Albert Speer, *Inside the Third Reich* (London, 1970), pp. 254-5.

4. *Ibid*. p. 258. Goebbels' comments in meeting of 27 February: *ibid*. Speer believed: *ibid*.

5. *Ibid*., p. 257. Goebbels' speech of 18 February 1943: 'Kundgebung des Gaues Berlin der NSDAP,' Helmut Heiber (ed.), *Goebbels-Reden Band 2: 1939-1945* (Dusseldorf, 1972), pp. 176-81. Plans to exploit anti-Bolshevik feeling: entry, 14 March 1943, Rudolf Semmler, *Goebbels—the man next to Hitler* (Ohio State University reprint, 1982 of London, 1947 edition), p. 76. Hitler's lack of interest: Speer, *Third Reich*, p. 293.

6. Hitler's discussion: 'Besprechung des Führers mit Generalfeldmarschall Keitel und General Zeitzler am 8.6.1943 auf dem Berghof,' BA MA RW 4/v. 507, p. 7. Herbst has argued: Ludolf Herbst, *Der Totale Krieg und die Ordnung der Wirtschaft. Die Kriegswirtschaft im Spannungsfeld von Politik, Ideologie und Propaganda 1939-1945* (Stuttgart, 1982), pp. 228, 241, 455.

7. Goebbels believed strong authority needed: entries, 2 March and 16 March 1943, Louis P. Lochner (ed.), *The Goebbels Diaries 1942-1943* (Garden City, N. Y., 1948), pp. 267, 301. Göring's position as Chairman: entry, 2 March 1943, *ibid.*, p. 267. Göring's authority essential: entry, 6 April 1943, BA NL 118/54, p. 5. Göring's position since 1941: R. J. Overy, *Goering the 'Iron Man'* (London, 1984), pp. 218-24. Reasons for his decline of power: *ibid.*, pp. 204-6. Hedonism: David Irving, *Göring: A Biography* (New York, 1989), pp. 354-5, 359-60, 370-1.

8. Goebbels believed in a union of a more and less radical group: entry, 1 April 1943, BA NL 118/54, p. 3.

9. 'Besprechung Reichsmarschall 15.-17. (einschl.) II.43 Reichsm. Polit. und Mil. Lage,' BA MA RL 2 I/22, p. 27. Goebbels' and Göring's relations strained: entry, 18 March 1943, Semmler, *Goebbels*, pp. 77-8. Speer makes first approach: Speer Chronik, February 1943, BA R 3/1737, p. 27.

10. Speer Chronik, March 1943, *ibid.*, p. 29. Speer claims he originated approach to Göring: Speer, *Third Reich*, p. 258. They discussed Ribbentrop's replacement: *ibid.*, p. 260. Victory had to be pursued politically: entry, 2 March 1943, Lochner (ed.), *Goebbels Diaries*, p. 266. Hitler's criticisms of Göring: entry, 9 March 1943, *ibid.*, pp. 279-82. Two further meetings in March: Speer Chronik, March 1943, BA R 3/1737, pp. 34, 37.

11. Goebbels and Speer's plans and the course of the meeting: Speer, *Third Reich*, pp. 264-5. Speer's explanation: *ibid.*, p. 265. Overy attributes: Overy, *Goering*, pp. 221-2. Fear of Hitler: Irving, *Göring*, p. 381.

12. Entry, 10 August 1943, Semmler, *Goebbels*, p. 97. Goebbels still wanted to revive Göring's authority: entry, 6 April 1943, BA NL 118/54, p. 5. Göring discredited by deterioration in air war: testimony of General Karl Bodenschatz, 8 March 1946, *Trial of the Major War Criminals Before the International Military Tribunal, Nuremberg, 14 November 1945-1 October 1946* (reprint, New York, 1971), vol. 9, pp. 30-3. Göring's standing with Hitler weakened: Dietrich Orlow, *The History of the Nazi Party: vol. II 1933-1945* (Newton Abbot, 1973), p. 420. Speer and Reimann have suggested: Speer, *Third Reich*, p. 256; Viktor Reimann, *The Man Who Created Hitler: Joseph Goebbels* (London, 1977), pp. 269-70.

13. Goebbels did not understand: entry, 2 April 1943, BA NL 118/54, p. 8. Perceptions of a Führer crisis: Dieter Rebentisch, *Führerstaat und Verwaltung im Zweiten Weltkrieg: Verfassungsentwicklung und Verwaltungspolitik 1939-1945* (Stuttgart, 1989), p. 402.

14. Goebbels—amended by Hitler and Bormann, 5 June 1943, 'Die Lage,' BA R 55/1487, pp. 37-8. Section on North Africa: *ibid.*, pp. 45-8. Goebbels favoured compulsory seizure: entry, 3 April 1943, BA NL 118/54, p. 6. Bormann advised Party leaders: Bormann, 5 April 1943, 'Rundschreiben Nr. 59/43,' BA NS 6/341. Hitler and Bormann may have been reflecting earlier public opinion: 'Meldungen aus dem Reich (Nr. 257),' 5 February 1942, in Heinz Boberach (ed.) *Meldungen aus dem Reich 1938-1945: Die geheimen Lageberichte des Sicherheitsdienstes der SS* (Herrsching, 1984), vol. 9, pp. 3272-3.

15. Speer reported Hitler supported total war: entry, 24 April 1943, Lochner (ed.), *Goebbels Diaries*, p. 342.

16. Bormann, 1 March 1943, 'Rundschreiben Nr. 37/43,' BA NS 6/340, p. 1, Bormann's own emphasis. Individual National Socialists to become 'the motor':

ibid., p. 3. Doubt and defeatism: Bormann, 24 June 1943, 'Anordnung A 43/43,' BA NS 6/341.

17. Hitler repeated similar orders: Bormann, 28 May 1943, 'Rundschreiben Nr. 82/43,' BA NS 18/736, pp. 1-2; Bormann, 24 June 1943, 'Anordnung A 43/43,' BA NS 6/341. A loss of heart among Party members: Orlow, *Nazi Party*, II, pp. 413, 415. Treatment of wives and children of leaders when reporting: Bormann, 28 May 1943, 'Rundschreiben Nr. 82/43,' BA NS 6/341, pp. 1-2. The Party in Bavaria was discredited: Elke Fröhlich, 'Teil VII Stimmung und Verhalten der Bevölkerung unter den Bedingungen des Krieges. B. Berichte des Sicherheitsdienstes 1940-1944,' in Martin Broszat, Elke Fröhlich and Falk Wiesemann (eds.), *Bayern in der NS-Zeit: soziale Lage und politisches Verhalten der Bevölkerung im Spiegel vertraulicher Berichte* (Munich, 1977), pp. 595-6.

18. Use of adjutants: Bormann, 24 March 1943, 'Rundschreiben Nr 47/43,' BA NS 6/340, pp. 1-2. Women to be trained as civilian motor drivers: Bormann, 22 March 1943, 'Rundschreiben Nr. 45/43,' BA NS 6/340, pp. 1-3. Hitler's policy on printing papers and magazines: Bormann, 16 May 1943, 'Rundschreiben Nr. 77/43,' BA NS 6/341, pp. 1-10.

19. Ulrich Herbert, *Fremdarbeiter: Politik und Praxis des "Ausländer-Einsatzes" in der Kriegswirtschaft des Dritten Reiches* (Berlin, 1985), p. 238. Goebbels' biographers' views: Roger Manvell and Heinrich Fraenkel, *Doctor Goebbels* (revised edition, London, 1968), chapters 6 and 7; Reimann, *Goebbels*, pp. 254, 268.

20. Berenice A. Carroll, *Design for Total War: Arms and Economics in the Third Reich* (The Hague, 1968), p. 242; suggestion Goebbels helped sabotage total war: *ibid.*, pp. 242-3. Herbst's study: Herbst, *Totale Krieg*, pp. 197-8. Janssen's analysis: Gregor Janssen, *Das Ministerium Speer: Deutschlands Rüstung im Krieg* (Frankfurt, 1968), pp. 274-5.

21. Goebbels spoke of total war: 30 January 1943, 'Kundgebung zum 10. Jahrestag der Machtübernahme,' in Heiber (ed.), *Goebbels-Reden*, 2, p. 161. The need to relinquish middle-class customs: *ibid.*, pp. 161, 165. Significant degree of voluntary sacrifice necessary: speech of 18 February 1943, *ibid.*, pp. 184-6. Public prepared to bear equally shared burdens: *ibid.*, pp. 187, 206. Specific measures: *ibid.*, pp. 192-3, 199-200, 204-5, respectively.

22. Optical measures foreshadowed: speech of 18 February 1943, Heiber, *Goebbels-Reden*, 2, pp. 189-90, 193, 195-6. Goebbels banned horse racing: submission from Goebbels to Hitler, 16 February 1943, BA R 43 II/658a, p. 1. Hitler's decision: note by Lammers, 4 March 1943, *ibid.*, pp. 1-2. Goebbels again approached Hitler: note (by Kritzinger?), 11 March 1943, and Lammers to Agriculture Minister and others, 24 March 1943, *ibid.*, pp. 1-2.

23. Kaltenbrunner told Himmler: Kaltenbrunner to Himmler, 12 May 1943, 'Hebung der Arbeitswilligkeit,' BA NS 19/2636, p. 3.

24. Goebbels' concept of total war: speech of 18 February 1943, Heiber, *Goebbels-Reden*, 2, p. 196. Germans need to counter Soviet measures: *ibid.*, pp. 184-5.

25. Goebbels criticised Sauckel's approach: entry, 2 April 1943, BA NL 118/54, p. 8. The number of women in this age group in Britain in 1945 is taken from Central Statistical Office, *Statistical Digest of the War* (London, 1951), p. 2, while the numbers employed as a result are taken from H. M. D. Parker, *Manpower: A Study of Wartime Policy and Administration* (London, 1957), p. 292.

26.   Martin Bormann to Gerda Bormann, 14 February 1943, in H. R. Trevor-Roper (ed.), *The Bormann Letters: The Private Correspondence Between Martin Bormann and His Wife from January 1943 to April 1945* (London, 1954), p. 5.

27.   Savings from closure of Prussian Finance Ministry: submission to Lammers, 2 February 1943, 'Durchführung des Führererlasses vom 13. Januar 1943 auf dem Gebiete der Verwaltung,' BA R 43 II/654a, p. 1. Hitler opposed: 'Niederschrift über die Besprechung des Ausschusses vom 16 März 1943, 16 Uhr,' *ibid.*, p. 4. The June meeting: 'Niederschrift über die Besprechung des Ausschusses vom 24. Juni 1943, II Uhr,' *ibid.*, pp. 4-5. Prussian Finance Ministry not dissolved until July 1944: second 'Pressekommuniqué,' undated, BA R 43 II/666b, p. 10.

28.   Entry, 23 January 1943, BA NL 118/50, p. 31.

29.   Goebbels wanted a National Socialist 'senate': entry, 15 May 1943, Semmler, *Goebbels*, p. 86. Goebbels wants stronger authority: entries, 2 and 16 March 1943, Lochner (ed.), *Goebbels Diaries*, pp. 269 and 301 respectively. Berger's comment: Berger to Himmler, 29 January 1943, BA NS 19/2687, pp. 1-2.

30.   Bormann's appointment: Lammers to all ORBs, 8 May 1943, 'Sekretär des Führers,' BA NS 6/159, pp. 1-2. Bormann assumes much of Lammers' power: Orlow, *Nazi Party*, II, p. 422. Bormann explained to Himmler: Bormann to Himmler, 1 May 1943, BA NS 19/1205, pp. 1-2. Bormann aware Goebbels not pleased: Bormann, 8 May 1943, 'Aktenvermerk für Pg. Dr Klopfer und Pg. Friedrichs,' BA NS 6/159, p. 2. Goebbels believed: Speer, *Third Reich*, pp. 254, 258.

31.   Entry, 6 April 1943, BA NL 118/54, p. 5. Alleged Goebbels-Bormann alliance: Speer, *Third Reich*, p. 267. Undermining press restrictions: entry, 2 April 1943, BA NL 118/54, pp. 7-8.

32.   Bormann's criticism of press publicity: Bormann, 5 May 1943, 'Rundschreiben Nr. 71/43,' BA NS 6/341. Party Chancellery objections: signature, 17 March 1943, 'Notiz für Pg. Tiessler,' 'Arbeitseinsatz von Frauen prominenter Parteigenossen-Ihre Vorlage vom 27.2.1943,' BA NS 18/736. Tiessler's response: T[iessler], 24 March 1943, 'Notiz für Pg. Witt,' *ibid.*

33.   Speer Chronik, March 1943, BA R 3/1737, p. 33. Number of meetings: Rebentisch, *Führerstaat und Verwaltung*, p. 479. Ausschuss meeting: 'Niederschrift über die Besprechung des Ausschusses vom 16. März 1943, 16 Uhr,' BA R 43 II/654a, pp. 2, 6. On the earlier numbers in the environmental planning office, see submission to Lammers, 2 February 1943, 'Durchführung des Führererlasses vom 13. Januar 1943 auf dem Gebiete der Verwaltung,' *ibid.*, p. 2.

34.   Decisions of 24 June meeting: 'Niederschrift über die Besprechung des Ausschusses vom 24. Juni 1943, II Uhr,' BA R 43 II/654a, pp. 3, 9-10. Unrest caused by business closures: Herbst, *Totale Krieg*, pp. 219-20, 225. Carroll's claim: Carroll, *Design for Total War*, pp. 242-3. Measures need to take into account overall aim: entry, 3 April 1943, BA NL 118/54, pp. 6, 8.

35.   Fernschreiben Bormann to all Gauleiters, 'Stillegung von Betrieben,' BA R 43 II/662. Four categories of business: Herbst, *Totale Krieg*, p. 215. Guidelines strictly enforced: Fritz Nadler, *Ein Stadt im Schatten Streichers: Bisher unveröffentlichte Tagebüchblätter Dokumente und Bilder vom Kriegsjahr 1943* (Nuremberg, 1969), pp. 135-6; Paul Sauer, *Württemberg in der Zeit des Nationalsozialismus* (Ulm, 1975), p. 371. Some cases of businesses pursuing peacetime production: Rudolf

Jordan, *Erlebt und Erlitten: Weg eines Gauleiters von München bis Moskau* (Leoni am Starnberger See, 1971), p. 243. Suggestions that closures acquired own momentum: Stuckart to Kritzinger, 17 March 1943, BA R 43 II/662; Sauckel to Lammers, 19 May 1943, 'Einsatz von Männern und Frauen auf Grund der Stillegungsverordnung vom 29. Januar 1943,' BA R 43 II/662a. Complaints were received from people whose businesses were closed: submission to Lammers, 8 April 1943, '1.) Vermerk,' 'Durchführung des Führererlasses vom 13. Januar,' BA R 43 II/662a. Closures free materials, power and labour: unsigned note, '1./ Vermerk,' 4 June 1943 and unsigned note, '1.) Vermerk,' 'Ausschusssitzung,' 23 June 1943, BA R 43 II/662. Shutdowns led to unemployment: submission to Lammers, 8 April 1943, 'Durchführung des Führererlasses vom 13. Januar 1943,' BA R 43 II/654b, p. 1. Policy caused unrest: Herbst, *Totale Krieg*, pp. 219-20, 230-1. Tiessler's proposal: T[iessler], submission to Goebbels, 'Der Nationalsozialismus bejaht den Mittelstand,' BA NS 18/266. Stuckart on political porcelain: Stuckart to Kritzinger, 17 March 1943, BA R 43 II/662. Some Gauleiters combat closures: Gerhard Hetzer, 'Unternehmer und leitende Angestellte zwischen Rüstungseinsatz und politischer Säuberung,' in Martin Broszat, Klaus-Dietmar Henke, and Hans Woller, (eds.), *Von Stalingrad zur Währungsreform: zur Sozialgeschichte des Umbruchs in Deutschland* (Munich, 1989), p. 553. Most pursue combing out: Rebentisch, *Führerstaat und Verwaltung*, pp. 489-90. Stürtz told Lammers: Gauleiter Mark Brandenburg to Lammers, 5 May 1943, BA R 43 II/662, pp. 1-4.

36. Some 2 million more called up: Ursula von Gersdorff, *Frauen im Kriegsdienst 1914-1945* (Stuttgart, 1969), p. 154. Lammers' claims of numbers saved: unsigned note, 23 July 1944, 'Ergebnis der Chef Besprechung,' BA R 43 II/664a, p. 1. Post-war comments: Rebentisch, *Führerstaat und Verwaltung*, p. 480. Rebentisch estimates: *ibid.*, note 376, p. 493. Numbers given up by Reichsarbeitsdienst: Hierl to Lammers, 11 March 1943, 'Durchführung des Führererlasses vom 13.1.1943 über Einsatz für Aufgaben der Reichsverteidigung,' BA R 43 II/660, pp. 1-2. Numbers freed by Post Ministry: Ohnesorge to Lammers, 9 March 1943, 'Führererlass vom 13.1.43,' BA R 43 II/660, pp. 1-2. Post Ministry proposals for total war are to be found on BA R 48/6 and R 48/7.

37. Some measures had foundered on resistance: unsigned note, 23 July 1944, 'Ergebnis der Chef Besprechung,' BA R 43 II/664a, p. 1. Hitler alters means of implementing policies: entry, 25 April 1943, Willi A. Boelcke (ed.), *Deutschlands Rüstung im Zweiten Weltkrieg: Hitlers Konferenzen mit Albert Speer 1942-1945* (Frankfurt, 1969), p. 252. Rebentisch's judgements: Rebentisch, *Führerstaat und Verwaltung*, p. 493.

38. Many of those freed not re-employable: Sauckel to Hitler, 15 April 1943, Document 407(vi)-RS, *TMWC*, vol. 26, pp. 7-8. Half a million women left work force: Schmelter, 'III Besprechung im Stralsund,' 3 May 1944, BA MA RL 3/6, p. 38. Further 0.7 million employed part time: unsigned, 'Vermerk über Vortrag des GBA. Gauleiter Sauckel beim Führer am 18. November 1943,' BA R 43 II/654, p. 2. Similar problems arose in Britain: Penny Summerfield, *Women Workers in the Second World War: Production and Patriarchy in Conflict* (second edition, London, 1989), pp. 33-5, 117. Railways' use of women: signature, 30 March 1943, '1.) Vermerk,' 'Beschäftigung von Angehörigen der Dienstnehmer öffentlicher Verwaltungen in deren Bereich,' BA R 43 II/658b, p. 1. Post office: signature to

Presidents Reichspostdirektionen, 4 February 1943, 'Verwendung von Frauen im Bahnpostdienst,' BA R 48/55, pp. 1-2, and other papers on this file.

39. Some less committed: Marlis G. Steinert, *Hitler's War and the Germans: Public Mood and Attitude during the Second World War* (Ohio, 1977), pp. 199-200. Industry attitudes: Stephen Salter, 'The Mobilisation of German Labour, 1939-1945. A Contribution to the History of the Working Class in the Third Reich,' (unpublished D. Phil. thesis, Oxford, 1983), p. 79. Sauckel's instructions: Marie-Luise Recker, *Nationalsozialistische Sozialpolitik im Zweiten Weltkrieg* (Munich, 1975), p. 183. Koonz claims that officials reluctant to enforce: Claudia Koonz, *Mothers of the Fatherland: Women, the Family and Nazi Politics* (London, 1987), p. 398. Popular opinion believed this: 'Meldungen . . . (Nr. 356),' 4 February 1943, in Boberach (ed.), *Meldungen aus dem Reich*, vol. 12, pp. 4751-2; 'Meldungen . . . (Nr. 366),' 11 March 1943; 'Meldungen . . . (Nr. 373),' 5 April 1943, all in Boberach (ed.), *Meldungen aus dem Reich*, vol. 13, pp. 4934, 5079. Lack of mechanism to ensure women do not slip out: Dörte Winkler, *Frauenarbeit im "Dritten Reich"* (Hamburg, 1977), p. 141. Bürckel's policy: Fernschreiben Tiessler to Witt, 22 April 1943, 'Einsatz der Partei beim Arbeitseinsatz der Frauen,' BA NS 18/742, pp. 1-2. Women's evasion: Wolfgang Werner, *'Bleib übrig!' Deutsche Arbeiter in der nationalsozialistischen Kriegswirtschaft* (Dusseldorf, 1983), p. 280; Stefan Bajohr, *Die Hälfte der Fabrik: Geschichte der Frauenarbeit in Deutschland 1914 bis 1945* (Marburg, 1979), pp. 292-3.

40. Many women unsuited to work: Steinert, *Hitler's War and the Germans*, p. 199. Many women not in areas where labour needed: Beck, *Under the Bombs*, p. 42. British figures: W. K. Hancock and M. M. Gowing, *British War Economy* (London, 1949), note 1 p. 308.

41. Perceptions of unequal treatment strengthened: Steinert, *Hitler's War and the Germans*, pp. 199, 201. Middle-class unrest: *ibid.*, pp. 198-201. Goebbels' intention to use class animus: *ibid.*, pp. 197-8. Popular reaction to the measures on women's employment: 'Meldungen . . . (Nr. 356),' 4 February 1943, pp. 4751-2; 'Meldungen . . . (Nr. 358),' 11 February 1943, pp. 4756-9, all in Boberach (ed.), *Meldungen aus dem Reich*, vol. 12; 'Meldungen . . . (Nr. 366),' 11 March 1943, pp. 4788-94; 'Meldungen . . . (Nr. 378),' 22 April 1943, all in Boberach (ed.), *Meldungen aus dem Reich*, vol. 13, pp. 5171-4. Popular reaction to the closure of businesses: 'Meldungen . . . (Nr. 366),' 11 March 1943, pp. 4939-43; 'Meldungen . . . (Nr. 372),' 1 April 1943, all in Boberach (ed.), *Meldungen aus dem Reich*, vol. 13, pp. 5040-4. Support of neither group secured: Herbst, *Totale Krieg*, p. 230. Bombing attributed to total war: Steinert, *Hitler's War and the Germans*, pp. 201-2.

42. Belief only upper-class women evading employment probably false: Tim Mason, 'Zur Frauenarbeit im NS-Staat,' *Archiv für Sozialgeschichte*, vol. 19, 1979, p. 583. In 1939, 58 per cent outside paid employment had working-class husbands: Ingrid Schupetta, *Frauen- und Ausländererwerbstätigkeit in Deutschland von 1939 bis 1945* (Cologne, 1983), pp. 146-7.

43. Sauckel's labour recruitment: Edward Homze, *Foreign Labor in Nazi Germany* (Princeton, N. J., 1967), pp. 146-7. Commission suspends its activities: Fernschreiben von Unruh to Hitler, 15 March 1943, BA Rep. 312 Nr. 27. Fromm opposes proposals: Waeger, Chef des Rüstungsamts, Reich Ministry of Bewaffnung und Munition to von Unruh, 1 March 1943, 'Vereinigung der Rohstoffstelle des Chef H Rüst u. BdE mit der des Wa A,' and Fromm, Chef des

Heeresrüstung and Befehlshaber des Ersatzheeres to von Unruh, 5 March 1943, 'Vereinfachung der Rohstoffbewirtschaftung,' BA Rep. 312 Nr. 27. Von Unruh inspected Heereswaffenamt: signature to von Schulenburg, Regierungspräsidenten, attachment, 17 March 1943, 'Bericht über die Prüfung des Geschäftsbetriebes in Heeres-Waffenamt,' BA Rep. 312 Nr. 27, p. 4. Other measures he proposed are set out in Chef OKW to von Unruh, 15 March 1943, 'Einschränkung des Arbeiten des Reichspatentamts,' BA Rep. 312 Nr. 6 Heft 2, pp. 1-2. Von Unruh authorised call-up in General Government: With to Himmler via Persönliche Stab, 26 February 1943, 'Heranziehung der Volksdeutschen aus dem Generalgouvernement zum Wehrdienst,' BA NS 19/2648. SS officials suggested reduction of staff not great: Krüger to Himmler, 19 January 1943, 'Personalangelegenheiten,' BA NS 19/2648, pp. 2-3. Administration used argument: Ifland, submission to Bormann, 17 May 1943, 'Vorlage an Reichsleiter Bormann,' 'Personalverhältnisse in Generalgouvernement,' BA NS 19/2648, pp. 1-2.

44. With to Himmler, 22 May 1943, 'Vereinheitlichung des Bauwesens bei allen Wehrmachtsteilen einschliesslich Waffen-SS,' BA NS 19/2065, pp. 1-6.

45. Difficulties of quotas for Ohnesorge: Keitel to Ohnesorge, 21 March 1943, BA NS 19/3658, pp. 1-2. Ohnesorge would do anything to win war: Berger to With, 25 March 1943, *ibid.* Keitel told Ohnesorge: Keitel to Ohnesorge, 21 March 1943, pp. 1-2; see also With to Himmler, 2 April 1943, 'Anrechnung von 4000 Mann Fronthilfe der deutschen Reichspost auf die Auflage Plan,' *ibid.* Ohnesorge's appeal for help: Fernschreiben Ohnesorge to Himmler, 18 March 1943, *ibid.* Berger's comment and Himmler's response: Berger to With, 25 March 1943, *ibid.*

46. Bormann's handwritten comment on Bereichsleiter Ifland, 4 April 1943, 'Vorlage an Reichsleiter Bormann,' BA NS 6/780, p. 1. Von Unruh's meeting: Bereichsleiter Ifland, 4 April 1943, 'Vorlage an Reichsleiter Bormann,' *ibid.*, p. 1.

47. Hitler decreed on 10 May: Bormann, 3 June 1943, 'Rundschreiben Nr. 86/43,' BA NS 6/796. Designed to prevent staff being moved: Ifland, 'Vorlage an Reichsleiter Bormann,' 19 February 1943, *ibid.*, pp. 1-2. Von Unruh reported to Bormann: von Unruh to Bormann for Hitler, 15 June 1943, 'Bericht Nr. 1. Frankreich,' *ibid.*, pp. 1-6. Suggestions inspections not rigorous enough: Rebentisch, *Führerstaat und Verwaltung*, pp. 473-4.

48. Bereichsleiter Ifland, 26 May 1943, 'Vorlage an Reichsleiter Bormann,' 'Sicherstellung des Wehrersatzes aus den UK-Gestellten: Mitwirkung der Reichsverteidigungskommissare,' BA NS 6/780, pp. 1-2, 6-7, 12-13.

49. Bormann to Ifland, 29 May 1943, *ibid.*, p. 1. Any further drafts from armaments sector: *ibid.*, p. 2.

50. *Ibid.*, p. 3.

51. Bormann, 5 April 1943, 'Anordnung A 25/43,' BA NS 6/341, p. 1. Bormann's emphasis.

52. Policy of qualitative superiority: Alan S. Milward, *The German Economy at War*, (London, 1967), p. 101. Bottlenecks: *ibid.*, pp. 104-5, 110-11. Single shifts because of shortages: Salter, 'Mobilisation of German Labour,' pp. 162-3. Working hours: Wolfgang Franz Werner, 'Belastungen der deutschen Arbeiterschaft in der zweiten Kriegshälfte,' in Ulrich Borsdorf and Mathilde Jamin (eds.), *Überleben im Krieg. Kriegserfahrungen in einer Industrieregion 1939-1945* (Hamburg, 1989), p. 36. Labour mobilisation engineers: Salter, 'Mobilisation of German Labour,' p. 95.

53. Speer wins control: KTB Chef WiAmt, 19 February 1943, 'Telefonat Amtschef—GFM Keitel,' KTB Chef WiAmt, 16 February 1943, BA MA RW 19/186. Speer opposes evacuation of armaments firms: entry, 6 April 1943, BA NL 118/54, p. 6.
54. Concern at call-up of 200,000: Speer to Zeitzler, 26 February 1943, BA R 3/1606, pp. 3-7. On the overall training programmes: papers on BA R 41/225, BA R 41/224, BA R 41/226, BA R 41/227. Firms reluctant to train German women: signature, 29 September 1941, 'Vermerk,' BA R 41/227, pp. 1-2. Difficult to get overview of training: Reichsgruppe Industrie to Reichswirtschaftskammer, 6 January 1940, 'Umschulung,' BA R 11/1226, p. 1. *Schwerpunkt* programme and later decree: Speer Chronik, February 1943, BA R 3/1737, p. 24. Speer's proposals to Hitler: Speer Chronik, June 1943, *ibid.*, p. 79.
55. SS use of building materials: Speer to Himmler, 30 May 1943, 'Baueisenkontingent für SS, insbesondere KL-Lager Auschwitz,' BA NS 19/994, pp. 1-2; Speer to Himmler, 5 April 1943, BA NS 19/1542, pp. 1-2. On the wider question of the allocation of resources, see Markus K. Billson, III, 'inside albert speer: secrets of moral evasion', *The Antioch Review*, vol. 37, 1979, p. 467; Matthias Schmidt, *Albert Speer—The End of a Myth* (London, 1985), pp. 189-94.

Chapter 5

1. Sicilian campaign: Peter Calvocoressi, Guy Wint and John Pritchard *Total War: The Causes and Courses of the Second World War*, Peter Calvocoressi, *Volume I: The Western Hemisphere* (second edition, London, 1989), p. 396-7. Dismissal of Mussolini: *ibid.*, pp. 399-400. German leadership surprised: entries for 25, 26 and 27 July 1943, Louis P. Lochner (ed.), *The Goebbels Diaries 1942-1943* (Garden City, N. Y., 1948), pp. 403-7, 410-11. Baird judges German propaganda at its most equivocal: Jay W. Baird, *The Mythical World of Nazi War Propaganda, 1939-1945* (Minneapolis, Minn., 1974), p. 208.
2. Marlis G. Steinert, *Hitler's War and the Germans: Public Mood and Attitude during the Second World War* (Ohio, 1977), p. 217. Further crisis of morale and a loss of support for the government: Baird, *Nazi War Propaganda*, pp. 209-10. Himmler admitted a wave of defeatism: 'Rede des Reichsführer-SS bei der SS-Gruppenführertagung in Posen am 4. Oktober 1943,' BA NS 19/4010, pp. 38-9; 'Rede des Reichsführer-SS vor den Reichs- und Gauleitern in Posen am 6. Oktober 1943,' *ibid.*, p. 20.
3. 'Rede von Reichsminister Speer auf der Tagung der Reichsredner und Gaupropagandaleiter am 24.9.1943 (Krolloper),' BA R 3/1548, p. 2. Discontented elements might be encouraged: entry, 27 July 1943, Lochner (ed.), *Goebbels Diaries*, p. 411. Jodl's parallel: 'Vortrag des Chefs des Wehrmachtführungsstabes vor den Reichs- und Gauleitern,' 7 November 1943, BA MA RW 4/v. 38, p. 3. Leaders agree workers remain loyal: entry, 27 July 1943, Lochner (ed.), *Goebbels Diaries*, p. 411; Speer's comments in 'Rede . . . auf der Tagung der Reichsredner,' 24 September 1943, BA R 3/1548, p. 2; Himmler in 'Rede . . . vor den Reichs- und Gauleitern,' 6 October 1943, BA NS 19/4010, p. 13. Speer on exemplary attitude of workers: 'Rede . . . auf der Tagung der Reichsredner,' 24 September 1943, BA R 3/1548, p. 1. Himmler claimed more defeatism in upper classes: 'Rede . . . bei der SS-Gruppenführertagung,' 4 October 1943, BA NS 19/4010, pp. 40-1. On the

reliability of the workers see Himmler, "Sicherheitsfragen von Reichsführer-SS Himmler. Vortrag gehalten auf der Befehlshabertagung in Bad Schachen am 14. Oktober 1943,' BA NS 19/4010, p. 7. On the absence of Jews: 'Rede . . . bei der SS-Gruppenführertagung,' 4 October 1943, BA NS 19/4010, p. 66; 'Rede . . . vor den Reichs- und Gauleitern,' 6 October 1943, BA NS 19/4010, p. 16. On the absence of Communist cells: 'Sicherheitsfragen von Reichsführer-SS . . . in Bad Schachen,' 14 October 1943, BA NS 19/4010, p. 7, and 'Rede des Reichsführer-SS vor der deutschen Presse in Weimar am 4. Dezember 1943,' BA NS 19/4011, p. 5.

4. Hitler responded more calmly: entry, 27 July 1943, Lochner (ed.), *Goebbels Diaries*, p. 407. Ordered Himmler to use severe measures: *ibid.*, p. 411. Men with international links removed: 'Erlass des Führers über die Fernhaltung international gebundener Männer von massgebenden Stellen in Partei, Staat und Wehrmacht vom 19. Mai 1943,' BA NS 6/345, pp. 1-2. Hitler sought to reduce privileges of leadership: Bormann, 30 September 1943, 'Rundschreiben Nr. 141/43,' BA NS 6/342, pp. 1-2. Order had to be repeated: Bormann, 'Rundschreiben Nr. 166/43,' BA NS 19/343, pp. 1-2.

5. Himmler's appointment: Albert Speer, *Inside the Third Reich* (London, 1970), p. 311. Population sees it as measure to ensure internal order: Kaltenbrunner to Himmler, 26 October 1943, 'Meldungen zur Ernennung des Reichsführer-SS zum Reichsminister des Innern,' BA NS 19/3270, p. 1 and 'Anlage,' pp. 1-7. Himmler's view of his tasks: 'Rede . . . bei der SS-Gruppenführertagung,' 4 October 1943, BA NS 19/4010, pp. 60-1. Himmler to secure mood and attitude: *ibid.*, p. 102. Slightest sign of trouble would need to be punished: 'Rede . . . bei der SS-Gruppenführertagung,' 4 October 1943, *ibid.*, p. 43.

6. Himmler to Bormann, 14 December 1943, BA NS 19/798. Himmler made examples of defeatists: 'Rede . . . bei der SS-Gruppenführertagung,' 4 October 1943, BA NS 19/4010, pp. 40-1. 150 death sentences: 'Rede des Reichsführers SS Reichsinnenminister Himmler auf der Tagung der RPÄ-Leiter am 28. Januar 1944,' BA NS 19/4012, p. 51. No uprising or difficulties would occur: 'Rede . . . vor den Reichs- und Gauleitern,' 6 October 1943, BA NS 19/4010, p. 15. Units should not be set up without Hitler's order: Himmler Schnellbrief to Reich defence commissioners, 22 July 1943, 'Erfassung aller wehrfähigen Männer für kriegswichtige Dienste in der Heimat,' BA NS 19/798, p. 1. Himmler and Bormann stop Wahl: Bormann to Himmler, 18 October 1943, pp. 1-4; Himmler to Bormann, 28 November 1943, 'Bildung einer Heimatschutztruppe in Gau Schwaben,' pp. 1-2; Himmler to Bormann, 14 December 1943, pp. 1-2; all in BA NS 19/798.

7. Himmler wants central authority but not over-centralisation of small issues: 'Abschrift Rede des Reichsführer-SS vor den Reichs- und Gauleitern, Posen, Rathaus, 6. Oktober 1943,' BA NS 19/4010, p. 31. He had strengthened state authority: *ibid.*, pp. 3-4. Nepotism order ignored: Dieter Rebentisch, *Führerstaat und Verwaltung im Zweiten Weltkrieg: Verfassungsentwicklung und Verwaltungspolitik 1939-1945* (Stuttgart, 1989), p. 509. Speer's hopes to use Himmler and their failure: Speer, *Third Reich*, pp. 312-14. Himmler refused to intervene: Brandt to With, 9 August 1943, BA NS 19/342.

8. Need to stamp out corruption and alcoholism: 'Rede . . . bei der SS-Gruppenführertagung,' 4 October 1943, BA NS 19/4010, pp. 91-3. Himmler's opinions on bans: *ibid.*, pp. 38-9. Himmler did not have power to change behaviour:

Hans Kehrl, *Krisenmanager im Dritten Reich. 6 Jahre Frieden 6 Jahre Krieg Errinerungen* (Dusseldorf, 1973), pp. 307-8. Military training in Niederlausitz: Himmler to Lammers, 29 September 1943, 'Errichtung eines Truppenübungsplatzes in der Niederlausitz,' and other papers on BA NS 19/1373.

9.   Energy and fanaticism secret weapons: Manfred Messerschmidt, 'Die Wehrmacht im NS-Staat,' in Karl Dietrich Bracher, Manfred Funke and Hans-Adolf Jacobsen (eds.), *Nationalsozialistische Diktatur 1933-1945: eine Bilanz* (Dusseldorf, 1983), p. 474. Goebbels worried about possible alienation: E. K. Bramsted, *Goebbels and National Socialist Propaganda 1925-1945* (East Lansing, Mich., 1965), pp. 274-5. Party to keep closer contact to public: Bormann, 15 September 1943, 'Anordnung Nr. 53/43,' BA NS 6/167, pp. 1-3. *Kampfzeit* the model: Bormann to Wahl, 18 October 1943, BA NS 19/798, p. 2. Party members called on to set good example: Bormann, 'Rundschreiben Nr. 133/43,' BA NS 6/342, pp. 1-3. This partly due to their public reception: Baird, *Nazi War Propaganda*, pp. 209-10. Goebbels now critical of Hitler's loyalty to party comrades: entries, 27 September and 23 October 1943, Wilfred von Oven, *Finale Furioso: Mit Goebbels bis zum Ende* (first published 1948-50, Tübingen, 1974), pp. 141-2, 161-2.

10.   Bormann agrees to proposal: see his handwritten comments on Schütt's (?) submission of 27 August 1943, 'Vorlage,' 'Generalappelle zur propagandistischen Aktivierung der Parteigenossen,' BA NS 6/793, p. 6. Schütt's criticisms of Goebbels' propaganda are on p. 1. General membership parades: Bormann, 29 September 1943, 'Anordnung Nr. 55/43,' BA NS 6/167, pp. 1-2. Quarterly propaganda marches: Bormann, 30 September 1943, 'Anordnung A56/43,' *ibid.*, pp. 1-2; on the strengthening of feelings of purpose, see undated speech by Ley, from its context the end of 1943, BA NS 6/793, p. 3. Gaus reported success: Lindau, 'Auszug aus den Berichten der Gaue über die Durchführung von Generalmitgliederappellen und Propagandamärschen,' BA NS 6/793, pp. 1-2. Bormann claimed successful war effort: Bormann, 6 December 1943, 'Anordnung A64/43,' BA NS 6/343, pp. 1-3. Public morale and attitudes: Steinert, *Hitler's War and the Germans*, pp. 213, 217.

11.   Berger (?) to Himmler, 11 September 1943, BA NS 19/750, p. 1. Soviet use of German officers: John Erickson, *The Road to Berlin: Stalin's War with Germany* (London, 1985), vol. 2, pp. 122-3. Hübner's proposals and Himmler: Hübner, May 1943, 'DENKSCHRIFT,' BA NS 19/750, pp. 1-28. On SS support for Hübner's proposals: SS-Hauptsturmführer Mischke, Head of Amt WVII, SS WVHA, to Himmler, 15 July 1943, 'Oberst Huebner,' pp. 1-4; Berger (?) to Himmler, 11 September 1943, 'Denkschrift über die Erziehung des deutschen Offizierkorps von Oberst Dr Hübner,' p. 1, BA NS 19/750. Berger attributes the plight: Berger to Brandt, 10 October 1943, 'Brief des Obersten Huebner,' *ibid.*, p. 1. Hitler agrees: Hübner to Obergruppenführer (presumably Berger), 13 October 1943, *ibid.*, pp. 1-2.

12.   Keitel, 6 February 1944, 'Führerbefehl vom 22.12.1943 für NS-Führung in der Wehrmacht,' BA NS 6/142, p. 1. Hitler decided: Bormann to Rosenberg, 30 November 1943, BA NS 6/142, pp. 1-2. Hitler ordered strengthening of ideological leadership: Hitler order, 22 December 1943, *ibid.*, pp. 1-2. Keitel's real attitude: handwritten note by Bormann, 'General Reinecke 21.12.43,' BA NS 6/761, pp. 1-2. Party officials believed Party had to participate: Passe, 18 December 1943, 'Besprechungsvorlage,' 'Politische Aktivierung der Wehrmacht,' BA NS 6/142,

pp. 1-6, and unsigned note, 21 December 1943, 'Unterhaltung mit Pg. Passe über "NS-Führungsoffizier",' BA NS 6/761, p. 1. The unsigned note is in Bormann's handwriting.

13. Dietrich Orlow, *The History of the Nazi Party: Vol. II 1933-1945* (Newton Abbot, 1973), p. 436. For a study of ideological training: Manfred Messerschmidt, *Die Wehrmacht im NS-Staat. Zeit der Indoktrination* (Hamburg, 1969).

14. Soviet war effort: John Erickson, *The Road to Stalingrad: Stalin's War with Germany*, vol. 1, (London, 1985), pp. 321-7; Alexander Werth, *Russia at War 1941-1945* (London, 1965), pp. 208-11; Alan S. Milward, *War, Economy and Society 1939-1945* (Berkeley, Calif., 1977), pp. 95-7, 220.

15. Hitler's admiration of Soviet war effort: entry, 20 March 1942, Lochner (ed.), *Goebbels Diaries*, p. 136. Inadequacy of Ausschuss compared: entry, 16 January 1943, BA NL 118/50, p. 9. Army's lack of revolutionary spirit: entries, 9 and 18 March, 10 May 1943, Lochner (ed.), *Goebbels Diaries*, pp. 280, 306-8, 368. Russian success due to commissars: Col. Hübner, May 1943, 'DENKSCHRIFT (Entwurf) über die weltanschauliche Schulung in der Wehrmacht (Heer),' BA NS 19/750, pp. 26-7. Himmler's view: 'Rede ... bei der SS-Gruppenführertagung,' 4 October 1943, BA NS 19/4010, p. 3.

16. Entry, 10 September 1943, Lochner (ed.), *Goebbels Diaries*, p. 437. Attempt by Hitler to transpose tactics of Kampfzeit: Jacobsen, 'Krieg in Weltanschauung und Praxis,' in Bracher et al. (eds.), *Nationalsozialistische Diktatur*, p. 438. Goebbels used 1930 and 1932 crises: entry, 14 December 1942, Lochner (ed.), *Goebbels Diaries*, p. 243; entry, 10 November 1942, Willi A. Boelcke (ed.), *The Secret Conferences of Dr Goebbels, October 1939-March 1943* (London, 1967), p. 296. Kampfzeit the model: Bormann to Wahl, 18 October 1943, BA NS 19/798, p. 2. Faith in victory result of Kampfzeit: Speer, *Third Reich*, pp. 357, 446.

17. Kursk and its consequences: Calvocoressi, *Total War*, I, pp. 500-1. German losses: Geoffrey Jukes, *Kursk: the clash of armour* (London, 1969), p. 152. Hitler always displayed confidence in victory: Speer, *Third Reich*, p. 292.

18. Berger's position in Ostministerium: Berger to Himmler, 27 July 1943, BA NS 19/3863, p. 1. Martin passes on reports: Berger to Himmler, 31 July 1943, 'Oberst Martin,' BA NS 19/738, pp. 1-2. Stuckart seeks help: Stuckart to Himmler, 10 July 1943, BA NS 19/950, p. 1. Hildebrandt forwards reports: SS-Obergruppenführer Hildebrandt, Head of the RSHA, to Himmler, 1 July 1943, BA NS 19/17, p. 1. Himmler's response: Brandt to Hildebrandt, 23 July 1943, *ibid.* Himmler saw dangers in declaration: Himmler to Bormann, 13 July 1943, BA NS 19/195, p. 1. Decree recognised peasant landholdings as private property: Alexander Dallin, *German Rule in Russia 1941-1945: A Study of Occupation Policies* (second edition, London, 1981), pp. 360-1. Himmler objects: Himmler to Lammers, 13 July 1943, p. 1, and other correspondence on BA NS 19/195.

19. Himmler's lack of interest in Vlasov: 'Sicherheitsfragen ... in Bad Schachen,' BA NS 19/4010, p. 20. Himmler warned SS officers: 'Rede . . . bei der SS-Gruppenführertagung,' 4 October 1943, pp. 13-19; 'Rede ... vor den Reichs- und Gauleitern,' 6 October 1943, BA NS 19/4010, pp. 5-7. Wants all men and women taken by the Germans: Himmler to Chef Bandenkampf-Verbände, HSSPF Ukraine and Russia Centre, 10 July 1943, BA NS 19/1436. Hitler's view: 'Auszug aus der Ansprache des Führers an die Heeresgruppenführer am 1.7.43 abends (s. 55-61),'

BA MA RW 4/v. 700, p. 57. Dallin on Bormann: Dallin, *German Rule in Russia*, pp. 124-6, 159-61.

20. Entry, 10 September 1943, Lochner (ed.), *Goebbels Diaries*, p. 434. Strategy a system of substitutions: entry, 8 September 1943, *ibid.*, p. 426.

21. Entry, 11 November 1943, *ibid.*, p. 508.

22. German propaganda: Bramsted, *Goebbels and National Socialist Propaganda*, pp. 316-19, 325-34. Goebbels hoped emphasis on Bolshevism would split enemy coalition: Baird, *Nazi War Propaganda*, pp. 225-7. Japanese attempts to mediate: Ingeborg Fleischhauer, *Die Chance des Sonderfriedens: Deutschsowjetische Geheimgespräche 1941-1945* (Berlin, 1986), pp. 177-9. Göring's suggestion: David Irving, *Göring: A Biography* (New York, 1989), p. 394. Soundings of the Soviets in late 1943: Fleischhauer, *Chance des Sonderfriedens*, pp. 185-99. Peace feelers continue: *ibid.*, pp. 203-14.

23. Himmler and Goebbels agree with Guderian: Alan Clark, *Barbarossa: the Russian-German conflict 1941-45* (Harmondsworth, 1966), p. 408. Goebbels hoped for agreement with Russia: entry, 25 November 1943, von Oven, *Finale Furioso*, pp. 186-93. Goebbels' discussions with Hitler: entry, 10 September 1943, Lochner (ed.), *Goebbels Diaries*, pp. 435-7. Goebbels persuaded by Hitler and Hitler's changing views: entry, 23 September 1943, *ibid.*, pp. 467-78. Bormann echoed Hitler's views: entry, 30 November 1943, *ibid.*, p. 539. Only the most senior members of the leadership could discuss or consider such proposals without being accused of defeatism: Bormann to Funk, 14 September 1943, BA NS 19/2053.

24. Goebbels' hopes for strains among allies: entries, 2 and 3 November 1943, Lochner (ed.), *Goebbels Diaries*, pp. 493-4. Himmler notes Allied disagreements: 'Rede . . . bei der SS-Gruppenführertagung,' 4 October 1943, BA NS 19/4010, p. 33. Coalition would break up: *ibid.*, pp. 49-59. Germans must use political and military means: entry, 8 November 1943, Lochner (ed.), *Goebbels Diaries*, p. 502. Leaders aware of Himmler's contacts: entry, 8 November 1943, *ibid.*, p. 502. Suggestions he played a double game: Peter Hoffmann, *The History of the German Resistance 1933-1945* (Cambridge, Mass., 1977), pp. 295-6, 378-9. Berger told Himmler: Berger to Himmler, 30 July 1943, BA NS 19/2671.

25. Calvocoressi, *Total War*, I, p. 500.

26. Gutterer to Generalbevollmächtigte für den Reichsverwaltung, 6 September 1943, BA R 55/324, p. 1. Gutterer's emphasis. Himmler orders reductions and uk numbers: Dr Hein, 3 September 1943, 'Einberufungen zur Wehrmacht Erlass des Generalbevollmächtigten für die Reichsverwaltung vom 1.9.43,' *ibid.*, pp. 1-2. Direct approach to Olbricht: acting head of the personnel section, unnamed, to ORR Dr Collatz, Minister's office, 9 September 1943, *ibid.*, pp. 1-2. Goebbels halts von Ribbentrop and von Unruh: von Unruh Fernschreiben to Keitel, Lammers and Bormann, 27 July 1943, BA NS 19/342; Goebbels to Hitler, 24 November 1943, BA NL 118/106, pp. 1-3.

27. Party Chancellery uk positions: Orlow, *Nazi Party*, II, p. 426. Bormann's order: Bormann, 30 October 1943, 'Anordnung Nr. 5/43 g,' BA NS 6/345, p. 1. Hitler asked Party to give up more personnel: Hitler, 12 December 1943, 'Verfügung V7/43 g. Rs,' *ibid.*, pp. 1-2. Bormann frees lesser leaders: Orlow, *Nazi Party*, II, p. 426.

28. Hitler, 27 November 1943, 'OKW/WFSt/Org.Nr. 007436/43 gK,' BA MA RW 4/v. 488, p. 1. Hitler mentions étappe: *ibid.*, p. 1. Étappe in World War I: Albrecht Mendelssohn Bartholdy, *The War and German Society: The Testament of a Liberal* (first published 1937, New York, 1971), pp. 27, 286-7 note 5. Korherr's report: Dr Korherr, Inspector for Statistics, 15 December 1943, 'Statistische Unterlagen für den Reichsführer-SS. Einige Zahlen aus dem Ersten Weltkrieg zur damaligen mangelnden Mobilmachung der Kraftreserven bzw. zur Bürokratisierung der Kriegführung,' BA NS 19/2107, pp. 1-3.

29. Common misconception: Churchill's views quoted in Gavin Long, *The Final Campaigns* (Canberra, 1963), pp. 35-6. Air Marshal Milch shared this view, claiming in 1943 that only 25 per cent of the army of 8 million was at the front: R. J. Overy, *Goering the 'Iron Man'* (London, 1984), p. 158. Wehrmacht comparatively lean: Martin van Creveld, *Fighting Power—German and U.S. Army Performance, 1939-1945* (Westport, Conn., 1982), pp. 49-51, 53. Allocated comparatively few resources: *ibid.*, p. 164.

30. Hitler, 27 November 1943, 'OKW/WFSt/Org. Nr. 007436/43 gK,' BA MA RW 4/v. 488, pp. 1, 4. Keitel's supplementary orders: Field Marshal Keitel, 27 November 1943, 'Ausführungsbestimmungen zu den Führerbefehl vom 27.11,' *ibid.*, pp. 1-2. Simplifications of armed forces' pay, etc.: draft WFSt/Org (1. Staffel), 26 November 1943, 'Besprechungspunkte für Chef OKW mit dem Sonderbeauftragten des Führers, BdE und Amtschefs im OKW,' BA MA RW 4/v. 475, pp. 1-2; signature submission to Goebbels, undated, 'Einheitsabzug von Arbeitslohn,' BA R 55/77, pp. 1-4; Pohl to Himmler, 23 September 1943, 'Vereinheitlichung der Uniformen der Wehrmachtteile,' BA NS 19/315, pp. 1-3. Outcome of proposals to simplify armed forces' uniforms: Speer Chronik, July 1944, BA R 3/1740, p. 158.

31. Hitler decreed use of men and women in RAD: Bormann, 3 August 1943, 'Rundschreiben 110/43,' BA NS 6/342, p. 1. Women sought for anti-aircraft units: Bormann, 24 August 1943, 'Rundschreiben Nr. 116/43,' *ibid.*, p. 1. Bormann's guidance to Gauleiters: Bormann teletype to all Gauleiters, 9 September 1943, BA NS 6/358, pp. 1-2. Hitler turned down Sauckel and Bormann and Lammers agreed: note by Lammers on p. 2 of Bormann to Lammers, 21 November 1943, 'Vortrag des GBA., Gauleiter Sauckel, beim Führer am 18.11.1943,' BA R 43 II/654. Bormann and Gauleiters believed: Bormann, 'Vermerk über Vortrag des GBA., Gauleiter Sauckel, beim Führer am 18. November 1943,' 21 November 1943, *ibid.*, p. 1.

32. Amount of foreign labour obtained by Sauckel decreased: Willi A. Boelcke (ed.), *Deutschlands Rüstung im Zweiten Weltkrieg: Hitlers Konferenzen mit Albert Speer 1942-1945* (Frankfurt, 1969), note p. 324. Sauckel only meets quota by use of Italians: Edward Homze, *Foreign Labor in Nazi Germany* (Princeton, N. J., 1967), pp. 217-8. Numbers recruited: *ibid.*, p. 147. Speer and Sauckel disagree: Speer Chronik, September 1943, BA R 3/1738, p. 148. Sperrbetriebe: Speer Chronik, October 1943, *ibid.*, p. 156. Numbers of Sperrbetriebe: Rebentisch, *Führerstaat und Verwaltung*, p. 513. Speer won dispute: Speer Chronik, December 1943, BA R 3/1738, p. 204. Hitler's support: record of meeting of 16-17 December 1943, Boelcke (ed.), *Hitlers Konferenzen*, pp. 323-4.

33. Italian prisoners of war: Central Planning Fernschreiben to Sauckel, 16 September 1943, BA R 3/1597, p. 1. Speer approached Himmler: Speer to Himmler, 15

December 1943, BA R 3/1583. Speer asks for help and wants strict discipline: Speer to Keitel, 21 December 1943, BA R 3/1586, pp. 1-2. Speer's suggestions on punishment: Speer to Keitel, 18 December 1943, *ibid.*

34.   Armaments had to rely more on Germans: Sauckel to the Presidents of Landesarbeitsämter, 30 July 1943, 'Auskämmung des zivilen Sektors zugunsten der Kriegswirtschaft,' BA R 41/280, pp. 1-2. Some 9000 workers freed: text of speech given at the Posen Gauleiter meeting in October sent by Speer to all Reichs and Gauleiters, November 1943, BA R 3/1548, pp. 30-1. Speer and Sauckel set quotas: Dr Fremerey Schnellbrief to Reichstatthalter and others, 7 August 1943, 'Rundschreiben Nr. 436/44 LWA,' BA R 41/280, p. 1. Gauleiters to accelerate fulfilment: Bormann, 2 August 1943, 'Rundschreiben Nr. 109/43,' BA NS 6/342, p. 1. Consumer production to be taken over by firms: Sauckel to the Presidents of Landesarbeitsämter, 30 July 1943, 'Auskämmung des zivilen Sektors zugunsten der Kriegswirtschaft,' BA R 41/280, pp. 1-2.

35.   Homze, *Foreign Labor*, p. 222. Armaments production and quantitative superiority: Alan S. Milward, *The German Economy at War* (London, 1967), pp. 100-1. Hitler agrees to shut down less important production: entries, 11-12 September 1943 and 30 September-1 October 1943, Boelcke (ed.), *Hitlers Konferenzen*, pp. 293, 304. Speer on this plan in September: Speer Chronik, August and September 1943, BA R 3/1738, pp. 130, 137, 142-4. Planned to use men from armaments: Speer Chronik, September 1943, BA R 3/1738, p. 149. Speer claimed to free 40,000 workers: text of speech given at Posen in October sent by Speer to all Reichs and Gauleiters, November 1943, BA R 3/1548, p. 33. Sauckel proved right: Bormann, 17 August 1944, 'Aktenvermerk für Pg. Friedrichs, II M., Pg. Dr Klopfer, Pg. Schütt, Berlin,' BA NS 6/785, pp. 2-3.

36.   Speer told the Gauleiters: Speer to all Reichs- and Gauleiters, November 1943, BA R 3/1548, p. 28-9. Speer's attempt to mobilise Himmler: Speer, *Third Reich*, pp. 312-13. Speer used SD reports: Speer to all Reichs- and Gauleiters, November 1943, BA R 3/1548, pp. 25, 29.

37.   Control over electricity production: Bormann, 20 August 1943, 'Rundschreiben Nr. 119/43,' BA NS 6/342, pp. 1-2. Power to use Italian armaments: Speer Chronik, September 1943, BA R 3/1738, p. 144. Speer's additional powers: 'Niederschrift über Vorträge der Reichsminister Funk und Speer vor einen Kreis der Wirtschaftspresse in Reichswirtschaftsministerium am 7. September 1943 abends,' BA R 3/1965, pp. 1-2. Bormann's explanations and assurances: Bormann Fernschreiben to all Gauleiters, 14 September 1943, 'Unterstützung des Reichsministers für Rüstung und Kriegsproduktion bei Durchführung seiner Sofort-Massnahmen zur Steigerung unserer Rüstungskraft,' BA NS 6/786, pp. 1-2. Plans to close firms in armaments centres: Speer to all Reichs- and Gauleiters, November 1943, BA R 3/1548, pp. 15-17.

38.   Homze, *Foreign Labor*, p. 220. Speer's three speeches: 'Niederschrift über Vorträge der Reichsminister Funk und Speer vor einem Kreis der Wirtschaftspresse in Reichswirtschaftsministerium am 7. September 1943 abends,' BA R 3/1965, pp. 4-5; 'Rede von Reichsminister Speer auf der Tagung der Reichsredner und Gaupropagandaleiter an 24.9.1943 (Krolloper),' BA R 3/1548, pp. 7-9; text of speech given at Posen in October sent by Speer to all Reichs and Gauleiters, November 1943, BA R 3/1548, pp. 17-22. Production of goods and his proposed solution: 'Rede von Reichsminister Speer auf der Tagung der

Reichsredner und Gaupropagandaleiter an 24.9.1943 (Krolloper),' BA R 3/1548, p. 8. Further production in simplest styles: *ibid.*, p. 12.

39. Earl R. Beck, *Under the Bombs: the German Home Front 1942-1945* (Lexington, 1986), p. 99. Details of home front shortages: *ibid.*, pp. 78, 99-100; Wolfgang Werner, *'Bleib übrig!' Deutsche Arbeiter in der nationalsozialistischen Kriegswirtschaft* (Dusseldorf, 1983), pp. 213-16; Arvid Fredborg, *Behind the Steel Wall* (London, 1944), p. 180. Figures on consumer goods of elastic demand: Willi A. Boelcke, *Die deutsche Wirtschaft 1930-1945: Interna des Reichswirtschaftsministeriums* (Dusseldorf, 1983), pp. 308, also pp. 309, 322. Gauleiters' resistance understandable: *ibid.*, pp. 283, 325.

40. Public reaction to rumours: Beck, *Under the Bombs*, p. 45-6. Boelcke on Speer: Boelcke, *deutsche Wirtschaft*, p. 317. Goebbels' attitude: entries, 29 April 1942, 12 March, 13 March, and 10 May 1943, Lochner (ed.), *Goebbels Diaries*, pp. 196, 295, 296, 367.

41. Speer to all Reichs- and Gauleiters, November 1943, BA R 3/1548, p. 36. Only the most decisive measures would master the situation: *ibid.*, pp. 1-2, 28. Purpose of speech: Speer Chronik, October 1943, BA R 3/1738, p. 156. Gauleiters' and Hitler's reactions: entry, 22-23 May 1944, Boelcke (ed.), *Hitlers Konferenzen*, p. 367.

42. Mierzejewski on Speer's organisation of economy: Alfred C. Mierzejewski, *The Collapse of the German War Economy, 1944-1945: Allied Air Power and the German National Railway* (Chapel Hill, N.C., 1988), pp. 17, 19, 178. German industry's dependence on Ruhr and Silesia: *ibid.*, pp. 22-4.

43. *Ibid.*, p. 86.

44. Intensified organisational disputes: Keitel to Himmler, 3 September 1943, 'Freiwillige des Geburtsjahrganges 1926,' BA NS 19/4; Brandt to Fromm, 22 October 1943, BA NS 19/973. Gauleiters could be divided into two groups: Speer Chronik, October 1943, BA R 3/1738, p. 171.

45. Bormann undermining position with Hitler: Speer, *Third Reich*, p. 313. Speer on closing the State Porcelain Factory: Speer to Bormann, 20 December 1943, BA R 3/1573, p. 1. Hitler's opposition to ban on landscape postcards: Bormann to Lammers, 24 April 1943, BA R 43 II/609a. Decision not to call up staff employed on his building projects: Mussehl to Killy, 12 February 1943 and Mussehl to Killy, 16 February 1943, BA R 43 II/660. Rivalry ensured that building in Linz did not get under way: Evan Burr Bukey, *Hitler's Hometown: Linz, Austria 1908-1945* (Bloomington, 1986), p. 200.

46. Bormann's rebuke: Bormann to Speer, 18 August 1943, 'Konzentration der Kriegswirtschaft,' BA R 43 II/610, pp. 1-2.

47. Speer Fernschreiben to Bormann, 18 September 1943, BA R 3/1573, pp. 1-2.

48. Speer on fortifications and labour shortage: Speer Fernschreiben to Bormann, 18 September 1943, BA R 3/1573, pp. 1-2. Speer's accumulation of offices: Karl Dietrich Bracher, 'Die Speer Legende,' *Neue Politische Literatur*, vol. 15, 1970, p. 430. Speer speaks of himself as successor: Kehrl, *Krisenmanager*, pp. 334-6.

49. Women wearing trousers in public prompted these comments: Bormann, 5 July 1943, 'Rundschreiben Nr. 99/43,' BA NS 6/342, p. 2.

50.   'Rede . . . bei der SS-Gruppenführertagung,' 4 October 1943, BA NS 19/4010, p. 64. School for *SS-Helferinnen*: *ibid.*, pp. 108-10. He wanted system of clear responsibility: *ibid.*, pp. 89, 97.

51.   Ohlendorf's appointment: Ludolf Herbst, *Der Totale Krieg und die Ordnungder Wiirtschaft. Die Kriegswirtschaft im Spannungsfeld von Politik, Ideologie und Propaganda 1939-1945* (Stuttgart, 1982), pp. 187, 260, 273. Ohlendorf's criticisms of self-responsibility: Boelcke, *deutsche Wirtschaft*, p. 303. Ohlendorf claimed at Nuremberg: Boberach, 'Einführung,' in Heinz Boberach (ed.), *Meldungen aus dem Reich 1938-1945: Die geheimen Lageberichte des Sicherheitsdienstes der SS* (Herrsching, 1984), vol. 1, p. 32. Himmler ignored Berger's suggestion: Berger to Himmler, 7 December 1943, 'SS-Brigadefuehrer Ohlendorf,' BA NS 19/786.

52.   Hitler ordered a greater use of SS prisoners to build A-4: entry for 19-22 August 1943, Boelcke (ed.), *Hitlers Konferenzen*, p. 291. Himmler will take over A-4: Himmler to Speer, 21 August 1943, BA NS 19/3734. Programme of building underground factories: Overy, *Goering*, pp. 226-7.

53.   'Rede . . . bei der SS-Gruppenführertagung,' 4 October 1943, BA NS 19/4010, p. 3. Himmler on Jewish labour and firms: 'Rede . . . vor den Reichs- und Gauleitern,' 6 October 1943, p. 19; and 'Rede . . . bei der SS-Gruppenführertagung,' 4 October 1943, BA NS 19/4010, pp. 82, 89. Himmler refused to make 30,000 ethnic Germans available: Himmler to Milch, 4 October 1943, BA NS 19/3597.

54.   Entry, 25 July 1943, Lochner (ed.), *Goebbels Diaries*, p. 404. Propaganda campaigns: Bramsted, *Goebbels and National Socialist Propaganda*, pp. 275-6. 'Thirty articles of war for the German people:' *ibid.*, pp. 286-8. '*Totaler Krieg*' office: signature to Oberlehrer Hickl, 29 December 1943, BA R 55/583, p. 1. National Socialism had to undergo renovation: entry, 10 September 1943, Lochner (ed.), *Goebbels Diaries*, p. 438. Goebbels distancing himself from Hitler: entry, 1 September 1943, von Oven, *Finale Furioso*, pp. 119-20.

55.   Air war increases: Calvocoressi, *Total War*, I, pp. 520-2. Bombing raids on Hamburg: Gerald Kirwin, 'Allied Bombing and Nazi Domestic Propaganda,' *European History Quarterly*, vol. 15, 1985, p. 350. Speer's estimates: Williamson Murray, *Luftwaffe* (Baltimore, 1985), p. 164. Effects on life and morale: Beck, *Under the Bombs*, pp. 60-74. Goebbels gained popularity because of visiting bombed areas: entries, 23 June and 10 August 1943, von Oven, *Finale Furioso*, pp. 40-2, 101-8. *Luftkriegsschädenausschuss* in his ministry: Walkenhorst, 8 July 1943, 'Notiz für Pg. Friedrichs,' 'Stellungnahme zum Schreiben Dr Leys,' BA NS 6/166, pp. 2-3. Organisations represented in the Luftkriegsschädenausschuss listed in Ellgering, 6 August 1943, 'LK. Mitteilung Nr. 15,' BA R 55/447, pp. 2-5. Goebbels' instructions on evacuation: Goebbels Schnellbrief to Bormann, Speer, Ley and others, 29 July 1943, *ibid.* Evacuation of industry to take precedence: Goebbels to all Gauleiters, 26 August 1943, 'LK-Mitteilung Nr. 30,' *ibid.*, p. 1. Requests Gauleiters refrain from taking own measures: Halm to members of the Luftkriegsschädenausschuss, 9 August 1943, 'LK-Mitteilung Nr. 16,' and Goebbels Schnellbrief to Gauleiters, 23 December 1943, 'LK-Mitteilung Nr. 78,' *ibid.*, pp. 1-2. SS building brigades: Pohl to Himmler, 14 July 1943, 'Einsatz von Maschinen und Baggern für die Baubrigade in Westdeutschland,' and SS WVHA, 9 November 1943, 'Einsatz der SS-Baubrigaden Bericht Nr. 5,' BA NS 19/14, pp. 1-6. Party measures and drafting of 15-year-olds: Beck, *Under the Bombs*, pp. 88-9.

56. Rudolf Jordan, *Erlebt und Erlitten: Weg eines Gauleiters von München bis Moskau* (Leoni am Starnberger See, 1971), p. 225. Pressure on resources and personnel: Bormann, 27 July 1943, 'Rundschreiben Nr. 39/43g,' pp. 1-2; and Siebel, KR-Fernschreiben, Party Chancellory IIM to Major Böhme, Luftwaffe General Staff, 27 July 1943, BA NS 6/66, pp. 1-3. Effects on productivity: Speer, 'Rede ... auf der Tagung des Reichsredner,' 24 September 1943, BA R 3/1548, p. 1. Speer called for means to be found to enable workers to return to work as soon as possible after air raids: *ibid.*, p. 5. Consumer goods production barely met needs of 10 per cent: Boelcke (ed.), *Hitlers Konferenzen*, note p. 316. Speer advised Hitler: entry, 6-7 December 1943, *ibid.*, p. 315. Speer and Goebbels concerned about production but Goebbels believed popular morale good: entries, 10 September, 27 and 29 November 1943, Lochner (ed.), *Goebbels Diaries*, pp. 436, 462, 532, 537. German propaganda: Bramsted, *Goebbels and National Socialist Propaganda*, pp. 316-19, 325-34.

57. Home front would hold out: Goebbels to Hitler, Christmas 1943, BA NL 118/106, p. 3. Goebbels' disillusionment: entry, 7 August 1943, Semmler, *Goebbels*, p. 96.

Chapter 6

1. Speer's plans to bomb electricity works: Speer to Himmler, 14 March 1944, BA R 3/1583. Military developments on the Eastern front: John Erickson, *The Road to Berlin: Stalin's War with Germany* (London, 1985), vol. 2, chapters 4 and 5.

2. Bombing: Williamson Murray, *Luftwaffe* (Baltimore, 1985), pp. 223-4, 229. Effect on daily life: Earl R. Beck, *Under the Bombs: The German Home Front, 1942-1945* (Lexington, 1986), pp. 108-12. Morale affected: 'SD-Berichte ... vom 4. Mai 1944 (Grüne Serie),' in Heinz Boberach (ed.), *Meldungen aus dem Reich 1938-1945: Die geheimen Lageberichte des Sicherheitsdienstes der SS* (Herrsching, 1984), vol. 17, pp. 6510-11. Public reaction: Marlis G. Steinert, *Hitler's War and the Germans: Public Mood and Attitude during the Second World War* (Ohio, 1977), pp. 234-5, 239. Demand for weapons of retaliation: Murray, *Luftwaffe*, p. 283.

3. Importance of maintaining public morale: Goebbels, 'Die politische und militärische Lage,' BA NS 19/1870, pp. 14, 16, 21. Greater use of purchases in occupied territories: Bormann, 11 January 1944, 'Bekanntgabe 9/44g,' BA NS 19/1897, pp. 1-2. Additional rations and use of foreign workers: Goebbels, 'Die politische und militärische Lage,' BA NS 19/1870, p. 15. Resources diverted into countering bombing: R. J. Overy, *The Air War 1939-1945* (London, 1980), p. 122. Resources equivalent to fighter aircraft: Murray, *Luftwaffe*, p. 284. Workers to be redirected to secure transport: Speer to Gauleiter Greiser, 11 January 1944, BA R 3/1581, pp. 1-2. He opposed efforts by Gauleiters to build new headquarters: Speer to Gauleiter Meyer, 11 March 1944, BA R 3/1590, pp. 1-2. Speer told Gutterer: Speer to Gutterer, 13 January 1944, *ibid.*, p. 1.

4. Party's important role: Rudolf Jordan, *Erlebt und Erlitten: Weg eines Gauleiters von München bis Moskau* (Leoni am Starnberger See, 1971), p. 205. Party formations: Bormann, 16 February 1944, 'Bekanntgabe 43/44,' BA NS 6/350, pp. 1-3. Activities of inter-departmental bombing committee: Goebbels to all Gauleiters, 3 March 1944, 'LK-Mitteilung Nr. 100,' pp. 1-2 and various *Lk-Mitteilungen* all in BA R 55/447. Reich inspection set up: 'Erlass des Führers über die Errichtung

einer Reichsinspektion der zivilen Luftkriegsmassnahmen. Vom 21. Dezember 1943,' BA NS 6/346, pp. 1-2. Hitler agreed to common measures: Goebbels to all Gauleiters, 28 January 1944, 'Reichsinspektion zur Durchführung zivilen Luftkriegsmassnahmen,' BA R 55/447, pp. 1-4. Experienced Gaus provide advice: signature to M-Beauftragten of all Gaus, 26 January 1944, 'Erfahrungsberichte aus dem Gebiete des Luftschutzes,' BA NS 6/294, pp. 1-9. SS building brigades: Pohl to Head of Amtsgruppe C and others, 28 February 1944, 'Aufstellung der 5. SS-Baubrigade,' BA NS 19/14. Resources tied down by the bombing: Albert Speer, *Inside the Third Reich* (London, 1970), pp. 278-9. Administrative problems in Britain: Tom Harrisson, *Living through the Blitz* (London, 1976), pp. 154-5, 165-8, 232-3, 292-9.

5.   Developments in Normandy: Peter Calvocoressi, Guy Wint and John Pritchard *Total War: The Causes and Courses of the Second World War*, Peter Calvocoressi, *Volume I: The Western Hemisphere* (second edition, London, 1989), pp. 539-42. Effects of failure on morale: 'Meldungen . . . vom 6. Juli 1944,' Boberach (ed.), *Meldungen aus dem Reich*, vol. 17, p. 6626. Upsurge in morale soon dissipated: 'Meldungen . . . vom 19. Juni 1944' and 'Meldungen . . . vom 28. Juni 1944,' *ibid.*, vol. 17, pp. 6595-7, 6613.

6.   Hopes attached to defeating invasion: entry, 10 April 1944, Rudolf Semmler, *Goebbels—the man next to Hitler* (Ohio State University reprint, 1982 of London, 1947 edition), p. 119; Goebbels' notes of Jodl's speech of 6 May 1944 to the Cabinet on the military situation, untitled, undated, BA NL 118/107, p. 15. Germany might gain breathing space: Gerhard Weinberg, 'World War II: The Allies, 1941-1945,' in Gerhard Weinberg, *World in the Balance: Behind the Scenes of World War II* (Hanover, 1981), p. 45. Germany would have to end war with USSR: entry, 12 April 1944, Semmler, *Goebbels*, pp. 119-21.

7.   Goebbels less influenced by Hitler's optimism: Elke Fröhlich, 'Hitler und Goebbels im Krisenjahr 1944. Aus den Tagebüchern des Reichspropagandaministers,' *Vierteljahrshefte für Zeitgeschichte*, vol. 38, 1990, pp. 197-9. Goebbels' discussions with Hitler in March: entry, 16 March 1944, Wilfred von Oven, *Finale Furioso: Mit Goebbels bis zum Ende* (first published 1948-50, Tübingen, 1974), pp. 256-60. Lack of record in Goebbels' diaries: Fröhlich, 'Hitler und Goebbels im Krisenjahr 1944,' p. 195. Memorandum: entry, 2 May 1944, Semmler, *Goebbels*, p. 122. Details of memorandum: entry, 12 April 1944, *ibid.*, pp. 119-29.

8.   Entry, 4 March 1945, Hugh Trevor-Roper (ed.), *Final Entries 1945: The Diaries of Joseph Goebbels* (New York, 1978), pp. 46.

9.   Treatment of Goebbels' memorandum: entry, 2 May 1944, Semmler, *Goebbels*, pp. 128-9. Memorandum not mentioned on 5 June: entry, 6 June 1944, *ibid.*, pp. 127-8. Hitler on Britain, Ribbentrop: Fröhlich, 'Hitler und Goebbels im Krisenjahr 1944,' pp. 215-16.

10.   Entry, 2 May 1944, Semmler, *Goebbels*, p. 128. Bormann on Goebbels' speech: Bormann, 21 March 1944, 'Bekanntgabe 64/44 g. Rs,' BA NS 6/350. Goebbels' speech: Goebbels, 23 February 1944, 'Die politische und militärische Lage,' BA NS 19/1870, ruling out capitulation, p. 5, on the difficulties of the air war and ways of overcoming them, pp. 30-40, and on the loss of production, p. 16. Explanation of developments in the East: *ibid.*, pp. 25-7. Differences of opinion and Kampfzeit parallel: *ibid.*, pp. 30-40. Proposals to increase birth rate: Bormann, 29 January

1944, 'Vermerk für Pg. Dr Friedrichs und Pg. Dr Klopfer,' 'Sicherung der Zukunft des deutschen Volkes,' BA NS 6/518, pp. 1-9.

11. The Wednesday Group and Goebbels' hopes: entry, 16 March 1944, von Oven, *Finale Furioso*, p. 255; entry, 2 June 1944, Semmler, *Goebbels*, pp. 125-7. Bormann's clique the greatest danger: entry, 16 March 1944, von Oven, *Finale Furioso*, p. 255. No chance of forming an opposition: entry, 2 June 1944, Semmler, *Goebbels*, pp. 126. Goebbels organises declaration of loyalty: Fröhlich, 'Hitler und Goebbels im Krisenjahr 1944,' p. 200.

12. Fröhlich, 'Hitler und Goebbels im Krisenjahr 1944,' p. 199.

13. Enemy had reached maximum armaments production: 'Rede des Reichsführer-SS Heinrich Himmler vor den Führern der 13.SS-Freiw.b.h. Gebirgs Division (Kroatien) im Führerheim Westlager, Truppenübungsplatz Neuhammer am 11. Januar 1944,' BA NS 19/4012, p. 12. More conscious of Soviet military strength: 'Rede des Reichsführer-SS auf der Ordensburg Sonthofen am 5. Mai 1944,' BA NS 19/4013, p. 10. Strength of home front: 'Rede des Reichsführers SS Reichsinnenminister Himmler auf der Tagung der RPÄ-Leiter am 28. Januar 1944,' BA NS 19/4012, pp. 2-3, 47-52. He fulfilled his promise to Hitler: *ibid.*, p. 54. Criminals and communists not free to undermine: *ibid.*, pp. 2-7, 25-27. Germans could not have withstood bombing: 'Rede . . . auf der Ordensburg Sonthofen am 5. Mai 1944,' BA NS 19/4013, p. 28. Maintenance of internal order main precondition: *ibid.*, p. 31. Parallels with 1932: 'Rede . . . auf der Tagung der RPÄ-Leiter,' 28 January 1944, BA NS 19/4012, p. 82. Victory to side whose nerve held: *ibid.*, p. 84.

14. 'Rede . . . auf der Ordensburg Sonthofen am 5. Mai 1944,' BA NS 19/4013, pp. 50-3.

15. Ohlendorf claimed at Nuremberg: Robert E. Conot, *Justice at Nuremberg* (New York, 1983), p. 255. Himmler's disclosures of the Final Solution attributed to increasing psychological strain: Hans Mommsen, 'The Realization of the Unthinkable: The "Final Solution of the Jewish Question" in the Third Reich,' in Gerhard Hirschfeld (ed.), *The Policies of Genocide: Jews and Soviet Prisoners of War in Nazi Germany* (London, 1986), p. 131, note 14.

16. Himmler authorises SS operation: Alexander Dallin, *German Rule in Russia 1941-1945: A Study of Occupation Policies* (second edition, London, 1981), pp. 602-6. Frauenfeld's paper: Frauenfeld, 10 February 1944, 'Denkschrift über die Probleme der Verwaltung der bes. Ostgebiete,' BA NS 19/1478, pp. 1-34; Bormann to Himmler, 18 February 1944, *ibid.*, pp. 1-2. Himmler and Bormann's views: Himmler's handwritten notes dated 26 March 1944 on the back page of Bormann's letter, *ibid.*

17. Numbers of Jews killed in 1944: Michael R. Marrus, *The Holocaust in History* (London, 1987), p. 56. Negotiations with Hungarian Jews: Raul Hilberg, *The Destruction of the European Jews*, vols. 1 to 3 (revised and definitive edition, New York, 1985), vol. 2, pp. 843-7; see also vol. 3, pp. 1132-9; affidavit of Dr Reszö Kastner, 13 September 1945, Document 2605-PS, *Trial of the Major War Criminals Before the International Military Tribunal, Nuremberg, 14 November 1945-1 October 1946* (reprint, New York, 1971), vol. 31, p. 13.

18. Speer's suggestion that Gebhardt's treatment of him was suspicious seems to be post-war exaggeration: Speer, *Third Reich*, chapter 23—Illness, and a detailed rebuttal of Speer's claims in Matthias Schmidt, *Albert Speer—The End of a Myth*

(London, 1985), chapter 6. Gebhardt's own reports to Himmler give no indication of anything suspicious: Gebhardt to Himmler, 21 February 1944, pp. 1-2; Meine to Gebhardt, 26 February 1944; and Himmler to Gebhardt, 20 March 1944, all in BA NS 19/1867. Speer's illness and behaviour: Speer Chronik, January to March 1944, BA R 3/1739, pp. 15, 21-3, 37.

19. Speer, 25 January 1944, 'Führer-Vorlage: 1,' BA R 3/1515, pp. 1-6. Goebbels sought to assure Hitler of his loyalty: entry, 12 April 1944, Semmler, *Goebbels*, p. 121.

20. Second submission: Speer, 25 January 1944, 'Führer Vorlage: 2,' BA R 3/1515, p. 1. Third submission: Speer, 25 January 1944, 'Führer-Vorlage: 3,' *ibid.*, pp. 1-2. Speer asked in addition: Speer, 25 January 1944, 'Führer-Vorlage: 4,' *ibid.*, pp. 1-2.

21. Speer's conclusions about his ministry and illness: 'Amtschef- Besprechung am 10. Mai 1944,' BA R 3/1549, p. 5. Dorsch's position: Gregor Janssen, *Das Ministerium Speer: Deutschlands Rüstung im Krieg* (Frankfurt, 1968), p. 42. Dorsch had provided politically damaging material about other members of the Ministry; Goebbels, as the man responsible for the politics and attitudes of officials, supported Speer: Speer to Dorsch, 27 January 1944, pp. 1-8, and Speer, 29 January 1944, 'Führer-Vorlage: 5,' BA R 3/1515, pp. 7-9. Speer's refusal and Milch's intervention: Janssen, *Ministerium Speer*, pp. 157-64; Schmidt, *Speer Myth*, pp. 95-8. Chronik's conclusion: Speer Chronik, April 1944, BA R 3/1739, p. 56. Speer moved to reassert authority: 'Amtschef-Besprechung am 10. Mai 1944,' BA R 3/1549, pp. 6-7.

22. Hitler did not respond: Speer, *Third Reich*, p. 330. Schmidt's interpretation: Schmidt, *Speer Myth*, pp. 87-8. Hitler's visits: Speer Chronik, March 1944, BA R 3/1739, pp. 35-6. Hitler's hints to Speer: Speer, *Third Reich*, pp. 343-4. Speer disregards Himmler's order: Speer Chronik, May 1944, BA R 3/1739, p. 89.

23. Final period of increase in German production: Ludolf Herbst, *Der Totale Krieg und die Ordnung der Wirtschaft. Die Kriegswirtschaft im Spannungsfeld von Politik, Ideologie und Propaganda 1939-1945* (Stuttgart, 1982), note p. 343. Speer met all 1942 targets: Speer Chronik, January 1944, BA R 3/1739, p. 2. Fuel situation deteriorating: Keitel to Speer, 25 March 1944, BA R 3/1987, pp. 5-6.

24. Jeffrey R. Fear, 'The Armament Industry in Schwaben 1939-1945: Its Effect on the Regional, Economic and Social Structure,' (Honours Thesis, University of Michigan, 1983), p. 37. Gau economic advisers move to contest his control of labour: Dietrich Orlow, *The History of the Nazi Party: vol. II 1933-1945* (Newton Abbot, 1973), p. 460. Speer's response to Klopfer's visit: Speer Chronik, February 1944, BA R 3/1739, p. 21. Speer's role in allocating resources: Speer to Schwarz, 11 March 1944, 'Barackenkontingent der Partei für das I. und II. Quartal 1944,' BA R 3/1600. Speer protested at use of armaments workers: Speer Fernschreiben to Bormann, 14 April 1944, BA R 3/1573. Party criticism on 1 May holiday: Bormann to Speer, 12 May 1944, BA R 3/1573. Speer agreed to Goebbels' request: Speer to Goebbels, 27 May 1944, BA R 3/1580.

25. Attachment, SD submission, 'Bekämpfung der Korruption,' Bormann, 6 May 1944, 'Bekanntgabe 103/44 g,' 'Bekämpfung der Korruption,' BA NS 6/350, p. 1. SS criticism of rings and committees: Reichsgeschäftsführer des Ahnenerbe to Brandt, 6 May 1944, 'Erhaltung der Firma H. Hensoldt u. Söhne als Familienbetrieb,' BA NS 19/3054. Rings and committees compete: Peter Hayes,

Industry and Ideology: IG Farben in the Nazi Era (Cambridge, 1987), p. 320. Ministry often lacks expertise: Stephen Salter, 'The Mobilisation of German Labour, 1939-1945. A Contribution to the History of the Working Class in the Third Reich,' (unpublished D. Phil. thesis, Oxford, 1983), p. 307. Potential for corruption in the system: Alan S. Milward, *The German Economy at War* (London, 1967), pp. 90-1. Ohlendorf's claims: Conot, *Nuremberg*, p. 251. Reluctance of firms to allow access: Herbst, *Totale Krieg*, p. 9. Carroll's suggestion: Berenice A. Carroll, *Design for Total War: Arms and Economics in the Third Reich* (The Hague, 1968), pp. 244-5, 248. Eigruber's problems: Eigruber to Speer, 24 February 1944, 'Betriebsstillegungen,' BA R 3/1577. Florian on armaments industry intervention: Gauleiter Florian to Speer, 2 June 1944, 'Arbeitseinsatzlage im Gau Düsseldorf,' BA R 3/1578, p. 3. Speer challenged attacks: Speer Chronik, January 1944, BA R 3/1739, p. 14.

26. Bormann's comments dated 29 June on a copy of Fernschreiben Friedrichs to Bormann, BA NS 6/780, p. 1. Party leaders want greater Party involvement in examining uk positions: Bormann, 20 May 1944, 'Aktenvermerk für Pg. Friedrichs und Pg. Klopfer,' 'Uk-Stellungen,' *ibid.* Some Gaus such as North Westphalia and Pomerania already had such a system: Friedrichs, 8 June 1944, 'Vorlage an den Reichsleiter,' 'Einschaltung der Partei bei Uk-Stellungen—Bildung von Gaukommissionen,' *ibid.*, p. 7. Bormann predicted Speer's response: Bormann, 20 May 1944, 'Aktenvermerk für Pg. Friedrichs und Pg. Klopfer,' 'Uk-Stellungen,' *ibid.* Bormann suspicious of Speer's claims: Bormann's comments dated 29 June on a copy of Fernschreiben Friedrichs to Bormann, *ibid.*, pp. 1-3, quotation on p. 1. Hitler's intervention necessary: Fernschreiben Bormann to Friedrichs and Klopfer, 29 June 1944, 'Sicherstellung des fuer die Wehrmacht notwendigen Ersatzes,' *ibid.*, pp. 4-8.

27. Ruhrstab showed Gauleiters not necessarily an obstacle: Speer Chronik, June 1944, BA R 3/1739, p. 115. Hoffmann's evidence of industry waste: Hoffmann to Bormann, 9 August 1942, 'Bericht Nr. 1,' p. 13; Hoffmann to Bormann, 27 August 1942, 'Bericht Nr. 4 Distrikt Krakau,' BA NS 6/795, p. 3.

28. Appointment of Geilenberg: Beck, *Under the Bombs*, p. 131. Drop in fighter production: Alfred C. Mierzejewski, *The Collapse of the German War Economy, 1944-1945: Allied Air Power and the German National Railway* (Chapel Hill, N.C., 1988), pp. 14-15. Appointment of Saur: Milward, *German Economy*, p. 142. Saur was an engineer who had worked for Todt since 1937 and entered the Munitions Ministry in 1940. His office oversaw continuing technical developments of weapons and he headed the final production of the weapons and munitions programme: Janssen, *Ministerium Speer*, p. 41. Jägerstab raises production: Speer Chronik, March 1944, BA R 3/1739, pp. 31-2. Milch attributed rises in productivity: Milch speech, 'III Besprechung in Stralsund 3. Mai 1944, 18.10 Uhr in der Kaserne des Heeres-Flak-Ersatzabteilung 61,' BA MA R L 3/6, pp. 90-3. Speer's opinion of the Jägerstab: Speer Chronik, May 1944, BA R 3/1739, p. 93. Speer's control of air armaments industry: Göring decree, 20 June 1944, BA R 3/1551.

29. Milward, *German Economy*, pp. 127-8. Dispersal forced in February 1944: Edward R. Zilbert, *Albert Speer and the Nazi Ministry of Arms: Economic Institutions and Industrial Production in the German War Economy* (East Brunswick, N. J., 1981), pp. 242-4. Speer's earlier opposition to dispersal: Milward, *German Economy*, pp. 125-6.

30. Wolfgang Werner, *'Bleib übrig!' Deutsche Arbeiter in der nationalsozialistischen Kriegswirtschaft* (Dusseldorf, 1983), pp. 282-3, 285-6. Speer concentrates production: Oberstleutnant Stieff to Chef H Rüst u BdE, undated, 'Konzentration der Rüstung,' p. 1, and 'Anlage 12,' 'Kontingentierung und Abstimmung des Rüstungsprogramms,' BA MA RH 2/1378, p. 2.

31. Beck, *Under the Bombs*, p. 121; other shortages, pp. 122-3. Transfer of firms to more important production: Speer Chronik, January 1944, BA R 3/1739, pp. 17-18. Resistance in cigarette industry overcome: Speer Chronik, March 1944, BA R 3/1739, p. 40. Haegert's appointment: Speer to Bouhler, 3 February 1944, BA R 3/1573.

32. Speer informed Bormann on 26 January: Speer to Bormann, 26 January 1944, BA R 3/1573, pp. 1-2. Rafelsberger's appointment and tasks: Funk and Speer to Rafelsberger, 15 January 1944; Speer to Rafelsberger, 20 January 1944, BA R 3/1573. Bormann requested advice: Bormann to Speer, 27 February 1944, 'Rationalisierung des Rechnungswesens und der Wirtschaftsverwaltung,' *ibid.* Speer's reply: Speer to Bormann, 9 March 1944, *ibid.*, pp. 1-2. End of Rafelsberger's commission: Speer to Rafelsberger, 28 August 1944, *ibid.*, pp. 1-2.

33. Himmler to Kehrl, 5 April 1944, BA NS 19/1802, pp. 1-2. SS firms: Milward, *German Economy*, pp. 156-7. Schieber was the head of Speer's office for the provision of raw material and labour requirements for armaments, the *Rüstungslieferungsamt*: Janssen, *Ministerium Speer*, p. 41. Schieber's view of Himmler's attitude: Dr Walter Schieber to Speer, 7 May 1944, BA R 3/1631, pp. 1-3. Himmler's claims on prisoner production: 'Rede Himmlers vor Vortretern der deutschen Justiz,' 25 May 1944, BA NS 19/4014, p. 11. Kehrl's letter: Kehrl to Ost-Gesellschaft für Pflanzenkautschuk und Guttapercha m.b.H., 14 March 1944, BA NS 19/1802.

34. Himmler Fernschreiben to Pohl, 19 February 1944, 'Rüstungsfertigung in Grossziegelwerk Oranienbg,' BA NS 19/443. Since August 1940 Jüttner had headed the SS Leadership Main Office (SS-Führungshauptamt, FHA), which was 'practically an SS general staff for military training and operations': Robert Lewis Koehl, *The Black Corps: The Structure and Power Struggles of the Nazi SS* (Madison, 1983), p. 194. Himmler on arming SS with mortars: Himmler to SS-Obergruppenführer Jüttner, SSFHA, 8 February 1944, BA NS 19/1542. Pohl plans to expand use of Oranienburg: Pohl to Himmler, 1 March 1944, 'Rüstungsfertigung im Grossziegelwerk Oranienburg,' BA R 3/1594. Pohl investigated caves: Pohl to Himmler, 24 January 1944, 'Höhlenbau in den SS-eigenen Steinbrüchen,' pp. 1-2, and Pohl to Brandt, 17 February 1944, 'Tunnel Krosno und Frystak sowie Spala,' BA NS 19/317. SS more willing to build underground factories: Milward, *German War Economy*, p. 145.

35. Speer believed labour failed most: Speer Chronik, June 1944, BA R 3/1739, pp. 125-9. Sauckel promised Hitler 4 million foreign workers: 4 January 1944, Document 1292-PS, *TMWC*, vol. 27, p. 107. Invasion ends hopes of more foreign workers: Janssen, *Ministerium Speer*, p. 225. Numbers employed in armaments decreased: 'Stichworte für Ministerrede anlässlich der nächsten Rüstungstagung,' 19 June 1944, BA R 3/1551, p. 1. Speer and Sauckel's meetings: Speer Chronik, BA R 3/1739, pp. 97, 136. Hitler leaves decision to Speer: Liebel to Lammers, 12 May 1944, 'Arbeitseinsatz in Frankreich,' BA R 3/1588, p. 2.

36. Speer orders his office to give up personnel: Speer to Himmler and Speer to Lammers, 14 February 1944, 'Abgabe von Wehrpflichtigen für den Fronteinsatz,' BA R 3/1583 and BA R 3/1588 respectively. Speer supported Backe's proposals: Speer to Backe, 7 January 1944, 'Ernährungsindustrie,' BA R 3/1572, pp. 1-2. Reichspost staff cuts: Bormann, 11 March 1944, 'Bekanntgabe 62/44g,' BA NS 6/350, p. 2.

37. Speer planned to set up a reserve: Speer Chronik, June 1944, BA R 3/1739, p. 128. Speer's Ministry believed additional two million workers could be found: unsigned undated briefing note for Speer, 'Notiz für eine Rede des Herrn Reichsministers Speer,' 'Mobilisierung von Leistungsreserven,' BA R 3/1551, pp. 1-4. Speer saw evidence that German reserves were not exhausted: Speer speech, 'Rede Reichsminister Speer auf der Rüstungstagung 24.6. in Linz,' BA R 3/1551, p. 31. Fostering outwork: see papers in BA R 12 I/339. Hostility to outwork: Beck, *Under the Bombs*, p. 142. Speer approaches Himmler for concentration camp prisoners: Speer? to Himmler, 23 February 1944, 'Einsatz von Kz-Häftlingen für den Rüstungswirtschaft,' BA R 3/1583, pp. 1-2; Speer Chronik, June 1944, BA R 3/1739, p. 136.

38. His claims to Sauckel on employment of women: Speer to Sauckel, 28 January 1944, BA R 3/1597. Effect of pay scales in industry and administration, and de facto equal pay: Salter, 'Mobilisation of German Labour,' pp. 148-50. Hitler agrees to lengthen labour service for some girls: Lammers, 1 April 1944, Institut für Zeitgeschichte, *Akten der Parteikanzlei Teil I* (Munich, 1983-1985), 101 06173. Hitler's views in meeting on equal pay: 'Besprechung beim Führer im Berghof am 25.4.1944 mit Lammers, M.B., Ley, Sauckel, Fischböck, Abetz, Liebel, Speer,' BA NS 6/778, pp. 1-6. The record notes that Speer arrived after discussion on the issue concluded. Economic implications: Salter, 'Mobilisation of German Labour,' pp. 150-1. Speer plans for home production: Schmelter, Armaments Ministry, 'III Besprechung im Stralsund,' 3 May 1944, BA MA R L 3/6, p. 38.

39. Bormann and Lammers on Sauckel's proposals: correspondence on BA R 43 II/654, especially Bormann to Lammers, 7 April 1944, 'Entwurf einer Zweiten Verordnung über die Meldung von Männern und Frauen für Aufgaben der Reichsverteidigung,' and Bormann to Sauckel, 7 April 1944, pp. 1-3. Model's proposals: Generaloberst Model, Heeresgruppe Nord, to Himmler, 10 February 1944, and attached reports, 'Woher weitere Soldaten für die Front?' and 'Zur Frauenarbeit auf dem Lande,' BA NS 19/3552, pp. 1-4.

40. Speer to Vögler, Director of the Vereinigte Stahlwerke, 15 March 1944, BA R 3/1604, pp. 1-2. End to exemptions of fathers of large families: Beck, *Under the Bombs*, p. 116. Percentages of men soldiers: Werner, *'Bleib übrig!'* p. 275. Von Unruh to free men from the replacement army: Keitel to von Unruh and Fromm, 3 March 1944, 'Sonderkommission zur Überprüfung der Personaleinsparung des Ersatzheeres,' BA MA RW 4/v. 475, pp. 1-2. Speer on appointing the industrialists: Speer to Vögler, Director of the Vereinigte Stahlwerke, 15 March 1944, BA R 3/1604, pp. 1-2. Speer's promise to Goebbels: entry, 11 July 1944, von Oven, *Finale Furioso*, p. 391. Pohl told Himmler: Pohl to Himmler, 13 April 1944, 'Führerbefehl vom 27.11.1943 (Vereinfachung Wehrmachtsverwaltung),' BA NS 19/1752, pp. 1-2.

41. Mussehl to Killy, 27 April 1944, BA R 43 II/681, p. 27.

42. Röhnert: Janssen, *Ministerium Speer*, p. 353, note 101. Pohl judged Frank had largely taken over: Pohl to Himmler, 24 April 1944, 'Vereinfachung der Wehrmachtsverwaltung,' BA NS 19/1752, p. 1. Ziegler plans war ministry: attachment to Pohl's letter to Himmler of 24 April 1944, SS-Gruppenführer Frank, 21 April 1944, 'Bericht über die 1. Kommissionsitzung,' BA NS 19/1752, p. 1. Von Unruh's advocacy unsuccessful: Mussehl to Killy, 27 April 1944, BA R 43 II/681, p. 22.

43. Himmler's objections to planned unified administration: Himmler to Pohl, 15 May 1944, 'Vereinfachung der Wehrmachtsverwaltung,' BA NS 19/1752, p. 1. Himmler advocates administrative simplification: 'Reichsführer-SS Heinrich Himmler zum Vortrag des Reichsleiters Fiehler,' 13 February 1944, p. 2; and 'Rede des Reichsführer-SS Heinrich Himmler auf der Tagung der Oberbürgermeister,' BA NS 19/4012, pp. 3-4. Difficulties over transfer of welfare responsibilities: Berger to Himmler, 26 April 1944, 'Übergabe der Versorgung an das Reichsarbeitsministerium,' BA NS 19/287, pp. 1-2. Unification of nine *Verordnungsblätter*: Himmler order, 4 January 1944, BA NS 19/2934. Himmler advised this was not possible: SS-Hauptsturmführer Berg, 7 August 1944, 'Vermerk für SS-Standartenführer Dr Brandt,' BA NS 19/2934, pp. 1-2.

44. Speer's advice to Gauleiter Meyer: Speer to Gauleiter Meyer, 23 January 1944, BA R 3/1590, p. 2.

45. Bormann creates *Arbeitsstab*: Bormann, 7 January 1944, 'Anordnung 6/44,' BA NS 6/346, pp. 1-2. Bormann wanted work to begin quickly: Bormann Fernschreiben to Friedrichs, undated, 'NS-Fuehrungsstab, Aufnahme der Arbeit, Vorlage vom 4.2,' BA NS 6/761. Reinecke's description: 'Besprechung des Führers mit General Reinicke [sic] am 7. Januar 1944 in der Wolfsschanze,' BA NS 6/162, p. 4.

46. Orlow, *Nazi Party*, II, p. 461. Hitler saw National Socialist leadership as decisive: 'Rede des Hauptbereichleiters Ruder auf der Tagung der Reichsleiter, Gauleiter und Verbändeführer am 23.2.1944 in München,' BA NS 6/346, p. 2. Bormann agreed: he strengthened the emphasis given to the importance of NSFOs in his corrections to a draft letter to the Gauleiters; untitled draft letter to Gauleiters, BA NS 6/761, pp. 1-2. Hitler claimed his experience showed: 'Besprechung des Führers mit General Reinicke am 7. Januar 1944 in der Wolfsschanze,' BA NS 6/162, pp. 3, 7, 8. Hitler had in fact not been an instruction officer but a contact person (*V-Mann*): Michael H. Kater, 'Hitler in a Social Context,' *Central European History*, vol. 14, 1981, p. 249. Hitler warned: 'Besprechung des Führers mit General Reinicke am 7. Januar 1944 in der Wolfsschanze,' BA NS 6/162, p. 21. Bormann aware of the need to choose correct workers: Bormann, unheaded note to Friedrichs, 1 March 1944, on a submission by Ruder, 'Vorlage,' 'Mitarbeiter für den Arbeitsstab,' BA NS 6/522, p. 1. Bormann on use of Gaubeauftragte and common orientation: Bormann, 28 February 1944, 'Anordnung 53/44,' BA NS 6/142.

47. Party Chancellery view of NSFOs: 'Rede des Hauptbereichsleiters Ruder auf der Tagung der Reichsleiter, Gauleiter und Verbändeführer am 23.2.1944 in München,' BA NS 6/346, p. 4. Hitler's order: Hitler, 19 June 1944, 'Verfügung 9/44,' BA NS 6/78, pp. 1-2. Bormann's agreement to all personnel and technical measures: 'Rede des Hauptbereichleiters Ruder. . .,' 23 February 1944, BA NS 6/346, p. 2. Belief ideological fanaticism could outweigh material strength: see,

for example, 'Der Krieg als Weltanschauungskampf von Dr Goebbels. Rede vor der Generalität in Posen am 25. Januar 1944,' BA MA RW 4/v. 413, p. 15. Himmler appointed inspector: Himmler decree, 1 January 1944, 'Inspektor für Weltanschauliche Erziehung,' BA NS 19/750.

48. Bormann to Speer, 1 March 1944, BA R 3/1611, p. 1. SS and Hitler Youth described by Party Chancellery: Berger to Brandt, 27 May 1944, 'I. Besprechung in Reichsministerium für die besetzten Ostgebiete,' BA NS 19/2181, p. 6. Bormann's willingness to prevent information from reaching Hitler—he allegedly misled Hitler on six cases of youth policy: Berger to Himmler, 23 April 1944, 'Zusammenarbeit Reichsjugendführung/Parteikanzlei,' BA NS 19/2185. Bormann criticised SD attempts: Bormann to Himmler, 27 April 1944, 'Einflussnahme des SD auf die Personalpolitik,' BA NS 19/1903, p. 2.

49. Popular hostility to Party: Franz W. Seidler, *"Deutscher Volkssturm" : Das letzte Aufgebot 1944/45* (Munich, 1989), p. 9. National Socialist family evenings: Bormann, 3 April 1944, 'Anordnung 74/44,' BA NS 6/346, pp. 1-5. Need to serve as an example in fulfilling war service: Bormann, 24 January 1944, 'Anordnung 15/44,' *ibid.*, p. 1. Need for strong nerves and bravery: Bormann, 17 May 1944, 'Führungshinweis Nr. 17,' BA NS 6/358, p. 1. Friedrichs' speech: speech by Friedrichs to Gau- and Reichsleiters, 23 March 1944, BA NS 6/784, p. 1.

50. Party's role in combatting bombing: Friedrichs to M-Beauftragten of NSDAP Gauleitungen, 'Luftkriegseinsatz der Partei,' BA NS 6/294, pp. 1-2. Party's role in event of invasion: Bormann, 31 May 1944, 'Rundschreiben 123/44 g. Rs,' BA NS 6/350, pp. 1-6. Numbers in Party organisations: Seidler, *"Deutscher Volkssturm,"* p. 26.

Chapter 7

1. German territorial losses in East: entry, 1 July 1944, Wilfred von Oven, *Finale Furioso: Mit Goebbels bis zum Ende* (first published 1948-50, Tübingen, 1974), p. 376. Situation in late 1944: Peter Calvocoressi, Guy Wint and John Pritchard, *Total War: The Causes and Courses of the Second World War*, Peter Calvocoressi, *Volume I: The Western Hemisphere* (second edition, London, 1989), p. 503; John Erickson, *The Road to Berlin: Stalin's War with Germany* (London, 1985), vol. 2, chapters 5 and 6. Declining public morale: 'Tätigkeitsberichte' of the Reichspropagandaämter (RPÄ) dated 4 and 10 July 1944, in BA R 55/601, pp. 1-9 and pp. 1-10 respectively. Rations worsened: Wolfgang Werner, *'Bleib übrig!' Deutsche Arbeiter in der nationalsozialistischen Kriegswirtschaft* (Dusseldorf, 1983), p. 329.

2. War to be over by end of year: entry, 1 September 1944, Harold Macmillan, *War Diaries: Politics and War in the Mediterranean January 1943-May 1945* (London, 1984), p. 514. Progress in Western campaign: Calvocoressi, *Total War*, I, pp. 543-7. Evacuations in West: Marlis G. Steinert, *Hitler's War and the Germans: Public Mood and Attitude during the Second World War* (Ohio, 1977), pp. 277-8.

3. Failings of the Luftwaffe: Williamson Murray, *Luftwaffe* (Baltimore, 1985), pp. 276-7. Effectiveness of strategic bombing increased: R. J. Overy, *The Air War 1939-1945* (London, 1980), p. 122. Attacks on railroads and oil industry: Murray, *Luftwaffe*, pp. 251-2, 256-7, 261. Problems with transport: Speer to Hitler, 11

November 1944, BA R 3/1528, pp. 1-13. Effects on Saar: Alfred C. Mierzejewski, *The Collapse of the German War Economy, 1944-1945: Allied Air Power and the German National Railway* (Chapel Hill, N.C., 1988), p. 89.

4. Deputy Gauleiter of Hanover-Ost, Peper, to Party Chancellery, 12 August 1944, 'Luftlage und Industrieschäden,' BA R 3/1573, p. 2. Firma Bosch: Paul Sauer, *Württemberg in der Zeit des Nationalsozialismus* (Ulm, 1975), p. 361. More room for production by closing other firms: *ibid.*, p. 359.

5. Himmler's meeting with Vlasov: signature, 19 September 1944, 'Vermerk für SS-Ogruf. v. Herff,' BA NS 34/11, p. 1. Moves too late: Andreyev, *Vlasov*, p. 60. Propaganda Ministry attitudes: Taubert to Naumann, 22 September 1944, BA R 55/1438, pp. 1, 5.

6. Goebbels impressed by worsening military situation: Elke Fröhlich, 'Hitler und Goebbels im Krisenjahr 1944. Aus den Tagebüchern des Reichspropagandaministers,' *Vierteljahrshefte für Zeitgeschichte*, vol. 38, 1990, p. 219. Meeting of 21 June 1944: *ibid.*, pp. 200-5.

7. Goebbels prepared groundwork: Peter Longerich, 'Joseph Goebbels und der totale Krieg: eine unbekannte Denkschrift des Propagandaministers vom 18. Juli 1944,' *Vierteljahrshefte für Zeitgeschichte*, vol. 35, 1987, p. 298. Hitler's agreement to discussion: entry, 6-8 July 1944, Willi A. Boelcke (ed.), *Deutschlands Rüstung im Zweiten Weltkrieg: Hitlers Konferenzen mit Albert Speer 1942-1945* (Frankfurt, 1969), p. 390. Meeting of Reich and Party Chancelleries: unsigned note, 13 July 1944, 'Aktivierung des Einsatzes deutscher Arbeitskräfte,' Institut für Zeitgeschichte, *Akten der Parteikanzlei Teil I* (Munich, 1983-1985), 101 10846-8. Bormann advised Gauleiters: Fernschreiben Bormann to Gauleiters, 19 July 1944, BA R 3/1573, pp. 1-2. Sauckel ordered men and women to report to labour offices: Klaus Mammach, *Der Volkssturm: Das letzte Aufgebot 1944/45* (Cologne, 1981), p. 17.

8. Fröhlich, 'Hitler und Goebbels im Krisenjahr 1944,' p. 206. Speer and Goebbels meet: *ibid.* Speer and Goebbels agree: Dieter Rebentisch, *Führerstaat und Verwaltung im Zweiten Weltkrieg: Verfassungsentwicklung und Verwaltungspolitik 1939-1945* (Stuttgart, 1989), pp. 513-14.

9. Speer's letter to Hitler: Speer to Hitler, 12 July 1944, BA R 3/1522, pp. 1-10.

10. Speer's second letter: Speer to Hitler, 20 July 1944, 'Denkschrift II,' ibid., pp. 1-2. Speer's claims on taxes and trains: speech to the Hauptausschuss Waffen, 10 August 1944, p. 14; Speer speech to the meeting of the Hauptausschuss Munition, 11 August 1944, pp. 12-14; speech by Speer to a meeting of the chairmen of armaments commissions, Berlin, 10 August 1944, BA R 3/1554, p. 5. Speer claimed 1.4 million still employed as household help: speech by Speer to a meeting of the chairmen of armaments commissions, 10 August 1944, BA R 3/1554, p. 18.

11. Speer's second letter to Hitler: Speer to Hitler, 20 July 1944, 'Denkschrift II,' BA R 3/1522, pp. 1-2.

12. Speer's figures doubtful: Rebentisch, *Führerstaat und Verwaltung*, p. 516 note 50. Lammers objected to Speer's claim: addendum to 23 July 1944, 'Ergebnis der Chef Besprechung,' BA R 43 II/664a. Reich Chancellery still protesting in November: submission to Lammers, 4 November 1944, 'Pressekommuniqué "Totaler Krieg",' BA R 43 II/666b, pp. 2-3. Rebentisch notes: Rebentisch, *Führerstaat und Verwaltung*, p. 514.

13. Speer to Hitler, 20 July 1944, 'Denkschrift II,' BA R 3/1522, pp. 12-15.

14. *Ibid.*, p. 8. Organisation of armed forces: *ibid.*, pp. 4-5, 19-21. Organisational simplification of Wehrmacht needed: *ibid.*, pp. 12-13, 15, 21. OKW had not strength: *ibid.*, pp. 19-21.

15. Speer compares war effort unfavourably to World War I: 'Vortrag von Reichsminister Speer beim Kaiserlich—Japanischen Botschafter Oshima am 8. August 1944,' BA R 3/1553, p. 1; speech to meeting of Hauptausschuss Waffen, BA R 3/1554, pp. 3-4. Specific comments to Gauleiters: 'Reichsminister Speer auf der Gauleiter-Tagung am 3. August 1944 in Posen,' BA R 3/1553, pp. 2-3; see also Speer to Hitler, 20 July 1944, 'Denkschrift II,' BA R 3/1522, pp. 6-8, 18. Sauckel stated, however, that the percentage of women employed in 1939 was greater than that in 1914: 'Ausführungen des Generalbevollmächtigten für den Arbeitseinsatz auf der Reichs- und Gauleiter-Tagung am 5./6. Febr. 27.1943 in Posen,' Document 1739-PS, *Trial of the Major War Criminals Before the International Military Tribunal, Nuremberg, 14 November 1945-1 October 1946* (reprint, New York, 1971), vol. 27, p. 595. Speer claims time Germans had to prepare: 'Minister Speer auf der Gauleiter-Tagung am 3. August 1944 in Posen,' BA R 3/1553, p. 3; speech to Hauptausschuss Waffen, BA R 3/1554, p. 4.

16. War a technical war: 'Reichsminister Speer auf der Gauleiter-Tagung am 3. August 1944 in Posen,' BA R 3/1553, p. 1; Speer, speech to a meeting of the Hauptausschuss Waffen, 10 August 1944, BA R 3/1554, p. 3; 'Tagung der Reichspropagandaämter am 28. u. 29. Aug. 1944 Vortrag von Reichsminister Speer: Die deutsche Rüstung und der totale Kriegseinsatz,' BA R 3/1554, p. 1. Only armaments, food and transport important: speech to the Hauptausschuss Waffen, 10 August 1944, BA R 3/1554, p. 12. Speer's call for proletarianisation: Albert Speer, *Inside the Third Reich* (London, 1970), p. 255.

17. W. K. Hancock and M. M. Gowing, *British War Economy* (London, 1949), p. 308; see also p. 457. Many women live in areas with no work: Earl R. Beck, *Under the Bombs: The German Home Front 1942-1945* (Lexington, 1986) , p. 42. Salter implies: Stephen Salter, 'The Mobilisation of German Labour, 1939-1945. A Contribution to the History of the Working Class in the Third Reich,' (unpublished D. Phil. thesis, Oxford, 1983), p. 78. German experience with transfers: Werner, *'Bleib übrig!'* pp. 282-3, 286, 292.

18. Text of Goebbels' memorandum: Longerich, 'Joseph Goebbels und der totale Krieg,' pp. 305-14.

19. *Ibid.*, pp. 300-1.

20. Goebbels on the office and Party role: Goebbels to Hitler, 18 July 1944, BA NL 118/107, pp. 5-22. Goebbels' private judgement of the failings of the Party membership: entries, 27 September and 23 October 1943, von Oven, *Finale Furioso*, pp. 141-2, 161-2.

21. Goebbels to Hitler, 18 July 1944, BA NL 118/107, p. 32.

22. Berenice A. Carroll, *Design for Total War: Arms and Economics in the Third Reich* (The Hague, 1968), p. 242.

23. Paper prepared by Reich Chancellery: untitled undated notice, attached to Lammers to Dietrich, 26 July 1944, 'Erlass des Führers über den totalen Kriegseinsatz,' BA R 43 II/664a, pp. 1-5.

24. Schmelter claims further 1.8 million men available: Gregor Janssen, *Das Minister-ium Speer: Deutschlands Rüstung im Krieg* (Frankfurt, 1968), p. 274.
25. Longerich, 'Joseph Goebbels und der totale Krieg,' p. 303. Goebbels' memoran-dum an attempt to create co-ordinating body: *ibid.*, p. 302. Longerich sees an attempt to take over internal leadership: *ibid.*, p. 304.
26. Goebbels' role in suppressing the revolt: Speer, *Third Reich*, pp. 382-9. Speer exaggerates suspicions: Matthias Schmidt, *Albert Speer—The End of a Myth* (London, 1985), chapter 7, especially pp. 102, 108-10. Goebbels' friends involved: entry, 5 August 1944, von Oven, *Finale Furioso*, pp. 447-8; Jay W. Baird, *The Mythical World of Nazi War Propaganda, 1939-1945* (Minneapolis, Minn., 1974), pp. 200, 237. Those too bound to Hitler: Fröhlich, 'Hitler und Goebbels im Krisenjahr 1944,' p. 205.
27. Entry, 23 July 1944, Semmler, *Goebbels*, p. 147. The crisis Hitler mentioned and Hitler turns to Goebbels' plans: Fröhlich, 'Hitler und Goebbels im Krisenjahr 1944,' p. 205. Goebbels' technique of putting his views to Hitler repeatedly: entry, 23 January 1943, BA NL 118/50, p. 31. Goebbels' visit to Hitler's headquarters and its results: entry, 23 July 1944, Semmler, *Goebbels*, pp. 140-7; entries, 25 July 1944, von Oven, *Finale Furioso*, pp. 431-7.
28. Dietrich Orlow, *The History of the Nazi Party: Vol. II 1933-1945* (Newton Abbot, 1973), p. 469.
29. Account of the meeting: unsigned note, 23 July 1944, 'Ergebnis der Chef Besprechung,' BA R 43 II/664a, pp. 1-8. Speer's call for radical measures: Berger Fernschreiben to Himmler, 21? July 1944, BA NS 19/2844, p. 2. Challenges to Speer's figures: Fröhlich, 'Hitler und Goebbels im Krisenjahr 1944,' p. 206. Goebbels' belief about implementation of Hitler's 1943 order: Berger Fernschreiben to Himmler, 21? July 1944, BA NS 19/2844, pp. 2-3.
30. Account of the meeting: unsigned note, 23 July 1944, 'Ergebnis der Chef Besprechung,' BA R 43 II/664a, pp. 4-7. Longerich's view: Longerich, 'Joseph Goebbels und der totale Krieg,' p. 304.
31. Hitler's decree: 'Erlass des Führers über den totalen Kriegseinsatz vom 25. Juli 1944,' and attached an additional decree of the same day naming Goebbels as plenipotentiary, pp. 2-4 of Bormann, 26 July 1944, 'Rundschreiben 153/44,' BA NS 6/347.
32. Decree extended to occupied territories: Lammers Schnellbrief to ORBs, 26 July 1944, 'Erlass des Führers über den totalen Kriegseinsatz,' BA R 43 II/664a, p. 1. Wehrmacht excluded: Lammers, 23 July 1944, 'Verstärkter Kriegseinsatz,' *ibid.*, p. 1. Hitler agreed with Lammers on Reich, Presidential and Party Chancelleries: Lammers, 25 July 1944, 'Totaler Kriegseinsatz,' *ibid.*, p. 2. Goebbels' earlier unsuccessful attempt: Goebbels Fernschreiben to Lammers, 24 July 1944, *ibid.* Offices directly under Hitler: the general building inspector for the Reich capital (*Generalbauinspektor für die Reichshauptstadt*), the general building inspector for the capital of the movement (*Generalinspektor für die Hauptstadt der Bewegung*), the head of the building control office for Linz (*Reichsbaurat für die Stadt Linz a.d. Donau*) and Hitler's general inspector for motoring (*Generalinspektor des Führers für das Kraftfahrwesen*). Lammers assured Goebbels this no obstacle: Lammers to Goebbels, 26 July 1944, 'Erlass des Führers über den totalen Kriegseinsatz,' BA R 43 II/664a, p. 2.

33. Goebbels' powers weaken Speer and Göring: Fröhlich, 'Hitler und Goebbels im Krisenjahr 1944,' p. 207. Rebentisch's view: Rebentisch, *Führerstaat und Verwaltung*, pp. 516, 520. Hitler's position: *ibid.*, p. 517; Fröhlich, 'Hitler und Goebbels im Krisenjahr 1944,' p. 207.

34. Hitler deputises Bormann to implement total war in Party: Hitler, 20 July 1944, 'Verfügung 10/44,' BA NS 6/347. Bormann's interpretation: Bormann, 19 August 1944, 'Anordnung 183/44,' BA NS 6/347, pp. 1-2. Party simplifications: sixth in a series of undated press communiqués, BA R 43 II/666b, pp. 1-3. Party uk positions: Rebentisch, *Führerstaat und Verwaltung*, pp. 527-8.

35. Himmler's views on Ersatzheer: Himmler to Gauleiter Mutschmann of Saxony, 31 July 1944, and Mutschmann to Himmler, 25 July 1944, BA NS 19/1872, pp. 1-2. Himmler chief of army armaments: Speer Chronik, July 1944, BA R 3/1740, p. 169. 500,000 troops raised: Burton Wright III, 'Army of Despair: The German Volkssturm 1944-1945' (Florida State University, Ph.D. thesis, 1982), p. 73. Volksgrenadier divisions formed: *ibid.*, pp. 72-3.

36. Pohl to Himmler, 17 August 1944, BA NS 19/3191, quotation on p. 1, on Ziegler p. 2. Hitler deputised Himmler to inspect armed forces: Hitler order, 2 August 1944, 'WFSt/Org. (1) Nr. 05699/44 geh,' *ibid.*, pp. 1-2. Himmler believed more men could be brought to front: 'Rede des Reichsführers-SS in Grafenwoehr am 25.7.1944,' BA NS 19/4015, p. 26. Pohl ordered to start work immediately: Himmler order, 5 August 1944, and Himmler to Pohl, 19 August 1944, BA NS 19/3191. Pohl estimated 70,000 to 75,000 would be freed: Pohl to Himmler, 3 October 1944, *ibid.*, p. 4.

37. Himmler takes over Ziegler's responsibility: Keitel to Himmler, October 1944, 'Reform der Organisation und Verwaltung,' ibid., pp. 1-2. Pohl suggested to Himmler: Pohl to Himmler, 14 November 1944, 'Vereinfachung der Wehrmachtverwaltung,' ibid., pp. 1-2. Himmler's attitude and instructions: Himmler to Pohl, 13 October 1944, ibid., pp. 1-2. Berger wanted Himmler to take over reinforcements: Berger to Himmler, 1 August 1944, 'Befehl des Oberkommandos der Wehrmacht,' BA NS 19/2409, p. 1.

38. Goebbels' appointment to inspect armed forces and views on numbers to be saved: entry, 11 December 1944, von Oven, *Finale Furioso*, pp. 520-3.

39. Himmler's attitude: Klopfer, Fernschreiben to Bormann, 2 September 1944, 'Generalgouverneur Dr Frank (Aufrechterhaltung des Generalgouvernements),' BA NS 6/166, p. 3.

40. Testimony of Prince Friedrich Christian zu Schaumburg-Lippe, Robert W. Kempner, *Das Dritte Reich im Kreuzverhör: aus den Vernehmungsprotokollen des Anklagers* (Dusseldorf, 1984), p. 160. Triumvirate of Goebbels, Bormann and Himmler: 'Tagebuchauszug Werner Beumelburg vom 30.7.1944 in Neu-Fahrland bei Potsdam,' note of meeting with Kreipe, BA MA RL 2 I/21, p. 2. Lammers unable to see Hitler: Lammers to Bormann, 1 January 1945, Document 753-D, *TMWC*, vol. 35, p. 495. Hitler's health deteriorating: entry, 10 November 1944, von Oven, *Finale Furioso*, p. 510. Weber's prediction and Hitler's charismatic authority weakened: Ian Kershaw, *The 'Hitler Myth': Image and Reality in the Third Reich* (Oxford, 1989), pp. 9, 200.

41. Orlow, *Nazi Party*, II, p. 464.

42. Plot explained all setbacks: Bormann to Gauleiter Eggeling, Halle/Saale, 8 September 1944, 'Stimmung der Bevölkerung,' BA NS 6/153, p. 2. Arrests of pre-National Socialist politicians: Beck, *Under the Bombs*, p. 145. Popular reaction to the plot against Hitler: RPÄ reports, 24 July 1944, pp. 1, 10; 25 July 1944, p. 10; and 7 August 1944, BA R 55/601, p. 1. Reports suggest working-class mood optimistic and receptive: RPÄ report, 5 December 1944, BA R 55/601, p. 2; 'Meldungen . . . 28. Juli 1944,' and 'Bericht an das Reichsministerium für Volksaufklärung und Propaganda vom 19. März 1945,' Boberach (ed.), *Meldungen aus dem Reich*, vol. 17, pp. 6684-8, 6732.

43. Propaganda Ministry proposals: Franz W. Seidler, *"Deutscher Volkssturm": Das letzte Aufgebot 1944/45* (Munich, 1989), p. 35. Goebbels' and Schepmann's plans: Orlow, *Nazi Party*, II, p. 474. Bormann persuades Hitler: Seidler, *"Deutscher Volkssturm,"* p. 36. Formation of the Volkssturm: Bormann, 19 October 1944, 'Anordnung 336/44,' BA NS 6/98; Hitler, 25 September 1944, 'Erlass über die Bildung des Deutschen Volkssturmes,' BA NS 6/168, pp. 1-3. Speer promised all the weapons needed: entry, 18 October 1944, von Oven, *Finale Furioso*, p. 500. Bormann's close involvement in all details of its establishment: see papers in BA NS 6/313 and NS 6/763. Organisation of Volkssturm by party: Orlow, *Nazi Party*, II, p. 474.

44. Bormann, 26 September 1944, 'Rundschreiben 270/44,' BA NS 6/98, p. 1. Volkssturm purely Party matter: Bormann to Lammers, 5 January 1945, Document 753-D, *TMWC*, vol. 35, p. 501. Volkssturm symbol of national unity and participation: Bormann, 27 October 1944, 'Rundschreiben 353/44,' BA NS 6/98.

45. Unsigned, 10 October 1944, 'Vorlage an Herrn Reichsleiter Bormann,' 'Führerbefehl für die Verstärkung der nationalsozialistischen Führung in der Wehrmacht,' BA NS 6/140, pp. 1-2.

46. Kuhn to Wächter, Head of the Propaganda Staff, Propaganda Ministry, 24 October 1944, 'Vorschlag zur Aktivierung der Partei im Endkampf,' BA R 55/621. Frontier Gaus build fortifications: Bormann, 6 October 1944, 'Rundschreiben 302/44 g. Rs,' BA NS 6/352, pp. 1-2; Bormann, 19 November 1944, 'Anordnung 405/44g,' BA *ibid.* Responsibility in operational area: 'Erlass des Führers über die Befehlsgewalt in einem Operationsgebiet innerhalb des Reiches. Vom 13. Juli 1944,' BA MA RW 4/v. 703, pp. 1-2. Civilian Reich defence commissioner: 'Zweiter Erlass Führers über die Befehlsgewalt in einem Operationsgebiet innerhalb des Reiches. Vom 20. September 1944,' *ibid.*, pp. 1-2.

47. Submission to Lammers, 4 October 1944, 'Weiblicher Kriegshilfsdienst,' BA R 43 II/666c, p. 1. Goebbels' initial proposals: submission to Lammers, 28 October 1944, 'Weiblicher Wehrhilfsdienst,' *ibid.*, p. 1.

48. Submission to Lammers, 17 November 1944, 'Weiblicher Wehrhilfsdienst,' *ibid.*, p. 4. Reich Chancellery concern and discussion: submission to Lammers, 28 October 1944, 'Weiblicher Wehrhilfsdienst,' *ibid.*, p. 3. Views of other leaders: Sauckel Schnellbrief to Reichsarbeitsführer, 24 October 1944, 'Wehrmachteinsatz des RAD,' *ibid.*, p. 1; OKW WF St/Org (II) to Naumann, Lammers, Bormann, Stuckart, 2 October 1944, 'Entwurf für den Erlass des Führers über den Wehrhilfsdienst der weiblichen Jugend,' *ibid.*, p. 1. Bormann and Sauckel agree: submission to Lammers, 2 November 1944, *ibid.*, pp. 1-2. Bormann's view: Bormann Fernschreiben to Lammers, 4 November 1944, 'Entwurf eines Fuehrererlasses über den weiblichen Wehrhilfsdienst,' *ibid.*, p. 4. On Lammers'

conservative position, see, for example, the exclamation mark he placed against a statement by Bormann that women might be trained to use weapons on Bormann to Goebbels, 16 November 1944, 'Einziehung von Frauen und Maedchen zum truppenmaessigen Wehrmachtseinsatz,' *ibid.*, p. 3. Lammers completely persuaded by Bormann: Lammers to Goebbels, 11 November 1944, 'Entwurf eines Führererlasses über den weiblichen Wehrhilfsdienst,' *ibid.*, p. 4. Bormann on Wehrmacht's use of labour: Bormann to Goebbels, 16 November 1944, 'Einziehung von Frauen und Maedchen zum truppenmaessigen Wehrmachtseinsatz,' *ibid.*, pp. 3-4.

49. Female auxiliary armed service corps planned: submission to Lammers, 27 November 1944, 'Wehrmachthelferinnenkorps,' *ibid.*, pp. 1-2. All women's auxiliaries combined: Jeff M. Tuten, 'Germany and the World Wars,' in Nancy Loring Goldman (ed.), *Female Soldiers—Combatants or Noncombatants? Historical and Contemporary Perspectives* (Westport, Conn., 1982), p. 56.

50. Nancy Loring Goldman, 'Introduction,' to *ibid.*, p. 6. Women used to build fortifications and free men for front: Bormann Fernschreiben to Goebbels, 27 September 1944, 'Weiblicher Kriegshilfsdienst,' BA R 43 II/666c, p. 1. Hitler's decision on women and the Volkssturm: Bormann, 30 November 1944, 'Anordnung 422/44,' BA NS 6/98.

51. Himmler orders an end to extermination: Document 3762-PS, *TMWC*, vol. 33, pp. 68-9; Document 2605-PS, *ibid.*, vol. 31, p. 13; affidavit of SS-Standartenführer Kurt Becher, read on 12 April 1946, *ibid.*, vol. 11, p. 334. Numbers of Jews dead in 1945: Michael R. Marrus, *The Holocaust in History* (London, 1987), p. 56.

52. Entry, 16 October 1944, von Oven, *Finale Furioso*, pp. 497-9.

53. Entry, 2 September 1944, Semmler, *Goebbels*, pp. 148-9.

54. Von Oven dates the letter as written on 21 September 1944: entry, 21 September 1944, *Finale Furioso*, pp. 479-82. Goebbels' undated letter: Goebbels to Hitler, BA NL118/107, pp. 1-5.

55. Goebbels' undated letter: Goebbels to Hitler, BA NL118/107, pp. 5-7.

56. *Ibid.*, pp. 8-11, 13.

57. Hitler's response and Goebbels' reaction: entry, 18 October 1944, von Oven, *Finale Furioso*, pp. 501-2.

58. Orlow, *Nazi Party*, II, p. 491. Tiessler's suggestion: Walter Tiessler, 'Licht und Schatten oder Schonungslose Wahrheit (1922-1945),' IfZ ED 158, p. 152.

59. 'Tagebuchauszug Werner Beumelburg vom 30.7.1944 in Neu-Fahrland bei Potsdam,' BA MA RL 2 I/21, p. 3. Attempts to foresee difficulties seen as defeatism, such as Ley's criticisms of Gauleiter Meyer entertaining the possibility of having to give up the left bank of the Rhine: Ley to Hitler, 30 November 1944, BA NS 6/135, p. 3. Göring does not dare suggest peace negotiations: entry, 12 October 1944, diary of General Kreipe, Chief of the Luftwaffe General Staff, BA MA RL 2 I/21, pp. 31, 37. Hitler on attacking Russia: Ingeborg Fleischhauer, *Die Chance des Sonderfriedens: Deutschsowjetische Geheimgespräche 1941-1945* (Berlin, 1986), pp. 194-5.

60. Entries, 15 October 1944 and 19 January 1945, von Oven, *Finale Furioso*, pp. 496, 545-6.

61. Entry, 27 July 1944, *ibid.*, p. 439.

Chapter 8

1. Arnhem and Ardennes offensive: Peter Calvocoressi, Guy Wint and John Pritchard, *Total War: The Causes and Courses of the Second World War*, Peter Calvocoressi, *Volume I: The Western Hemisphere* (second edition, London, 1989), pp. 547-9. Eastern front: John Erickson, *The Road to Berlin: Stalin's War with Germany*, Vol. 2 (London, 1985), pp. 564-6. Bombing and economy: Alfred C. Mierzejewski, *The Collapse of the German War Economy, 1944-1945: Allied Air Power and the German National Railway* (Chapel Hill, N. C., 1988), pp. 103, 107-8.

2. Decline of armaments production: Speer, 27 January 1945, 'Nr: M1362/45 g.Rs,' BA R 3/1587, p. 23. Policies to concentrate armaments production: 'Erlass des Führers über die Konzentration der Rüstung und Kriegsproduktion vom 19.6.1944,' 16 July 1944, pp. 1-3, and Speer, 20 July 1944, '1. Anordnung zum Erlass des Führers über die Konzentration der Rüstung und Kriegsproduktion vom 19. Juni 1944,' BA R 43 II/607, pp. 1-3.

3. Mierzejewski, *Collapse of the German War Economy*, p. 97, see also pp. 95-6. Speer and Hitler agree in August: *ibid.*, p. 94. Elasticity of supply: *ibid.*, pp. xiii-xiv.

4. Goebbels' immediate measures: 'Führerinformation Nr. A1457 30. Juli 4 über den totalen Kriegseinsatz,' BA R 43 II/666b, pp. 4-8. Hitler agrees to extend women's labour: Bormann to Lammers, 23 August 1944, 'Massnahmen zum totalen Kriegseinsatz,' BA R 43 II/654. Working hours: Wolfgang Werner, *'Bleib übrig!' Deutsche Arbeiter in der nationalsozialistischen Kriegswirtshaft* (Dusseldorf, 1983), pp. 335-7.

5. Signature to the head of the propaganda section, 28 August 1944, 'Wochenübersicht über Zuschriften zum totalen Kriegseinsatz,' BA R 55/623, p. 1; other details, pp. 2-4. Main suggestions: undated 'Entwurf,' containing a list of suggestions from Feldpost Nr. 08000, *ibid.* Propaganda Ministry comments in January 1945: Bade to the head of the propaganda section with attachments, 24 January 1945, BA R 55/1394, pp. 1-3. Morale continued to decline: 'Meldungen . . . vom 17. August 1944,' in Heinz Boberach (ed.), *Meldungen aus dem Reich 1938-1945: Die geheimen Lageberichte des Sicherheitsdienstes der SS* (Herrsching, 1984), vol. 17, pp. 6705-6.

6. Calls for appropriate lifestyle: Goebbels undated circular to all ORBs, 'Lebensstil im totalen Krieg,' BA R 43 II/665, pp. 1-3. Ban on hunting invitations: Bormann, 15 September 1944, 'Rundschreiben 245/44,' BA NS 6/348, pp. 1-2. Public criticism of new uniforms: RPÄ reports collected in 'Tätigkeitsbericht,' 30 October 1944, BA R 55/601, p. 9.

7. Staff of 50: Dieter Rebentisch, *Führerstaat und Verwaltung im Zweiten Weltkrieg: Verfassungsentwicklung und Verwaltungspolitik 1939-1945* (Stuttgart, 1989), p. 518. Organisation and tasks of the committees: office of the Reichsbevollmächtigter für den totalen Krieg, 1 August 1944, 'Aufgabenverteilung,' BA R 43 II/665, pp. 1-2. Faust's good connections: Rebentisch, *Führerstaat und Verwaltung*, p. 517. Committees work quickly: entry, 27 July 1944, Wilfred von Oven, *Finale Furioso: Mit Goebbels bis zum Ende* (first published 1948-50, Tübingen, 1974), pp. 440-1.

8. Attachment to Naumann to Killy, BA R 43 II/666b, pp. 2-3.

9. Bormann notifies Party leaders of Goebbels' appointment: Bormann, 27 June 1944, 'Rundschreiben 153/44,' BA NS 6/347, pp. 1-6. Bormann sets up a special staff: Klaus Mammach, *Der Volkssturm: Das Letzte Aufgebot 1944/45* (Cologne, 1981), p. 23. Bormann's views on Goebbels' draft decree: Bormann Fernschreiben to Goebbels, 8 August 1944, 'Einschaltung der Gauleiter bei der Durchführung des totalen Kriegseinsatzes,' BA R 43 II/666a. Gau and Kreis commissions: Speer to Bormann, 5 September 1944, enclosing Hanke to all Kreisleiters, 30 August 1944, BA R 3/1615, pp. 1-6. Some Gauleiters cooperate successfully: Speer to Bormann, 5 September 1944, BA R 3/1615, p. 1.

10. Gauleiters had responsibility: Goebbels and Bormann, '1. Ausführungs-bestimmung zu der Anordnung für die Durchführung des totalen Kriegseinsatzes vom 16. August 1944, vom 27. August 1944,' BA R 43 II/666a. Bormann opposed ORB attempts: Bormann Fernschreiben to Goebbels, 24 August 1944, 'Eingehende Vorschriften des Obersten Reichsbehörden gegenüber den Gauleitern zur Durchführung des totalen Kriegseinsatzes,' *ibid.* Speer suggested Gauleiters have armaments responsibilities: Speer to Lammers, 23 September 1944, BA R 3/1768, pp. 1-2. Bormann opposed and saw Party influence as strongest: Bormann, 16 December 1944, 'Rundschreiben 457/44,' BA NS 6/349, p. 3.

11. Gauleiters approach Goebbels: Goebbels Fernschreiben to Hoffmann, 13 January 1945, 'Reform der Post Verteilung,' BA R 55/622, pp. 1-3 and other correspondence on this file. Goebbels' radio conferences with Gauleiters: Naumann to section heads, 7 December 1944, BA R 55/711. Gauleiters seek support in 1945: entry, 21 January 1945, von Oven, *Finale Furioso*, pp. 546-7.

12. Hitler orders creation of new divisions: Keitel to Goebbels, 11 November 1944, 'Wehrersatz August bis Oktober 1944,' BA MA RW 6/v. 415. Wehrmacht demands and uk reserves: 'Führerinformation Nr. A.1.462 vom 9. August 1944 über den Stand der Planungen für den totalen Kriegseinsatz,' BA R 43 II/666b, pp. 1-2.

13. Hitler informed: Rebentisch, *Führerstaat und Verwaltung*, p. 520. Goebbels' August 1944 submission: 'Führerinformation Nr. A.1.462 vom 9. August 1944 über den Stand der Planungen für den totalen Kriegseinsatz,' BA R 43 II/666b, pp. 2-5.

14. *Ibid.*, p. 7. Workers given up in order of priority: *ibid.*, pp. 5-7. Further 850,000 workers from educational courses: *ibid.*, pp. 8-12.

15. Goebbels' proposals for film: *ibid.*, pp. 12-20. Only 5000 staff saved: Mammach, *Volkssturm*, p. 18.

16. Goebbels' plans for cultural sector: 'Führerinformation Nr. A 1 467 II. August 4 über die totalen Kriegsmassnahmen auf dem Kulturellensektor,' *ibid.*, pp. 1-25. The implementation of restrictions in entertainment: unsigned undated (August 1944) note, 'Truppenbetreuung durch NS.-Gemeinschaft "Kraft durch Freude",' BA R 43 II/648a, pp. 1-2.

17. Harlan's claim: David Welch, *Propaganda and the German Cinema 1933-1945* (revised edition, Oxford, 1987) p. 234, cites Harlan's memoirs as evidence. Propaganda importance of film's message: *ibid.*, pp. 225-34. Growing defeatism and crisis of confidence: 'Bericht an das Reichsministerium für Volksaufklärung und Propaganda vom 28. März 1945,' Boberach (ed.), *Meldungen aus dem Reich*, vol. 17, pp. 6732-3; Gerald Kirwin, 'Allied Bombing and Nazi Domestic Propaganda,' *European History Quarterly*, vol. 15, 1985, pp. 356-7.

18. Submission to Lammers, 11 August 1944, 'Freimachung von Kräften der Reichspost für den totalen Kriegseinsatz,' BA R 43 II/665, pp. 1-4.
19. Bormann advised Goebbels of Hitler's response: Bormann to Goebbels, 14 August 1944, 'Planungen für den totalen Kriegseinsatz. Ihre Vorlage vom 9.8.44,' *ibid.*, pp. 1-2. Bormann told Ohnesorge: Bormann, Fernschreiben to Ohnesorge, 14 August 1944, *ibid.*, p. 2; Ohnesorge, 12 August 1944, 'Deutsche Reichspost und totaler Kriegseinsatz,' *Amtsblatt Nr. 258*, August 1944, Institut für Zeitgeschichte, *Akten der Parteikanzlei Teil I* (Munich, 1983-1985), 114 0007-11. Bormann points out to Ohnesorge: Bormann, Fernschreiben to Ohnesorge, 14 August 1944, BA R 43 II/665, p. 2. Goebbels proposes to overcome Hitler's objections: 'Führerinformation Nr. A I 465 17. August 1944 über Massnahmen des totalen Kriegseinsatzes,' BA R 43 II/666b, pp. 2-3. Goebbels opposed hometown papers: 'Führerinformation Nr. A 1 467 11. August 4 . . . ,' *ibid.*, p. 22.
20. Most measures introduced in two weeks: entry, 16 August 1944, von Oven, *Finale Furioso*, p. 459. Bormann unsuccessful in overcoming Hitler's opposition: 'Niederschrift über die Besprechung des Ausschusses vom 24. Juni 1943, 11 Uhr,' BA R 43 II/654a, pp. 4-5. Press communiqué announces dissolution of Prussian Finance Ministry and restriction of educational facilities: second 'Pressekommuniqué' (undated), BA R 43 II/666b, pp. 1-10. These communiqués are undated and have been numbered according to their order in the file. Restrictions on commercial life: third undated 'Pressekommuniqué,' BA R 43 II/666b, pp. 1-13. Staff unsuited to armaments work to be used: undated seventh 'Pressekommuniqué,' BA R 43 II/666a, p. 2. Employment of domestic servants: 'Anlage,' 'Sauckel, 'Erlass zur 7. Durchführungsverordnung vom 23.2.1943, Einsatz von Hausgehilfinnen,' in Bormann, 11 September 1944, 'Bekanntgabe 236/44,' BA NS 6/348, pp. 2-3. New rules would free 300,000 to 400,000 domestic servants: E. K. Bramsted, *Goebbels and National Socialist Propaganda 1925-1945* (East Lansing, Mich., 1965), pp. 353-4. Sauckel agrees to release 200,000 women: speech by Speer to meeting of chairmen of armaments commissions, 10 August 1944, BA R 3/1554, pp. 6-7. Effects of extension of reporting: Stephen Salter, 'The Mobilisation of German Labour, 1939-1945. A Contribution to the History of the Working Class in the Third Reich,' (unpublished D. Phil. thesis, Oxford, 1983), p. 84.
21. Measures adopted after 11 August: Mammach, *Volkssturm*, p. 20; first 'Pressekommuniqué,' undated, BA R 43 II/666b, pp. 11-13. Continuing simplifications: Willikens to Lammers, Bormann and others, 14 October 1944, IfZ *APK*, 101 02148-9; signature to Lammers, 4 September 1944, 101 02143; 'Verordnung über ausserordentliche Massnahmen im Pacht-, Landbewirtschaftungs- und Entschuldungsrecht aus Anlass des totalen Krieges. Vom. 11. Oktober 1944,' IfZ *APK*, 101 02259-62; Marrenbach to Naumann, 26 August 1944, IfZ *APK*, 117 08516-20. 42 per cent of Reich health office given up: Dr Gussmann to Pg. Vogt, Planungsausschuss, 1 September 1944, 'Überprüfung des Reichsgesundheitsamtes,' BA R 55/1221, pp. 1-2. The post office had freed over 250,000 men: Berger to Himmler, 14 July 1944, BA NS 19/3168, p. 2. Railways gave up 57,904 workers: signature to VO Transport head, 17 November 1944, 'Personalabgaben der Reichsbahn an die Wehrmacht,' BA MA RW 4/v.865. Goebbels orders end to planning: Schmidt-Leonhardt to all section heads, 27 October 1944, 'Einstellung von Planungsarbeiten,' BA R 55/711, pp. 1-2. Contin-

ued economies and reduction of positions in Propaganda Ministry: Prummer (?) to section heads, 9 August 1944, BA R 55/558; Esser to Goebbels, 10 September 1944, pp. 1-2; Naumann to Esser, 18 September 1944; *Der Fremdenverkehr*, September 1944 Nr. 19, in BA R 55/983, p. 3. Hayler's appointment: Bormann, 10 September 1944, 'Rundschreiben 230/44,' BA NS 6/348.

22. RR. Schmerling, 21 October 1944, '3 Monate "Totaler Kriegseinsatz." Eine systematische Darstellung der bisher getroffenen Massnahmen und ergangenen gesetzlichen Bestimmungen,' BA R 3/149, p. 6. Measures taken pp. 1-6.

23. Rebentisch, *Führerstaat und Verwaltung*, p. 523. Rebentisch suggests: *ibid.*, p. 518.

24. Orlow's argument: Dietrich Orlow, *The History of the Nazi Party*, Vol. II, 1933-1945 (Newton Abbot, 1973), pp. 469-70. Simplifications continue: Bisse and Jahoff, Reichsstelle für den Aussenhandel to Lammers, 21 September 1944, IfZ *APK*, 101 03325-6; see also measures listed in footnote 21.

25. Rebentisch, *Führerstaat und Verwaltung*, pp. 519-20.

26. Semler on problems: entry, 22 September 1944, Rudolf Semmler, *Goebbels—the Man Next to Hitler* (Ohio State University reprint, 1982, of London, 1947 edition), pp. 151-3. Armaments firms' reactions: Rebentisch, *Führerstaat und Verwaltung*, p. 522. Closures initially create unemployment: entry, 1 September 1944, von Oven, *Finale Furioso*, p. 463. Hierl believed unemployment would continue: entry, 10 September 1944, *ibid.*, pp. 473-4. Similar unemployment arose in Britain: Penny Summerfield, *Women Workers in the Second World War: Production and Patriarchy in Conflict* (second edition, London, 1989), p. 32.

27. Salter noted: Salter, 'Mobilisation of German Labour,' p. 108. Disagreement about numbers involved: undated, 'Stellungnahme WFSt/Org,' BA MA RW 4/v. 26. From August to October 1944 451,800 men were made available: Keitel to Goebbels, 11 November 1944, 'Abrechnung über den Wehrersatz August-Oktober 1944,' BA MA RW 6/v. 415, p. 3. German losses and men to front: Mammach, *Volkssturm*, pp. 21-2.

28. 'Deutsche Volkswirtschaft,' 'Wehrmacht-Ersatzplan 1945,' BA MA RW 6/v. 416, p. 3. Justice Ministry employees: Rebentisch, *Führerstaat und Verwaltung*, p. 524. German men available for employment: undated, 'A. Bevölkerung,' in 'Wehrmacht-Ersatzplan 1945,' BA MA RW 6/v. 416, pp. 1-3. 6.5 million in uk positions: 'B. b) Deutsche Volkswirtschaft,' *ibid.*, p. 4. Women in employment: *ibid.*, pp. 2-4. Work force in agriculture: 'B c) Landwirtschaft,' *ibid.*, p. 1. Local female labour force in industry: 'B e) Industrie (Gesamtbereich),' *ibid.*, pp. 2-3.

29. 'B. b) Deutsche Volkswirtschaft,' *ibid.*, pp. 2-3. Work force in agriculture: 'B c) Landwirtschaft,' *ibid.*, p. 1. Local female and male labour force in industry: 'B e) Industrie (Gesamtbereich),' *ibid.*, pp. 2-3.

30. 'B m) Wehrmachtbereich und Rüstungssicherung,' *ibid.*, p. 5. Reduction of staff in administrative sector: 'B i) Verwaltung,' *ibid.*, pp. 2-3. AWA assumes more women can be employed: *ibid.*, pp. 3-4. Employment in armaments sector: 'B m) Wehrmachtbereich und Rüstungssicherung,' *ibid.*, pp. 1-2.

31. Other statistical authorities' views: Dr Luyken, draft 1943 speech, 'Aktuelle Tagesfragen der Statistik,' BA R 41/284, p. 15. Percentage of women employed in agriculture: Ingrid Schupetta, *Frauen- und Ausländererwerbstätigkeit in Deutschland von 1939 bis 1945* (second edition, Darmstadt, 1988), p. 39.

Mithelfende Familienangehoerigen in agriculture: Stefan Bajohr, *Die Hälfte der Fabrik: Geschichte der Faruenarbeit in Deutschland 1914 bis 1945* (Marburg, 1979), p. 21. Women handled most agricultural work in war: Kurt Wagner, Gerhard Wilke, 'Dorffleben im Dritten Reich: Körle in Hessen,' in Detlev Peukert and Jürgen Reulecke (eds.), with the collaboration of Adelheid Gräfin zu Castell Rüdenhausen, *Die Reihen fast geschlossen: Beiträge zur Geschichte des Alltags unterm Nationalsozialismus* (Wuppertal, 1981), p. 101. Domestic servants as agricultural workers on farms: Tim Mason, 'Zum Frauenarbeit im NS-Staat,' *Archiv für Sozialgeschichte*, vol. 19, 1979, p. 583. Domestic servants allow small businesses to continue: Stephenson, ' "Emancipation" and its Problems: War and Society in Württemberg 1939-45,' *European History Quarterly*, vol. 17, 1987, p. 352.

32. Different historians' views: R. J. Overy, ' "Blitzkriegwirtschaft"? Finanzpolitik, Lebensstandard und Arbeitseinsatz in Deutschland 1939-1942,' *Vierteljahrshefte für Zeitgeschichte*, vol. 36, 1988, pp. 429-30; Tilla Siegel, *Leistung und Lohn in der nationalsozialistischen "Ordnung der Arbeit"* (Opladen, 1989), pp. 172-3; Marie-Luise Recker, *Nationalsozialistische Sozialpolitik im Zweiten Weltkrieg* (Munich, 1985), p. 193. The British figures are taken from W. K. Hancock and M. M. Gowing, *British War Economy* (London, 1949), note, p. 372; American figures from Alan S. Milward, 'Arbeitspolitik und Productivität in der deutschen Kriegswirtschaft unter vergleichendem Aspekt,' in Friedrich Forstmeier and Hans-Erich Volkmann (eds.), *Kriegswirtschaft und Rüstung 1939-1945* (Dusseldorf, 1977), p. 88. German percentage of women employed increased by one per cent: Leila J. Rupp, 'Women, Class, and Mobilization in Nazi Germany,' *Science and Society*, vol. 43, 1979, p. 53. German figures are taken from Burton H. Klein, *Germany's Economic Preparations for War* (Cambridge, Mass., 1959), p. 68 and Rupp, 'Women, Class and Mobilization in Nazi Germany,' p. 53. In *Mobilizing Women* Rupp gives lower figures for German female participation rates (35.6 per cent in 1943), but her figures are taken as a percentage of all German women, not only those of working age, and she admits that they underestimate the German participation rate: Leila J. Rupp, *Mobilizing Women for War: German and American Propaganda, 1939-1945* (Princeton, N. J., 1978), pp. 184-6. If Koonz's higher figure of female participation in 1939 (49.2 per cent) is used, then German female participation rose above 50 per cent during the war: Claudia Koonz, *Mothers of the Fatherland: Women, the Family and Nazi Politics* (London, 1987), note 47 p. 471. Overy's arguments: Overy, ' "Blitzkriegswirtschaft"?,' p. 426. German women as percentage of civilian work force: Rupp, *Mobilizing Women*, pp. 185-6. Soviet women's employment: Alan S. Milward, *War, Economy and Society 1939-1945* (Berkeley, Calif., 1977), p. 220.

33. Women's voluntary work: 'Nachrichten der Reichsfrauenführung für die Mai-Ausgabe vom Parteiarchiv,' [1941], BA NS 44/37, pp. 3-4. Women volunteers adapt materials from winter clothing campaign: Bramsted, *Goebbels and National Socialist Propaganda*, p. 250. Volunteer numbers hard to assess: Georg Tidl, *Die Frau im Nationalsozialismus* (Vienna, 1984), pp. 112-13. Bormann claimed these age groups already in war work: Bormann Fernschreiben to Lammers, 4 November 1944, 'Entwurf eines Fuehrererlasses über den weiblichen Wehrhilfsdienst,' BA R 43 II/666c, p. 4. Main untapped group: Schupetta, *Frauen- und Ausländerer-werbstätigkeit*, pp. 137-8.

34. Berger's proposals: Berger to Naumann, 16 August 1944, BA NS 19/2844, pp. 1-6. Ohlendorf approaches Speer: Albert Speer, *The Slave State: Heinrich Himmler's Masterplan for SS Supremacy* (London, 1981), pp. 72-3.

35. Entry, 28 November 1953, Speer, *Spandau: The Secret Diaries* (London, 1978), p. 235. Speer's initial response positive: speech to Tagung Hauptausschuss Waffen, 10 August 1944, BA R 3/1554, p. 13. Speer promised equipment: entry, 16 August 1944, von Oven, *Finale Furioso*, p. 459. Speer saw possibility to gain 1.3 million: speech by Speer to armaments commissioners, 19 September 1944, BA R 3/1555, p. 6. Speer ordered suggestions: Speer decree to section heads, 27 July 1944, BA R 3/1634, pp. 1-3. Speer's ministry's August suggestions: signature, 4 August 1944, 'Vorschläge zur Gewinnung zusätzlicher Arbeitskräfte in Zuge der totalen Kriegsmassnahmen,' BA R 3/1580, pp. 1-3. Goebbels wants overall reduction of administrative work: Stuckart Schnellbrief to ORBs, 18 September 1944, IfZ *APK*, 114 0005-6. Staffing of Armaments Ministry reduced by 30 per cent: Speer decree to section heads, 27 July 1944, BA R 3/1634, pp. 1-3.

36. Speer to Gauleiter Wegener, 11 August 1944, BA R 3/1605, pp. 1-2.

37. Speer wants film and theatre tradesmen in armaments: Speer to Goebbels, 11 August 1944, BA R 3/1580. Speer on Hungarian Jewish prisoners: Speer to Goebbels, August 1944, *ibid.*, pp. 1-2.

38. Speer to Keitel, 11 August 1944, BA R 3/1615, pp. 1-2.

39. Goebbels to all Gauleiters, 11 August 1944, pp. 1-2, and the attachment, Speer to Betriebsführer, 8 August 1944, BA R 3/1615, pp. 3-4.

40. Speer protests at Gauleiters' refusal: Speer Fernschreiben to Bormann, 18 September 1944, BA R 3/1615, pp. 1-2. Hitler orders fortifications: Franz W. Seidler, *"Deutscher Volkssturm": Das letzte Aufgebot 1944/45* (Munich, 1989), p. 33. Bormann orders their return: Speer Chronik, September 1944, BA R 3/1740, p. 258.

41. Goebbels advised Gauleiters of creation of new fighting divisions: Goebbels Fernschreiben to all Gauleiters, 17 August 1944, 'Aufstellung neuer Kampfdivisionen,' BA R 3/1615, pp. 1-3. Speer claimed Gauleiters not keeping their agreement: Speer to Goebbels, 25 August 1944, *ibid.*, p. 2. Middle-level armaments officers experienced pressure from Gauleiters: Speer Chronik, August 1944, BA R 3/1740, p. 228.

42. 'Telefongespräch Reichsminister Speer-MinRat Dr. Klein vom Reichsbevollmächtigten für den totalen Kriegseinsatz am 1. September 1944,' BA R 3/1615, pp. 1-6.

43. Goebbels and Speer clash, and Goebbels' subsequent reaction: entry, 1 September 1944, von Oven, *Finale Furioso*, pp. 462-4. Results of Speer's appeal to Hitler: entry, 3 September 1944, *ibid.*, pp. 467-9.

44. Speer to Goebbels, 4 September 1944, BA R 3/1615, pp. 1-4.

45. Speer refuses responsibility for production breaches: Speer to all Gauleiters, 5 September 1944, 'Einberufungsaktion,' *ibid.*, pp. 1-2. Speer advises guidelines still in force: Speer to Rüstungsinspektionen, 5 September 1944, *ibid.* Telegram to all Gauleiters from Speer, Goebbels and Bormann: Speer, Goebbels and Bormann Fernschreiben to all Gauleiters, 8 September 1944, *ibid.*, pp. 1-4.

46. Speer Chronik for August 1944, BA R 3/1740, p. 228. German losses in West: Seidler, *"Deutscher Volkssturm,"* p. 27. Bormann lacked sympathy for Speer's

demands: letter Martin Bormann to Gerda Bormann, 8-9 September 1944, H. R. Trevor-Roper (ed.), *The Bormann Letters: The Private Correspondence between Martin Bormann and His Wife from January 1943 to April 1945* (London, 1954), p. 104. He believed that armaments, railways and the post never made numbers requested available: Bormann to Himmler, 2 July 1944, 'Wehrersatz aus der Landwirtschaft,' BA NS 19/3631. In September Speer told Goebbels: Speer to Goebbels, 15 September 1944, BA R 3/1615, p. 3. Troops without weapons: speech by Speer to armaments commissioners, 19 September 1944, BA R 3/1555, p. 4.

47. Speer to Goebbels, 15 September 1944, BA R 3/1615, p. 3. Goebbels' hopes for levée en masse: Albert Speer, *Inside the Third Reich* (London, 1970), p. 419.

48. Speer Chronik, September 1944, BA R 3/1740, p. 252.

49. Speer's concern to protect his own power base: Matthias Schmidt, *Albert Speer— The End of a Myth* (London, 1985), p. 122. Speer wants women in armaments industry exempted: Speer to Goebbels, 20 September 1944, BA R 3/1580. Speer believed they could not dispense with Reichspatentamt: Speer to Goebbels, 23 September 1944, *ibid.*, pp. 1-3. Speer requested Goebbels to abandon plans to form a committee: Speer to Goebbels, 25 September 1944, *ibid.*, pp. 1-2.

50. Mierzejewski, *Collapse of the German War Economy*, p. 96. Speer's letter to Hitler: Exhibit Speer-1, 20 September 1944, *Trial of the Major War Criminals before the International Military Tribunal, Nuremberg, 14 November 1945-1 October 1946* (official text, reprint of 1947-49 edition, New York, 1971), vol. 41, pp. 394-401, allegations of Bormann and Goebbels at p. 395.

51. Speer, *Third Reich*, p. 398. Speer faced disobedience and less co-operation: Mierzejewski, *Collapse of the German War Economy*, pp. 90, 96, 113-14. Speer pointed out: Exhibit Speer-1, *TMWC*, vol. 41, pp. 394, 398. Bormann told Speer: Speer, *Third Reich*, p. 398. Speer able to gain a note from Hitler: Hitler, 23 September 1944, 'An die Betriebsführer der deutschen Rüstung und Kriegsproduktion,' BA R 3/1615. Bormann's advice to Gauleiters to evade Hitler's order: Orlow, *Nazi Party*, II, p. 472.

52. Hitler advised by Planungsausschuss: Dr Klein, Planungsausschuss, 25 September 1944, 'Führerinformation,' BA R 3/1615, p. 1. Response of industrialists at August meeting: Speer Chronik, August 1944, BA R 3/1740, p. 230. Speer reprimanded Gauleiters: Speer Fernschreiben to Gauleiter Rainer of Kärnten, 9 October 1944, BA R 3/1595.

53. Gauleiter's opinions asked: Dr Klein, Planungsausschuss, 25 September 1944, 'Führerinformation,' BA R 3/1615, p. 2. Speer's own submission argued: Speer, 26 September 1944, 'Stellungnahme zur Führerinformation v. Dr Goebbels,' BA R 3/1527, pp. 1-2.

54. Bormann's claims: Bormann, 1 October 1944, 'Rundschreiben 293/44,' BA R 3/1615, pp. 1-2. Janssen's explanation: Gregor Janssen, *Das Ministerium Speer. Deutschlands Rüstung im Krieg* (Berlin, 1968), p. 280. Industry leaders had to face possibility: Bormann, 1 October 1944, 'Rundschreiben 293/44,' BA R 3/1615, pp. 1-2.

55. Hitler agreed to giving up 60,000 earlier: Janssen, *Ministerium Speer*, p. 277. Speer objected: Speer Fernschreiben to Bormann, 3 October 1944, BA R 3/1573, pp. 1-2. Speer pointed out he had given up 50,000 voluntarily: Speer to Guderian, 3 October 1944, BA R 3/1581, pp. 1-2. Speer turned to Göring: Speer to Göring, 3 October

1944, BA R 3/1615, pp. 1-2. Speer objected to Hitler that decision serious: Speer to Hitler, 3 October 1944, BA R 3/1527, pp. 1-4. Goebbels later blamed Speer: entries for 4 and 13 October 1944, and 8 February 1945, von Oven, *Finale Furioso*, pp. 490-1, 495, 575-6.

56. Hitler places programmes under complete protection: Janssen, *Ministerium Speer*, p. 280. Speer must agree to co-responsibility of Gauleiters: Orlow, *Nazi Party*, II, p. 480.

57. Speer to Goebbels, 20 September 1944, BA R 3/1615, pp. 1-3.

58. Speer speech, 'Dienstbesprechung der Vorsitzer der Rüstungs-kommissionen, Rüstungsinspekteure und Wehrkreisbeauftragte,' 19 September 1944, BA R 3/1554, pp. 7-9.

59. Mierzejewski, *Collapse of the German War Economy*, p. 120. Munitions production first to drop: Alan S. Milward, *The German Economy at War* (London, 1967), p. 163. Reasons for falls in production: *ibid.*, pp. 163, 165, 180-1, 184-5. Mierzejewski's research: Mierzejewski, *Collapse of the German War Economy*, p. 119. 60. Speer described his position: Fernschreiben Berger to Himmler, 31 October 1944, BA NS 19/2058, p. 2. Speer criticised for earlier decisions: Bormann file note, 7 August 1944, 'Aktenvermerk für Pg. Friedrichs, IIM., Pg. Dr Klopfer, Pg. Schütt, Berlin,' BA NS 6/785, pp. 2-3. Speer claimed that armaments production was continuing to rise and that it was usually higher than US production: unsigned, 11 August 1944, 'Protokoll der Besprechung am 11. August 1944,' BA R 3/1987, pp. 3-8. No signs of production arriving at front: Bormann file note, 3 November 1944, 'Aktenvermerk für Pg. Dr Klopfer,' 'Rücksprache mit Reichsminister Speer,' BA NS 6/785, p. 2. Speer's production claims exaggerated: Willi A. Boelcke (ed.), *Deutschlands Rüstung im Zweiten Weltkrieg: Hitlers Konferenzen mit Albert Speer 1942-1945* (Frankfurt, 1969), pp. 7-8, 25. Reports large industrial firms transferring production: SS-Sturmbannführer Backhaus, Agriculture Minister's office, to Brandt, 26 August 1944, BA NS 19/830, p. 1; SS-Scharführer signature, 26 December 1944, 'Vermerk,' BA NS 19/488. Bormann's description of Speer: Bormann file note, 3 November 1944, 'Aktenvermerk für Pg. Dr Klopfer,' 'Rücksprache mit Reichsminister Speer,' BA NS 6/785, p. 2. Bormann saw Speer allying himself with Göring against Goebbels and Bormann: Martin Bormann to Gerda Bormann, 4 November 1944, Trevor-Roper (ed.), *Bormann Letters*, p. 146. Goebbels noted Bormann, Himmler and all Gauleiters opposed Speer: entry, 1 September 1944, von Oven, *Finale Furioso*, p. 464. Homze claims: Edward L. Homze, *Foreign Labor in Nazi Germany* (Princeton, N. J., 1967), p. 227.

61. Speer claims Goebbels came out as his enemy: entry, 28 November 1953, Speer, *Spandau*, p. 235.

62. Hitler decides in favour of one man then the other: Speer, *Third Reich*, p. 398. Guns and weapons needed: Janssen, *Ministerium Speer*, p. 277. Speer's assurances contributed to Goebbels' demands: entry, 18 October 1944, von Oven, *Finale Furioso*, p. 500. Speer defending his power base: Schmidt, *Speer Myth*, p. 123. Armaments previously gained staff: Boelcke (ed.), *Hitlers Konferenzen*, pp. 20-1.

Chapter 9

1. Account of military developments in 1945: Peter Calvocoressi, Guy Wint and John Pritchard, *Total War: The Causes and Courses of the Second World War*, Peter Calvocoressi, *Volume I: The Western Hemisphere* (second edition, London, 1989), pp. 561-9. Speer claims Hitler and Bormann still optimistic: Albert Speer, *Inside the Third Reich* (London, 1970), p. 419. Remaining civilian life disrupted: entries, 21 January, 29 January and 19 April 1945, Wilfred von Oven, *Finale Furioso: Mit Goebbels bis zum Ende* (first published 1948-50, Tübingen, 1974), pp. 549, 557-60, 647-9. Anti-fascist resistance: Martin Broszat, 'Teil II. Lage der Arbeiterschaft, Arbeiteropposition, Aktivität und Verfolgung der illegalen Arbeiterbewegung 1933-1944,' in Martin Broszat, Elke Fröhlich and Falk Wiesemann. (eds.), *Bayern in der NS-Zeit: soziale Lage und politisches Verhalten der Bevölkerung im Spiegel vertraulicher Berichte* (Munich, 1977), pp. 321-2, and document 'Bericht über die Vorgänge in Penzberg am 28.4.1945,' *ibid.*, pp. 322-5.

2. Some hoping for miracle weapons: Elke Fröhlich, 'Teil VII. Stimmung und Verhalten der Bevölkerung unter den Bedingungen des Krieges C. Berichte aus oberbayrischen Landeskreisen und Gemeinden 1944/45,' *ibid.*, p. 665. Speer disclaims responsibility for 'secret weapon' propaganda: Speer speech to 3. Lehrgang of commanding generals, 13 January 1945, BA R 3/1556, pp. 31-2; but see Matthias Schmidt, *Albert Speer—The End of a Myth* (London, 1985), pp. 112-17, for Speer's role in continuing this propaganda, and his role in maintaining Goebbels' belief in the new weapons, entry, 14 November 1944, Rudolf Semmler, *Goebbels—the Man Next to Hitler* (Ohio State University reprint, 1982, of London, 1947 edition), pp. 165-6. Hopes for collapse of enemy alliance: David Irving, *Göring: A Biography* (New York, 1989), p. 18. Last-minute peace negotiations: Leonidas E. Hill (ed.), *Die Weiszäcker-Papiere 1933-1950* (Frankfurt, 1974), pp. 388-404; Hansjakob Stehle, 'Deutsche Friedensfühler bei den Westmächten im Februar/März 1945,' in Karl Dietrich Bracher, Manfred Funke and Hans-Adolf Jacobsen (eds.), *Nationalsozialistische Diktatur 1933-1945: eine Bilanz* (Dusseldorf, 1983), pp. 509-28. Goebbels and Himmler agree, and Goebbels' plans: entry, 15 February 1945, Semmler, *Goebbels*, pp. 179-80; entry, 7 March 1945, Hugh Trevor-Roper (ed.), *Final Entries 1945: The Diaries of Joseph Goebbels* (New York, 1978), p. 71. SS continues to try to use Vlasov: Berger, Fernschreiben to Himmler, 28 January 1945, 'Gen. Wlassow,' BA NS 19/732. Himmler sees Vlasov as of great importance: Himmler, Fernschreiben to SS-Obergruppenführer Wolff, 30 January 1945, *ibid.*

3. Himmler Fernschreiben to Hofer, 18 February 1945, BA NS 19/3298. Himmler's responsibilities as commander of Army Group: 'Befehl des Führers vom 21.1.1945,' BA NS 6/354. Himmler's lack of success with Army Group Upper Rhine: Burton Wright III, 'Army of Despair: The German Volkssturm 1944-1945' (Florida State University, Ph. D. thesis, 1982), pp. 75-6. Himmler unsuccessful and replaced by Heinrici: Cornelius Ryan, *The Last Battle* (London, 1968), pp. 74-6, 82-5. This weakened Himmler's position: entries, 11 and 30 March 1945, Trevor-Roper (ed.), *Final Entries*, pp. 103, 281. Himmler replaced as head of army armaments and Speer's comments: Speer, *Third Reich*, p. 420 and note on same page.

4.   Signature, submission, 15 February 1945, 'Staatssekretärbesprechung am 15.2. 14.00 Uhr. Vortragsnotiz,' BA MA RW 4/ v. 703, p. 3. Effects of bombing on morale: von Hengl, head of the army NS-Führungstab, 8 April 1945, '1.) Ergebnis der Untersuchung bei Gauleiter Wegener und Heeresgruppe H Grund der Meldung des Gauleiters über Tätigkeit feindlicher Agenten in deutscher Offiziersuniform,' BA MA RW 6/ v. 406. Leaders recognise effects of bombing: entry, 12 March 1945, Trevor-Roper (ed.), *Final Entries*, p. 113. RPÄ reports suggest: Marlis G. Steinert, *Hitler's War and the Germans: Public Mood and Attitude during the Second World War* (Athens, Ohio, 1977), pp. 302-3. Protests at food shortages: Wolfgang Werner, *'Bleib übrig!' Deutsche Arbeiter in der nationalsozialistischen Kriegswirtschaft'* (Dusseldorf, 1983), p. 358. Local efforts at resistance: Steinert, *Hitler's War and the Germans*, p. 312.

5.   Millions of refugees: Earl R. Beck, *Under the Bombs: The German Home Front 1942-1945* (Lexington, Mass., 1986), p. 174. Central co-ordination more difficult: Dieter Rebentisch, *Führerstaat und Verwaltung im Zweiten Weltkrieg: Verfassungsentwicklung und Verwaltungspolitik 1939-1945* (Stuttgart, 1989), p. 529. Rebentisch has suggested: *ibid.*

6.   Increasing decentralisation and evacuation of ministries: Uwe D. Adam, 'Persecution of the Jews, Bureaucracy and Authority in the Totalitarian State,' *Leo Baeck Institute Year Book*, vol. 29, 1978, p. 141. Schools closed to make room for refugees: Bormann, 21 January 1945, 'Rundschreiben 16/45,' BA NS 6/353. Plans of meetings of state secretaries: signature, 8 March 1945, 'Vortragsnotiz,' 'Staatssekretärsbesprechung am 8.3.45,' pp. 1-2; signature, 6 March 1945, 'Vortragsnotiz,' 'Staatssekretärsbesprechung am 5.3.1945,' BA MA RW 4/v. 703, pp. 1-3. Himmler rejects Hofer's attempt to seek exemption; Himmler, Fernschreiben to Hofer, 18 February 1945, BA NS 19/3298.

7.   Bormann, 15 February 1945, 'Rundschreiben 81/45g,' BA NS 6/354, p. 1. February ban on evacuation of offices from Berlin: Hauptreferat Pro W (Dr Dorsch?), 21? February 1945, 'Verlagerungen,' BA R 55/622, pp. 1-2. Goebbels favour a policy of removal only with express approval: Naumann to Leiter Pro., 17 February 1945, *ibid.*, p. 1. Evacuation east of Rhine planned: signature, 15 February 1945, 'Vortragsnotiz,' 'Staatssekretärsbesprechung am 15.2. 1400 Uhr,' BA MA RW 4/ v. 703, pp. 2-3. Hitler orders evacuation of population behind area of Army Group West: Bormann to Gauleiter Essen and others, 24 March 1945, 'Räumungsmassnahmen im Westen,' BA MA RW 4/v. 704, pp. 1-2. Hitler's order on evacuation of threatened areas: Bormann to Gauleiter Essen, 24 March 1945, 'Räumungsmassnahmen im Westen,' *ibid.*, pp. 1-2. Bormann's advice: Bormann, 23 March 1945, 'Rundschreiben 166/45 g. RS,' BA NS 6/354, pp. 1-2. Instructions ignored because they could not be followed: entries, 13 March, 27 March and 4 April 1945, Trevor-Roper (ed.), *Final Entries*, pp. 124, 244, 314.

8.   Signature, WFSt/Qu. Nr. 003766/45 g. Kdos, 19 April 1945, 'Staatssekretärbesprechung am 18.4.1945,' BA MA RW 4/v. 703, pp. 1-3.

9.   Berger was urging need for central office: Berger to Himmler, 27 January 1945, 'Ersatzwesen,' BA NS 19/4, pp. 1-2. Hitler decides to call up 80,000 men a month: record for 3-5 January 1945, Willi A. Boelcke (ed.), *Deutschlands Rüstung im Zweiten Weltkrieg: Hitlers Konferenzen mit Albert Speer 1942-1945* (Frankfurt, 1969), p. 466. Goebbels inspects Luftwaffe: Goebbels to Hitler, 20 March 1945, BA NL 118/106, pp. 1-4. Himmler's order to all available SS leaders: SS-

Hauptsturmführer sig to Gen. v. Herff, Chef des SS-Personalhauptamtes, Schnellbrief, 31 March 1945, 'RFSS-Befehl: Freigabe von SS-Führern (kv. und bedingt kv.) durch die Hauptämter der SS,' BA NS 34/17. Bormann circular on legal sanctions: Bormann, 1 February 1945, 'Rundschreiben 50/45,' BA NS 6/353, pp. 1-3. Wehrersatzamt's conclusions about number called up: Wehrersatzamt Abt. E (Id), April 1945, 'Abrechnung über die Einberufungen in der Zeit vom 3.1.-27.3.45,' BA MA RW 4/v. 26, pp. 1-2.

10. Speer defending firms in January: Speer to Goebbels, 23 January 1945, 'Einberufungen von Wehrpflichtigen der Geb. Jahrg. 00 und älter aus der kriegswichtigen gewerblichen Wirtschaft,' BA R 3/1580, pp. 1-2. In February Speer told Goebbels: Speer to Goebbels, 15 February 1945, *ibid.*, pp. 1-2. On same day Speer countered Goebbels' assumption: Speer to Goebbels, 15 February 1945, *ibid.*, p. 1.

11. Speer on Front-OT: Speer to Keitel, 19 January 1945, 'SE VI-Aktion,' BA R 3/1586. Himmler inspects OT: Himmler to Speer, 14 February 1945, 'Überprüfung und Vereinfachung der Organisations- und Verwaltungsgrundlagen der OT,' BA NS 19/3374.

12. Speer's meeting with Naumann: Dr Schmelter, 15 February 1945, 'Vermerk über die Besprechung Reichsminister Speer—Staatsekretär Dr Naumann,' BA R 3/1580, p. 1. Bormann's subsequent circular: Bormann, 23 February 1945, 'Rundschreiben 100/45 g,' BA NS 6/354. Letter from Bormann, Goebbels and Speer: 'Anlage' to 'Rundschreiben 100/45g,' 17 February 1945, Bormann, Goebbels and Speer, *ibid.*, pp. 2-3.

13. Armed forces called up men to class of 1886: Bormann, 14 February 1945, 'Bekanntgabe 93/45g,' BA NS 19/772, pp. 1-3. Call up of 6000 16-year-olds: Bormann, 28 February 1945, 'Vermerk für Pg. Friedrichs und Pg. Dr Klopfer,' 'Verstärkung der kämpfenden Truppe,' BA NS 6/785, p. 1. Desertion increases: Manfred Messerschmidt, 'Krieg in der Trümmerlandschaft. "Pflichterfüllung" wofür?' in Ulrich Borsdorf and Mathilde Jamin (eds.), *Überleben im Krieg. Kriegserfahrungen in einer Industrieregion 1939-1945* (Hamburg, 1989), pp. 173-5. Bormann's concern about soldiers on leave: Bormann, 28 February 1945, 'Vermerk für Pg. Friedrichs und Pg. Dr Klopfer,' 'Verstärkung der kämpfenden Truppe,' BA NS 6/785, pp. 3-4. March order on seizing deserters: Bormann, 10 March 1945, 'Anordnung 129/45g,' BA NS 6/354, p. 1, Keitel's attached order, p. 4. Other members of leadership concerned: entries, 3 and 7 March 1945, Trevor-Roper (ed.), *Final Entries*, pp. 33-4, 70.

14. Bormann, 28 February 1945, 'Vermerk für Pg. Friedrichs und Pg. Dr Klopfer,' 'Verstärkung der kämpfenden Truppe,' BA NS 6/785, p. 1. These plans never realised: Jeff M. Tuten, 'Germany and the World Wars,' in Nancy Loring Goldman (ed.), *Female Soldiers—Combatants or Noncombatants? Historical and Contemporary Perspectives* (Westport, Conn., 1982), p. 56. Women equipped with hand weapons: Franz W. Seidler, *"Deutscher Volkssturm" : Das letzte Aufgebot 1944/45* (Munich, 1989), p. 69. Hitler orders first priority to protect women: Keitel, 23 March 1945, 'Einsatz von Frauen und Mädchen in der Wehrmacht,' BA MA RW 4/v. 865, pp. 1-2. Women used to build trenches: Klaus Mammach, *Der Volkssturm: Das Letzte Aufgebot 1944/45* (Cologne, 1981), p. 27. Women used in 'Werewolf' and others: Georg Tidl, *Die Frau im Nationalsozialismus* (Vienna, 1984), p. 26.

15. Weaknesses of fortifications and defensive lines: John D. Heyl, 'The Construction of the *Westwall*, 1938: An Exemplar for National Socialist Policymaking,' *Central European History*, vol. 14, 1981, p. 63. Hitler decides on use of labour at focal points: Bormann, 10 February 1945, 'Rundschreiben 66/45 g. Rs,' BA NS 6/354, pp. 1-3. Speer recommends use of Party: Speer, 15 January 1945, 'Bericht über die Reise nach den Westgebieten vom 15.-31. Dezember 1944,' BA MA RW 4/v. 497, p. 10.

16. Greater reliance on ideology: Bormann, Fernschreiben to all Reichsleiter, 7 April 1945, BA NS 6/134, p. 2. Concern from Himmler and Party Chancellery: Brandt to Berger, 25 January 1945, 'Einrichtung von NS-Führungsoffiziere mit Sondervollmachten,' BA NS 19/750, p. 1. Political activation and fanaticising most important: Bormann, 14 March 1945, 'Rundschreiben 148/45,' BA NS 6/353, pp. 1-3. Wants propaganda strengthened and Wehrmacht to speak to people: Ruder, 5 March 1945, 'Vermerk für Pg. Friedrichs Pg. Schütt,' BA NS 6/137. Noack suggested: Noack, 9 March 1945, 'Entwurf. Propagandaanweisung für die Wehrmacht,' BA NS 6/137, p. 3.

17. Walkenhorst's report: Walkenhorst, 10 April 1945, 'Vorlage,' 'NS-Führung in Heer, Luftwaffe und Marine,' BA NS 6/144, pp. 1-2. Officials believed Reinecke had failed: Ruder, 20 February 1945, 'Vorlage,' 'Nationalsozialistische Führung in der Wehrmacht,' *ibid.*, pp. 1-3. Bormann suggested a direct role: Ruder, 19 February 1945, 'Aktenvermerk,' 'Vortrag bei Reichsleiter Bormann am 17.2,' *ibid.*, p. 1.

18. Bormann's comments on the side of Hess's document, BA NS 6/144, pp. 1-2, quotation at p. 1. Opposing streams stronger than Party Chancellery: Bürgel, 4 April 1945, 'Vermerk für Pg. Walkenhorst,' 'NS-Führung in Heer, Luftwaffe und Marine,' *ibid.*, pp. 1-3. Uneasy interregnum because Hitler does not sign decree: Hess, 29 March 1945, 'Vorlage,' 'NS-Führung der Wehrmacht. Führerbefehl vom 13.3.45. Auflösung des NS-Führungsstabes beim OKW,' *ibid.*, p. 1.

19. Bormann, 10 March 1945, 'Anordnung 129/45 g,' BA NS 6/354, p. 3. Party leaders urged to carry out orders with determination: Bormann, 1 February 1945, 'Anordnung 48/45g,' *ibid.*, pp. 1-2.

20. Bormann, 15 April 1945, 'Rundschreiben 211/45,' BA NS 6/353. Political leaders had to report or be treated as deserters: Bormann, 12 February 1945, 'Anordnung 74/45,' *ibid.*, pp. 1-2. Bormann calls for exemplary leadership: Bormann, 23 February 1945, 'Anordnung 98/45,' *ibid.*, pp. 1-2.

21. Bormann, 21 March 1945, 'Anordnung 155/45,' *ibid.*, p. 1.

22. Entry, 7 February 1945, von Oven, *Finale Furioso*, p. 572. Political leaders had to fight or fall: Bormann Fernschreiben to all Reichsleiters, Gauleiters and Verbändeführer, 1 April 1945, 'Anordnung,' BA NS 6/353, p. 1. Bormann and Hitler unwilling to consider behind-the-lines resistance: Rudolf Jordan, *Erlebt und Erlitten: Weg eines Gauleiters von München bis Moskau*, (Leoni am Starnberger See, 1971), pp. 264-5. Leadership aware of failings of Gauleiters and Party: entries, 27 March 1945 and 3 April 1945, Trevor-Roper (ed.), *Final Entries*, pp. 251, 303-5; Speer's farewell letter to Hanke, 14 April 1945, BA R 3/1582.

23. Quoted, entry, 26 March 1945, von Oven, *Finale Furioso*, p. 623.

24. Failure of Party and civilian offices to withstand evacuation psychosis: Himmler to Hofmann HSSPF Südwest, 29 November 1944, BA NS 19/2230, pp. 1-2.

Proposal to use political leaders in endangered Gaus: Ruder, 24 February 1945, 'Vorlage,' 'Sondereinsatz der Parteikanzlei: zur Verstärkung der Partei in frontnähen Gebieten,' BA NS 6/169, p. 2; Bormann to Keitel, 15 March 1945, pp. 1-3 and Bormann to Henlein, 'Sondereinsatz der Partei-Kanzlei in frontnahen Gebieten,' BA NS 6/169, pp. 1-3. Berger criticised proposals: Berger to Brandt, 18 February 1945, 'Politische Kampfkommandanten,' BA NS 19/3833, pp. 1-2. Bormann refused to believe increasing hostility to the Party: Steinert, *Hitler's War and the Germans*, p. 308. Policy also involved sending Party leaders but was unsuccessful: Dietrich Orlow, *The History of the Nazi Party*, Vol. II, 1933-1945 (Newton Abbot, 1973), p. 480. SS ensure resistance continued: Ryan, *Last Battle*, pp. 227-8, 344, 379. Himmler pointed out he would have SS leaders shot: Himmler to Hofmann, 29 November 1944, BA NS 19/2230, pp. 1-2.

25. Bormann and Himmler's reactions to Dotzler's paper: Dotzler, 23 January 1945, 'Abschrift Vorschläge zum Aufbau einer Widerstandsbewegung in den von den Bolschewisten besetzten deutschen Ostgebieten,' pp. 1-3; Bormann to Himmler, 27 January 1945, pp. 1-4; Himmler to Bormann, 8 February 1945, BA NS 19/832. OKW aware Germans behind the lines did not resist: undated paper, 'Anlage 1. Bericht über die Lage in den besetzten deutschen Ostgebieten,' BA MA RW 4/v. 705, p. 9.

26. Germans had to reduce enemy's strength: Bormann, 10 March 1945, 'Rundschreiben 128/45 g. Rs,' BA NS 6/354, pp. 1-2. Enemy had to be taught no weapon against Werewolf: Bormann Fernschreiben to all Reichsleiter, Gauleiter and Verbändeführer, 7 April 1945, BA NS 6/134, pp. 1-2.

27. Entry, 2 April 1945, Trevor-Roper (ed.), *Final Entries*, p. 297. Doubts about serious functioning of Werewolf: Charles Whiting, *Werewolf: The Story of the Nazi Resistance Movement 1944-1945* (London, 1972), pp. 146-8, 188-9. Goebbels hopes it encourages popular resistance: entries, 29 and 31 March, 1, 2 and 3 April 1945, Trevor-Roper (ed.), *Final Entries*, pp. 269, 289, 296, 297, 304.

28. Entry, 27 March 1945, Trevor-Roper (ed.), *Final Entries*, p. 250. Goebbels wants withdrawal from Geneva Convention but is opposed: entries, 27 March 1945 and 30 March 1945, *ibid.*, pp. 250, 278.

29. Volkssturm not trained in partisan warfare: Wright, 'Army of Despair,' p. 22. Himmler pointed to need for training in partisan warfare: 'Rede des Reichsführers-SS in Grafenwoehr am 25.7.1944,' BA NS 19/4015, p. 19. Use of Volkssturm to counter army defeatism: 'Bericht des Dienstleiters der Partei-Kanzlei, Pg. Mauer, der sich als Oberstleutnant seit 30.1.45 zusammen mit den Parteigenossen Alt und Beringer im NSFO-Sondereinsatz im Bereich des Heeresgruppe Schörner befindet,' BA NS 6/169, pp. 1-2. Volkssturm men not to be withdrawn from important civilian activities: Bormann, Himmler and Keitel, 28 March 1945, 'Verwendung des Deutschen Volkssturms,' BA MA RW 4/v. 495, p. 1. Volkssturm units to be employed in direct enemy threat: Bormann, 1 March 1945, 'Rundschreiben 30/45,' with Anlage, pp. 1-2; 2 April 1945, 'Anordnung 50/45,' BA NS 6/99, pp. 1-2. Volkssturm not to interfere with emergency programme: Bormann, 28 January 1945, 'Anordnung 14/45g,' BA NS 6/99, p. 1. Problems for production: Marie-Luise Recker, *Nationalsozialistische Sozialpolitik im Zweiten Weltkrieg* (Munich, 1985), p. 288.

30. Volkssturm weapons' shortages: Seidler, *"Deutscher Volkssturm,"* pp. 193-207. Units not immediately in action lose weapons: Bormann, 11 March 1945, 'An-

ordnung 132/45 g. Rs,' BA NS 6/354, pp. 1-2. Key problem shortage of weapons: Seidler, *"Deutscher Volkssturm,"* pp. 331-2, 341. Inadequate training in use of weapons and selection of officers also problems: Bormann, 23 February 1945, 'Rundschreiben 28/45,' BA NS 6/99; Reimer Möller, 'Der Volkssturm im Kreis Steinburg,' in Erich Hoffmann and Peter Wulf (eds.), *"Wir bauen das Reich"*: *Aufstieg und erste Herrschaftsjahre des Nationalsozialismus in Schleswig-Holstein* (Münster, 1983), pp. 429-37. Party claims that army did not know how to use Volkssturm: 'Bericht des . . . Pg. Mauer,' BA NS 6/169, p. 2. Kissel's view: Wright, 'Army of Despair', p. 206. Reluctance to admit training in guerilla war needed: entry, 11 March 1945, von Oven, *Finale Furioso*, p. 606.

31.   Public attitudes to Volkssturm: Steinert, *Hitler's War and the Germans*, pp. 281, 434. More recent German studies: Seidler, *"Deutscher Volkssturm,"* pp. 14, 17-19, 372, 374.

32.   Volkssturm fought better in East than West: Wright, 'Army of Despair,' pp. 237-8, 210, 224. Younger men more committed than older: Alfons Heck, *A Child of Hitler* (New York, 1986), pp. 184-7, 190, 195-6. Effects of bombing on resistance in West: entries, 4 and 14 March 1945, Trevor-Roper (ed.), *Final Entries*, pp. 38, 134. Some women would have fought: Borek, OKW to Chef H Rüst and others, 7 December 1944, 'Freiwillige Meldungen von Frauen und Mädchen zum Einsatz mit der Waffe,' BA MA RH 15/120.

33.   Hopes for defence of Berlin like Moscow: entries, 28 February and 4 March 1945, Trevor-Roper (ed.), *Final Entries*, pp. 8-10, 41; 'Rede des Reichsführers-SS in Grafenwoehr am 25.7.1944,' BA NS 19/4015, p. 4.

34.   Armaments production still higher than 1943 average: Ludolf Herbst, *Der Totale Krieg und die Ordnung der Wirtschaft: die Kriegswirtschaft im Spannungsfeld von Politik, Ideologie und Propaganda 1939-1945* (Stuttgart, 1982), note 1, p. 343. Collapsed in some areas: Paul Sauer, *Württemberg in der Zeit des Nationalsozialismus* (Ulm, 1975), p. 482. Berlin Reich armaments centre: entry, 29 January 1945, von Oven, *Finale Furioso*, p. 559-60. Effects of territorial losses and raw material shortages: Alan S. Milward, *The German Economy at War* (London, 1967), pp. 183-4. Stepped-up Allied bombing against transportation: Alfred C. Mierzejewski, *The Collapse of the German War Economy, 1944-1945: Allied Air Power and the German National Railway* (Chapel Hill, N. C., 1988), pp. 125-140. Large numbers of workers kept to repair rail links: *ibid.*, pp. 134-5. Resulting production drops: *ibid.*, pp. 141, 146. Collapse of Ruhr by February: *ibid.*, p. 172. Speer's efforts hampered: *ibid.*, pp. 144-5. Other workers and management maintain production: Michael Fichter, 'Aufbau und Neuordnung: Betriebsräte zwischen Klassensolidarität und Betriebsloyalität,' in Martin Broszat, Klaus-Dietmar Henke and Hans Woller eds.), *Von Stalingrad zur Währungsreform: zur Sozialgeschichte des Umbruchs in Deutschland* (Munich, 1989), p. 480.

35.   Speer pointed out in January: Speer, 16 January 1945, 'Zur Vorlage beim Führer über Oberst von Below,' BA R 3/1522, pp. 1-3. By end of January Speer warned about Silesia: Speer, 30 January 1945, 'Auswirkungen—Verlust Oberschlesien,' BA R 3/1965, pp. 1-9; Speer, 30 January 1945, 'Zur Rüstungslage Februar-März 1945,' BA R 3/1535, pp. 1-10.

36.   Speer's paper of 15 March: Speer, 15 March 1945, 'Wirtschaftslage März-April 1945 und Folgerungen,' BA R 3/1536, pp. 1-10. Hitler's scorched earth order:

Hitler order, 20 March 1945, 'OKW/WFSt/Op/Qu Nr. 002711/45gKdos,' Exhibit Speer-25, *Trial of the Major War Criminals before the International Military Tribunal, Nuremberg, 14 November 1945-1 October 1946* (official text, reprint of 1947-49 edition, New York, 1971), vol. 41, pp. 430-1; order by the chief of Wehrmacht transportation, 29 March 1945, Exhibit Speer-26, pp. 431-2; a slightly modified form of the order issued on 30 March 1945 by Hitler, Speer Exhibit-28, pp. 433-4; Speer's implementation directives, 30 March 1945, all in *TMWC*, vol. 41, pp. 435-6.

37. Speer's attitude in September 1944: Milward, *German Economy*, p. 185. Speer on destruction and dismantling of bridges: Speer to General Staff of the Army, General of Engineers and Fortifications, 15 March 1945, BA R 3/1593. Hitler's order at Speer's suggestion in April: Bormann, 13 April 1945, 'Anordnung 209/45 g. Rs,' BA NS 6/354, pp. 1-2. Firms not evacuated to keep producing: Speer to Gauleiter Uiberreither of Steiermark, 4 December 1944, BA R 3/1603, p. 1.

38. Speer to Hitler, 29 March 1945, BA R 3/1538, p. 2.

39. *Ibid.*, p. 4.

40. Scorched earth order broke charisma: Orlow, *Nazi Party*, II, pp. 481-2. Goebbels opposed to scorched earth policy: entry, 14 March 1945, Trevor-Roper (ed.), *Final Entries*, p. 135. Those who helped Speer: Orlow, *Nazi Party*, II, pp. 481-2. Gauleiters who opposed Speer: *ibid.*. Speer would have been aware of effects of scorched earth policy: J. K. Galbraith, 'The Speer Interrogation: Last Days of the Third Reich,' *Atlantic*, July 1979, p. 51.

41. Göring's moves and arrest: Irving, *Göring*, pp. 11-22. Himmler's negotiations with Bernadotte and World Jewish Congress: Count Folke Bernadotte, *The Curtain Falls: Last Days of the Third Reich* (New York, 1945), pp. 46-59, 64-5. Himmler tries to negotiate with Eisenhower: *ibid.* pp. 87-8, 91-3, 105-119. Bormann's opinion of Doenitz's political reliability: Bormann, undated, 'Bekanntgabe,' 'Lageberichte des Oberbefehlshabers der Kriegsmarine,' BA NS 6/134; Orlow, *Nazi Party*, II, pp. 483-4. Himmler's unrealistic expectations: Speer, *Third Reich*, pp. 486, 495-6.

42. Goebbels prepares himself for possible defeat: Walter Tiessler, 'Licht und Schatten oder schonungslose Wahrheit (1922-1945),' IfZ ED 158, p. 180; entries, 27 August and 3 October 1943, von Oven, *Finale Furioso*, pp. 115, 153. Consolations of philosophy: Goebbels to Hitler, and attachment, 10 January 1945, BA NL 118/107, pp. 1-2. For detailed accounts of the last-minute manoeuvering, see Hugh Trevor-Roper, *The Last Days of Hitler* (new edition, London, 1967), *passim*, and James P. O'Donnell, *The Berlin Bunker* (London, 1979).

43. Speer edited files: Schmidt, *Speer Myth*, pp. 14-21. Speer's hopes of continuing as Minister: *ibid.*, pp. 14-15, 139-42.

Conclusion

1. Alan Clark, *Barbarossa: The Russian-German Conflict 1941-45* (Harmondsworth, 1966), p. 408.

2. Dieter Rebentisch, *Führerstaat und Verwaltung im Zweiten Weltkrieg: Verfassungsentwicklung und Verwaltungspolitik 1939-1945* (Stuttgart, 1989), pp. 533-4, 549.

3. For example, Martin Broszat, 'Teil I. Ein Landkreis in der Fränkischen Schweiz. Der Bezirk Ebermannstadt 1929-1945,' in Martin Broszat, Elke Fröhlich and Falk Wiesemann (eds.), *Bayern in der NS-Zeit: soziale Lage und politisches Verhalten der Bevölkerung im Spiegel vertraulicher Berichte* (Munich, 1977), p. 27-8.

4. Jeffrey Fear, 'Die Rüstungsindustrie im Gau Schwaben 1939-1945,' *Vierteljahrshefte für Zeitgeschichte*, vol. 35, 1987, p. 205.

5. Albert Speer, *Inside the Third Reich* (London, 1970), pp. 165, 168, 181.

6. Stephen Salter, 'The Mobilisation of German Labour, 1939-1945. A Contribution to the History of the Working Class in the Third Reich,' (unpublished D. Phil. thesis, Oxford, 1983), pp. 310-19.

7. 'Rede des Reichsführer-SS in Grafenwoehr am 25.7.1944,' BA NS 19/4015, p. 14.

8. Tim Mason, 'The Legacy of 1918 for National Socialism,' in Anthony Nicholls and Erich Matthias (eds.), *German Democracy and the Triumph of Hitler—Essays in Recent German History* (London, 1971), p. 223.

9. Signatur, submission, 15 February 1945, 'Staatssekretärbesprechung am 15.2. 14.00 Uhr Vortragsnotiz,' BA MA RW 4/v. 703, p. 3.

10. Paul Sauer, *Württemberg in der Zeit des Nationalsozialismus* (Ulm, 1975), pp. 365-6.

11. Johannes Volker Wagner, *Hakenkreuz über Bochum: Machtergreifung und nationalsozialistischer Alltag in einer Revierstadt* (Bochum, 1983), pp. 383-4; Adolf Klein, *Köln im Dritten Reich: Stadtgeschichte der Jahre 1933-1945* (Cologne, 1983), pp. 254, 258-9, 269-71; Hugo Ott, 'Das Land Baden im Dritten Reich,' Landeszentrale für Politische Bildung Baden-Württemberg (ed.), *Badische Geschichte: vom Grossherzogtum bis zur Gegenwart* (Stuttgart, 1979), pp. 204; Kurt Schnöring, 'Nacht über Wuppertal: Terror und Widerstand,' in Klaus Goebel, Michael Knieriem, Kurt Schnöring, and Volkmar Wittmütz, *Geschichte der Stadt Wuppertal* (Wuppertal, 1977), pp. 156-7; Sauer, *Württemberg*, pp. 350-60.

12. Gustav Stolper, Karl Häuser and Knut Borchardt, *The German Economy 1870 to the Present* (second edition, London, 1967), p. 163.

13. For details: Robert Cecil, *Hitler's Decision to Invade Russia 1941* (London, 1975), p. 118; Paul Kennedy, *The Rise and Fall of the Great Powers: Economic Change and Military Conflict from 1500 to 2000* (New York, 1987), pp. 352-3.

14. Albert Speer, *Inside the Third Reich* (London, 1970), p. 293.

BIBLIOGRAPHY

Archival Sources

Bayrisches Staatsarchiv, Munich

Bayerischen Staatskanzlei, MA.
Reichsstatthalter.
Staatsministerium des Innern, MInn.

Bundesarchiv Koblenz

Adjutantur des Führers, NS 10.
Der Beauftragte für den Vierjahresplan, R 26.
Deutsche Arbeitsfront, NS 5 I.
Hauptamt für Volkswohlfahrt (NSV), NS 37.
Kleine Ewerbungen.
Nachlass Goebbels, NL 118.
Parteikanzlei der NSDAP, NS 6.
Persönlicher Stab Reichsführer-SS, NS 19 and NS 19 neu. At the time I consulted these files, the Bundesarchiv was reorganising and recataloguing them. File numbers may since have been altered.
Reichsarbeitsministerium, R 41.
Reichsfrauenführung, NS 44.
Reichsgruppe Industrie, R 12 I.
Reichskanzlei, R 43 II. The main files consulted were in the 'Krieg' series.
Reichsministerium für Rüstung und Kriegsproduktion, previously Reichsministerium für Bewaffnung und Munition, R 3. The main files used were the files of the Ministerbüro Speer.
Reichsministerium für Volksaufklärung und Propaganda, R 55.
Reichspostministerium, R 48.
Reichspropagandaleitung, NS 18.
Reichswirtschaftskammer, R 11.
Reichswirtschaftsministerium, R 7.
SS Hauptamt, NS 31.
SS Personal Hauptamt, NS 34.
Statistisches Reichsamt, R 24.
Statistisches Reichsamt publications, RD 75.

von Unruh commission files, Rep. 312. These files are from the Hauptarchiv
Berlin-Dahlem, formerly the Prussian Geheimes Staatsarchiv. They are
few and very fragmented.

Bundesmilitärarchiv Freiburg

Oberkommando des Heer
Allgemeines Heeresamt, RH 15.
Chef des Heeresrüstung und Befehlshaber des Ersatzheeres, RH 14.
Generalstab des Heeres, RH 2.
Heereswaffenamt, RH 8 I.
Oberkommando der Wehrmacht
Allgemeines Wehrmachtamt, RW 6.
Wehrmachtführungsstab, RW 4.
Wehrwirtschafts- und Rüstungsamt, RW 19.
Nachlass Keitel, N 54.
Luftwaffe
Chef des Generalstabes, RL 2 I.
Generalluftzeugmeister, RL 3.
Generalstab der Luftwaffe, RL 2.
Reichsminister der Luftfahrt und Oberbefehlshaber der Luftwaffe, RL 1.

Institut für Zeitgeschichte

Akten der Parteikanzlei der NSDAP, Teil I, volumes 1 and 2, Munich, 1983-5.
Speer Interviews, ED 99 Band 9-13.
Walther Tiessler, 'Licht und Schatten oder schonungslose Wahrheit (1922-
1945),' ED 158.

Landesarchiv, Berlin

Arbeitsamt Berlin, Rep. 242.
Berliner Magistrat, Rep. 239.
Generalbauinspektor für die Reichshauptstadt, Pr. Br. Rep. 107.
Polizeipräsident in Berlin, Rep. 20.
Preussische Bau- und Finanzdirektion zu Berlin, Pr. Br. Rep. 42.
Staatspräsident der Reichshauptstadt, Berlin, Pr. Br. Rep. 57.

Geheimes Preussisches Staatsarchiv, Berlin-Dahlem

Preussisches Finanzministerium, Rep. 151.
Preussisches Ministerium für Wissenschaft, Kunst und Volksaufbildung, IHA
Rep. 76.
Preussisches Staatsministerium, Rep. 90.

Other Primary Sources

Banse, Ewald. *Wehrwissenschaft. Einführung in eine neue nationale Wissenschaft.* Leipzig, 1933.

Below, Nicolaus von. *Als Hitlers Adjutant 1937-45.* Mainz, 1980.

Bernadotte, Count Folke. *The Curtain Falls: Last Days of the Third Reich.* New York, 1945.

Boberach, Heinz (ed.). *Meldungen aus dem Reich 1938-1945: Die geheimen Lageberichte des Sicherheitsdienstes der SS,* volumes 1-17. Herrsching, 1984.

Boelcke, Willi A. (ed.). *Deutschlands Rüstung im Zweiten Weltkrieg: Hitlers Konferenzen mit Albert Speer 1942-1945.* Frankfurt, 1969.

Boelcke, Willi A. (ed.). *The Secret Conferences of Dr Goebbels October 1939-March 1943.* London, 1967.

Boelcke, Willi A. (ed.). *Wollt Ihr den totalen Krieg? Die geheimen Goebbels-Konferenzen 1939-43.* Stuttgart, 1989.

Dietrich, Otto. *The Hitler I Knew.* London, 1957.

Engelmann, Bernt. *In Hitler's Germany: Daily Life in the Third Reich.* New York, 1986.

Fredborg, Arvid. *Behind the Steel Wall.* London, 1944.

Fröhlich, Elke, on behalf of the Institut für Zeitgeschichte and in association with the Bundesarchiv (ed.). *Die Tagebücher von Joseph Goebbels Sämtliche Fragmente Teil I Aufzeichnungen 1924-1941, Band 1, 27.6.1924-31.12.1930, Band 3 1.1.1937-31.12.1939, Band 4 1.1.1940-8.7.1941.* Munich, 1987.

Galbraith, J. K. 'The Speer Interrogation: Last Days of the Third Reich,' *Atlantic.* July 1979: 50-7.

Genoud, François (ed.). *The Testament of Adolf Hitler: The Hitler-Bormann Documents February-April 1945,* second edition. London, 1962.

Goebbels, Joseph. *Das eherne Herz. Reden und Aufsätze aus den Jahren 1941/42.* Munich, 1943.

Goebbels, Joseph. *Der steile Aufstieg. Reden und Aufsätze aus den Jahren 1942/43.* Munich, undated.

Halder, Franz. *Hitler as War Lord.* London, 1950.

Heck, Alfons. *A Child of Hitler.* New York, 1986.

Heiber, Helmut (ed.). *Goebbels-Reden* Band 2: 1939-1945. Dusseldorf, 1972.

Heiber, Helmut (ed.). *Reichsführer! . . . Briefe an und von Himmler.* Stuttgart, 1968.

Hesse, Fritz. *Das Vorspiel zum Kriege: Englandberichte und Erlebnisse eines Tatzeugen 1935-1945.* Leoni am Starnberger See, 1979.

Hesse, Fritz. *Hitler and the English.* London, 1954.

Hierl, Constantin. *Grundlagen einer deutschen Wehrpolitik.* Munich, 1939.

Hill, Leonidas E. (ed.). *Die Weiszäcker-Papiere 1933-1950.* Frankfurt, 1974.

Hitler, Adolf. *Mein Kampf* (first published 1925 and 1927). Boston, 1943.

Hitler, Adolf. *Hitler's Secret Book* (written 1928). New York, 1961.

Jordan, Rudolf. *Erlebt und Erlitten: Weg eines Gauleiters von München bis Moskau*. Leoni am Starnberger See, 1971.

Kautter, Eberhard. *Wirtschaftsgeist, Sozialgeist, Wehrgeist*. Berlin, 1935.

Kehrl, Hans. *Krisenmanager im Dritten Reich 6 Jahre Frieden 6 Jahre Krieg Errinerungen*. Dusseldorf, 1973.

Kehrl, Hans. *Realitäten im Dritten Reich*. Historische Tatsachen Nr. 6. Vlotho, 1979.

Kempner, Robert W. *Das Dritte Reich im Kreuzverhör: aus den Vernehmungsprotokollen des Anklägers*. Dusseldorf, 1984.

Kersten, Felix. *The Kersten Memoirs 1940-1945*. London, 1956.

Khrushchev, Nikita. 'Double-bluffing the Little Corporal,' *The Australian*, 25 September 1990, p. 13. Extract from *Khrushchev Remembers: The Glasnost Tapes*.

Lochner, Louis P. (ed.). *The Goebbels Diaries 1942-1943*. Garden City, 1948.

Lochner, Louis P. *What About Germany?* London, 1943.

Ludendorff, Erich. *My War Memories 1914-1918* volume 2. London, undated.

Macmillan, Harold. *War Diaries: Politics and War in the Mediterranean January 1943-May 1945*. London, 1984.

Schellenberg, Walter. *The Labyrinth: Memoirs of Walter Schellenberg*. New York, 1956.

Scholtz-Klink, Gertrud. *Die Frau im Dritten Reich: Eine Dokumentation*. Tübingen, 1978.

Schroeder, Christa. *Er war mein Chef. Aus dem Nachlass der Sekretärin von Adolf Hitler*. Munich, 1985.

Semmler, Rudolf. *Goebbels—the Man Next to Hitler*. Ohio State University reprint, 1982, of London, 1947, edition.

Shirer, William. *Berlin Diary: The Journal of a Foreign Correspondent 1934-1941*. London, 1942.

Speer, Albert. *Inside the Third Reich*. London, 1970.

Speer, Albert. *Spandau: The Secret Diaries*. London, 1978.

Speer, Albert. *The Slave State: Heinrich Himmler's Masterplan for SS Supremacy*. London, 1981.

Steinbach, Lothar. *Ein Volk, ein Reich, ein Glaube? Ehemalige Nationalsozialisten und Zeitzeugen berichten über ihr Leben im Dritten Reich*. Bonn, 1983.

Taylor, Fred (ed.). *The Goebbels Diaries 1939-1941*. London, 1982.

Thomas, Georg. *Geschichte der deutschen Wehr- und Rüstungswirtschaft (1918-1943/45)*. Schriften des Bundesarchivs 14, Boppard, 1966.

Trevor-Roper, H. R. (ed.). *Final Entries 1945: The Diaries of Joseph Goebbels*. New York, 1978.

Trevor-Roper, H. R. (ed.). *The Bormann Letters: The Private Correspondence between Martin Bormann and His Wife from January 1943 to April 1945.* London, 1954.

Trial of the Major War Criminals before the International Military Tribunal, Nuremberg 14 November 1945-1 October 1946. Official Text, English edition, 42 volumes, reprint of 1947-49 edition New York, 1971.

von Oven, Wilfred. *Finale Furioso: Mit Goebbels bis zum Ende* First published 1948-50. Tübingen, 1974.

von Studnitz, Hans. Georg *While Berlin Burns: Diaries 1943-5.* London, 1964.

Wulf, Joseph. *Theater und Film im Dritten Reich Eine Dokumentation.* Frankfurt, 1989.

Secondary Sources

Books and Theses

Andreyev, Catherine. *Vlasov and the Russian Liberation Movement: Soviet Reality and Émigré Theories.* Cambridge, 1987.

Aron, Raymond. *The Century of Total War,* seventh printing. Boston, 1966.

Baird, Jay W. *The Mythical World of Nazi War Propaganda, 1939-1945.* Minneapolis, Minn., 1974.

Bajohr, Stefan. *Die Hälfte der Fabrik: Geschichte der Frauenarbeit in Deutschland 1914 bis 1945.* Marburg, 1979.

Balfour, Michael. *Propaganda in War 1939-1945: Organisations, Policies and Publics in Britain and Germany.* London, 1979.

Bartholdy, Albrecht Mendelssohn. *The War and German Society: The Testament of a Liberal* (first published 1937). New York, 1971.

Beck, Earl R. *Under the Bombs: The German Home Front 1942-1945.* Lexington, Mass., 1986.

Benz, Wolfgang. *Herrschaft und Gesellschaft im nationalsozialistischen Staat: Studien zur Struktur- und Mentalitätsgeschichte.* Frankfurt, 1990.

Berghahn, Volker. *Modern Germany.* Cambridge, 1982.

Best, Geoffrey. *War and Society in Revolutionary Europe 1770-1870.* London, 1982.

Boberach, Heinz, and Hans Booms (eds.). *Aus der Arbeit des Bundesarchivs: Beiträge zum Archivwesen, zur Quellenkunde und Zeitgeschichte.* Boppard am Rhein, 1978.

Boelcke, Willi A. *Die deutsche Wirtschaft 1930-1945: Interna des Reichwirtschaftsministeriums.* Dusseldorf, 1983.

Bond, Brian. *War and Society in Europe, 1870-1970.* London, 1984.

Borsdorf, Ulrich, and Mathilde Jamin (eds.). *Überleben im Krieg. Kriegserfahrungen in einer Industrieregion 1939-1945.* Hamburg, 1989.

Bower, Tom. *The Paperclip Conspiracy: The Battle for the Spoils and Secrets of Nazi Germany.* London, 1987.

Bracher, Karl Dietrich. *The Age of Ideologies: A History of Political Thought in the Twentieth Century.* London, 1984.

Bracher, Karl Dietrich. *Zeitgeschichtliche Kontroversen: Um Faschismus, Totalitarismus, Demokratie.* Munich, 1976.

Bracher, Karl Dietrich, Manfred Funke, and Hans-Adolf Jacobsen (eds.). *Nationalsozialistische Diktatur 1933-1945: eine Bilanz.* Dusseldorf, 1983.

Bramsted, E. K. *Goebbels and National Socialist Propaganda 1925-1945.* East Lansing, Mich., 1965.

Broszat, Martin. *The Hitler State.* London, 1981.

Broszat, Martin, Norbert Frei, in association with the Institut für Zeitgeschichte (eds.). *Ploetz Das Dritte Reich: Ursprüng Ereignisse Wirkungen.* Würzburg, 1983.

Broszat, Martin and Elke Fröhlich. *Bayern in der NS-Zeit II: Herrschaft und Gesellschaft im Konflikt Teil A.* Munich, 1979.

Broszat, Martin, Elke Fröhlich, and Anton Grossmann. *Bayern in der NS-Zeit IV: Herrschaft und Gesellschaft im Konflikt Teil C.* Munich, 1981.

Broszat, Martin, Elke Fröhlich and Falk Wiesemann. *Bayern in der NS-Zeit: soziale Lage und politisches Verhalten der Bevölkerung im Spiegel vertraulicher Berichte.* Munich, 1977.

Broszat, Martin, Klaus-Dietmar Henke, and Hans Woller (eds.). *Von Stalingrad zur Währungsreform: zur Sozialgeschichte des Umbruchs in Deutschland.* Munich, 1989.

Broszat, Martin, and Hartmut Mehringer. *Bayern in der NS-Zeit V: Die Parteien KPD, SPD, BVP in Verfolgung und Widerstand.* Munich, 1983.

Broszat, Martin, and Klaus Schwabe (eds.). *Die deutschen Eliten und der Weg in den Zweiten Weltkrieg.* Munich, 1989.

Bukey, Evan Burr. *Hitler's Hometown: Linz, Austria 1908-1945.* Bloomington, Ind., 1986.

Calvocoressi, Peter, Guy Wint, and John Pritchard. *Total War: The Causes and Courses of the Second World War*, Peter Calvocoressi, *Volume I: The Western Hemisphere*, second edition. London, 1989.

Carr, William. *Arms, Autarky and Aggression: A Study in German Foreign Policy, 1933-1939.* London, 1972.

Carr, William. *Poland to Pearl Harbor: The Making of the Second World War.* London, 1985.

Carroll, Berenice A. *Design for Total War: Arms and Economics in the Third Reich.* The Hague, 1968.

Cecil, Robert. *Hitler's Decision to Invade Russia 1941.* London, 1975.

Central Statistical Office. *Statistical Digest of the War.* London, 1951.

Clark, Alan. *Barbarossa: The Russian-German Conflict 1941-45.* Harmondsworth, 1966.

Creveld, Martin van. *Fighting Power—German and U.S. Army Performance, 1939-1945.* Westport, Conn., 1982.

Dallin, Alexander. *German Rule in Russia 1941-1945: A Study of Occupation Policies,* second edition. London, 1981.

Deist, Wilhelm, (ed.). *The German Military in the Age of Total War.* Leamington Spa, 1985.

Deist, Wilhelm. *The Wehrmacht and German Rearmament.* London, 1981.

Der alltägliche Faschismus: Frauen im Dritten Reich. Berlin, 1981.

Długoborski, Waclaw (ed.). *Zweiter Weltkrieg und sozialer Wandel: Achsenmächte und besetzte Länder.* Göttingen, 1981.

Erickson, John. *The Road to Stalingrad: Stalin's War with Germany,* volume 1. London, 1985.

Erickson, John. *The Road to Berlin: Stalin's War with Germany,* volume 2. London, 1985.

Fanning, William Jeffress, Jr. 'The German War Economy in 1941: A Study of Germany's Material and Manpower Problems in Relation to the Overall Military Effort.' Texas Christian University, Ph.D. diss., 1983.

Farquharson, John. *The Plough and the Swastika: The NSDAP and Agriculture in Germany 1928-45.* London, 1976.

Fear, Jeffrey R. 'The Armament Industry in Schwaben 1939-1945: Its Effect on the Regional, Economic, and Social Structure.' University of Michigan Honours Thesis, 1983.

Feldman, Gerald D. *Army, Industry and Labor in Germany, 1914-1918.* Princeton, N. J., 1966.

Fleischhauer, Ingeborg. *Die Chance des Sonderfriedens Deutsch-sowjetische Geheimgespräche 1941-1945.* Berlin, 1986.

Focke, Harald, and Uwe Reiner. *Alltag unterm Hakenkreuz Band I Wie die Nazis das Leben der Deutschen veränderten Ein aufklärendes Lesebuch* Hamburg, 1987.

Forstmeier, Friedrich, and Hans-Erich Volkmann(eds.). *Kriegswirtschaft und Rüstung 1939-1945.* Dusseldorf, 1977.

Forstmeier, Friedrich, and Hans-Erich Volkmann (eds.). *Wirtschaft und Rüstung am Vorabend des Zweiten Weltkrieges,* second edition. Dusseldorf, 1981.

Gersdorff, Ursula von. *Frauen im Kriegsdienst 1914-1945.* Stuttgart, 1969.

Gerth, H. H., and C. Wright Mills (eds.). *From Max Weber: Essays in Sociology,* new edition. New York, 1973.

Gillingham, John. *Industry and Politics in the Third Reich: Ruhr Coal, Hitler and Europe.* London, 1985.

Goebel, Klaus, Michael Knieriem, Kurt Schnöring, and Volkmar Wittmütz. *Geschichte der Stadt Wuppertal.* Wuppertal, 1977.

Goldman, Nancy Loring (ed.). *Female Soldiers—Combatants or Noncombatants? Historical and Contemporary Perspectives.* Westport, Conn., 1982.

Grill, Johnpeter Horst. *The Nazi Movement in Baden, 1920-1945.* Chapel Hill, N. C., 1983.

Halperin, M. H. *Bureaucratic Politics and Foreign Policy.* Washington, 1974.

Hancock, W. K., and M. M. Gowing. *British War Economy.* London, 1949.

Hardach, Gerd. *The First World War 1914-1918.* Harmondsworth, 1987.

Harrisson, Tom. *Living through the Blitz.* London, 1976.

Hayes, Peter. *Industry and Ideology: IG Farben in the Nazi Era.* Cambridge, 1987.

Heiber, Helmut. *Joseph Goebbels,* second edition. Munich, 1974.

Herbert, Ulrich. *Fremdarbeiter: Politik und Praxis des "Ausländer—Einsatzes" in der Kriegswirtschaft des Dritten Reiches.* Berlin, 1985.

Herbst, Ludolf. *Der Totale Krieg und die Ordnung der Wirtschaft: die Kriegswirtschaft im Spannungsfeld von Politik, Ideologie und Propaganda 1939-1945.* Stuttgart, 1982.

Hiden, John, and John Farquharson. *Explaining Hitler's Germany: Historians and the Third Reich.* Totowa, N.J., 1983.

Hilberg, Raul. *The Destruction of the European Jews,* volumes 1-3, revised and definitive edition. New York, 1985.

Hildebrand, Klaus. *The Third Reich.* London, 1984.

Hirschfeld, Gerhard, and Lothar Kettenacker (eds.). *The "Führer State": Myth and Reality. Studies on the Structure and Politics of the Third Reich.* Stuttgart, 1981.

Hirschfeld, Gerhard (ed.). *The Policies of Genocide: Jews and Soviet Prisoners of War in Nazi Germany.* London, 1986.

Hoffmann, Erich and Peter Wulf (eds.). *"Wir bauen das Reich": Aufstieg und erste Herrschaftsjahre des Nationalsozialismus in Schleswig-Holstein.* Munster, 1983.

Hoffmann, Peter. *The History of the German Resistance 1933-1945.* Cambridge, Mass., 1977.

Homze, Edward L. *Foreign Labor in Nazi Germany.* Princeton, N.J., 1967.

Howard, Michael. *Clausewitz.* Oxford, 1978.

Howard, Michael. *War in European History,* revised edition. Oxford, 1979.

Hüttenberger, Peter. *Die Gauleiter: Studie zum Wandel des Machtgefüges in der NSDAP.* Stuttgart, 1969.

Im Zeichen des Hakenkreuzes: Bielefeld 1933-1945. Eine Ausstellung des Stadtarchivs in der Studiengalerie der Kunsthalle 28. Januar—20. März 1983 Bielefeld, 1983.

Irving, David. *Göring: A Biography* New York, 1989.

Irving, David. *The Rise and Fall of the Luftwaffe: The Life of Luftwaffe Marshal Erhard Milch.* London, 1973.

Janssen, Gregor. *Das Ministerium Speer. Deutschlands Rüstung im Krieg.* Berlin, 1968.

Jukes, Geoffrey. *Hitler's Stalingrad Decisions.* Berkeley, Calif., 1985.

Jukes, Geoffrey. *Kursk: The Clash of Armour.* London, 1969.

Karlsruher Kinder im "Dritten Reich": Staatliche Kunsthalle Karlsruhe Ausstellung im Kindermuseum 2.10.1982—31.7.1983, second edition. Karlsruhe, 1983.

Kennedy, Paul. *The Rise and Fall of the Great Powers: Economic Change and Military Conflict from 1500 to 2000.* New York, 1987.

Kershaw, Ian. *The 'Hitler Myth': Image and Reality in the Third Reich.* Oxford, 1989.

Kershaw, Ian. *The Nazi Dictatorship: Problems and Perspectives of Interpretation,* second edition. London, 1989.

Kitchen, Martin. *The Silent Dictatorship: The Politics of the German High Command under Hindenburg and Ludendorff, 1916-1918.* London, 1976.

Klein, Adolf. *Köln im Dritten Reich: Stadtgeschichte der Jahre 1933-1945.* Cologne, 1983.

Klein, Burton H. *Germany's Economic Preparations for War.* Cambridge, Mass., 1959.

Kocka, Jürgen. *Facing Total War: German Society 1914-1918.* Leamington Spa, 1984.

Koehl, Robert Lewis. *The Black Corps: The Structure and Power Struggles of the Nazi SS.* Madison, Wisc., 1983.

Koonz, Claudia. *Mothers in the Fatherland: Women, the Family and Nazi Politics.* London, 1987.

Krausnick, Helmut, Hans Buchheim, Martin Broszat, and Hans-Adolf Jacobsen. *The Anatomy of the SS-State.* London, 1968.

Landeszentrale für politische Bildung Baden-Württemberg (ed.). *Badische Geschichte: Vom Grossherzogtum bis zur Gegenwart.* Stuttgart, 1979.

Lang, Jochen von. *Bormann: The Man who Manipulated Hitler.* London, 1979.

Lehker, Marianne. *Frauen im Nationalsozialismus: wie aus Opfern Handlanger der Täter wurden—eine nötige Trauerarbeit.* Frankfurt, 1984.

Lider, Julian. *Origins and Development of West German Military Thought Volume 1: 1949-1966.* Aldershot, 1986.

Long, Gavin. *The Final Campaigns.* Canberra, 1963.

Lötzke, K., and Brather, H. *Übersicht über die Bestände des Deutschen Zentralarchivs Potsdam.* Berlin, 1957.

Luard, Evan. *War in International Society: A Study in International Sociology.* New Haven, Conn., 1987.

Lusza, Radomír. *Austro-German Relations in the Anschluss Era.* Princeton, N.J., 1975.

Lynn, John A. *The Bayonets of the Republic: Motivation and Tactics in the Army of Revolutionary France, 1791-94.* Urbana, Ill., 1984.

Mammach, Klaus. *Der Volkssturm: Das letzte Aufgebot 1944/45.* Cologne, 1981.

Manvell, Roger and Heinrich Fraenkel. *Doctor Goebbels,* revised edition. London, 1968.

Manvell, Roger and Heinrich Fraenkel. *Heinrich Himmler,* second edition. London, 1969.

Marrus, Michael R. *The Holocaust in History.* London, 1987.

Martens, Stefan. *Hermann Göring "Erster Paladin des Führers" und "Zweiter Mann im Reich."* Paderborn, 1985.

Mason, Tim. *Arbeiterklasse und Volksgemeinschaft. Dokumente und Materialen zur deutscher Arbeiterpolitik 1936-1939.* Opladen, 1975.

Mason, Tim. 'The Legacy of 1918 for National Socialism,' in A. Nicholls and
    E. Matthias (eds.). *German Democracy and the Triumph of Hitler—Essays in Recent German History*. London, 1971, pp. 215-39.

McNeill, William H. *The Pursuit of Power: Technology, Armed Forces, and Society since A.D. 1000*. Oxford, 1983.

Meissner, Hans-Otto. *Magda Goebbels: A Biography*. London, 1980.

Merton, R. K., A. P. Gray, B. Hockey, and H. C. Selvin (eds.). *Reader in Bureaucracy*. New York, 1952.

Michalka, Wolfgang, (ed.), in association with the Militärgeschichtliches
    Forschungsamt. *Der Zweite Weltkrieg: Analysen, Grundzüge,
    Forschungsbilanz*. Munich, 1989.

Mierzejewski, Alfred C. *The Collapse of the German War Economy, 1944-
    1945: Allied Air Power and the German National Railway*. Chapel Hill,
    N. C., 1988.

Militärgeschichtliches Forschungsamt. *Das Deutsche Reich und der Zweite
    Weltkrieg*, volumes one to five/one. Stuttgart, 1979-1988.

Millett, Allan R., and Williamson Murray (eds.). *Military Effectiveness: Volume
    III: The Second World War*. Boston, 1988.

Milward, Alan S. *The German Economy at War*. London, 1967.

Milward, Alan S. *War, Economy and Society 1939-1945*. Berkeley, Calif., 1977.

Mollin, Gerhard. *Montankonzerne und "Drittes Reich": Der Gegensatz
    zwischen Monopolindustrie und Befehlswirtschaft in der deutschen
    Rüstung und Expansion 1936-1944*. Göttingen, 1988.

Mommsen, Wolfgang. *Die Nachlässe in den deutschen Archiven* Volume 1,
    Boppard, 1971; volume 2, Boppard, 1983.

Mommsen, Wolfgang. *The Age of Bureaucracy: Perspectives on the Sociology
    of Max Weber*. Oxford, 1974.

Murray, Williamson. *The Change in the European Balance of Power, 1938-
    1939: The Path to Ruin*. Princeton, N. J., 1984.

Murray, Williamson. *Luftwaffe*. Baltimore, Md., 1985.

Nadler, Fritz. *Ein Stadt im Schatten Streichers: Bisher unveröffentlichte
    Tagebüchblätter Dokumente und Bilder vom Kriegsjahr 1943*.
    Nuremberg, 1969.

Nef, John U. *War and Human Progress: An Essay on the Rise of Industrial Civilization*. Cambridge, Mass., 1952.

Niethammer, Lutz (ed.). *"Die Jahre weiss man nicht, wo man die heute
    hinsetzen soll": Faschismus-Erfahrungen im Ruhr-Gebiet.
    Lebensgeschichte und Sozialkultur im Ruhrgebiet 1930 bis 1960*, volume
    1, second edition. Bonn, 1986.

Noakes, Jeremy (ed.). *Government Party and People in Nazi Germany*, Exeter
    Studies in History no. 2. Exeter, 1980.

O'Donnell, James. *The Berlin Bunker*. London, 1979.

Orlow, Dietrich. *The History of the Nazi Party*, II 1933-1945. Newton Abbot,
    1973.

Overy, R. J. *Goering the 'Iron Man.'* London, 1984.

Overy, R. J. 'Hitler's War Plans And The German Economy,' in Robert Boyce and Esmonde M. Robertson (eds.). *Paths to War: New Essays on the Origins of the Second World War.* London, 1989, pp. 96-127.

Overy, R. J. *The Air War 1939-1945.* London, 1980.

Overy, R. J. *The Nazi Economic Recovery 1932-1938.* London, 1982.

Paret, Peter, (ed.). *Makers of Modern Strategy from Machiavelli to the Nuclear Age.* Princeton, N. J., 1986.

Parker, H.M.D. *Manpower: A Study of War-time Policy and Administration.* London, 1957.

Peukert, Detlev and Jürgen Reulecke (eds.) with the assistance of Adelheid Gräfin zu Castell Rüdenhausen. *Die Reihen fast geschlossen: Beiträge zur Geschichte des Alltags unterm Nationalsozialismus.* Wuppertal, 1981.

Posen, Barry R. *The Sources of Military Doctrine: France, Britain and Germany between the World Wars.* Ithaca, N.Y., 1984.

Rebentisch, Dieter. *Führerstaat und Verwaltung im Zweiten Weltkrieg: Verfassungsentwicklung und Verwaltungspolitik 1939-1945.* Stuttgart, 1989.

Recker, Marie-Luise. *Nationalsozialistische Sozialpolitik im Zweiten Weltkrieg.* Munich, 1985.

Reimann, Viktor. *The Man Who Created Hitler—Joseph Goebbels.* London, 1976.

Reitlinger, Gerald. *The Final Solution,* second edition. London, 1971.

Rupp, Leila J. *Mobilizing Women for War: German and American Propaganda, 1939-1945.* Princeton, N. J., 1978.

Ryan, Cornelius. *The Last Battle.* London, 1968.

Salter, Stephen. 'The Mobilisation of German Labour, 1939-1945. A Contribution to the History of the Working Class in the Third Reich.' Unpublished D.Phil. thesis, Oxford, 1983.

Sauer, Paul. *Württemberg in der Zeit des Nationalsozialismus.* Ulm, 1975.

Schmidt, Matthias. *Albert Speer—The End of a Myth.* London, 1985.

Schramm, Percy Ernst. *Hitler the Man and Military Leader.* London, 1972.

Schreiber, Gerhard. *Hitler Interpretationen 1923-1983: Ergebnisse, Methoden und Probleme der Forschung,* second edition. Darmstadt, 1988.

Schupetta, Ingrid. *Frauen und Ausländererwerbstätigkeit in Deutschland von 1939 bis 1945.* Cologne, 1983.

Seaton, Albert. *The German Army 1933-45.* London, 1983.

Seaton, Albert. *The Russo-German War 1941-45.* London, 1971.

Seebold, Gustav-Hermann. *Ein Stahlkonzern im Dritten Reich: Der Bochumer Verein 1927-1945.* Wuppertal, 1981.

Seidler, Franz W. *"Deutscher Volkssturm" : Das letzte Aufgebot 1944/45.* Munich, 1989.

Siegel, Tilla. *Leistung und Lohn in der nationalsozialistischen "Ordnung der Arbeit."* Opladen, 1989.

Steinert, Marlis G. *Hitler's War and the Germans: Public Mood and Attitude during the Second World War.* Athens, Ohio, 1977.

Stolper, Gustav, Karl Häuser, and Knut Borchardt. *The German Economy 1870 to the Present*, second edition. London, 1967.

Strawson, John. *Hitler as Military Commander*. London, 1971.

Summerfield, Penny. *Women Workers in the Second World War: Production and Patriarchy in Conflict*, second edition. London, 1989.

Sydnor, Charles W., Jr. *Soldiers of Destruction: The SS Death's Head Division, 1933-1945*. Princeton, N.J., 1977.

Sywottek, Jutta. *Mobilmachung für den totalen Krieg: Die propagandistische Vorbereitung der deutschen Bevölkerung auf den Zweiten Weltkrieg*. Opladen, 1976.

Szepansky, Gerda. *'Blitzmädel,' 'Heldenmutter,' 'Kriegerwitwe': Frauenleben im Zweiten Weltkrieg*. Frankfurt, 1989.

Thalmann, Rita. *Frausein im Dritten Reich*. Frankfurt, 1987.

Tidl, Georg. *Die Frau im Nationalsozialismus*. Vienna, 1984.

Toland, John. *Adolf Hitler*. New York, 1976.

Trevor-Roper, Hugh. *The Last Days of Hitler*, new edition. London, 1967.

Vogel, Walter and Gregor Verlande. *Findbücher zu Beständen des Bundesarchivs Band R 13 Bestand R 43 Reichskanzlei*. Koblenz, 1975.

Wagenführ, Rolf. *Die deutsche Industrie im Kriege 1939-1945*, second edition. Berlin, 1963.

Wagner, Johannes Volker. *Hakenkreuz über Bochum: Machtergreifung und nationalsozialistischer Alltag in einer Revierstadt*. Bochum, 1983.

Weinberg, Gerhard L. *World in the Balance: Behind the Scenes of World War II*. Hanover, 1981.

Welch, David. *Propaganda and the German Cinema 1933-1945*, second edition. Oxford, 1987.

Werner, Wolfgang. *'Bleib übrig!' Deutsche Arbeiter in der nationalsozialistischen Kriegswirtschaft*. Dusseldorf, 1983.

Werth, Alexander. *Russia at war 1941-1945*. London, 1965.

Whiting, Charles. *Werewolf: The Story of the Nazi Resistance Movement 1944-1945*. London, 1972.

Winkler, Dörte. *Frauenarbeit im "Dritten Reich."* Hamburg, 1977.

Wistrich, Robert. *Wer war wer im Dritten Reich? Ein biographisches Lexikon: Anhänger, Mitläufer, Gegner aus Politik, Wirtschaft, Militär, Kunst, und Wissenschaft*. Frankfurt, 1988.

Wright, Burton, III. *'Army of Despair: The German Volkssturm, 1944-1945.'* Florida State University Ph.D. thesis, 1982.

Zilbert, Edward R. *Albert Speer and the Nazi Ministry of Arms: Economic Institutions and Industrial Production in the German War Economy*. East Brunswick, N.J., 1981.

Articles

Adam, Uwe D. 'An Overall Plan for Anti-Jewish Legislation in the Third Reich?' *Yad Vashem Studies on the European Jewish Catastrophe and Resistance*, 11, 1976: 33-55.

Adam, Uwe D. 'Persecution of the Jews, Bureaucracy and Authority in the Totalitarian State.' *Leo Baeck Institute Year Book*, 29, 1978: 139-48.

Ball-Kaduri, Kurt J. 'Berlin wird judenfrei: die Juden in Berlin in den Jahren 1942/1943.' *Jahrbuch für die Geschichte Mittel- und Ostdeutschlands*, 22, 1973: 196-241.

Barkas, Janet. 'Face to face with the Planner of the Third Reich.' *Contemporary Review*, 222, 1973: 72-7.

Bauer, Yehuda. 'Genocide: Was it the Nazis' Original Plan?' *Annals*, AAPSS, 450, 1980: 35-45.

Berghahn, Volker. 'NSDAP und "geistige Führung" der Wehrmacht 1939-1943.' *Vierteljahrshefte für Zeitgeschichte*, 17, 1969: 17-71.

Bessel, Richard. 'Living with the Nazis: Some Recent Writing on the Social History of the Third Reich.' *European History Quarterly*, 14, 1984: 211-20.

Billson, Markus K., III. 'inside albert speer: secrets of moral evasion.' *The Antioch Review*, vol. 37, 1979.

Billson, Marcus K., III. 'A Conversation with Albert Speer.' *Dalhousie Review*, 58, 1978: 17-29.

Bracher, Karl Dietrich. 'Die Speer-Legende.' *Neue Politische Literatur*, 15, 1970: 429-31.

Bracher, Karl Dietrich. 'Nur die Niederlage verhinderte den Sklavenstaat.' *Frankfurter Allgemeine Zeitung*, 185, 13 August 1981: 6.

Davidson, Eugene. 'Albert Speer and the Nazi War Plants.' *Modern Age*, 10, 1965/66: 383-98.

Eichholtz, Dietrich. 'Die Vorgeschichte des "Generalbevollmächtigte für den Arbeitseinsatz" (mit Dokumenten).' *Jahrbuch für Geschichte*, 9, 1973: 339-83.

Erdmann, K. D. 'GWU in eigener Sache. Antwort an einen Dunkelmann: Wie informiert GWU ihre Leser?' *Geschichte in Wissenschaft und Unterricht*, 32, 1981: 197-8.

'Externus' 'Hildebrands Lied—oder: Wie die GWU ihre Leser informiert.' *Geschichtsdidaktik*, 5, 1980: 325-7.

Fear, Jeffrey. 'Die Rüstungsindustrie im Gau Schwaben 1939-1945.' *Vierteljahrshefte für Zeitgeschichte*, 35, 1987: 193-216.

Fröhlich, Elke. 'Hitler und Goebbels im Krisenjahr 1944. Aus den Tagebüchern des Reichspropagandaministers.' *Vierteljahrshefte für Zeitgeschichte*, 38, 1990: 195-225.

Funke, Manfred. 'Führer-Prinzip und Kompetenz-Anarchie im nationalsozialistischen Herrschaftssystem.' *Neue Politische Literatur*, 20, 1975: 60-7.

Gibbons, Robert. 'Dokumentation: Allgemeine Richtlinien für die politische und wirtschaftliche Verwaltung der besetzten Ostgebiete.' *Vierteljahrshefte für Zeitgeschichte*, 25, 1977: 252-77.

Gillingham, John. 'The "Deproletarianization" of German Society: Vocational Training in the Third Reich.' *Journal of Social History*, 19, 1986: 423-32.

Grill, Johnpeter Horst. 'Local and Regional Studies on National Socialism: A Review.' *Journal of Contemporary History*, 21, 1986: 253-94.

Groehler, Olaf and Erhard Moritz. 'Zur Kaderauslese des faschistischen Geheimen Meldedienstes 1944/45.' *Militärgeschichte*, 17, 1978: 582-94.

Hauerwas, Stanley. 'Among the Moved.' *Worldview*, 19, 1976: 47-9.

Hepp, Michael. 'Falschung und Wahrheit: Albert Speer und "Der Sklavenstaat".' *Mitteilungen*, 1, 1985: 1-68.

Herzstein, Robert E. 'La découverte du journal de Goebbels: quel est son intérêt historique?' *Revue d'histoire de la deuxième guerre mondiale*, 30, 1980: 49-58.

Heyl, John D. 'The Construction of the *Westwall*, 1938: An Exemplar for National Socialist Policymaking.' *Central European History*, 14, 1981: 63-78.

Hildebrand, Klaus. 'Die verfolgende Unschuld.' *Geschichte in Wissenschaft und Unterricht*, 32, 1981: 742-3.

Hildebrand, Klaus. 'Nationalsozialismus ohne Hitler? Das Dritte Reich als Forschungsgegenstand der Geschichtswissenschaft.' *Geschichte in Wissenschaft und Unterricht*, 31, 1980: 289-304.

Hildebrand, Klaus. 'Noch einmal: Zur Interpretation des Nationalsozialismus. Vergleichende Anmerkungen zu einer Tagung und einem Buch.' *Geschichte in Wissenschaft und Unterricht*, 32, 1981: 199-204.

Hillgruber, Andreas. 'Tendenzen, Ergebnisse und Perspektiven der gegenwärtigen Hitler-Forschung.' *Historische Zeitschrift*, 266, 1978: 600-21.

Hofer, Walther. 'Fifty Years On: Historians and the Third Reich.' *Journal of Contemporary History*, 21, 1986: 225-51.

Hofer, Walther. '50 Jahre danach, Über den wissenschaftlichen Umgang mit dem Dritten Reich.' *Geschichte in Wissenschaft und Unterricht*, 34, 1983: 1-28.

Horn, Wolfgang. 'Zur Geschichte und Struktur des Nationalsozialismus und der NSDAP.' *Neue Politische Literatur*, 18, 1973: 194-209.

Janssen, Gregor. 'Todt et Speer.' *Revue d'histoire de la deuxième guerre mondiale*, 21, 1971: 37-54.

John, Jürgen. 'Rüstungsindustrie und NSDAP-Organisation in Thüringen 1933 bis 1939.' *Zeitschrift für Geschichtswissenschaft*, 22, 1974: 412-22.

Kater, Michael H. 'Hitler in a Social Context.' *Central European History*, 14, 1981: 243-72.

Kirwin, Gerald. 'Allied Bombing and Nazi Domestic Propaganda.' *European History Quarterly*, 15, 1985: 341-62.

Knox, Macgregor. 'Conquest, Foreign and Domestic, in Fascist Italy and Nazi Germany.' *Journal of Modern History*, 56, 1984: 1-57.

Kretschmer, Rainer and Helmut J. Koch. 'Der Propagandaapparat des NS-Staates.' *Das Argument*, 12, 1970: 305-21.

Link, Werner. 'Das nationalsozialistische Deutschland und die USA 1933-1941.' *Neue Politische Literatur*, 18, 1973: 225-33.

Longerich, Peter. 'Joseph Goebbels und der totale Krieg: eine unbekannte Denkschrift des Propagandaministers vom 18. Juli 1944.' *Vierteljahrshefte für Zeitgeschichte*, 35, 1987: 289-314.

Marrus, Michael R. 'The History of the Holocaust: A Survey of Recent Literature.' *Journal of Modern History*, 59, 1987: 114-60.

Mason, Tim. 'Zur Frauenarbeit im NS-Staat.' *Archiv für Sozialgeschichte*, 19, 1979: 579-84.

Mommsen, Hans. 'Ein Erlass Himmlers zur Bekämpfung der Korruption in der inneren Verwaltung vom Dezember 1944.' *Vierteljahrshefte für Zeitgeschichte*, 16, 1968: 295-309.

Mommsen, Wolfgang J. 'Die "reine Wahrheit" über das nationalsozialistische Herrschaftssystem?' *Geschichte in Wissenschaft und Unterricht*, 32, 1981: 738-41.

Nuss, Karl, and Heinz Sperling. 'Eine Rüstungskonzeption des deutschen Generalstabes aus dem Jahre 1934.' *Militärgeschichte*, 17, 1978: 203-11.

Olsson, Sven-Olof. 'The documents of "Zentrale Planung" as a Basis for Research on the German War Economy.' *Scandinavian Economic History Review*, 24, 1976: 45-59.

Overy, R. J. '"Blitzkriegswirtschaft"? Finanzpolitik, Lebensstandard und Arbeitseinsatz in Deutschland 1939-1942.' *Vierteljahrshefte für Zeitgeschichte*, 36, 1988: 379-435.

Overy, R. J. 'Germany, "Domestic Crisis" and War in 1939.' *Past and Present*, No. 116, 1987: 138-68.

Overy, R. J. 'Hitler's War and the German Economy: A Reinterpretation.' *The Economic History Review*, 35, 1982: 272-91.

Overy, R. J. 'The Audit of War.' *Times Literary Supplement*, 4332, 11 April 1986: 393.

Peterson, E. N. 'The Bureaucracy and the Nazi Party.' *Review of Politics*, 28, 1966: 172-92.

Rupp, Leila J. 'Women, Class, and Mobilization in Nazi Germany.' *Science and Society*, 43, 1979: 51-69.

Saage, Richard. 'Das sozio-politische Herrschaftssystem des Nationalsozialismus Reflexionen zu Franz Neumanns "Behemoth".' *Jahrbuch des Instituts für Deutsche Geschichte*, 10, 1981: 341-62.

Schulz, Eberhard. 'Ein Günstling des Schicksals: Zu Albert Speers "Errinerungen".' *Merkur*, 23, 1969: 1157-64.

Stephenson, Jill. '"Emancipation" and Its Problems: War and Society in Württemberg 1939-45.' *European History Quarterly*, 17, 1987: 345-65.

Stephenson, Jill. 'Middle-class Women and National Socialist "Service".' *History*, 67, 1982: 32-44.

Stephenson, Jill. 'Women's Labor Service in Nazi Germany.' *Central European History*, 15, 1982: 241-65.

Stephenson, Jill. '"Reichsbund der Kinderreichen": The League of Large Families in the Population Policy of Nazi Germany.' *European Studies Review*, 9, 1979: 351-75.

Vago, Bela. 'The Intelligence Aspects of the Joel Brand Mission.' *Yad Vashem Studies on the European Catastrophe and Resistance*, 10, 1974: 111-28.

Volker, Ernst, Anita Kaun, and Hans-Jürgen Zeidler. 'Neuerschlossene Bestände im Militärarchiv der DDR (Zeitraum 1920-1945).' *Militärgeschichte*, 20, 1981: 582-94.

Winkler, Dörte. 'Frauenarbeit versus Frauenideologie: Probleme der weiblichen Erwerbstätigkeit in Deutschland 1930-1945.' *Archiv für Sozialgeschichte*, 17, 1977: 99-126.

Ziemke, Earl F. 'Germany and World War II: The Official History?' *Central European History*, 16, 1983: 398-407.

INDEX

view of von Unruh, 39, 78, 79
views misunderstood by Goebbels, 67-8
ways of influencing, 71-2
weakening health and authority, 140, 167, 173, 194
Hoess, Rudolf, 37
Hofer, Gauleiter, 175, 176
Hoffmann, Gauleiter Albert, 185
Hoffmann, Party Chancellery official, 38, 39, 42, 78, 116
Höhere SS- und Polizeiführer (Higher SS and Police Leaders) see HSSPF
Höhere SS- und Polizeiführer Russland-Mitte (Higher SS and Police Leader Russia Centre), 61
Höhere SS- und Polizeiführer Ukraine (Higher SS and Police leader Ukraine), 61
Home Guard, 183
Homze, Edward L., 95, 170
honour cross of the German mother, 52
Horchers' restaurant, 57, 66
horse racing, ban on, 69-70, 73
housing - policy differences, 67
HSSPF (Höhere SS- und Polizeiführer/) - Higher SS and Police Leaders, 61, 181
Hübner, Colonel, 87
Hungary, 116
  Jewish community, 111
  Jewish prisoners from, 162
I.G. Farben, 118
ideological education, 49, 50
Ifland, Otto, 38, 79
Imperial Germany
  and World War I, 12, 13, 14
indispensable workers see uk workers
industrialists, 167
  less co-operative with party, 167
  on giving up uk positions, 167-8
industry
  aircraft, 18, 116-17
  alleged corruption of, 115
  combing out of, 96, 97
  commended by Hitler, 167
  employing women, 76
  Party intervention in, 114, 116
  problems of, 80
  reluctance to work for regime, 167, 171
  transfers of staff within, 95-6, 97
  women in, 23, 24
industry restructuring see business closures
Inspector-General of Building for the Capital of the Reich, 3
instruction officer see Bildungsoffizier
intellectuals
  attitude to the war, 84
intentionalist interpretation see monocratic interpretation

inter-departmental bomb damage committee see Luftkriegsschädenausschuss
Interior Ministry, 3, 61, 85
  uk positions, 92
iron ore, 17
Italy, 9
  internment of army, 95
  overthrow of Mussolini, 83, 84, 193
    : effects in Germany, 83-6, 93, 103, 141, 193
  urges compromise peace, 36
Jacobsen, Hans-Adolf, 88-9
Jägerstab (Fighter Staff), 117
Janssen, Gregor, 69, 168
Japan, 28, 34
  proposes alliance with USSR, 143
  seeks compromise peace, 35-6, 49, 144
Jews, 12-13, 81, 84, 111
  Hitler and World War I, 12-13
  in Berlin, 35
  labour of, 37, 102, 162
Jodl, General Alfred, 30, 84
Jünger, Ernst, 12
Justice Ministry, 35, 52, 152, 157
  uk positions in, 92
Jüttner, Hans, 118-19, 174
Kaltenbrunner, Ernst, 70
Kammler, SS-Brigadeführer, 101
Kampfzeit (time of struggle)
  as model for total war, 57, 86, 88-9, 110, 179, 180, 183, 197
Kasserine Pass, 63
Kaufmann, Gauleiter Karl, 79, 185
KDF (Kraft durch Freude) - Strength through Joy, 152
Kehrl, Hans, 21, 43, 85, 97, 117, 118
Keitel, Field Marshal Wilhelm, 40, 45, 78, 80, 94, 95, 116, 121, 129, 137, 162, 167, 178, 182
  and Dreier Ausschuss, 47, 52, 51
  and Ohnesorge, 78
  on NSFOs, 87
  supports Goebbels' demands for labour, 165
Kersten, Felix, 186
Kharkov, 63, 89
Kiev, 89
Kissel, Major-General Hans, 182
Klein, Burton H., 18, 25
  Germany's Economic Preparations for War, 18
Klein, Ministerialrat, 164, 167, 168
Klopfer, Gerhard, 114, 129, 185
Koch, Erich, 65, 90, 128
Koerner, Paul (Pili), 33
Kolberg, 153
Korherr, Dr Richard, SS Inspector for Statistics, 93

Oberster Gerichtsherr - supreme justice authority, 35
occupation policy, 4
in USSR, 29, 30, 48, 65, 90
Oder position, 176
Oder river, 173
Office of the Four Year Plan, 17
officers for military ideological leadership (Wehrgeistige Führung), 87
officers for National Socialist leadership see NSFOs
Ohlendorf, Otto, 101, 111, 115, 161, 185
and Himmler's alleged plans to assassinate Hitler, 111
economic views, 101
Ohnesorge, Wilhelm, 39, 78, 154
and von Unruh, 78
oil industry, 116-17, 128
OKW (Oberkommando der Wehrmacht) - Supreme Command of the Armed Forces, 16, 80, 93, 139, 157, 181, 184
and armed forces' use of labour, 40, 52, 59-60
Olbricht, General Friedrich, 93
Operation Barbarossa, 27, 201
Oppeln, 184
opposition to Hitler, 92
optics of total war, 62, 149
Oranienburg concentration camp, 119
ORBs (Oberste Reichsbehörden) - supreme Reich authorities, 51, 135, 138, 150
Orel, 89
Orlow, Dietrich, 155-6, 164, 185
Oshima, Ambassador Hiroshi, 91, 143
Ostministerium (Ministry for the occupied Eastern territories), 49, 52, 58, 90, 92, 134, 140
OT (Organisation Todt), 21, 78, 113, 120, 139, 162, 177
outwork see Heimarbeit,
Overy, R.J., 17, 25, 54, 66, 159, 189
'Hitler's War and the German economy', 19
total war model, 19, 20
Panzerfäuste - anti-tank weapons, 176, 182
Paris, 127
partisans, 183
Party Chancellery, 52, 60, 72, 73, 85, 122, 123, 138, 139, 179, 191
and planned women's armed forces' auxiliary, 142-3
and women's registration for labour, 55, 56
uk numbers, 93
people's grenadier divisions see Volksgrenadier divisions,
people's storm, militia see Volkssturm
petroleum, 17
planning committee see Planungsausschuss
planning office see Planungsamt

Planungsamt - planning office, 97
Planungsausschuss - planning committee, 149, 150, 167
plenipotentiary for Reich administration see Generalbevollmächtigter für die Reichsverwaltung,
plenipotentiary for the economy see Generalbevollmächtigter für die Wirtschaft
Pohl, Oswald, 37, 101, 118, 119, 121, 139
Poland, 107-8
attack on, 21, 22
Poles, 181
police, 139, 158, 176
polycratic interpretation, 5-7
Pomerania, 116
popular community see Volksgemeinschaft
Posen, 98, 102, 174
Post Ministry, 52, 75, 76, 78
post office, 119, 152, 155, 165
proposed staff savings, 153, 154
Presidential Chancellery, 58, 138
price-fixing system for war contracts, 32
print media
restrictions on, 68
printing industry
restrictions on, 153
prisoners of war, 24, 38
Soviet, 29, 30, 34, 102
propaganda, 8, 11,
Propaganda Ministry, 2, 33, 34, 36, 40, 93, 114, 117, 128, 134, 148, 149, 151
and air defence, 43-4
and NSDAP, 142
and war clothing issues, 114
and women's employment, 40
proposes volunteer border guard, 141
staff reductions, 33-4, 42, 59, 60, 155
uk positions in, 92-3
propaganda, German, 1, 2, 3, 13, 30, 40, 74, 91, 93, 102, 128
and bombing, 103, 174
and campaign in USSR, 30
and Italian crisis, 83-4
and secret weapons, 174
and women's employment, 55-6
difficulties of, 63-4
lessons of World War I, 13
Speer attempts to control armaments propaganda, 113
treatment of Stalingrad, 48
Prussian Finance Ministry, 52, 71, 154, 196
Prützmann, SS-Obergruppenführer Hans, 181
public opinion, 67
qualitative superiority of armaments, 80, 96
Quebec conference of Roosevelt and Churchill (September 1944), 144
RAD (Reichsarbeitsdienst) - Reich labour service, 75, 94, 156